IMMORTAL RAIN

VOLUME 1

BY
KAORI OZAKI

LOS ANGELES • TOKYO • LONDON • HAMBURG

Translator - Michael Wert
English Adaptation - Stormcrow Hayes
Copy Editor - Troy Lewter
Retouch and Lettering - Vicente Rivera Jr.
Cover Artist - Anna Kernbaum

Editor - Nora Wong
Digital Imaging Manager - Chris Buford
Pre-Press Manager - Antonio DePietro
Production Managers - Jennifer Miller, Mutsumi Miyazaki
Art Director - Matt Alford
Managing Editor - Jill Freshney
VP of Production - Ron Klamert
President & C.O.O. - John Parker
Publisher & C.E.O. - Stuart Levy

E-mail: info@TOKYOPOP.com
Come visit us online at www.TOKYOPOP.com

A  Manga

TOKYOPOP Inc.
5900 Wilshire Blvd. Suite 2000
Los Angeles, CA 90036

Immortal Rain Vol. 1

Immortal Rain Volume 1 (originally published as "Meteor Methuselah"). ©1999 Kaori Ozaki.
All Rights Reserved. First published in Japan in 1999 by Shinshokan Publishing Co., Ltd., Tokyo, Japan.
English translation rights arranged through Shinshokan Publishing Co., Ltd.

English text copyright ©2004 TOKYOPOP Inc.

ISBN: 1-59182-722-1

First TOKYOPOP printing: June 2004

10 9 8 7 6 5 4 3

Printed in the USA

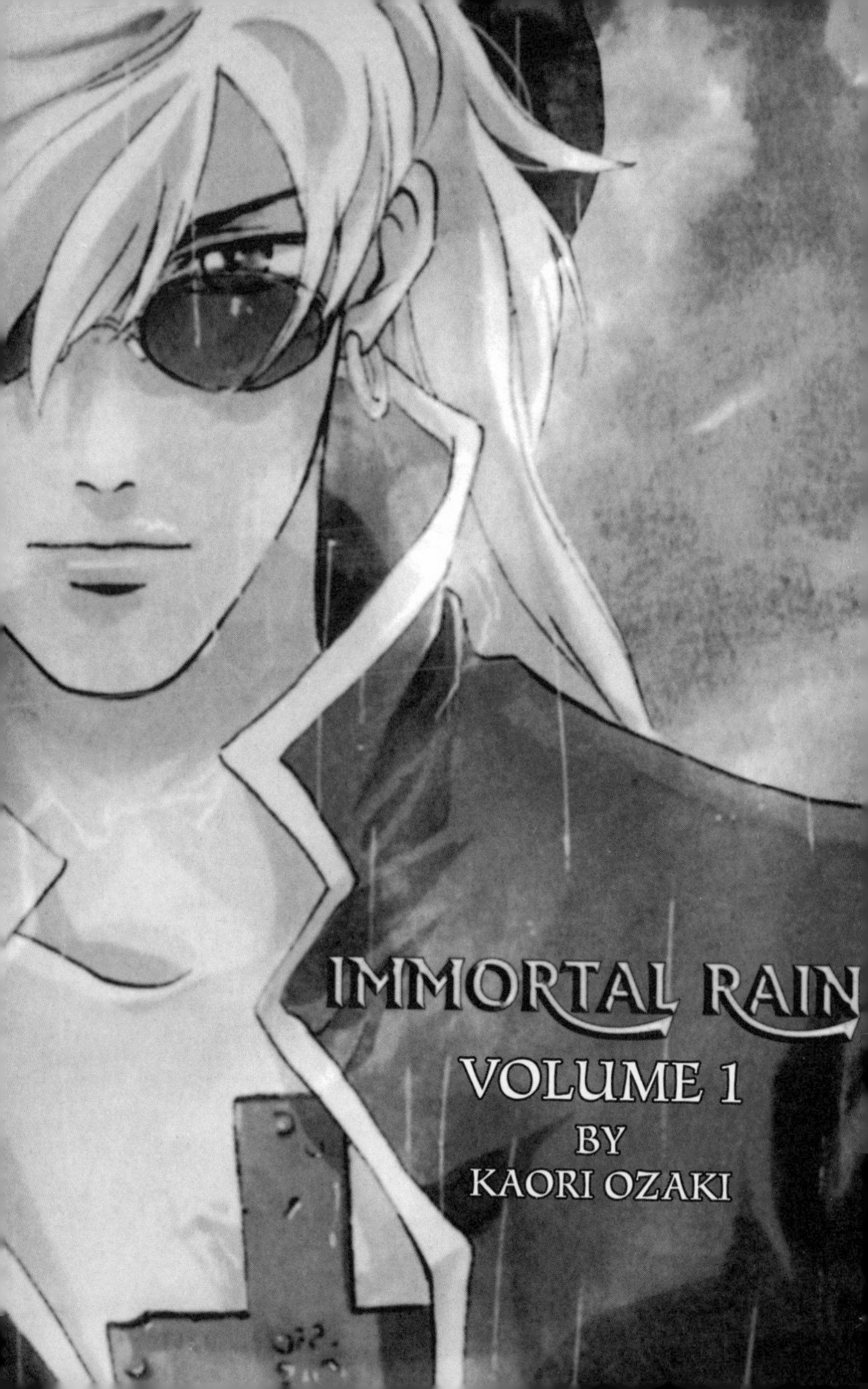
IMMORTAL RAIN
VOLUME 1
BY
KAORI OZAKI

◆ CONTENTS

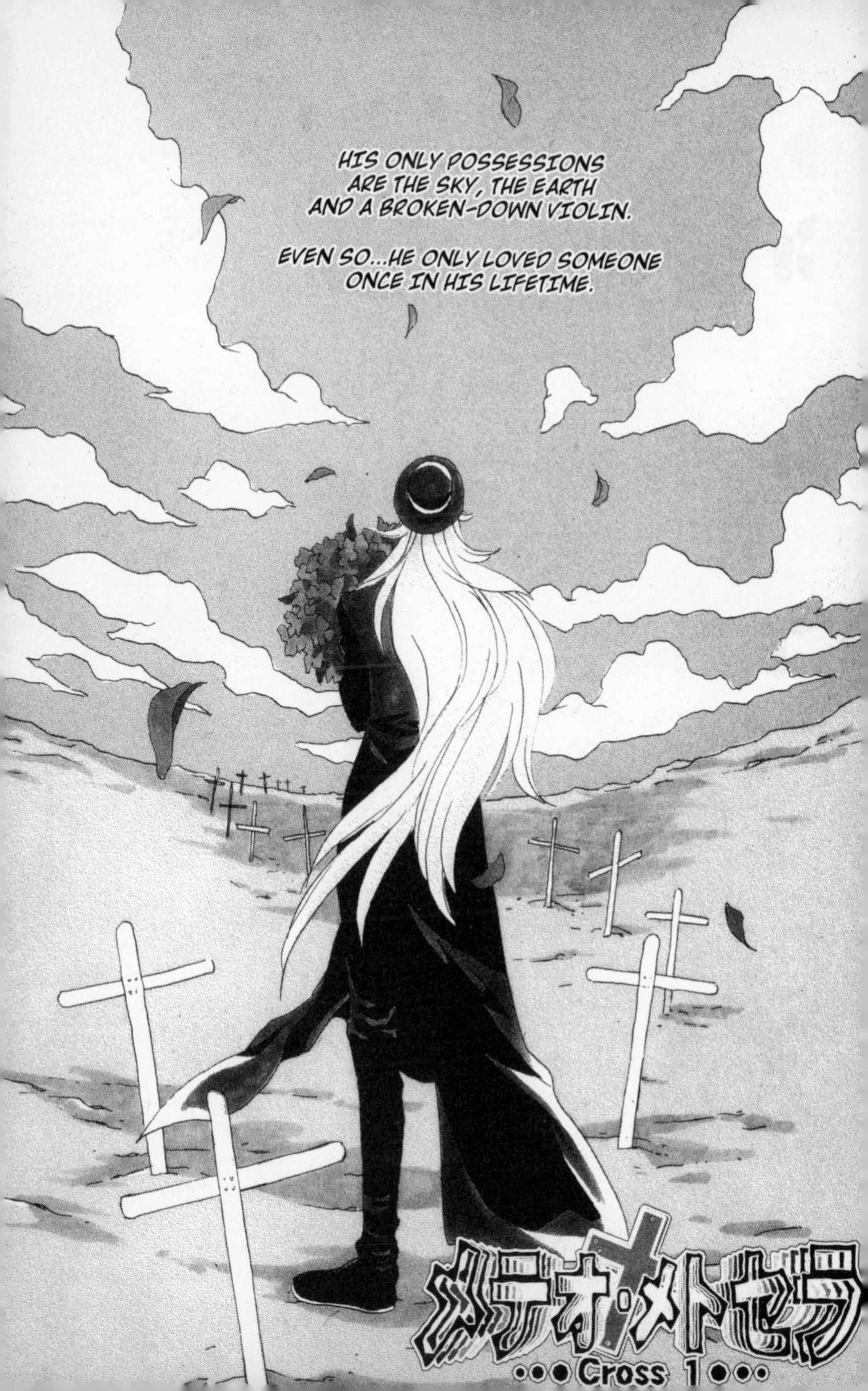
HIS ONLY POSSESSIONS ARE THE SKY, THE EARTH AND A BROKEN-DOWN VIOLIN.
EVEN SO...HE ONLY LOVED SOMEONE ONCE IN HIS LIFETIME.
バイオメトセラ
Cross 1

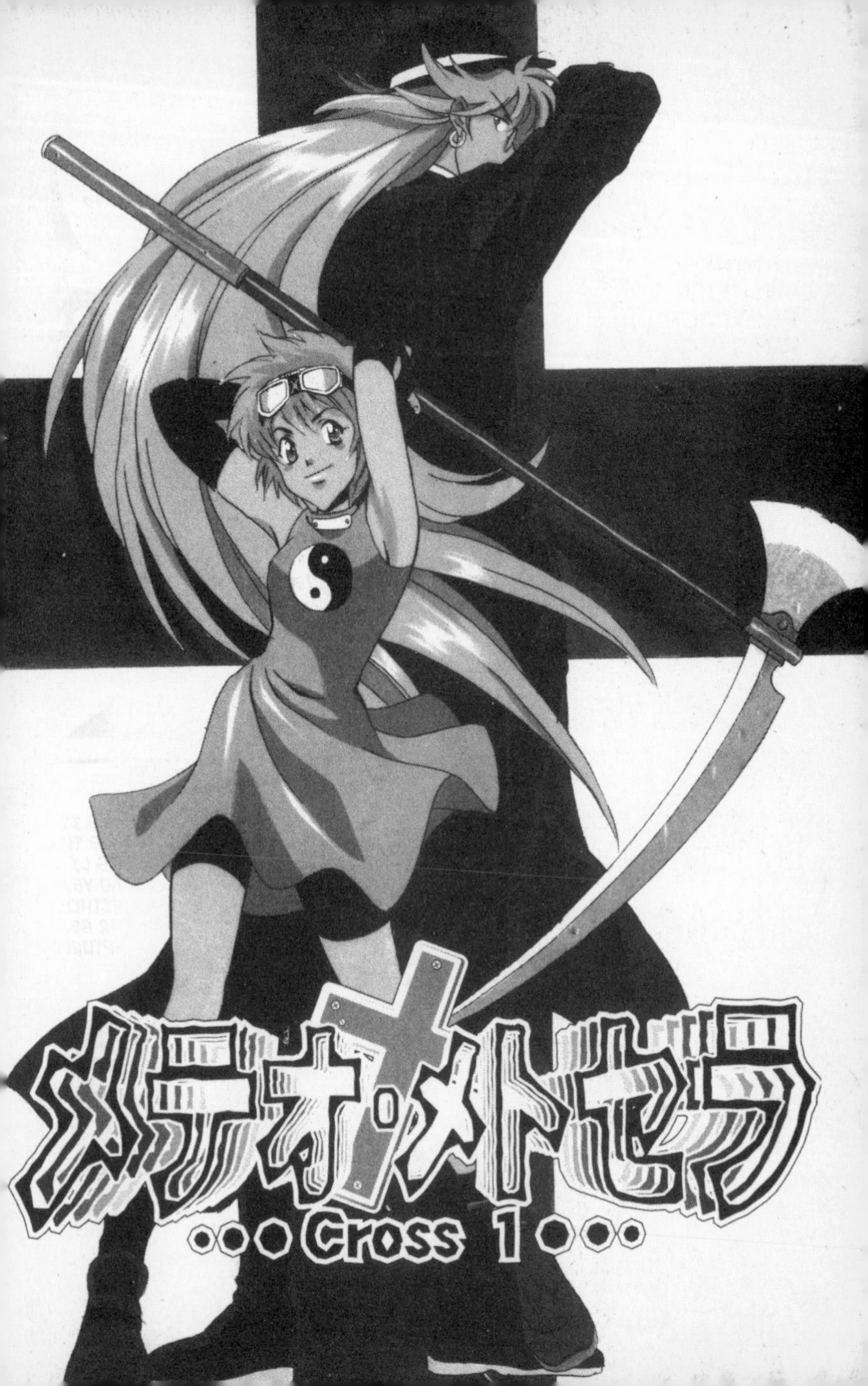
Cross 1

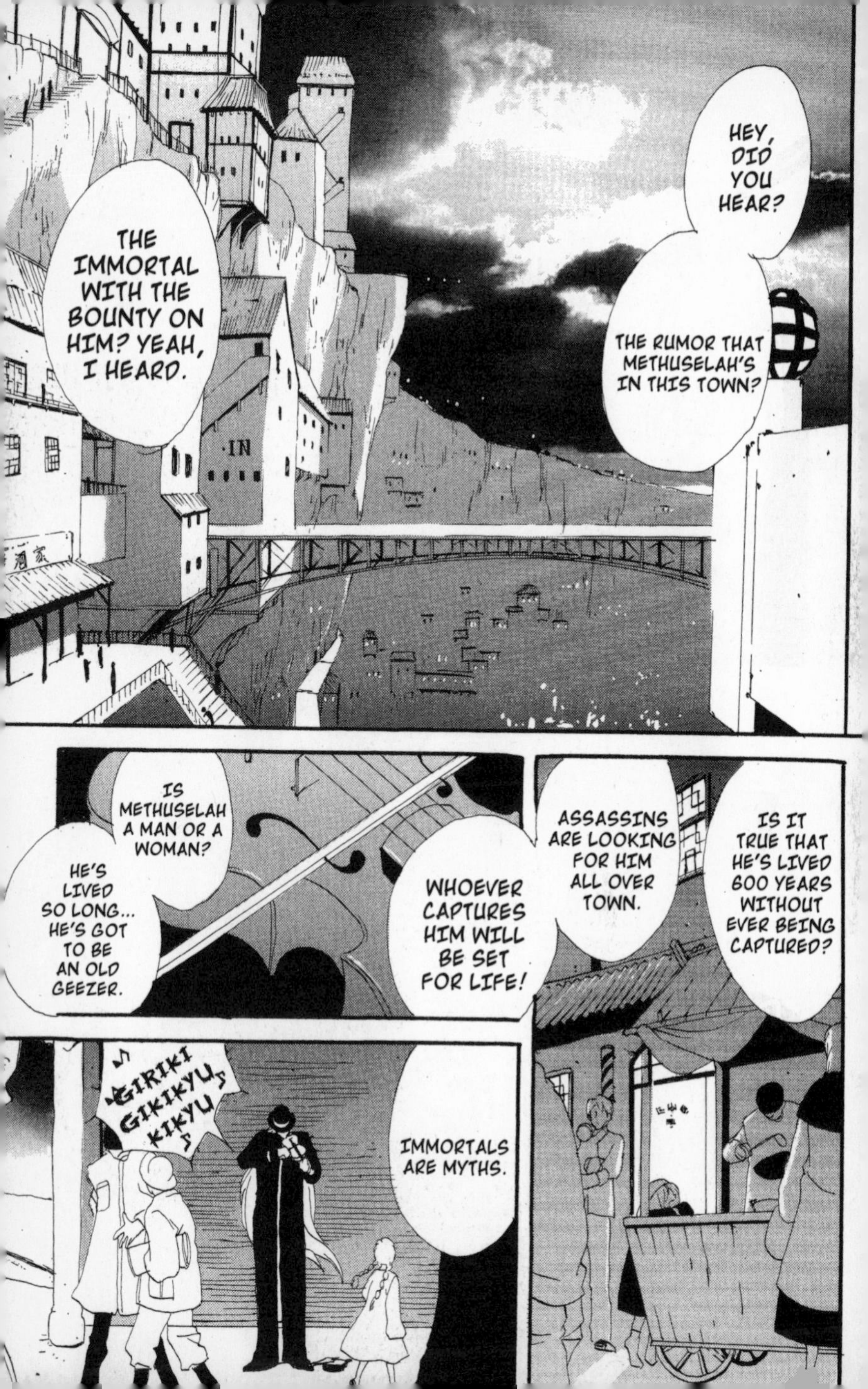
HEY, DID YOU HEAR?
THE RUMOR THAT METHUSELAH'S IN THIS TOWN?
THE IMMORTAL WITH THE BOUNTY ON HIM? YEAH, I HEARD.
IS IT TRUE THAT HE'S LIVED 600 YEARS WITHOUT EVER BEING CAPTURED?
ASSASSINS ARE LOOKING FOR HIM ALL OVER TOWN.
WHOEVER CAPTURES HIM WILL BE SET FOR LIFE!
IS METHUSELAH A MAN OR A WOMAN?
HE'S LIVED SO LONG... HE'S GOT TO BE AN OLD GEEZER.
IMMORTALS ARE MYTHS.
GIRIKI GIKIKYU KIKYU

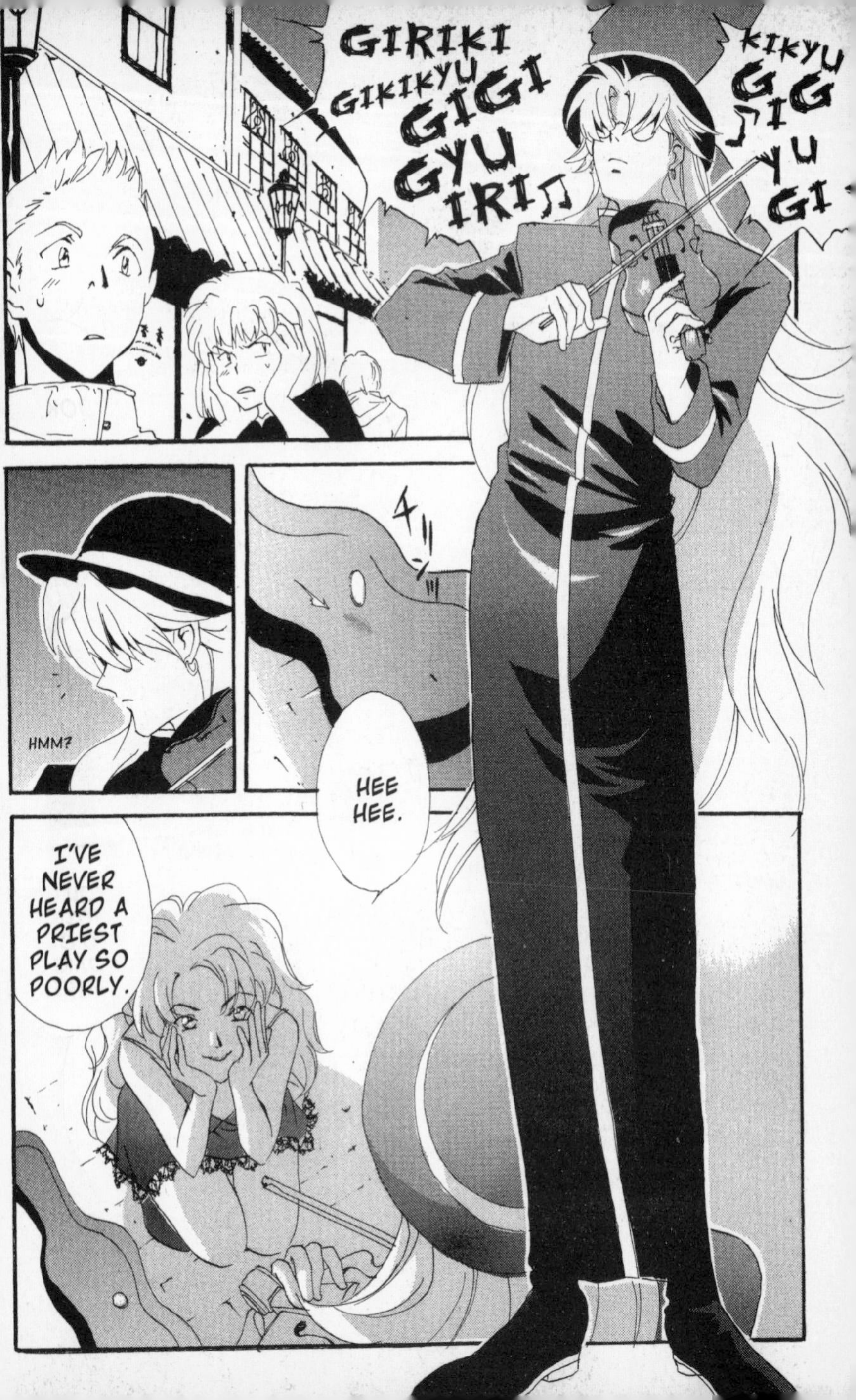
KIKYU GG GIG ♪I YU GI
GIRIKI GIKIKYU GIGI GYU IRI♫
HEE HEE.
HMM?
I'VE NEVER HEARD A PRIEST PLAY SO POORLY.

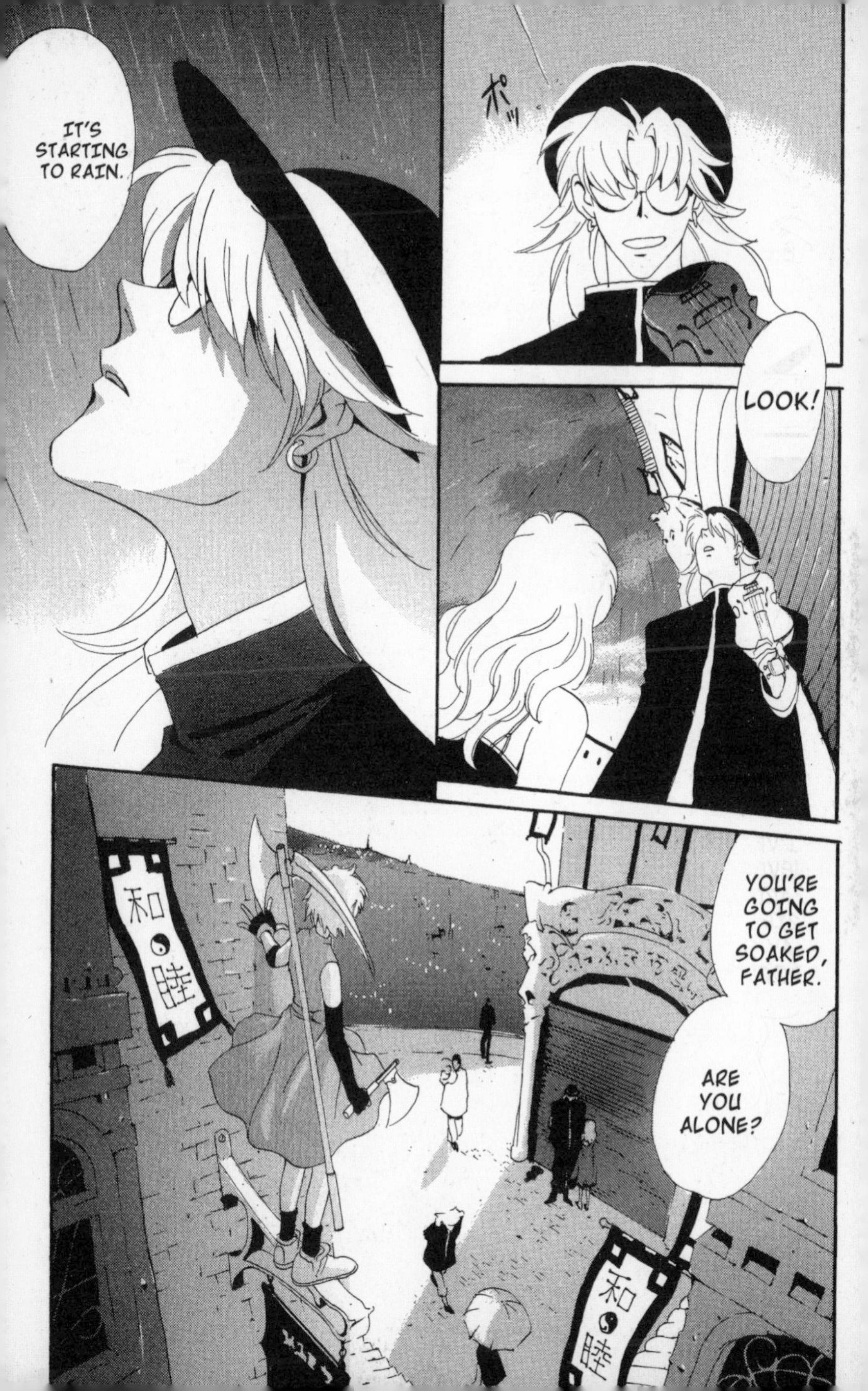
ポッ
LOOK!
IT'S STARTING TO RAIN.
YOU'RE GOING TO GET SOAKED, FATHER.
ARE YOU ALONE?
和睦
和睦

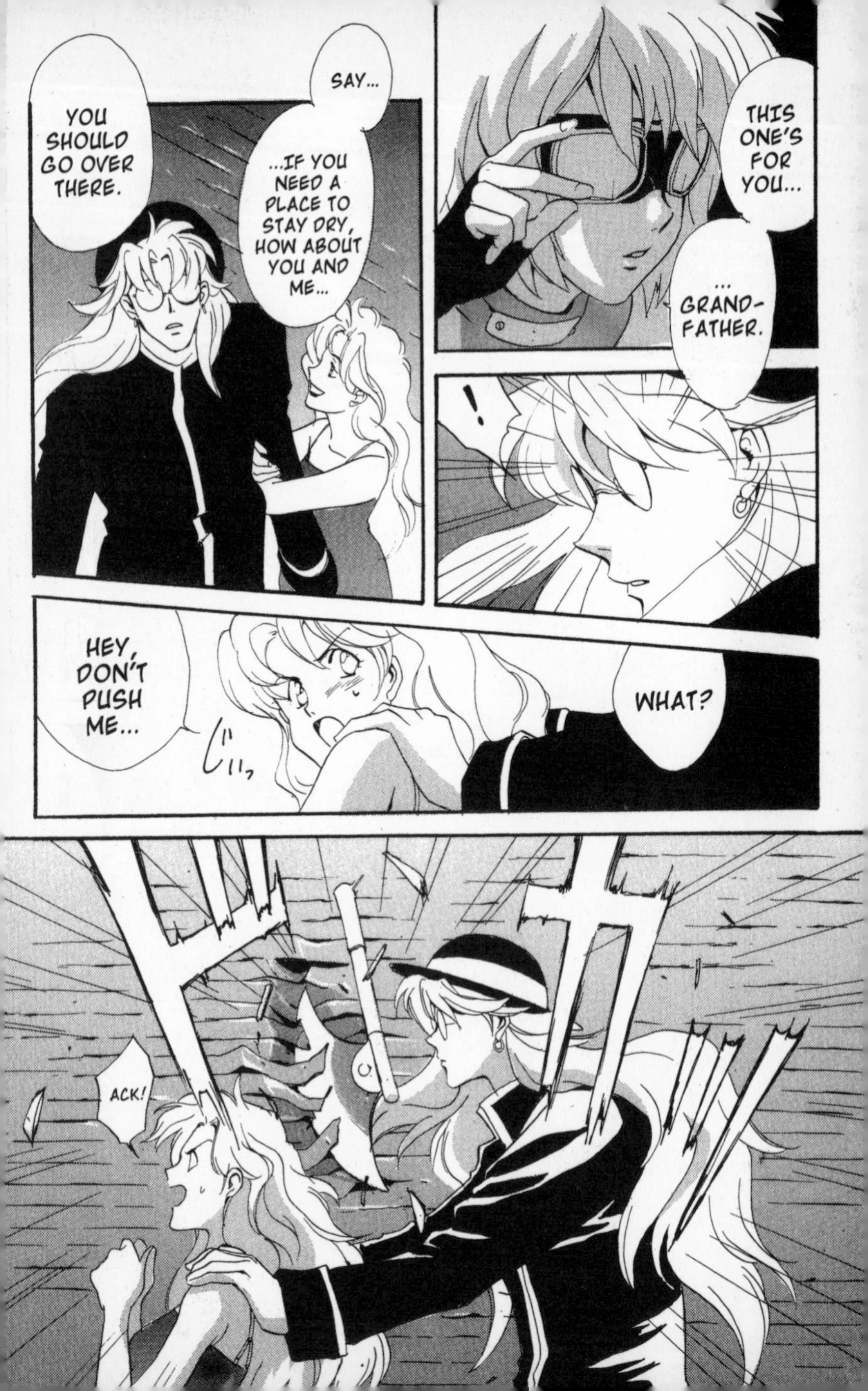
THIS ONE'S FOR YOU...
...GRAND-FATHER.
!
SAY...
...IF YOU NEED A PLACE TO STAY DRY, HOW ABOUT YOU AND ME...
YOU SHOULD GO OVER THERE.
WHAT?
HEY, DON'T PUSH ME...
ACK!

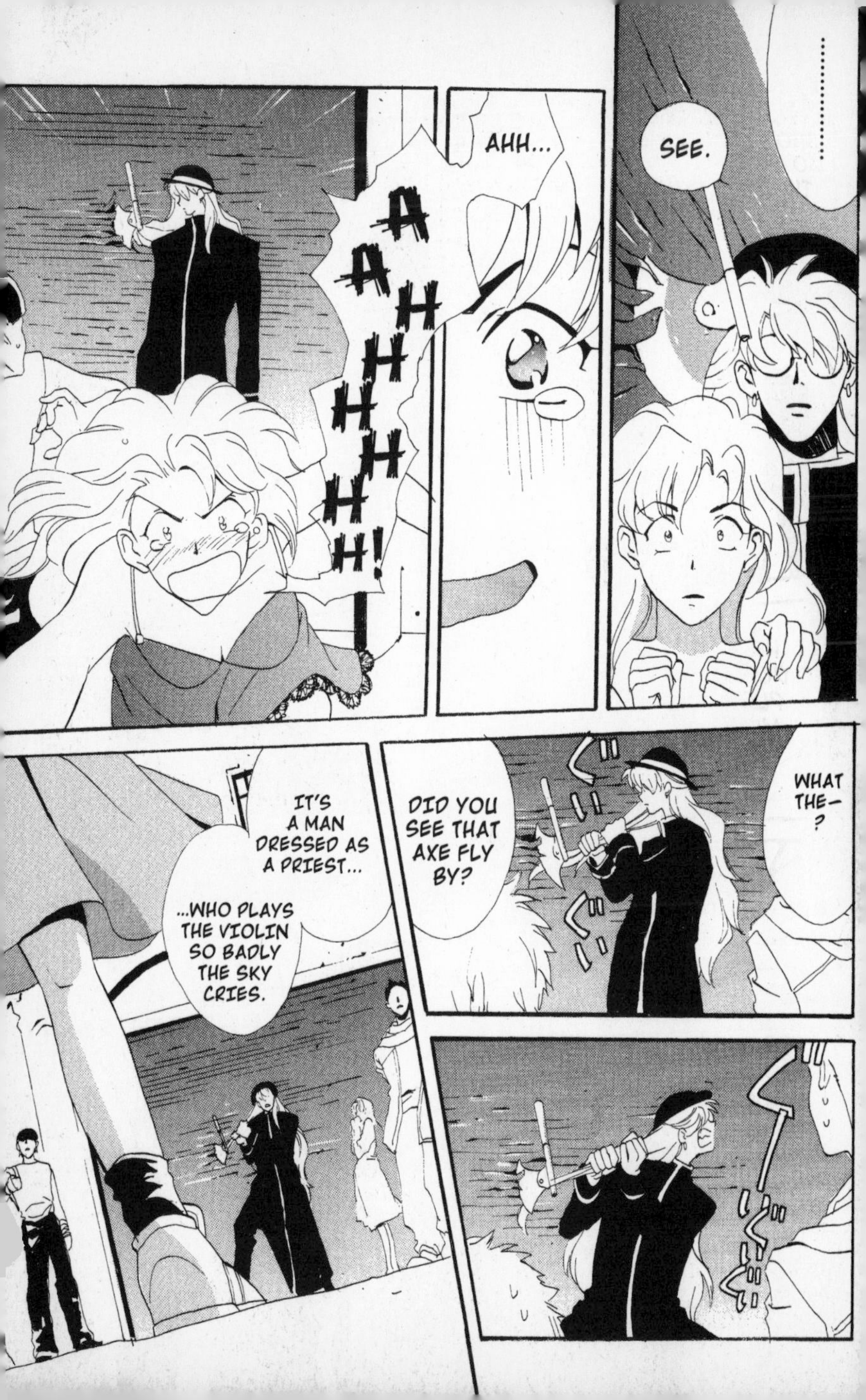
....
SEE.
AHH...
AAHHHHHHH!
WHAT THE–?
DID YOU SEE THAT AXE FLY BY?
IT'S A MAN DRESSED AS A PRIEST...
...WHO PLAYS THE VIOLIN SO BADLY THE SKY CRIES.

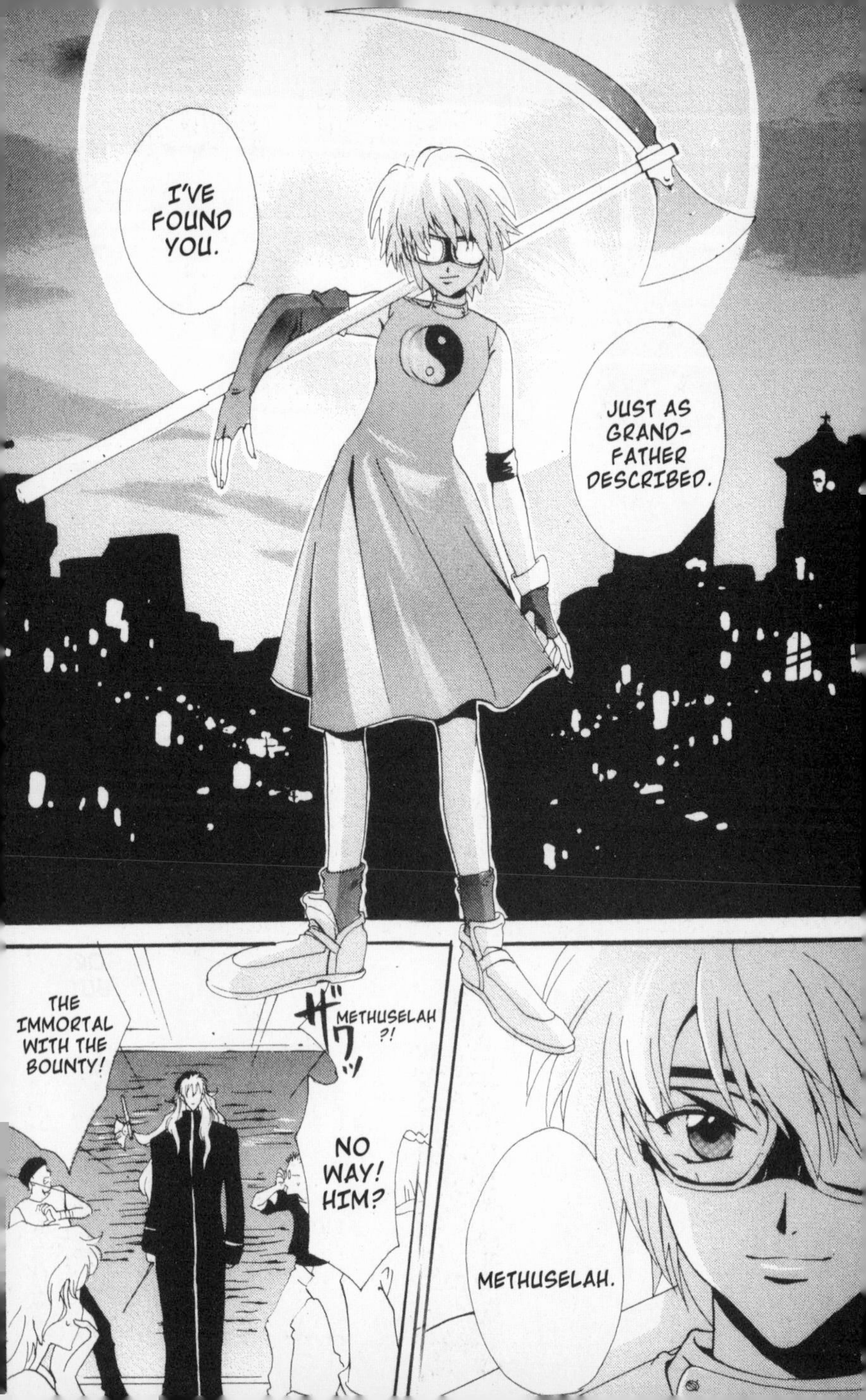
I'VE FOUND YOU.
JUST AS GRAND-FATHER DESCRIBED.
METHUSELAH.
METHUSELAH ?!
ザワッ
THE IMMORTAL WITH THE BOUNTY!
NO WAY! HIM?

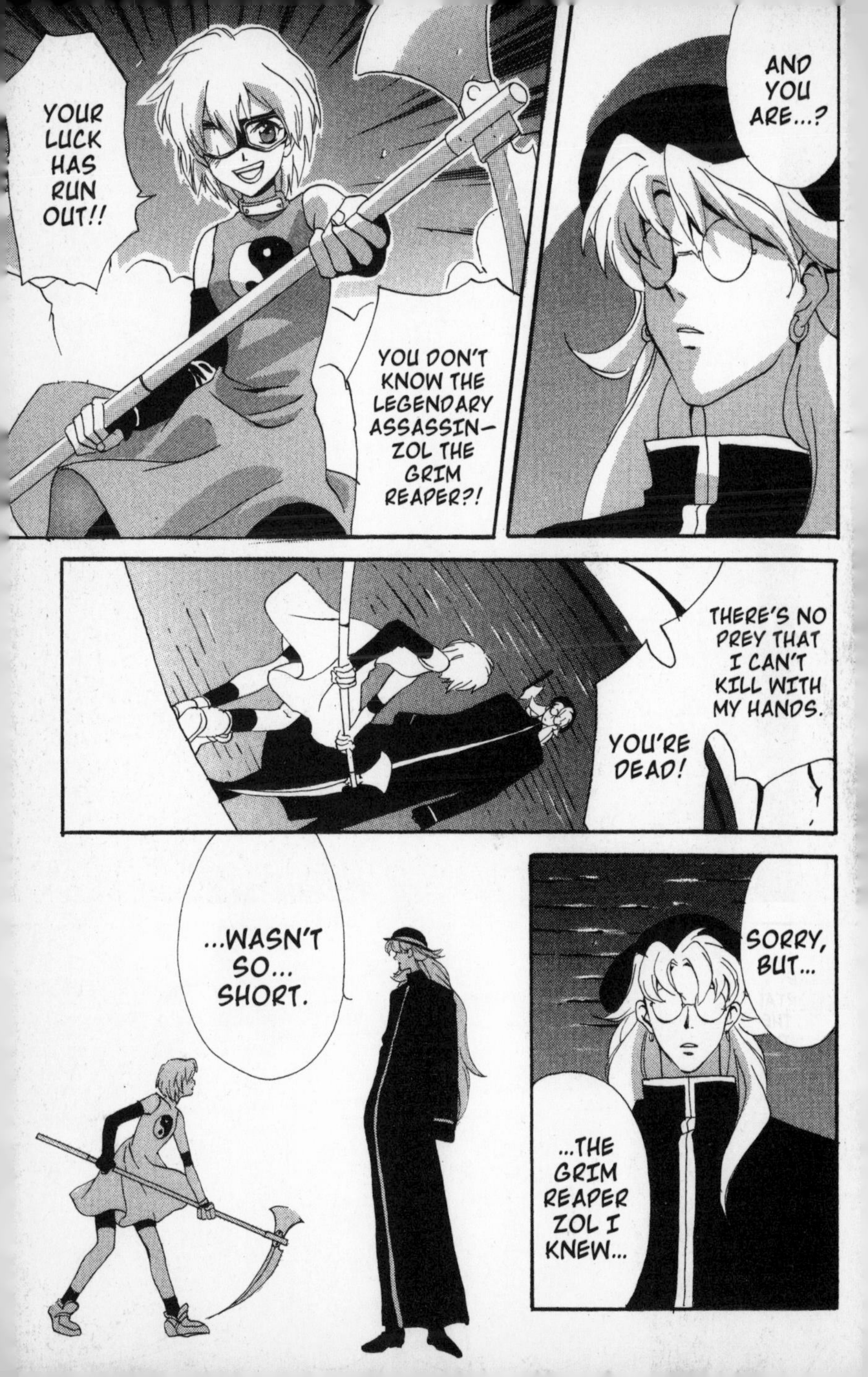
AND YOU ARE...?
YOUR LUCK HAS RUN OUT!!
YOU DON'T KNOW THE LEGENDARY ASSASSIN—ZOL THE GRIM REAPER?!
THERE'S NO PREY THAT I CAN'T KILL WITH MY HANDS.
YOU'RE DEAD!
SORRY, BUT...
...THE GRIM REAPER ZOL I KNEW...
...WASN'T SO... SHORT.

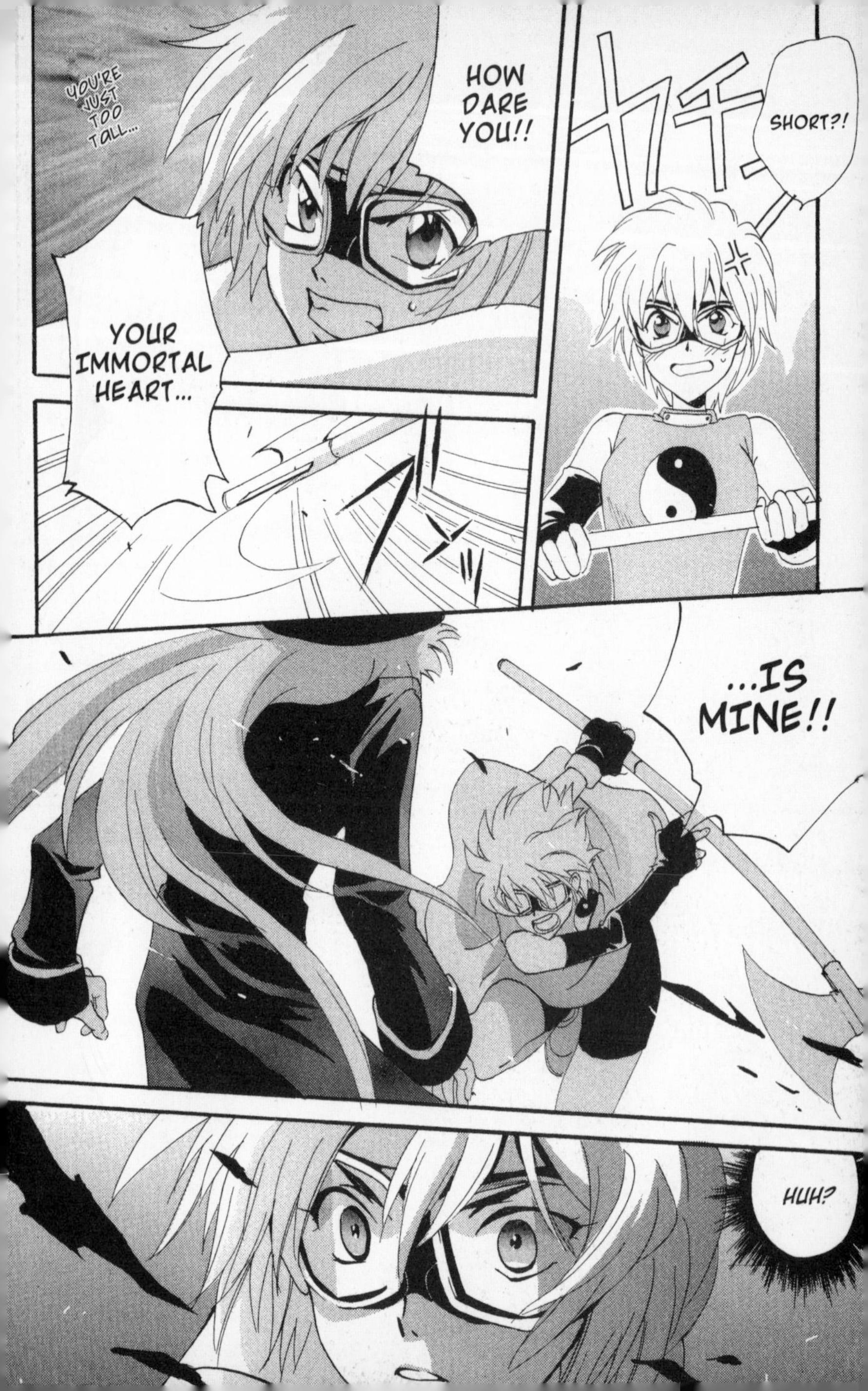
カチン
SHORT?!
HOW DARE YOU!!
YOU'RE JUST TOO TALL...
YOUR IMMORTAL HEART...
...IS MINE!!
HUH?

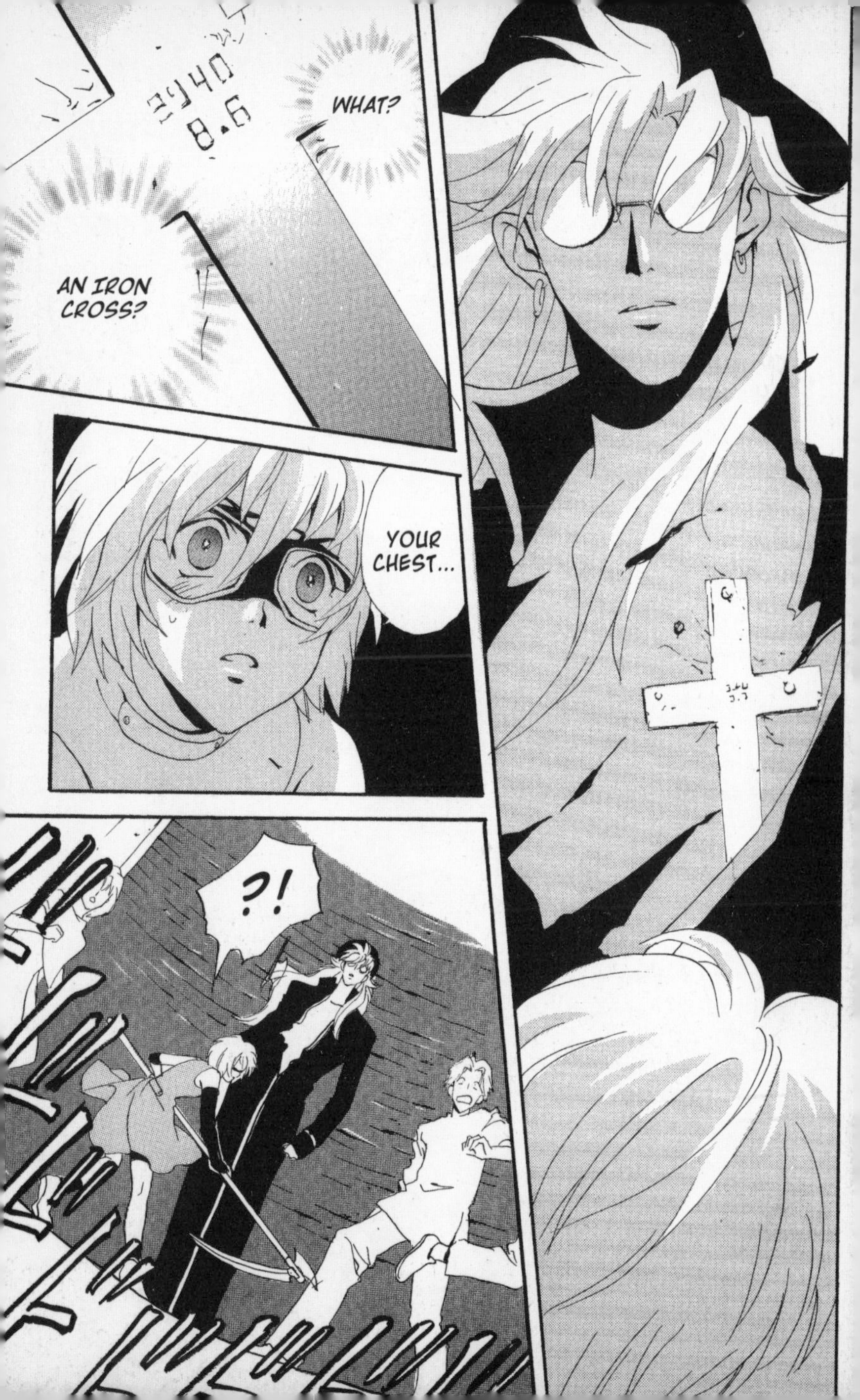
WHAT?
AN IRON CROSS?
YOUR CHEST...
?!

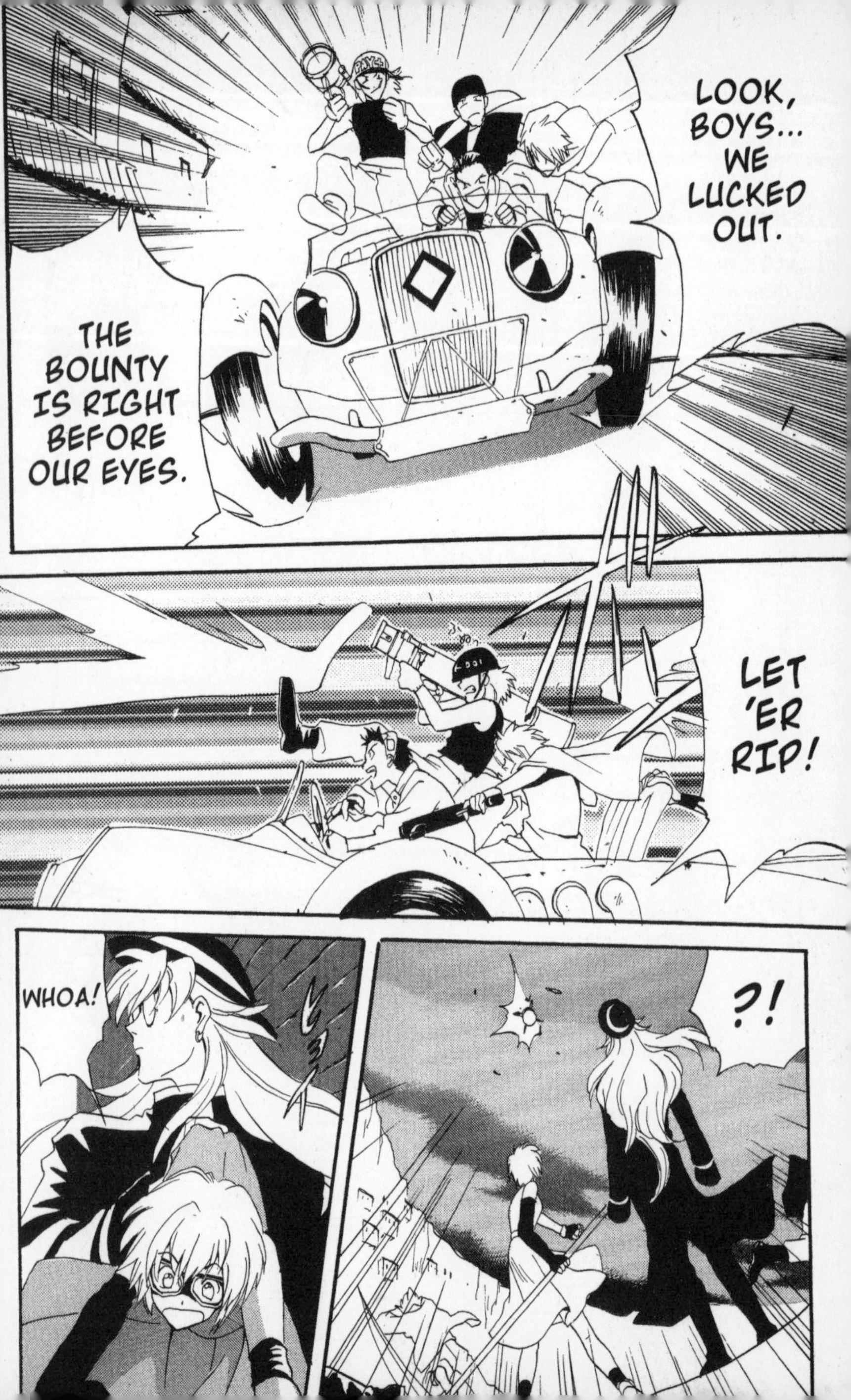
LOOK, BOYS... WE LUCKED OUT.
THE BOUNTY IS RIGHT BEFORE OUR EYES.
LET 'ER RIP!
?!
WHOA!

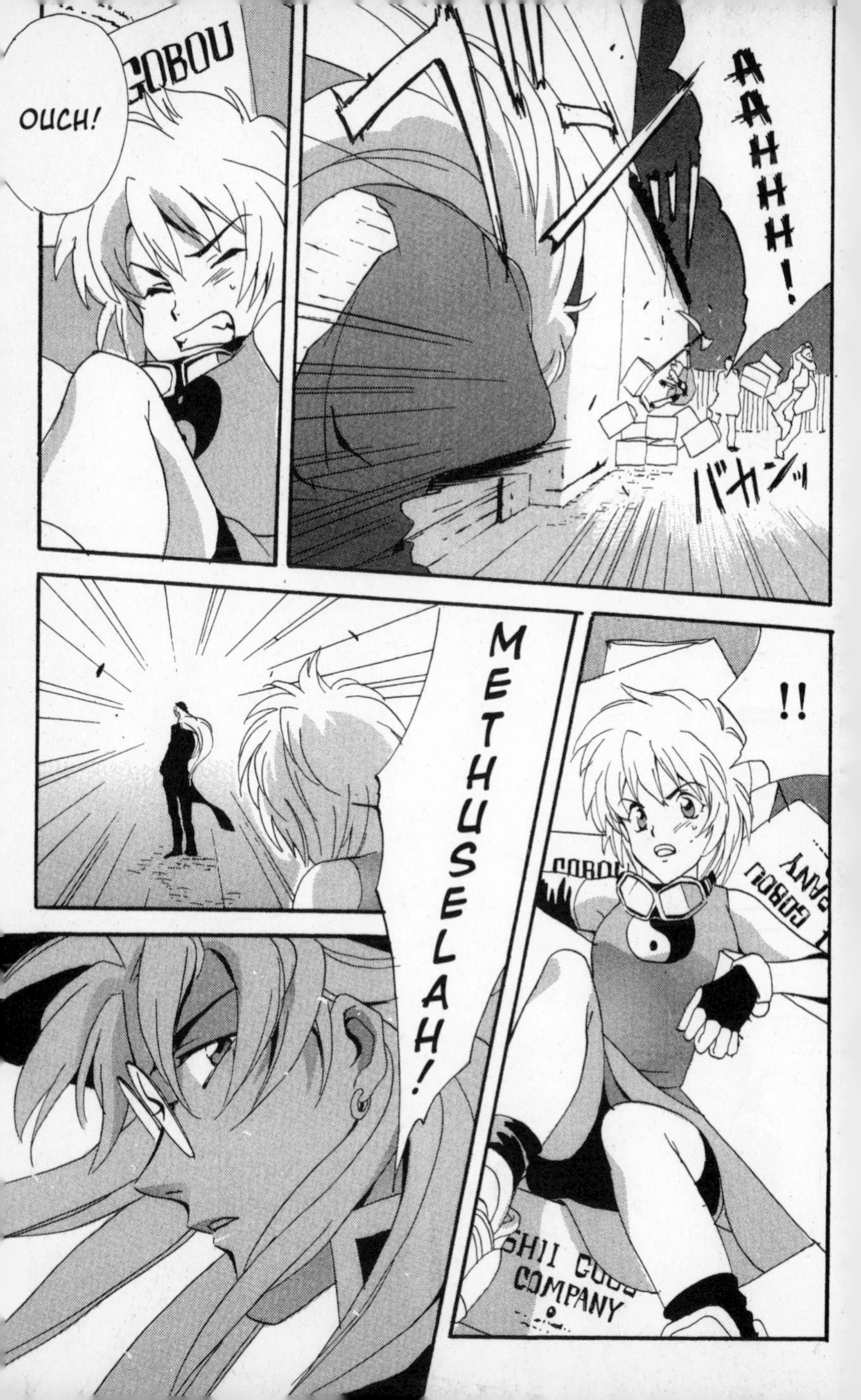
AAHHH!
バカンッ
GOBOU
OUCH!
!!
METHUSELAH!
COMPANY

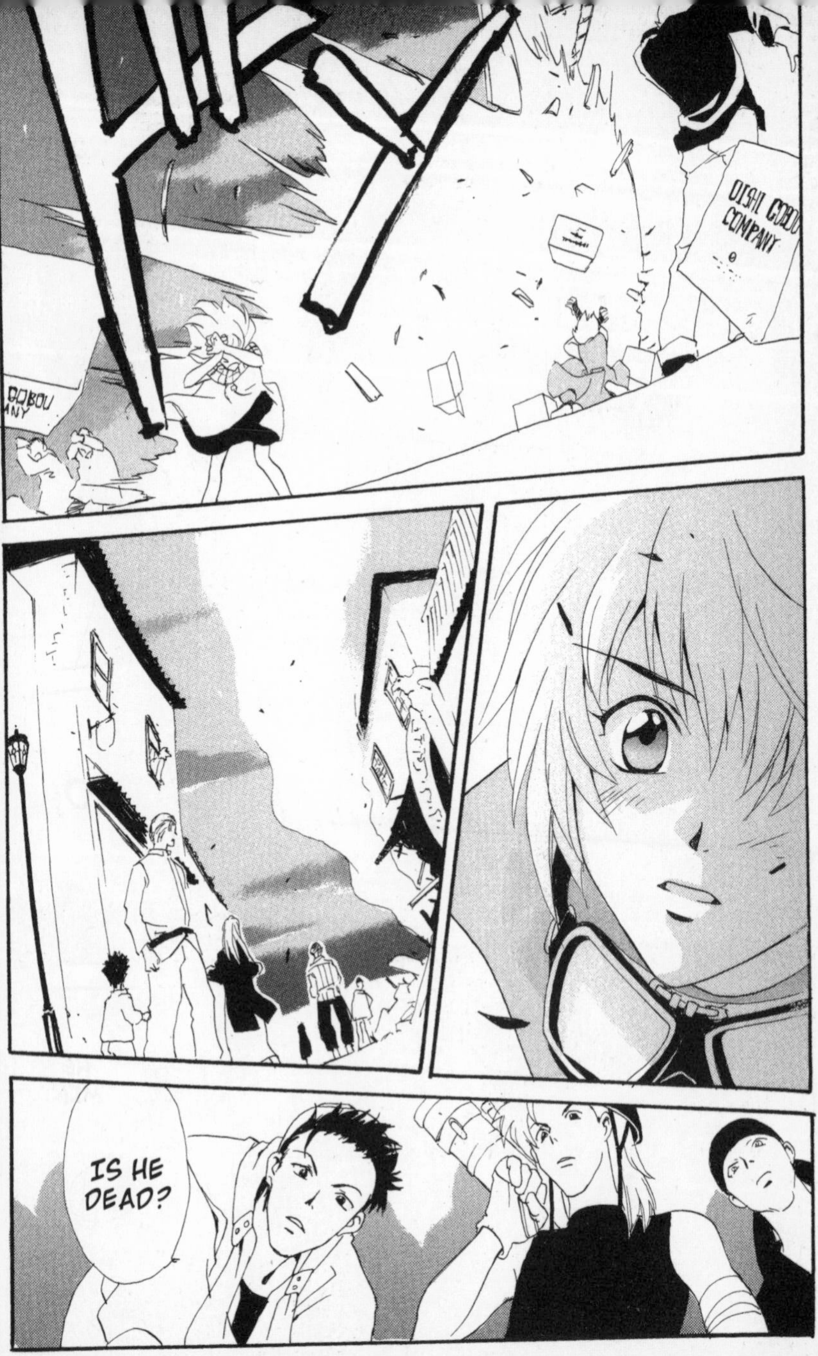
OISHI GOBOU
COMPANY
IS HE DEAD?

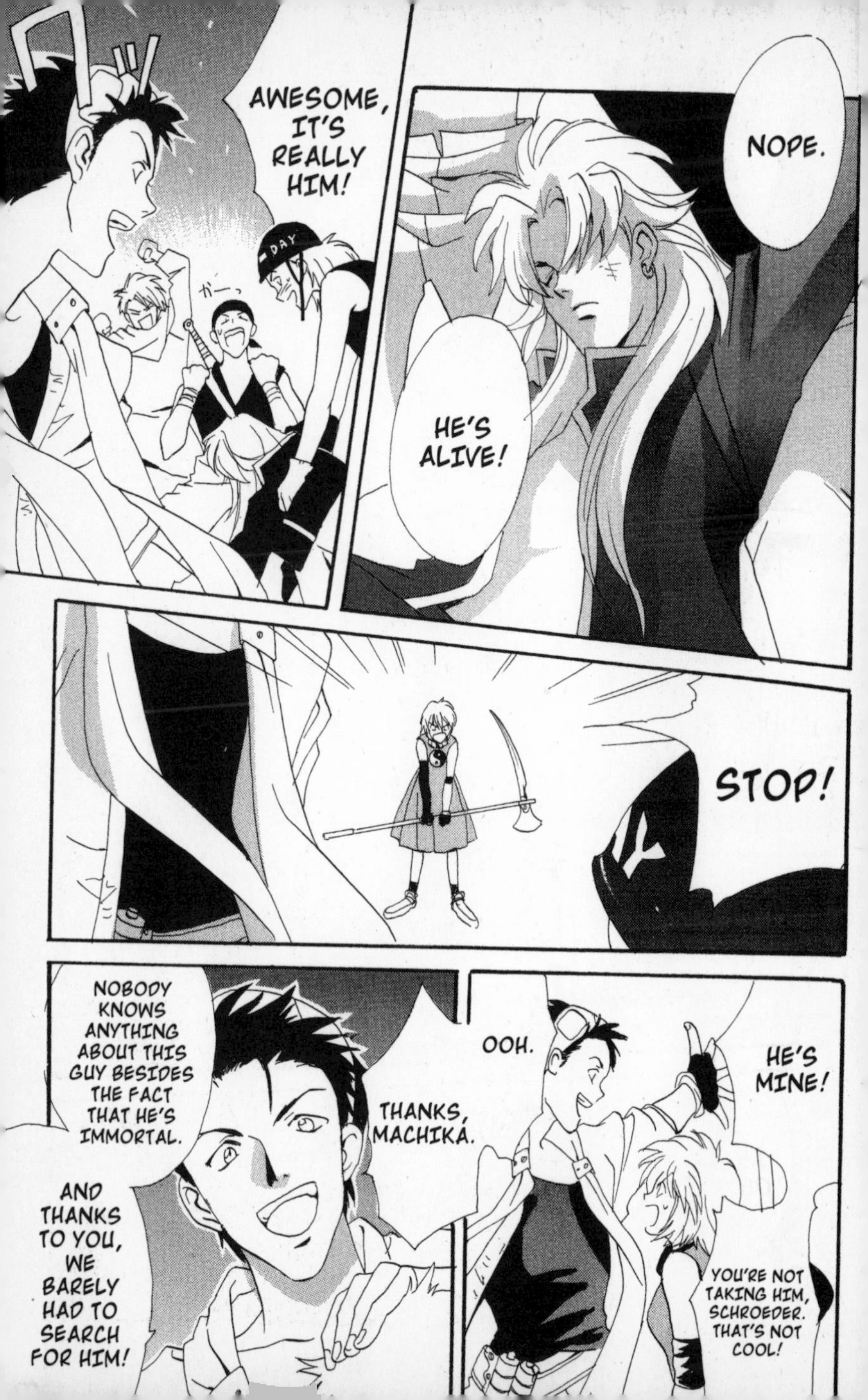
NOPE.
HE'S ALIVE!
AWESOME, IT'S REALLY HIM!
STOP!
HE'S MINE!
OOH.
YOU'RE NOT TAKING HIM, SCHROEDER. THAT'S NOT COOL!
THANKS, MACHIKA.
NOBODY KNOWS ANYTHING ABOUT THIS GUY BESIDES THE FACT THAT HE'S IMMORTAL.
AND THANKS TO YOU, WE BARELY HAD TO SEARCH FOR HIM!

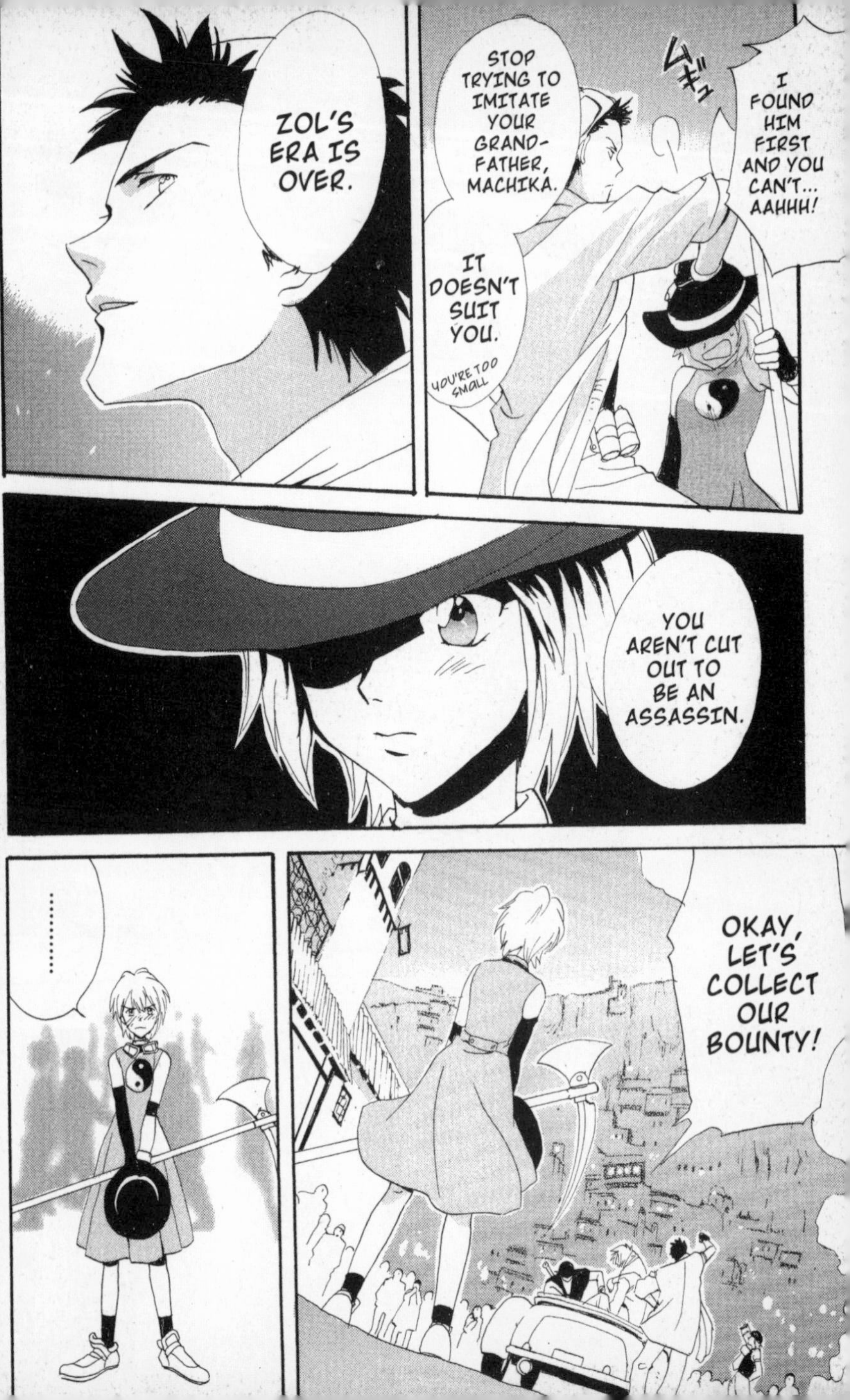
I FOUND HIM FIRST AND YOU CAN'T... AAHHH!
ムギュ
STOP TRYING TO IMITATE YOUR GRAND-FATHER, MACHIKA.
IT DOESN'T SUIT YOU.
YOU'RE TOO SMALL
ZOL'S ERA IS OVER.
YOU AREN'T CUT OUT TO BE AN ASSASSIN.
OKAY, LET'S COLLECT OUR BOUNTY!
......

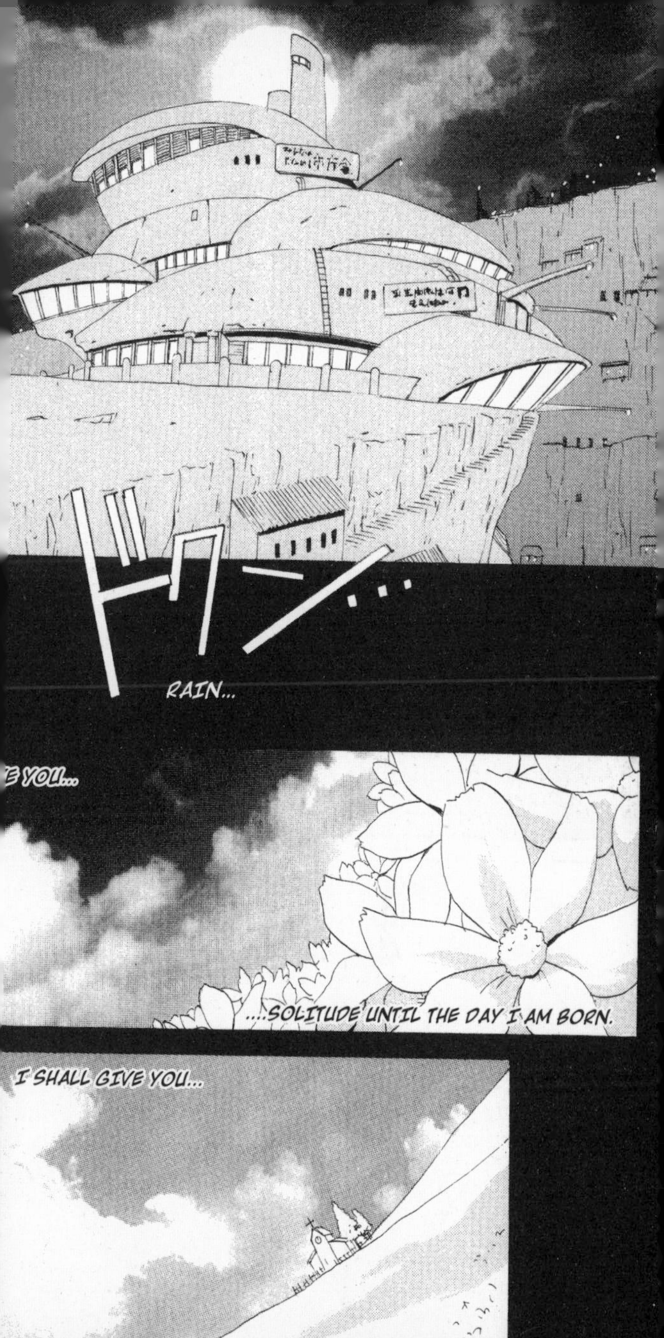
ドクーン...
RAIN...
E YOU...
....SOLITUDE UNTIL THE DAY I AM BORN.
I SHALL GIVE YOU...
...THE ENDS OF TIME...

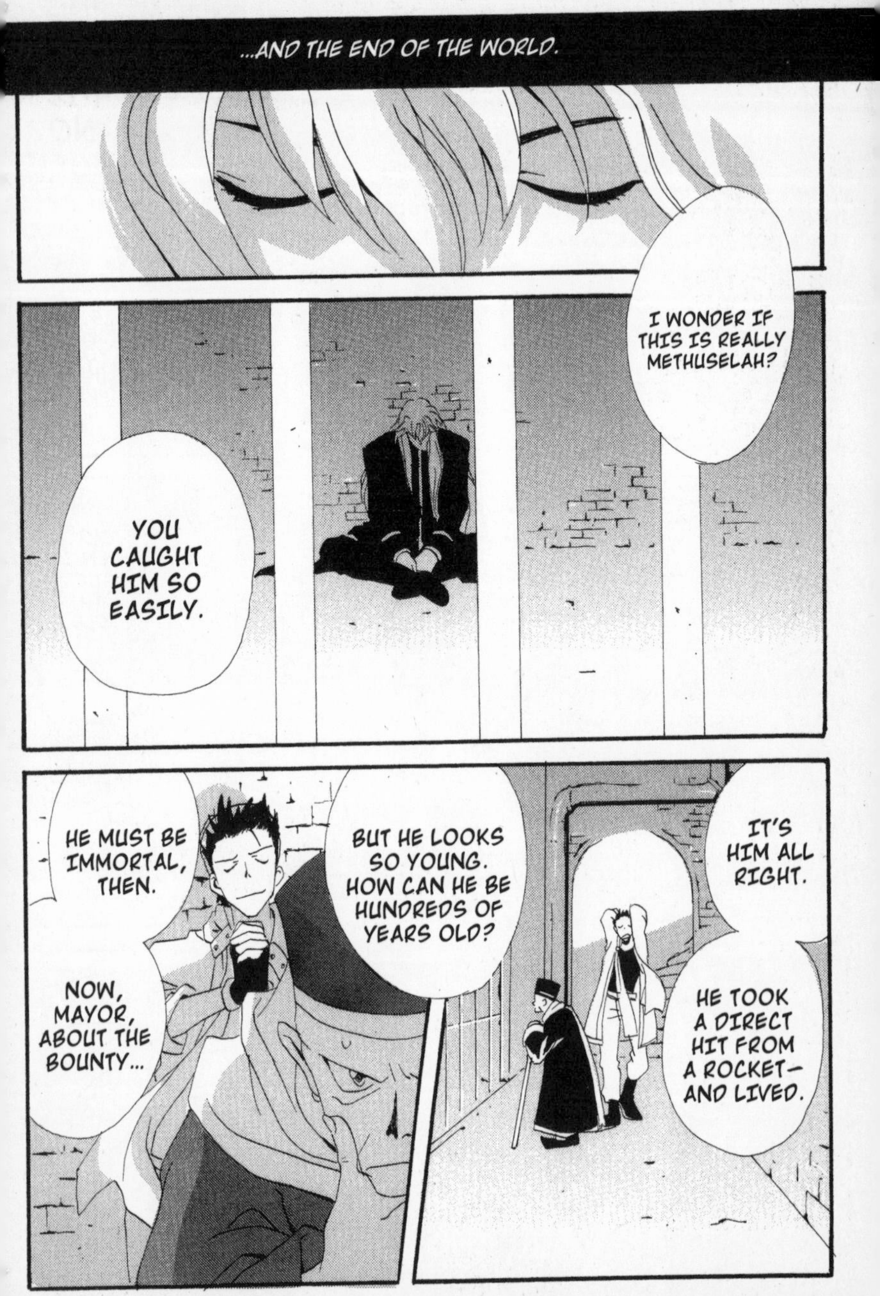
...AND THE END OF THE WORLD.
I WONDER IF THIS IS REALLY METHUSELAH?
YOU CAUGHT HIM SO EASILY.
IT'S HIM ALL RIGHT.
HE TOOK A DIRECT HIT FROM A ROCKET— AND LIVED.
BUT HE LOOKS SO YOUNG. HOW CAN HE BE HUNDREDS OF YEARS OLD?
HE MUST BE IMMORTAL, THEN.
NOW, MAYOR, ABOUT THE BOUNTY...

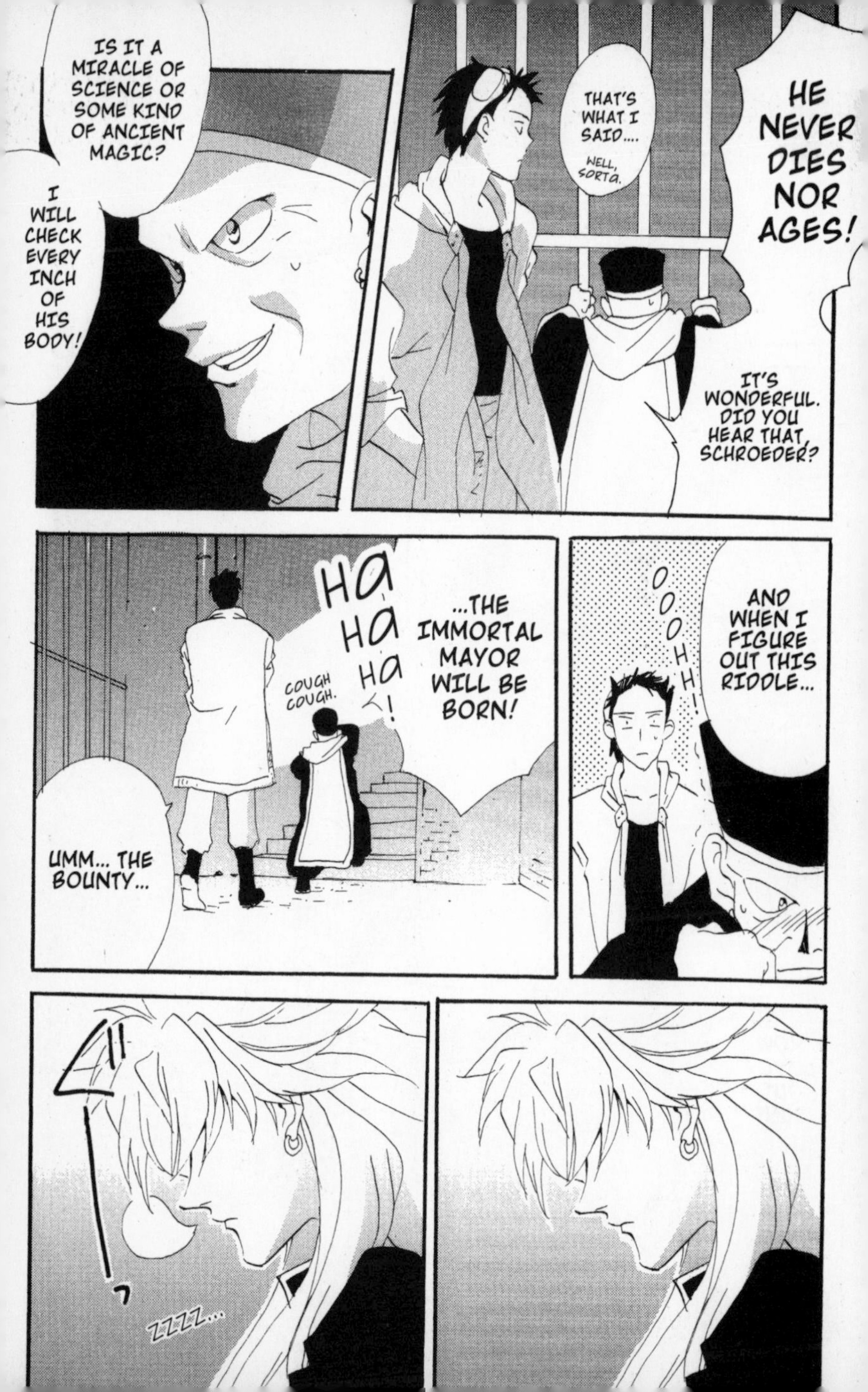
HE NEVER DIES NOR AGES!
THAT'S WHAT I SAID....
WELL, SORTA.
IT'S WONDERFUL. DID YOU HEAR THAT, SCHROEDER?
IS IT A MIRACLE OF SCIENCE OR SOME KIND OF ANCIENT MAGIC?
I WILL CHECK EVERY INCH OF HIS BODY!
AND WHEN I FIGURE OUT THIS RIDDLE...
OOOHH!
...THE IMMORTAL MAYOR WILL BE BORN!
HA HA HA!
COUGH COUGH.
UMM... THE BOUNTY...
ZZZZ...

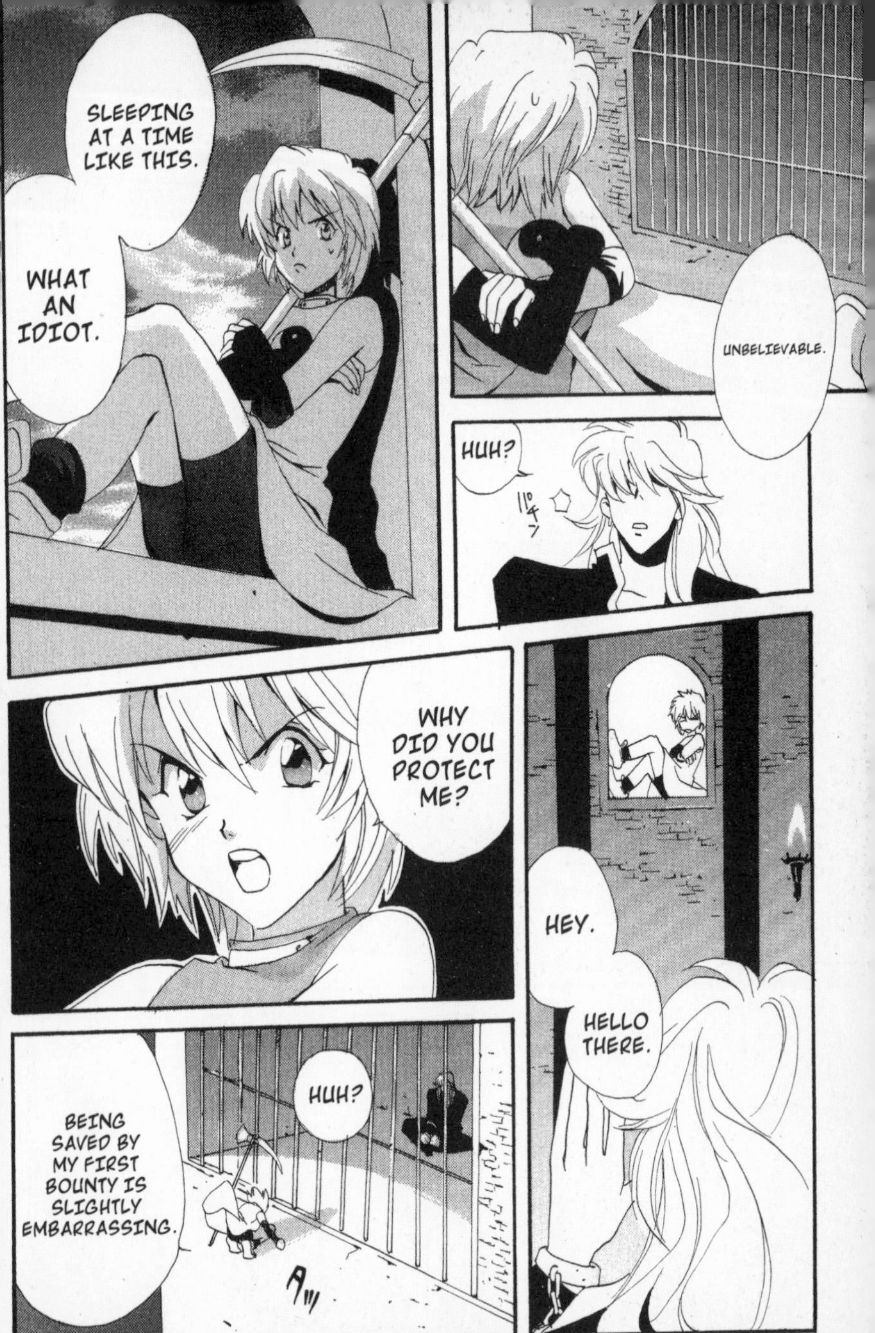
UNBELIEVABLE.
HUH?
SLEEPING AT A TIME LIKE THIS.
WHAT AN IDIOT.
HEY.
HELLO THERE.
WHY DID YOU PROTECT ME?
HUH?
BEING SAVED BY MY FIRST BOUNTY IS SLIGHTLY EMBARRASSING.

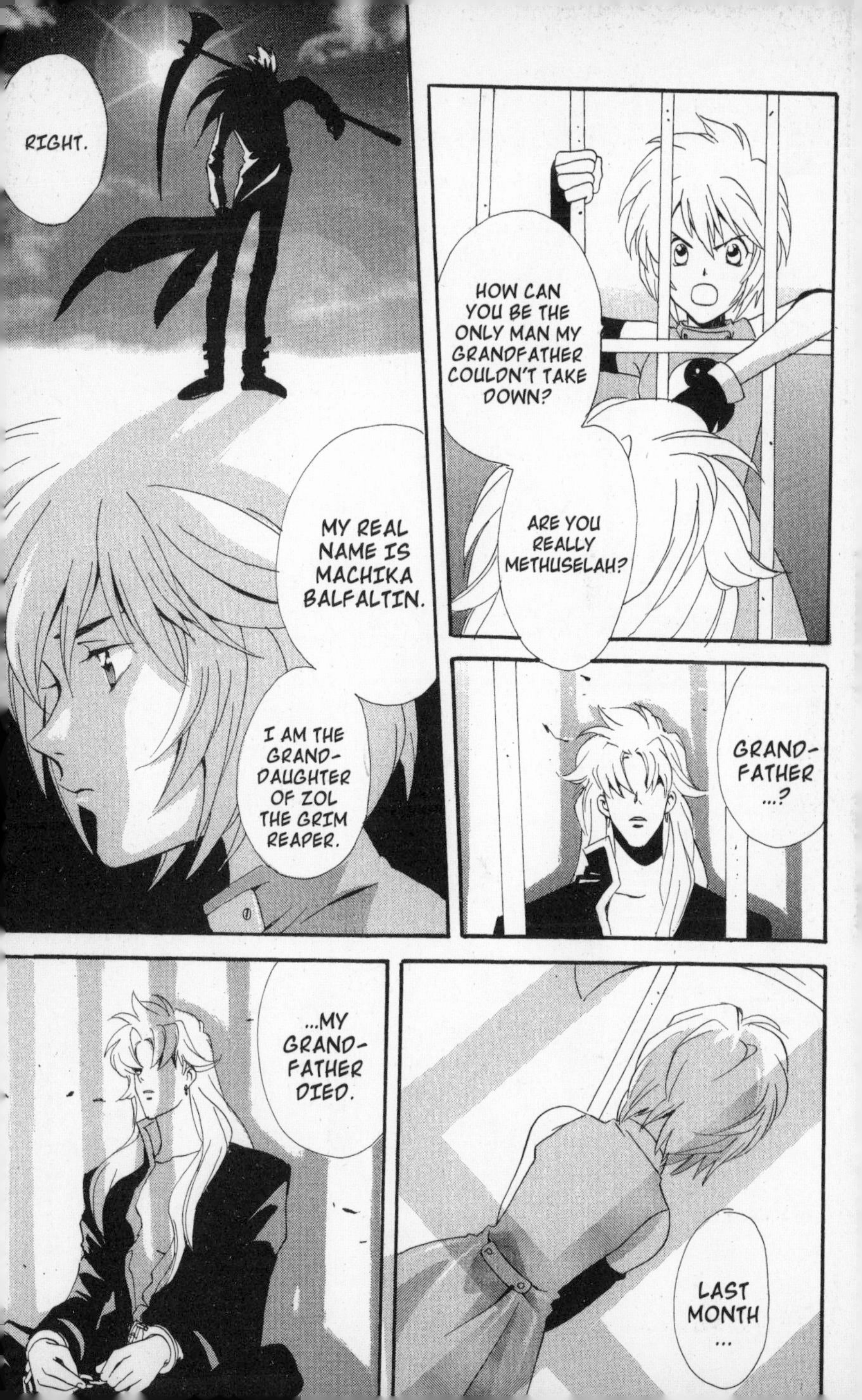
HOW CAN YOU BE THE ONLY MAN MY GRANDFATHER COULDN'T TAKE DOWN?
ARE YOU REALLY METHUSELAH?
RIGHT.
MY REAL NAME IS MACHIKA BALFALTIN.
I AM THE GRAND-DAUGHTER OF ZOL THE GRIM REAPER.
GRAND-FATHER ...?
LAST MONTH ...
...MY GRAND-FATHER DIED.

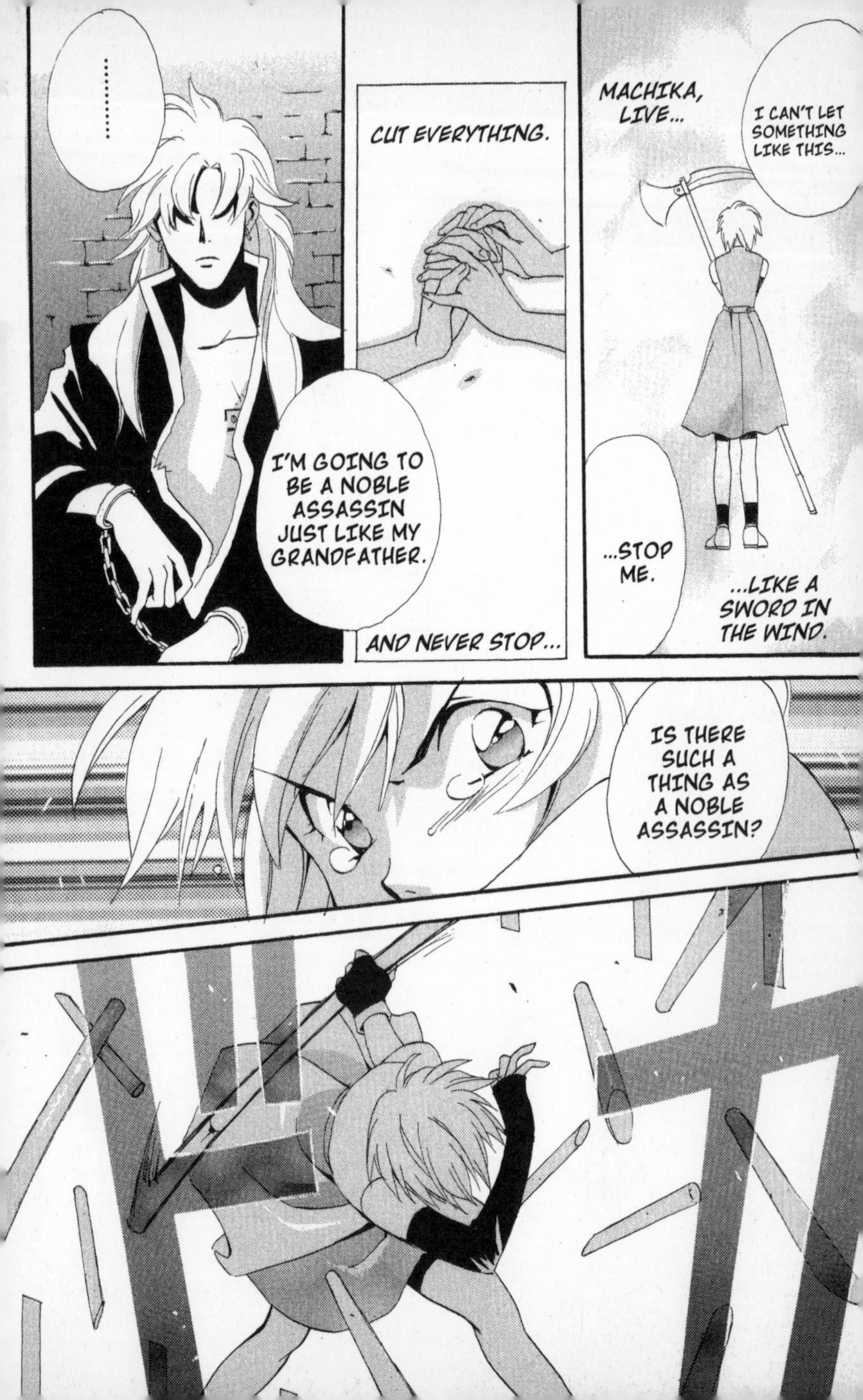
I CAN'T LET SOMETHING LIKE THIS...
MACHIKA, LIVE...
...STOP ME.
...LIKE A SWORD IN THE WIND.
CUT EVERYTHING.
I'M GOING TO BE A NOBLE ASSASSIN JUST LIKE MY GRANDFATHER.
AND NEVER STOP...
......
IS THERE SUCH A THING AS A NOBLE ASSASSIN?

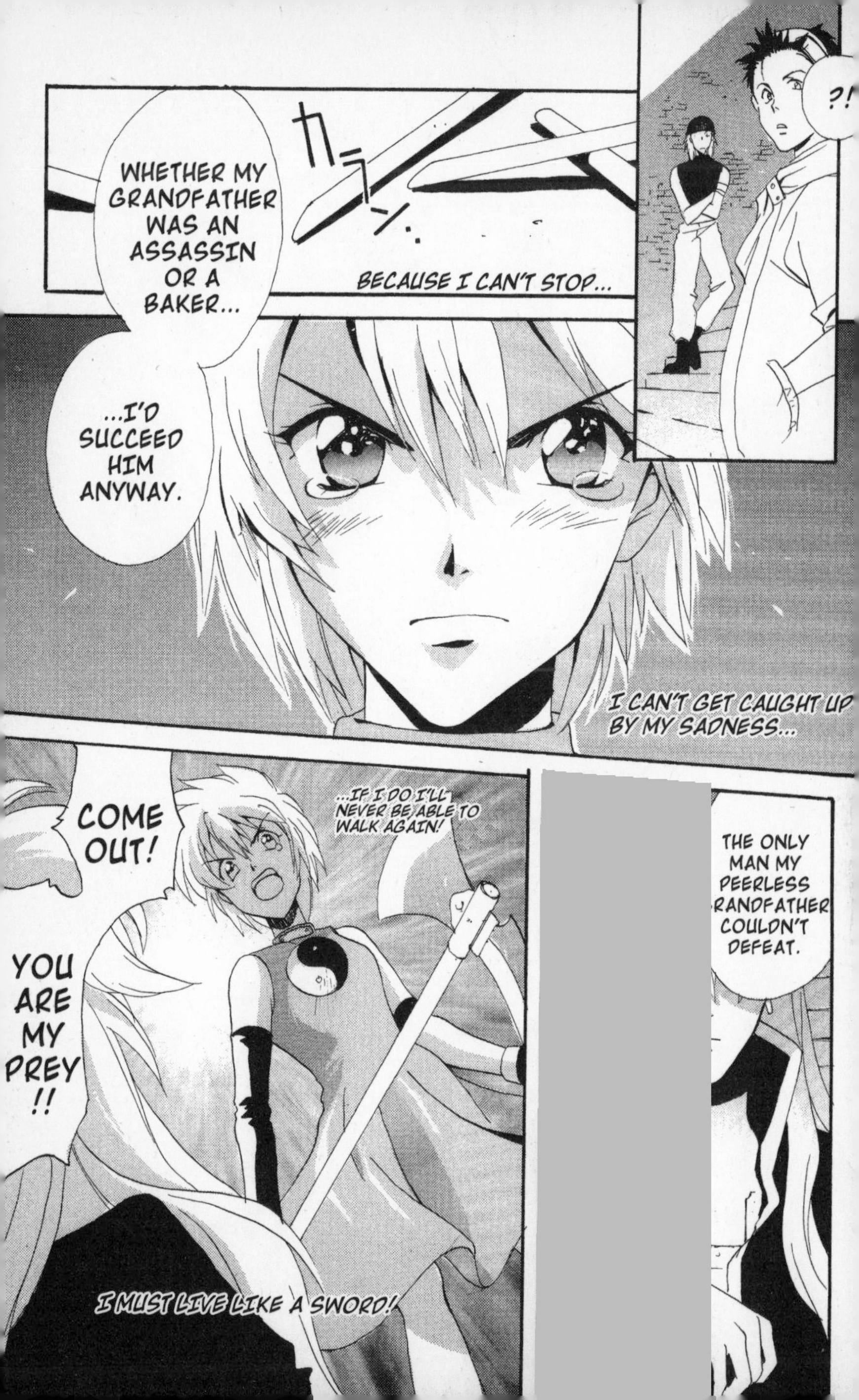
?!
カラーン..
BECAUSE I CAN'T STOP...
WHETHER MY GRANDFATHER WAS AN ASSASSIN OR A BAKER...
...I'D SUCCEED HIM ANYWAY.
I CAN'T GET CAUGHT UP BY MY SADNESS...
THE ONLY MAN MY PEERLESS GRANDFATHER COULDN'T DEFEAT.
COME OUT!
...IF I DO I'LL NEVER BE ABLE TO WALK AGAIN!
YOU ARE MY PREY !!
I MUST LIVE LIKE A SWORD!

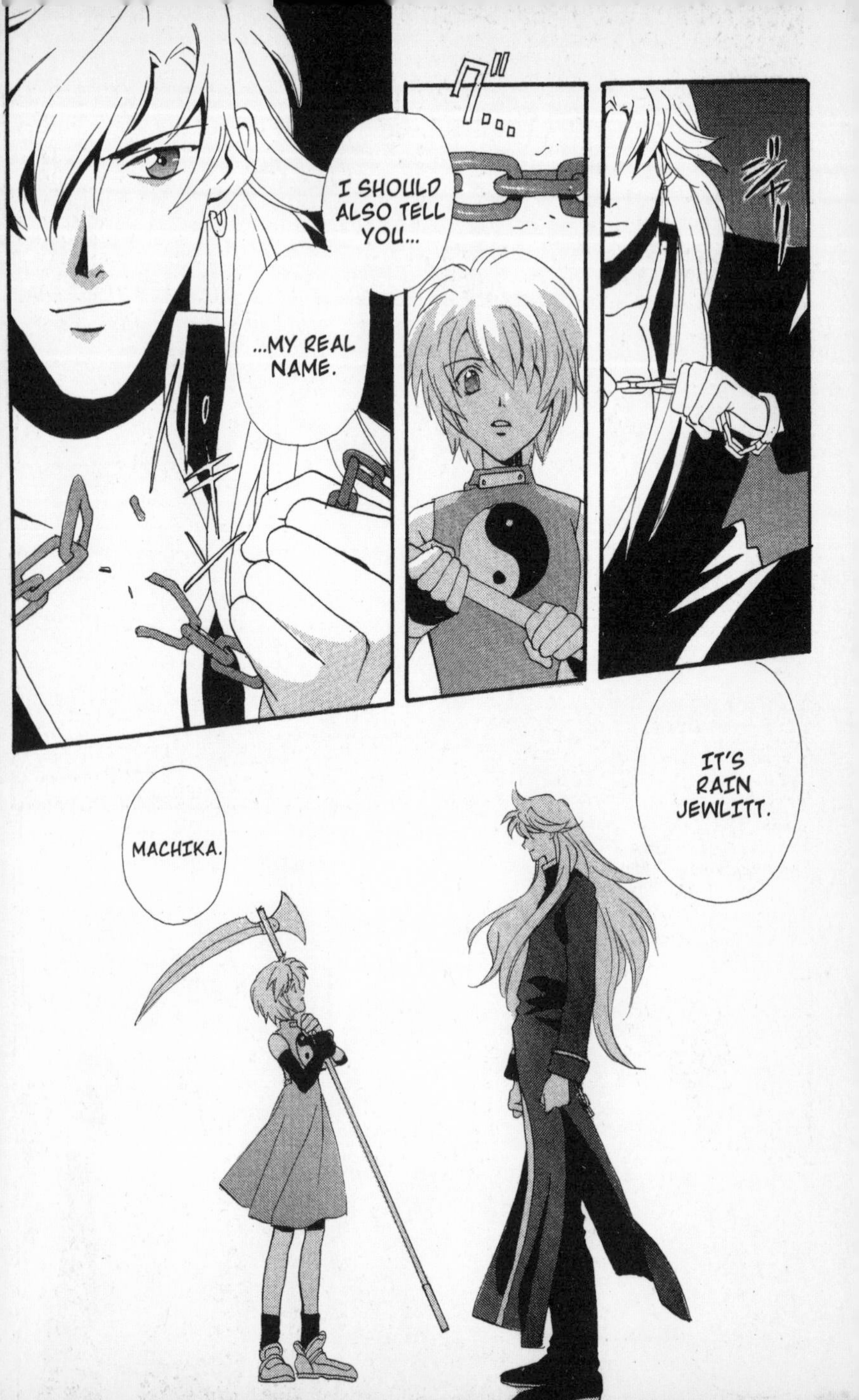
I SHOULD ALSO TELL YOU...
...MY REAL NAME.
IT'S RAIN JEWLITT.
MACHIKA.

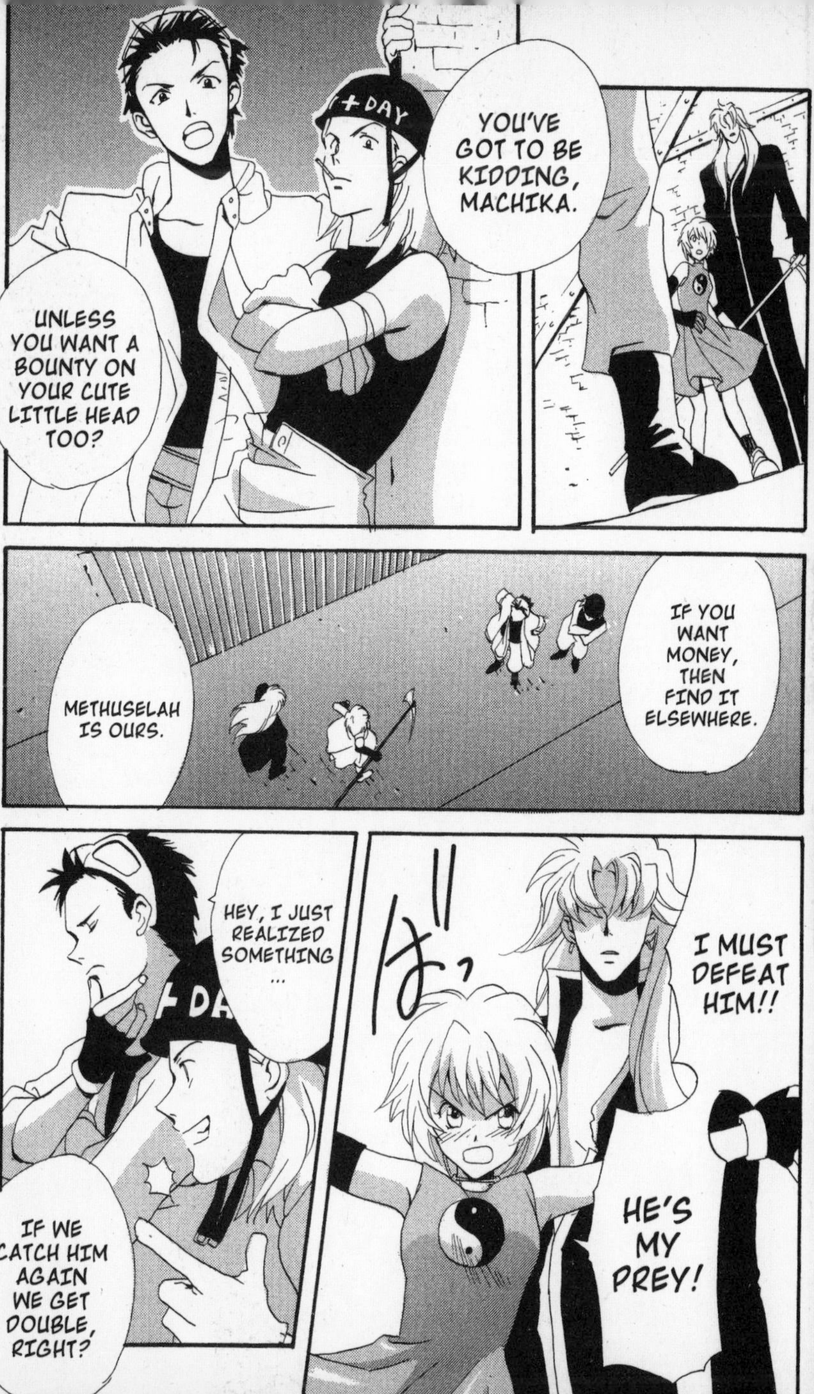
YOU'VE GOT TO BE KIDDING, MACHIKA.
UNLESS YOU WANT A BOUNTY ON YOUR CUTE LITTLE HEAD TOO?
IF YOU WANT MONEY, THEN FIND IT ELSEWHERE.
METHUSELAH IS OURS.
I MUST DEFEAT HIM!!
はっ
HE'S MY PREY!
HEY, I JUST REALIZED SOMETHING ...
IF WE CATCH HIM AGAIN WE GET DOUBLE, RIGHT?

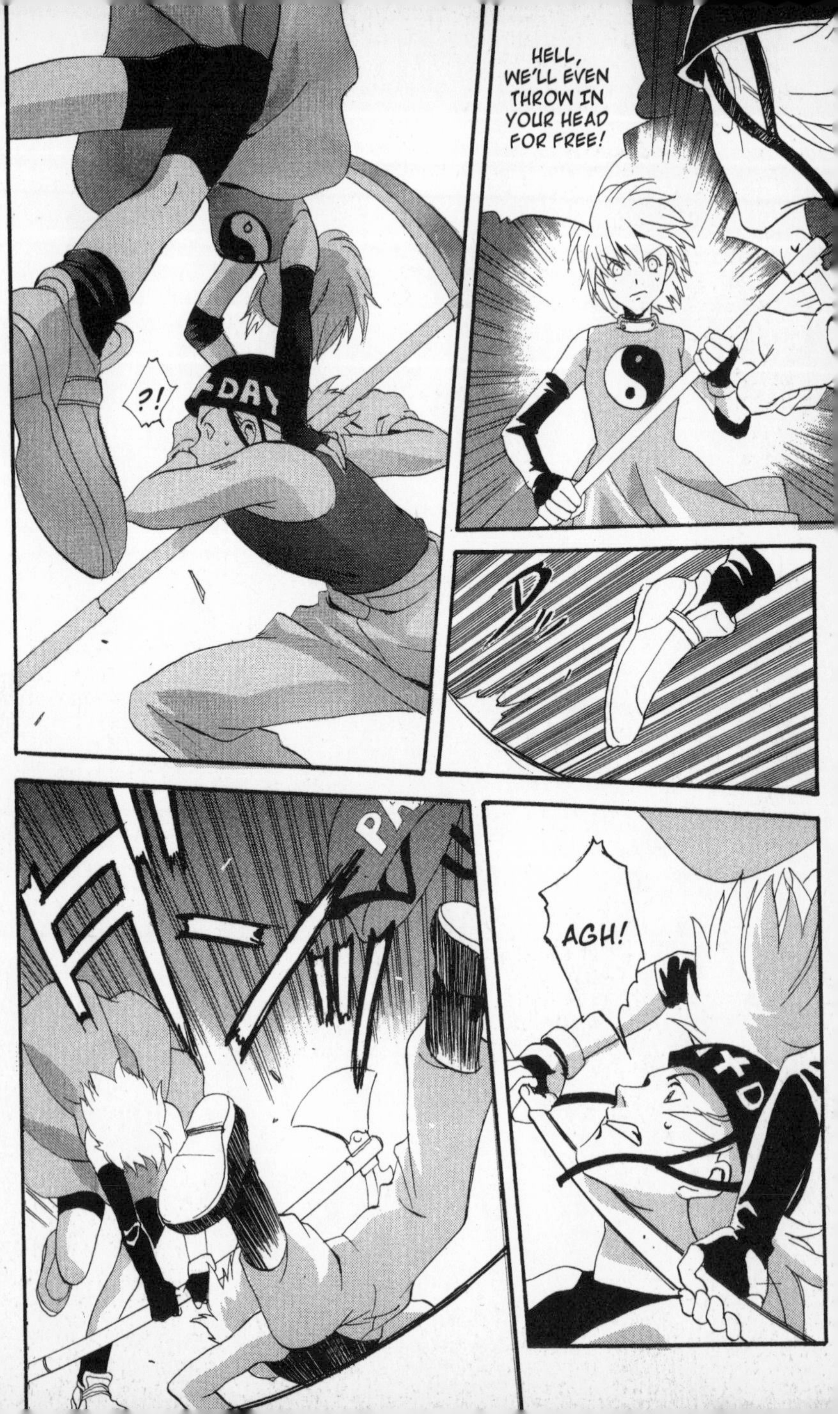
HELL, WE'LL EVEN THROW IN YOUR HEAD FOR FREE!
?!
AGH!

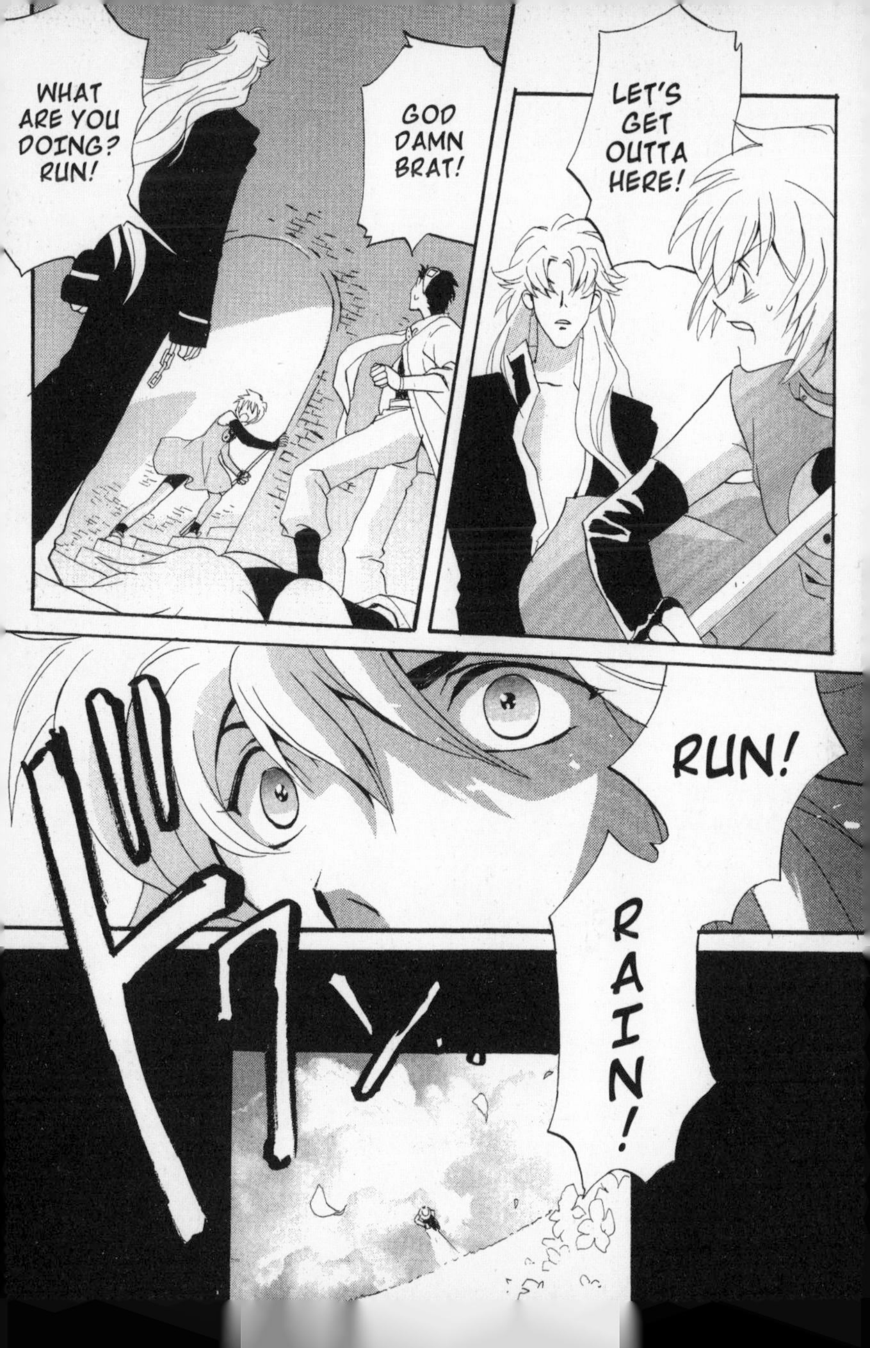
LET'S GET OUTTA HERE!
GOD DAMN BRAT!
WHAT ARE YOU DOING? RUN!
RUN!
RAIN!

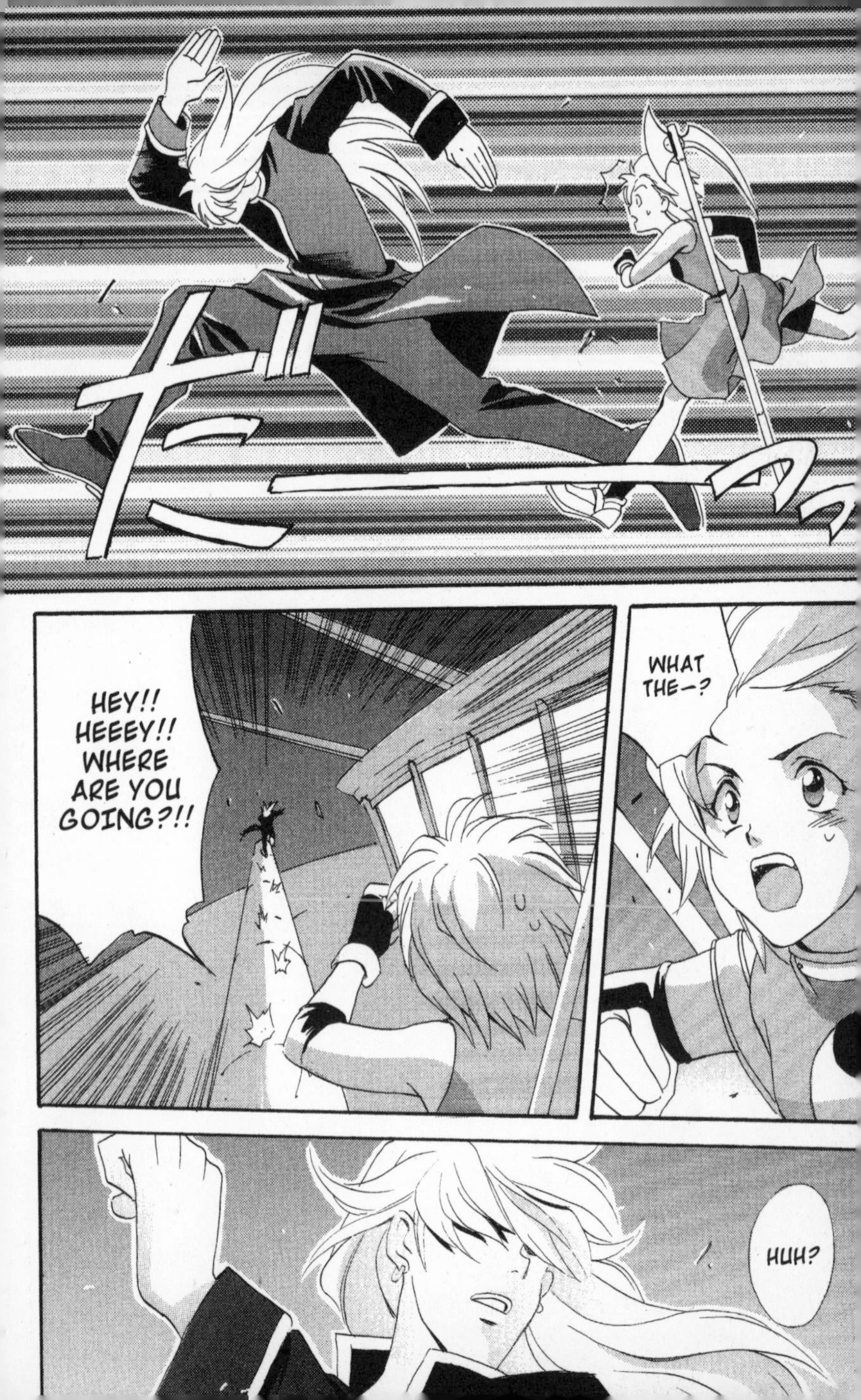
WHAT THE—?
HEY!! HEEEY!! WHERE ARE YOU GOING?!!
HUH?

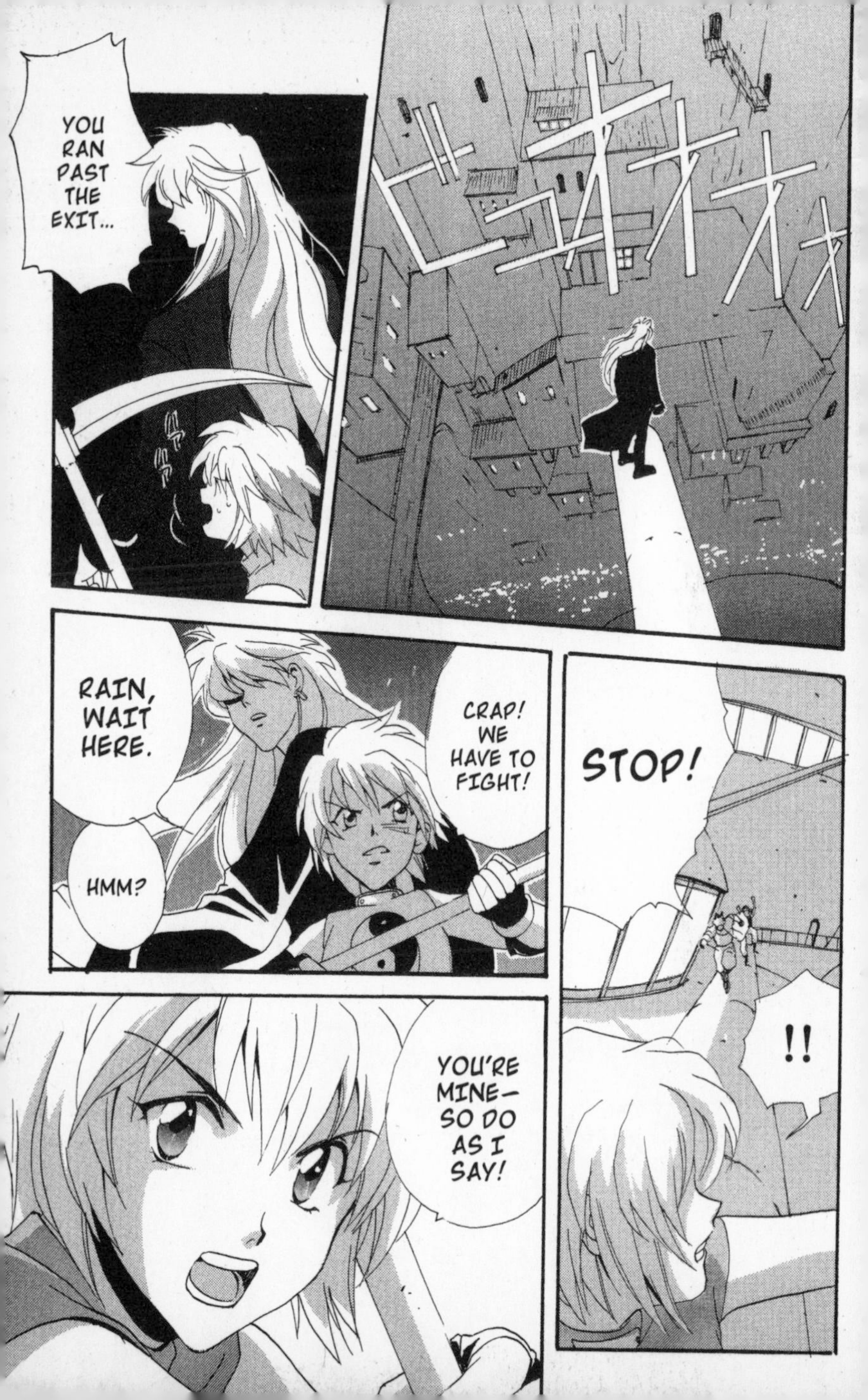
YOU RAN PAST THE EXIT...
STOP!
!!
CRAP! WE HAVE TO FIGHT!
RAIN, WAIT HERE.
HMM?
YOU'RE MINE— SO DO AS I SAY!

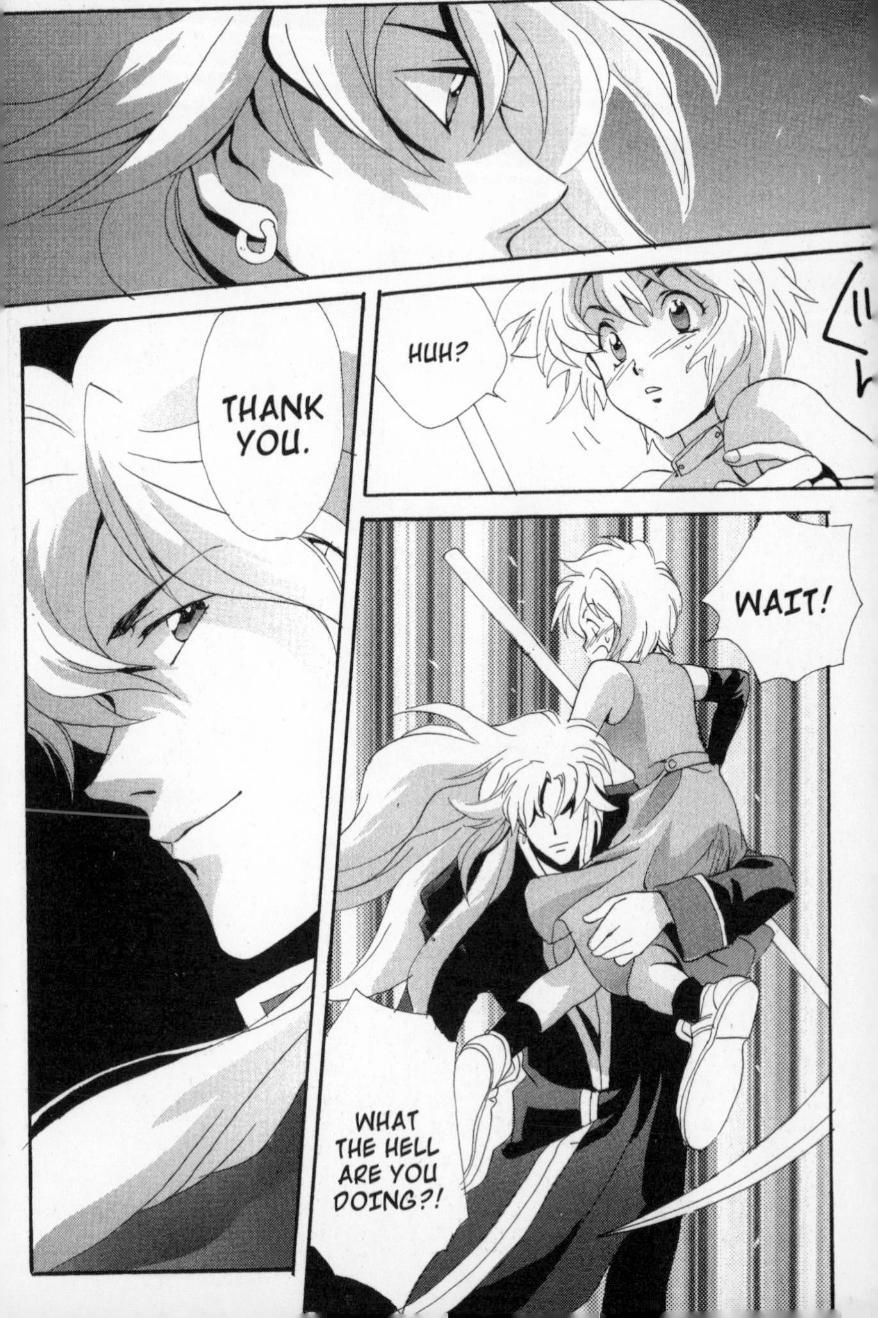
HUH?
WAIT!
WHAT THE HELL ARE YOU DOING?!
THANK YOU.

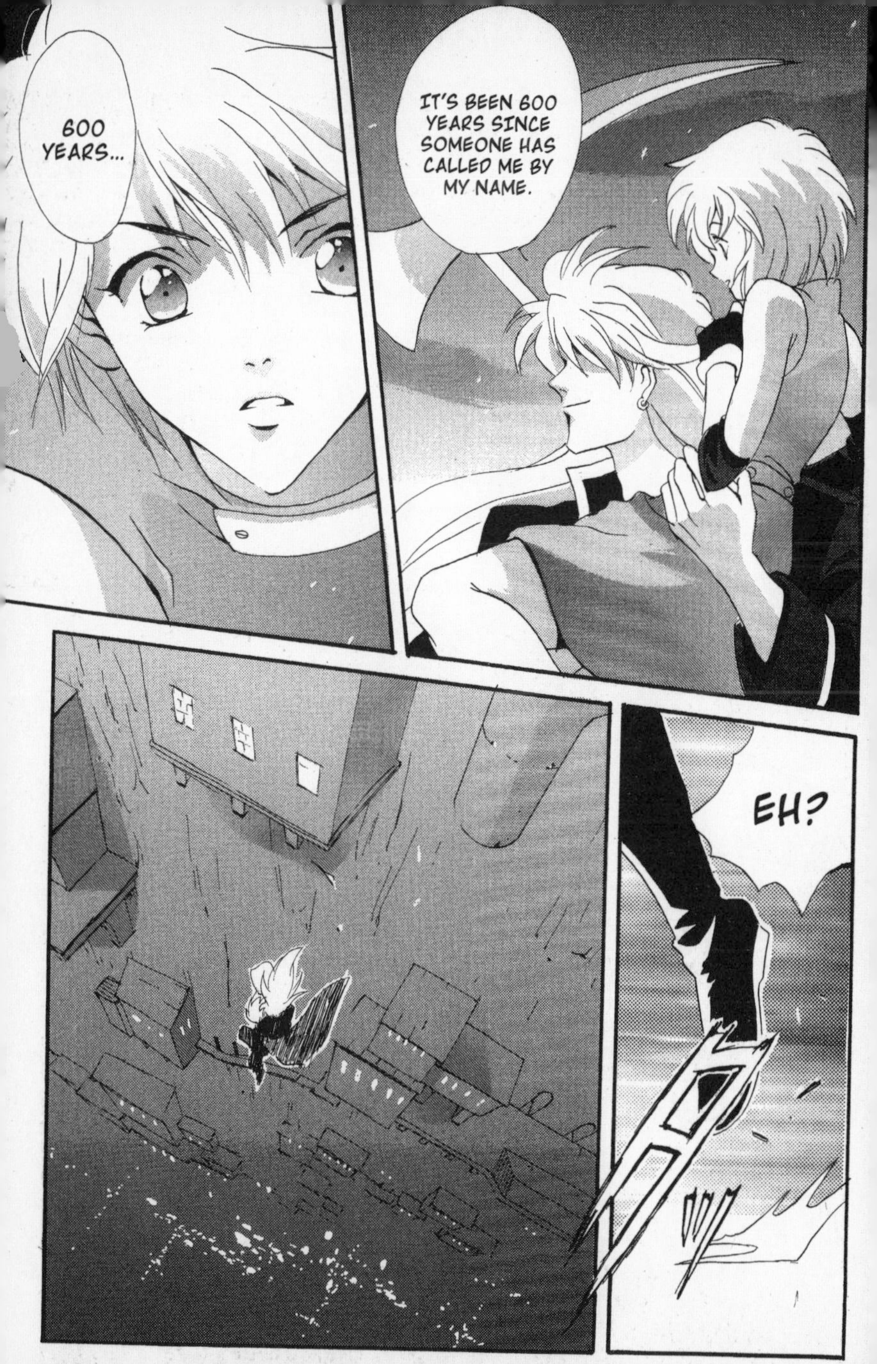
IT'S BEEN 600 YEARS SINCE SOMEONE HAS CALLED ME BY MY NAME.
600 YEARS...
EH?

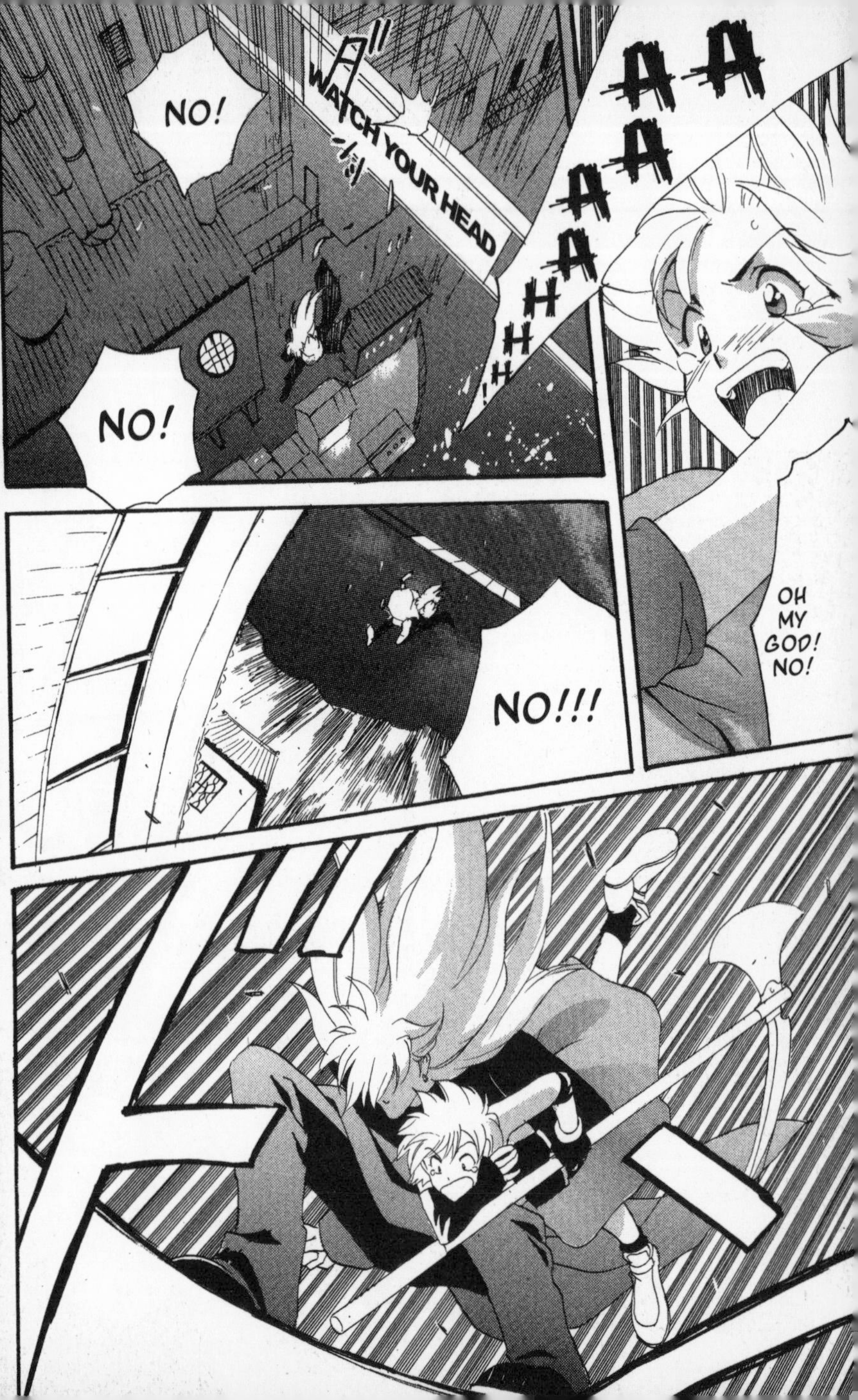

AAAAAAHHHH!
OH MY GOD! NO!
WATCH YOUR HEAD
NO!
NO!
NO!!!

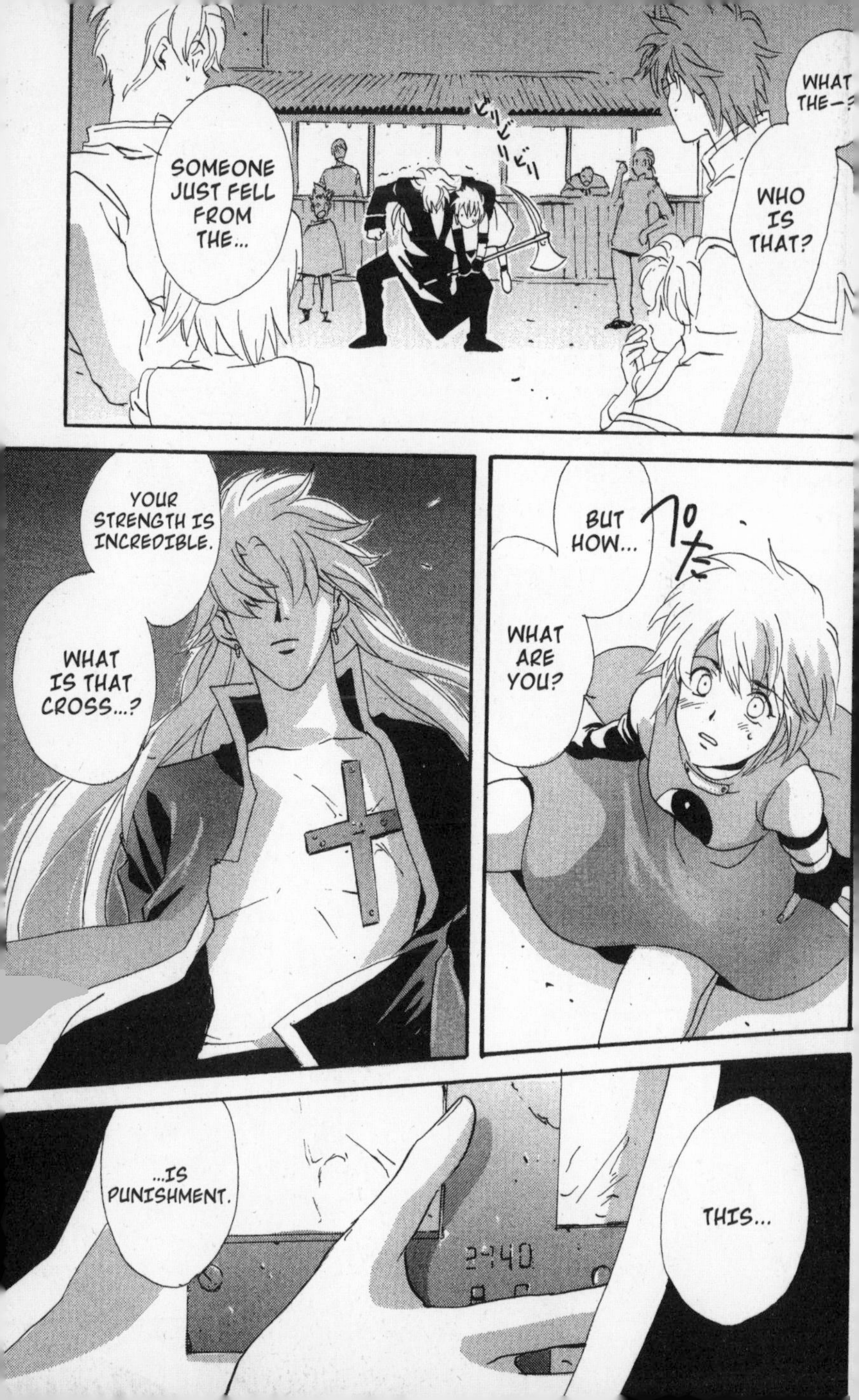
WHAT THE—?!
WHO IS THAT?
SOMEONE JUST FELL FROM THE...
BUT HOW...
WHAT ARE YOU?
YOUR STRENGTH IS INCREDIBLE.
WHAT IS THAT CROSS...?
THIS...
...IS PUNISHMENT.

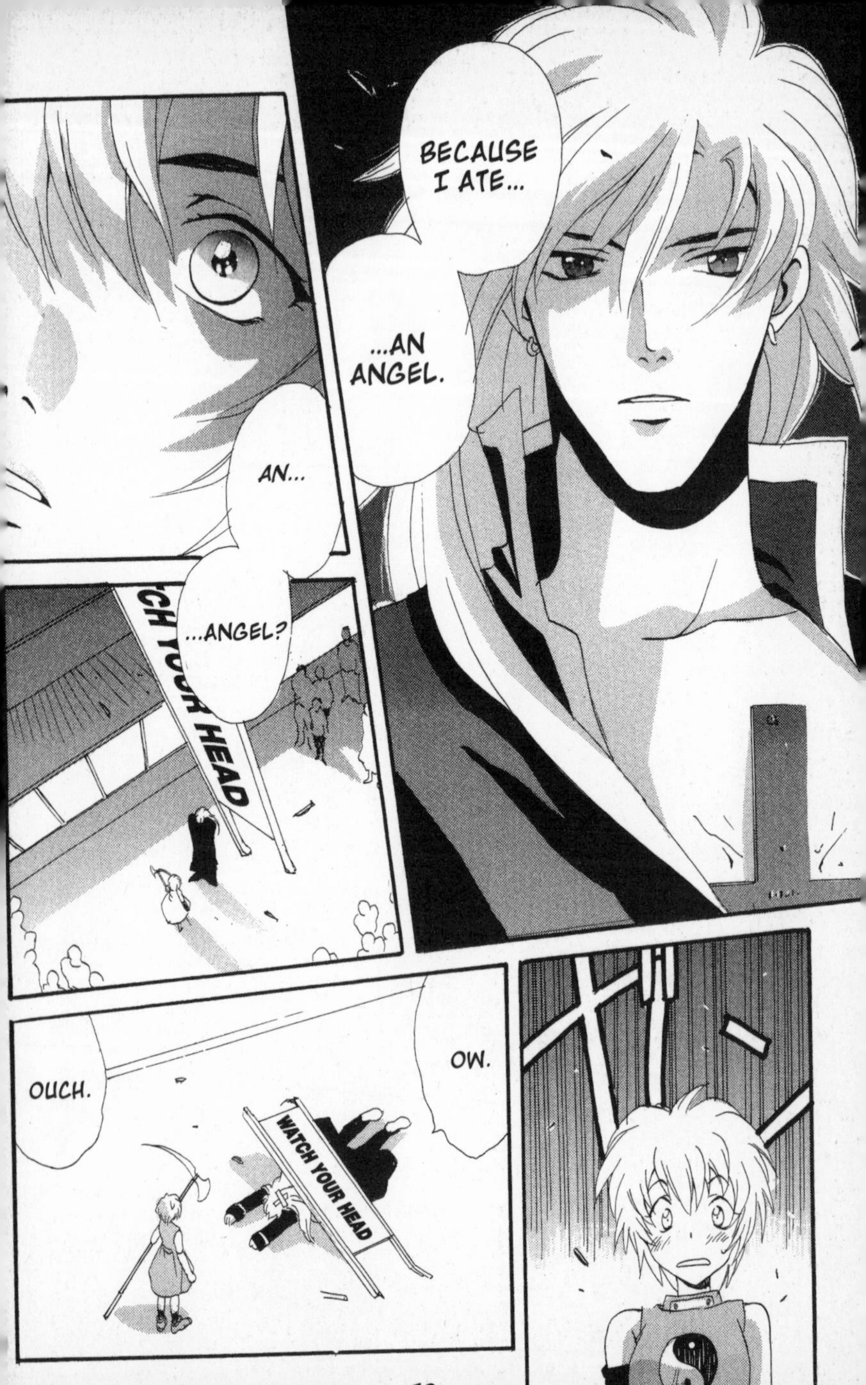
BECAUSE I ATE...
...AN ANGEL.
AN...
...ANGEL?
CH YOUR HEAD
OW.
OUCH.
WATCH YOUR HEAD

MACHIKA BALFALTIN

AGE : 14
HEIGHT : 150CM
BLOOD TYPE : O

COMMAND
FIGHT
CRY
FLEE

LV: 12
HP: 228/228
OFFENSE
STRENGTH: 59
DEFENSE
STRENGTH: 38
SPEED: 67
WIT: 33
LUCK: 29

EQUIPMENT
WEAPON: GRIM REAPER'S SICKLE /
       OFFENSE STRENGTH + 38
ARMOR: ONE PIECE /
       DEFENSIVE STRENGTH + 9
ACCESSORY: LEATHER KNUCKLES /
       OFFENSIVE STRENGTH + 8

DEATHBLOW TECHNIQUE COMMAND

HEADTHROW   ⇨Ⓟ+Ⓖ

SCORPION KICK (from behind enemy) ⇨⇦Ⓟ+Ⓚ

GRIM REAPER   ↙Ⓚ
SOMERSAULT

MACHIKA NEVER SURRENDERS AND NEVER GIVES
UP. NO MATTER THE ODDS. NEVER SAY DIE!

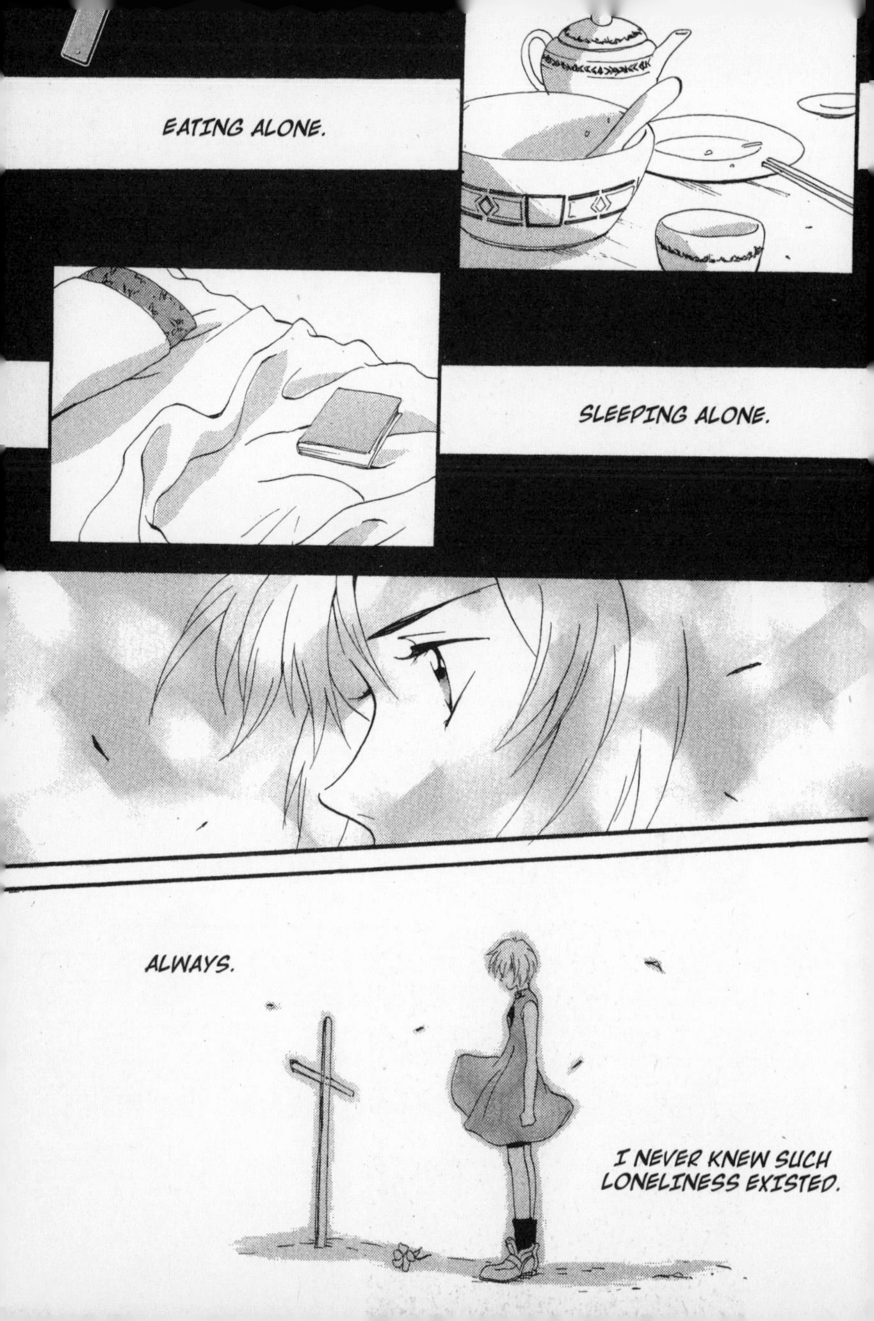
EATING ALONE.
SLEEPING ALONE.
ALWAYS.
I NEVER KNEW SUCH LONELINESS EXISTED.

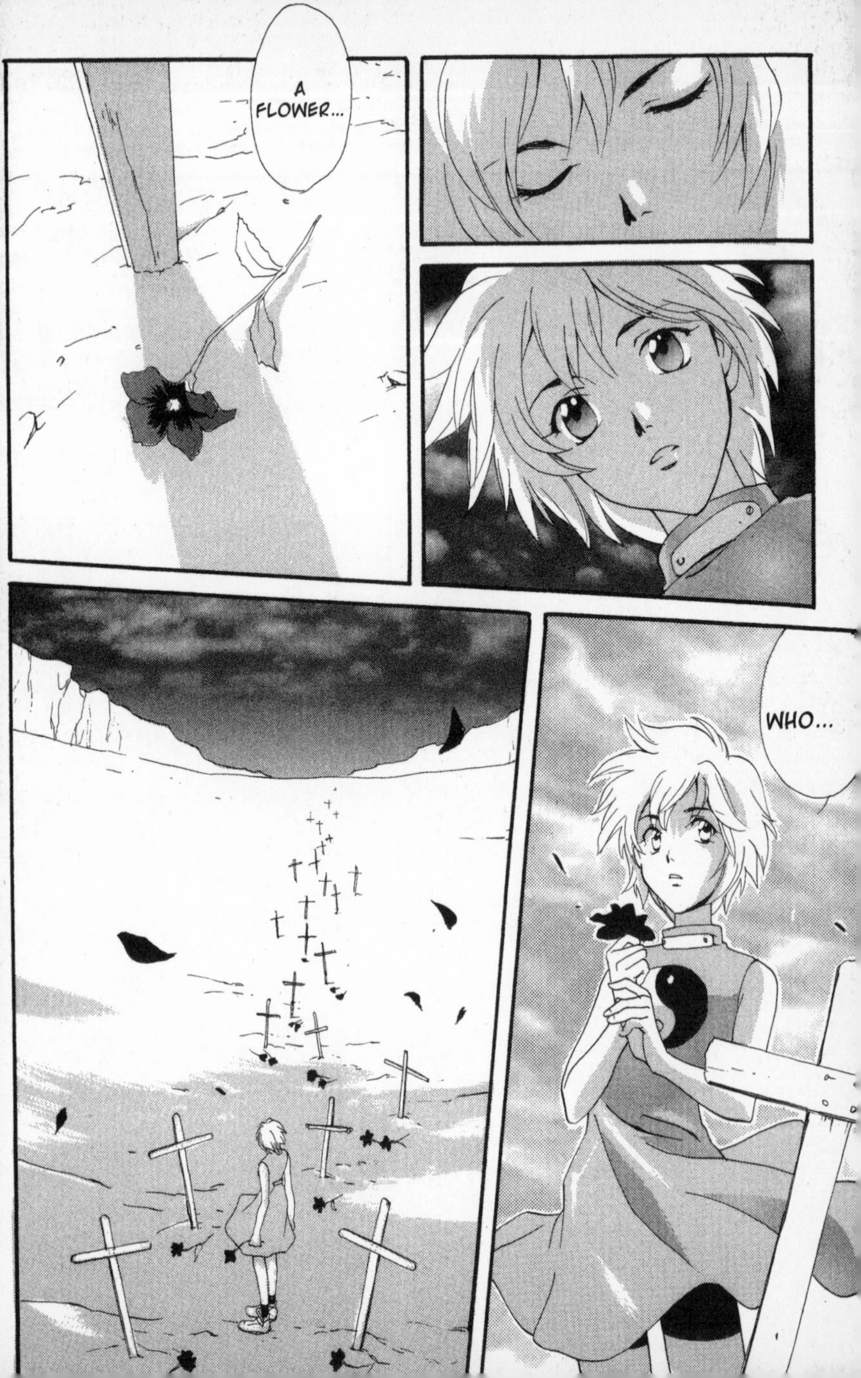
A FLOWER...
WHO...

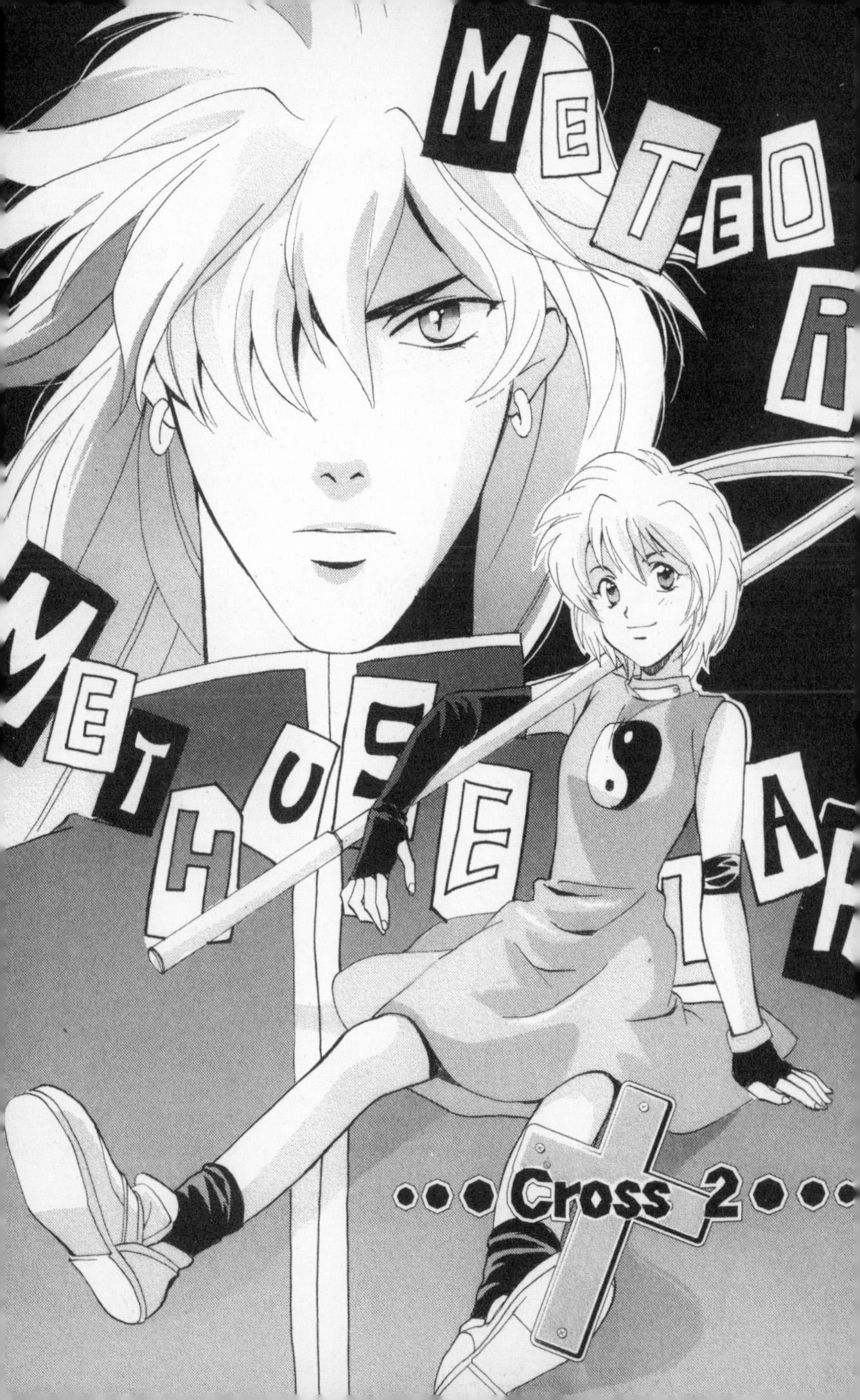
METEOR
METHUSELAH
Cross 2

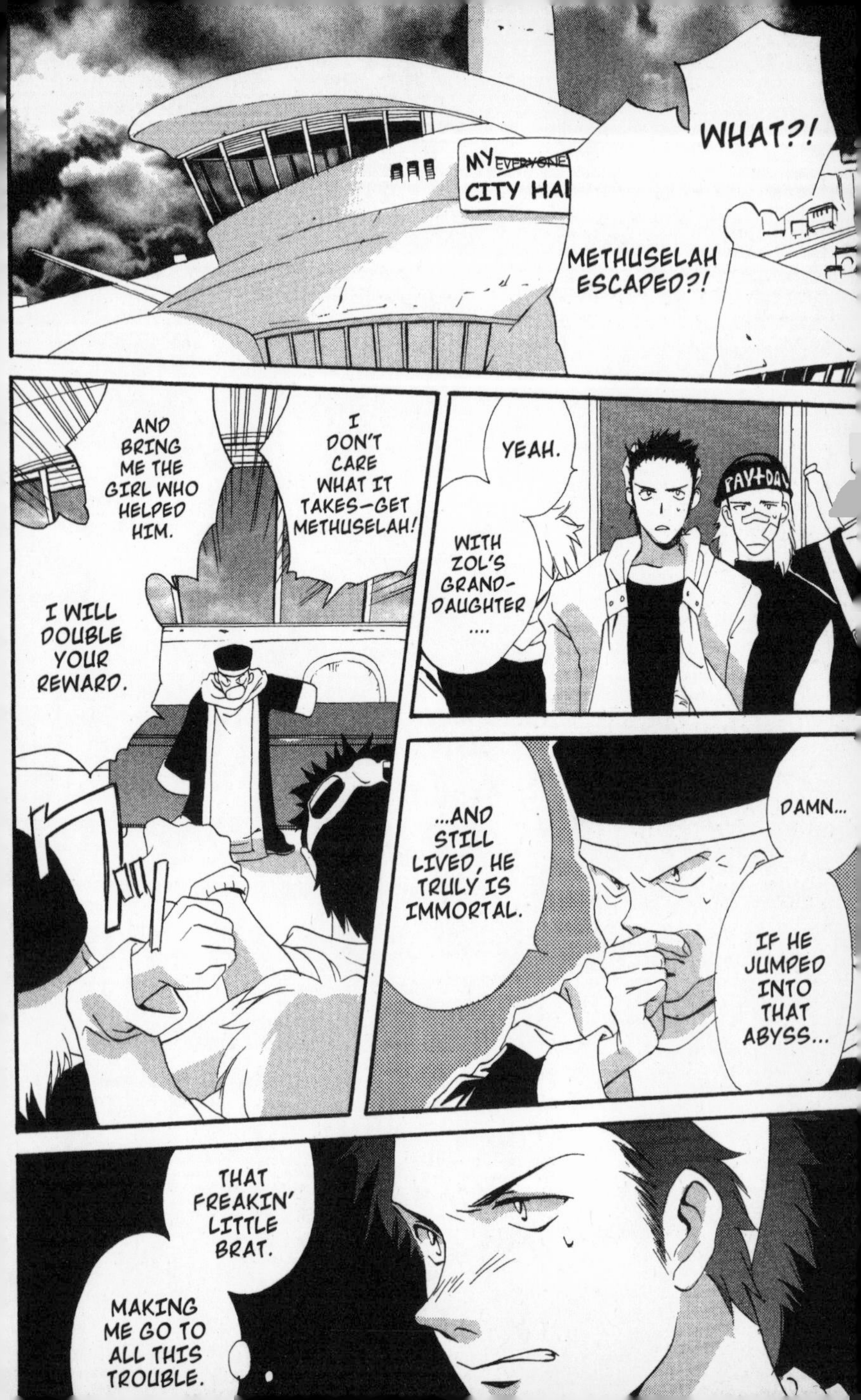
WHAT?!
MY EVERYONE
CITY HA
METHUSELAH ESCAPED?!
YEAH.
WITH ZOL'S GRAND-DAUGHTER....
DAMN...
IF HE JUMPED INTO THAT ABYSS...
...AND STILL LIVED, HE TRULY IS IMMORTAL.
I DON'T CARE WHAT IT TAKES—GET METHUSELAH!
AND BRING ME THE GIRL WHO HELPED HIM.
I WILL DOUBLE YOUR REWARD.
THAT FREAKIN' LITTLE BRAT.
MAKING ME GO TO ALL THIS TROUBLE.

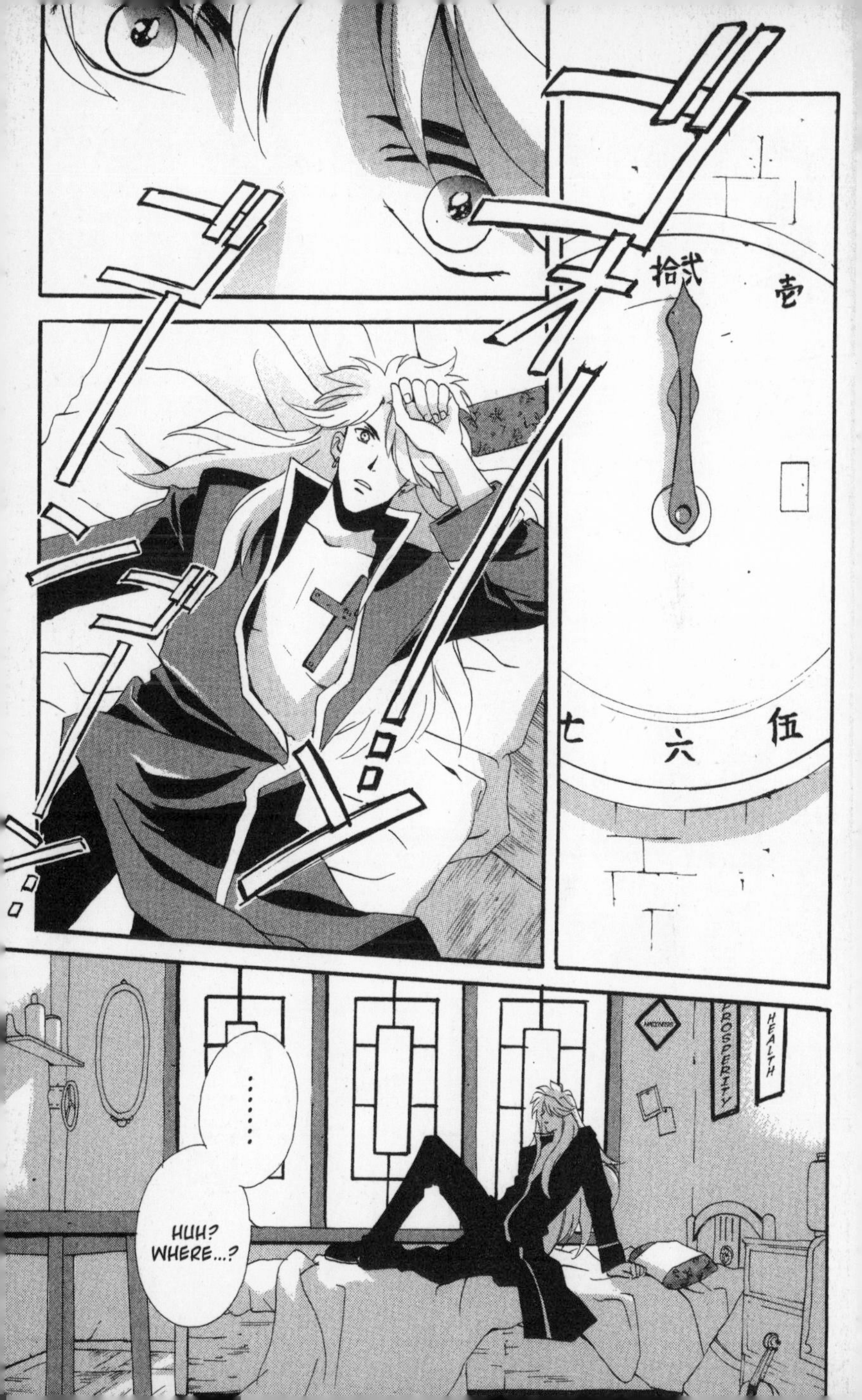

拾弐
壱
七
六
伍
PROSPERITY
HEALTH
......
HUH? WHERE...?

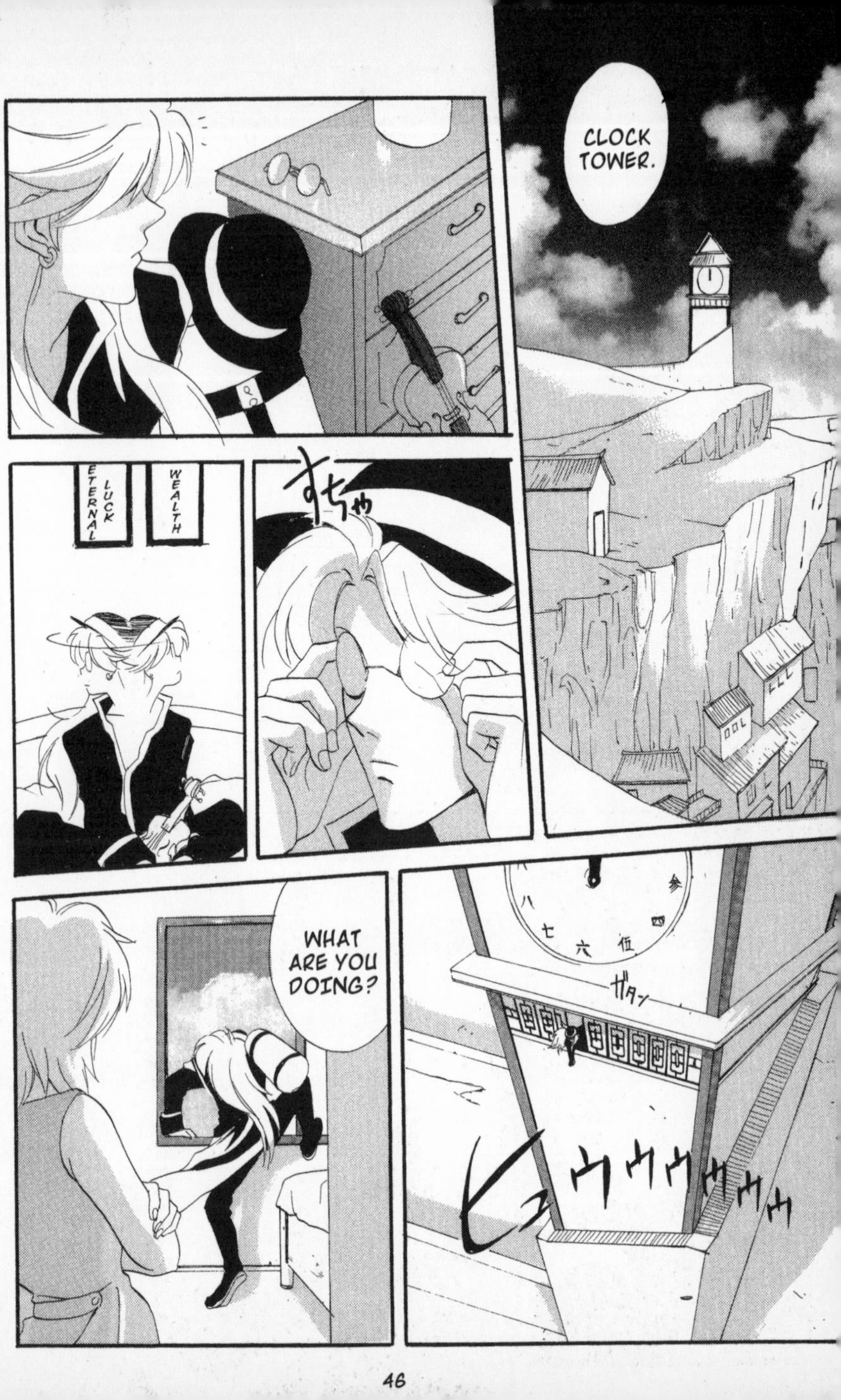
CLOCK TOWER.
すちゃ
WEALTH
ETERNAL LUCK
参 四 伍 六 七 八
ガタン
ヒュウウウウウウウ
WHAT ARE YOU DOING?

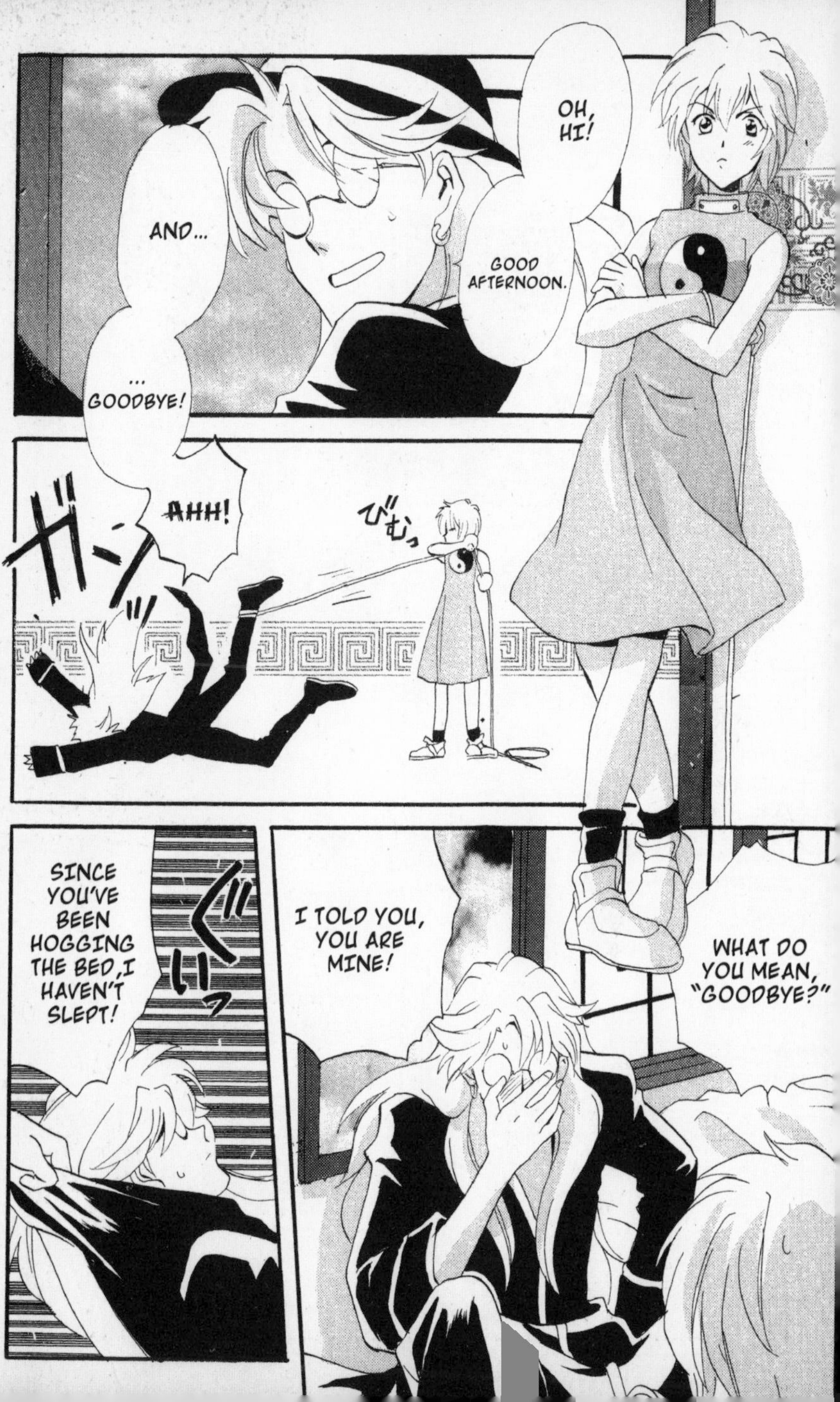
OH, HI!
GOOD AFTERNOON.
AND...
... GOODBYE!
びむっ
AHH!
ガーン
WHAT DO YOU MEAN, "GOODBYE?"
I TOLD YOU, YOU ARE MINE!
ぐいっ
SINCE YOU'VE BEEN HOGGING THE BED, I HAVEN'T SLEPT!

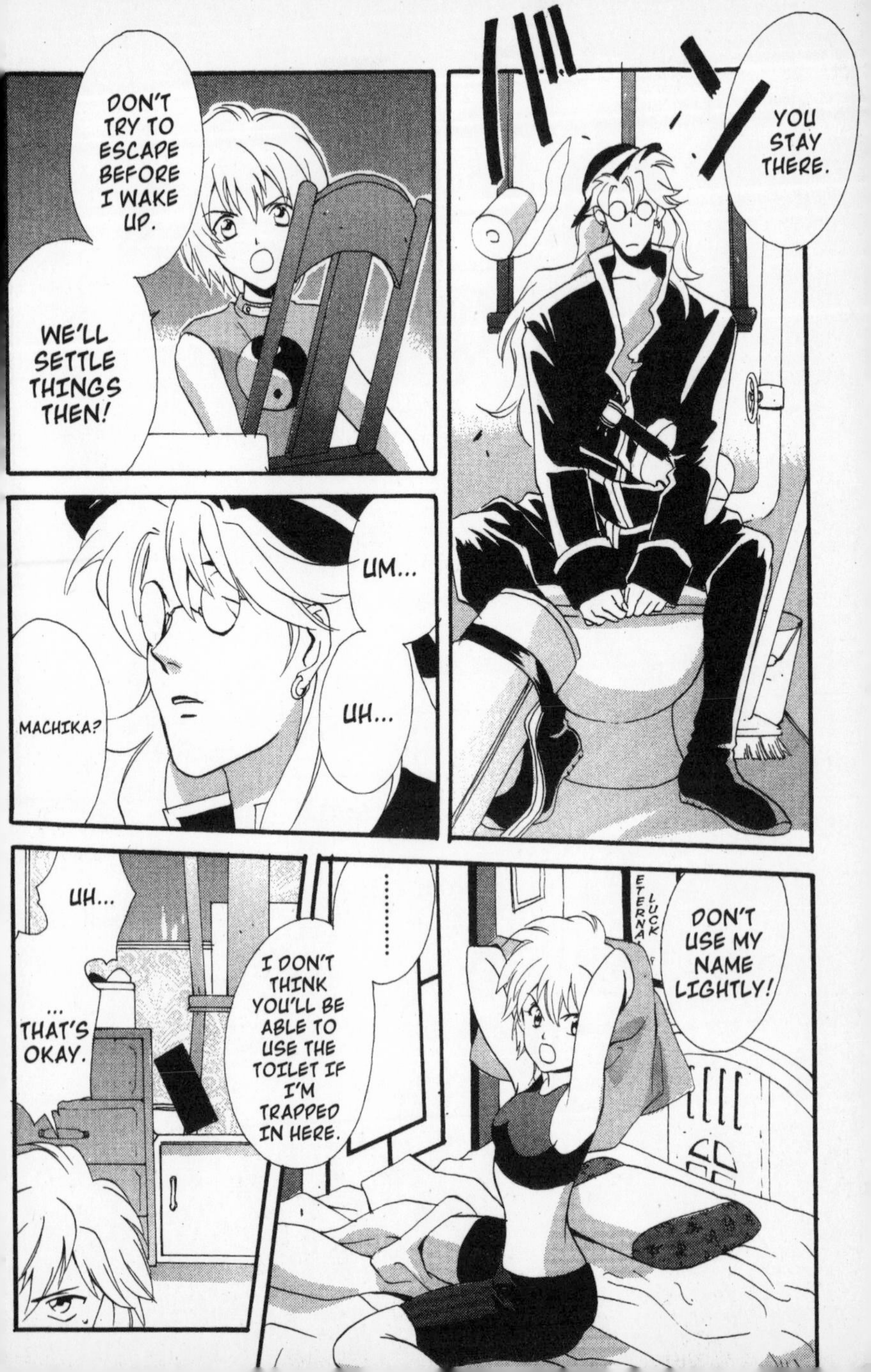
YOU STAY THERE.
DON'T TRY TO ESCAPE BEFORE I WAKE UP.
WE'LL SETTLE THINGS THEN!
UM...
UH...
MACHIKA?
ETERNAL LUCK
DON'T USE MY NAME LIGHTLY!
......
I DON'T THINK YOU'LL BE ABLE TO USE THE TOILET IF I'M TRAPPED IN HERE.
UH...
... THAT'S OKAY.

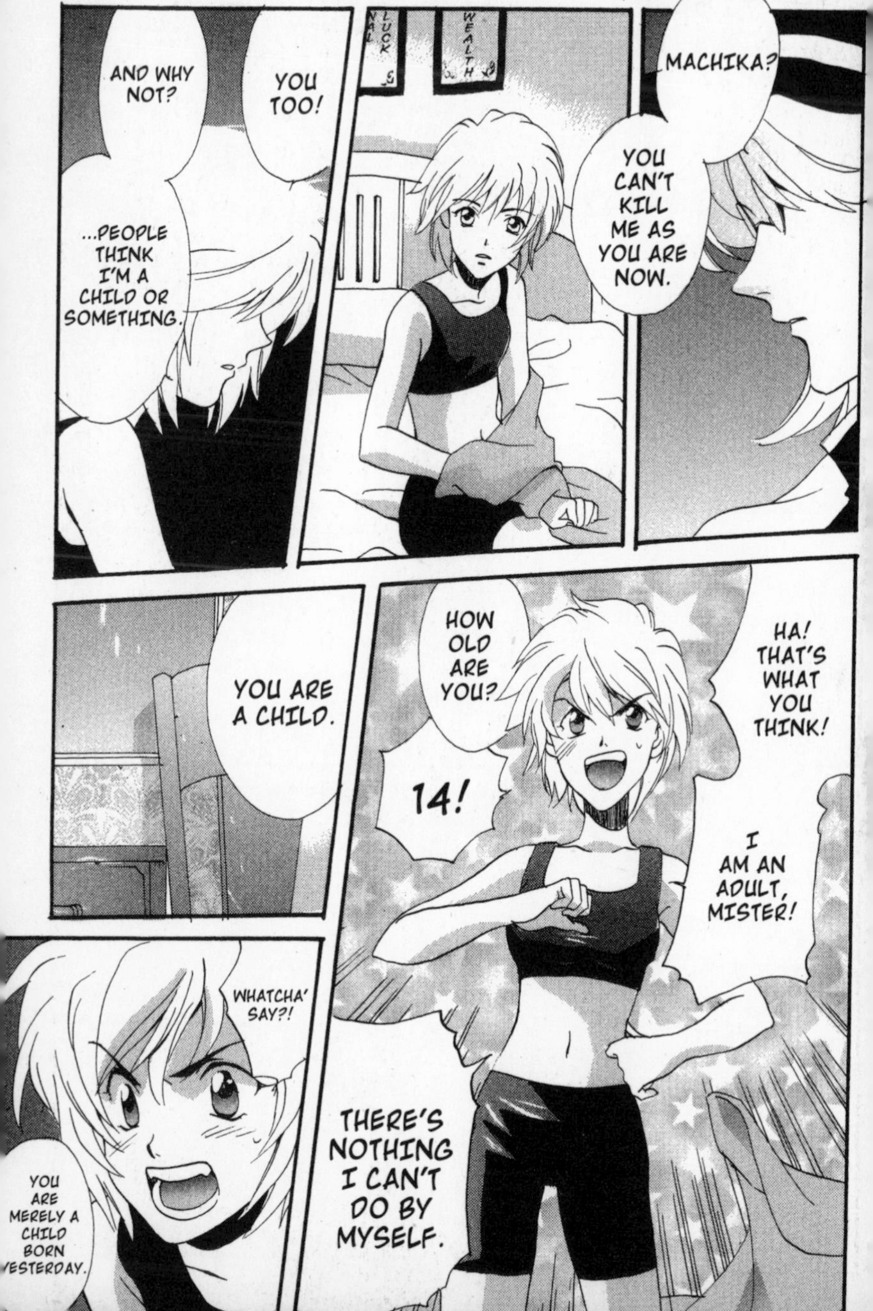

MACHIKA?
YOU CAN'T KILL ME AS YOU ARE NOW.
LUCK
WEALTH
YOU TOO!
AND WHY NOT?
...PEOPLE THINK I'M A CHILD OR SOMETHING.
HA! THAT'S WHAT YOU THINK!
I AM AN ADULT, MISTER!
HOW OLD ARE YOU?
14!
THERE'S NOTHING I CAN'T DO BY MYSELF.
YOU ARE A CHILD.
WHATCHA' SAY?!
YOU ARE MERELY A CHILD BORN YESTERDAY.

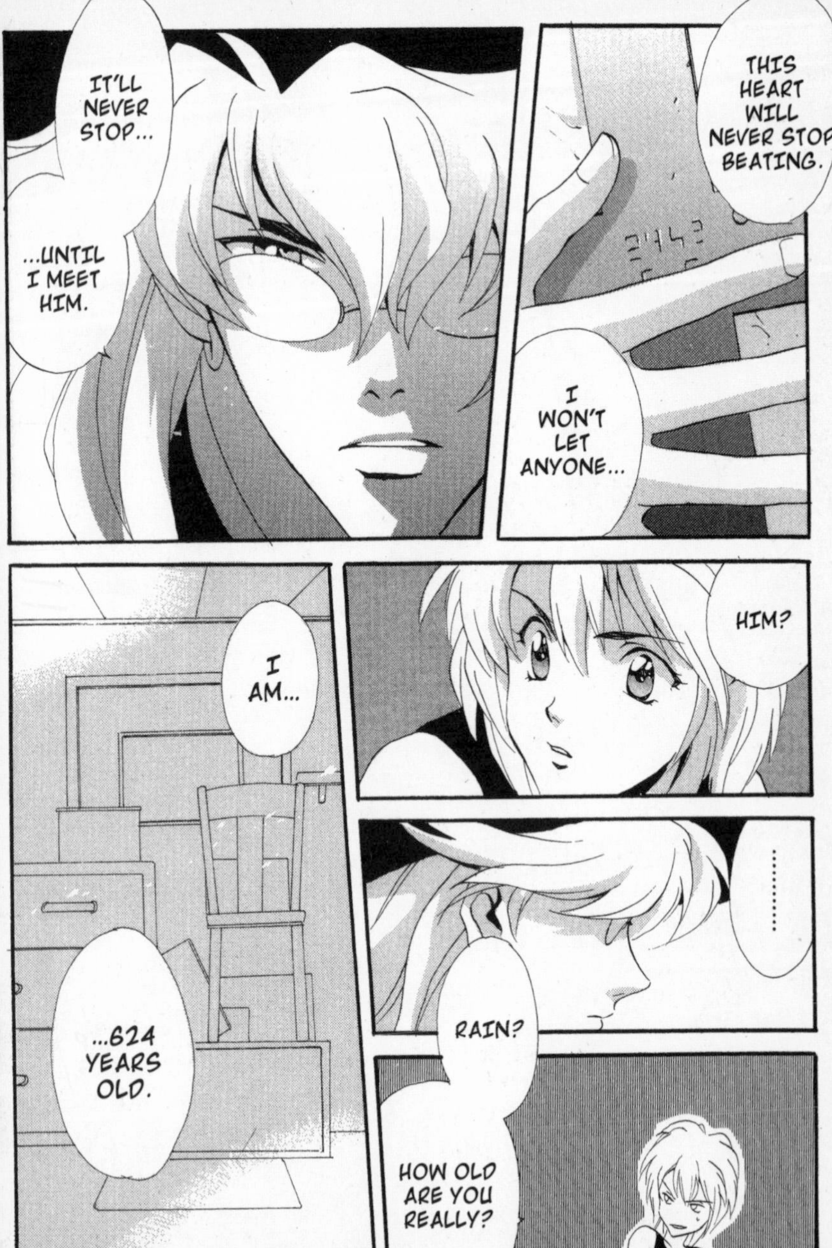
THIS HEART WILL NEVER STOP BEATING.
I WON'T LET ANYONE...
IT'LL NEVER STOP...
...UNTIL I MEET HIM.
HIM?
......
RAIN?
HOW OLD ARE YOU REALLY?
I AM...
...624 YEARS OLD.

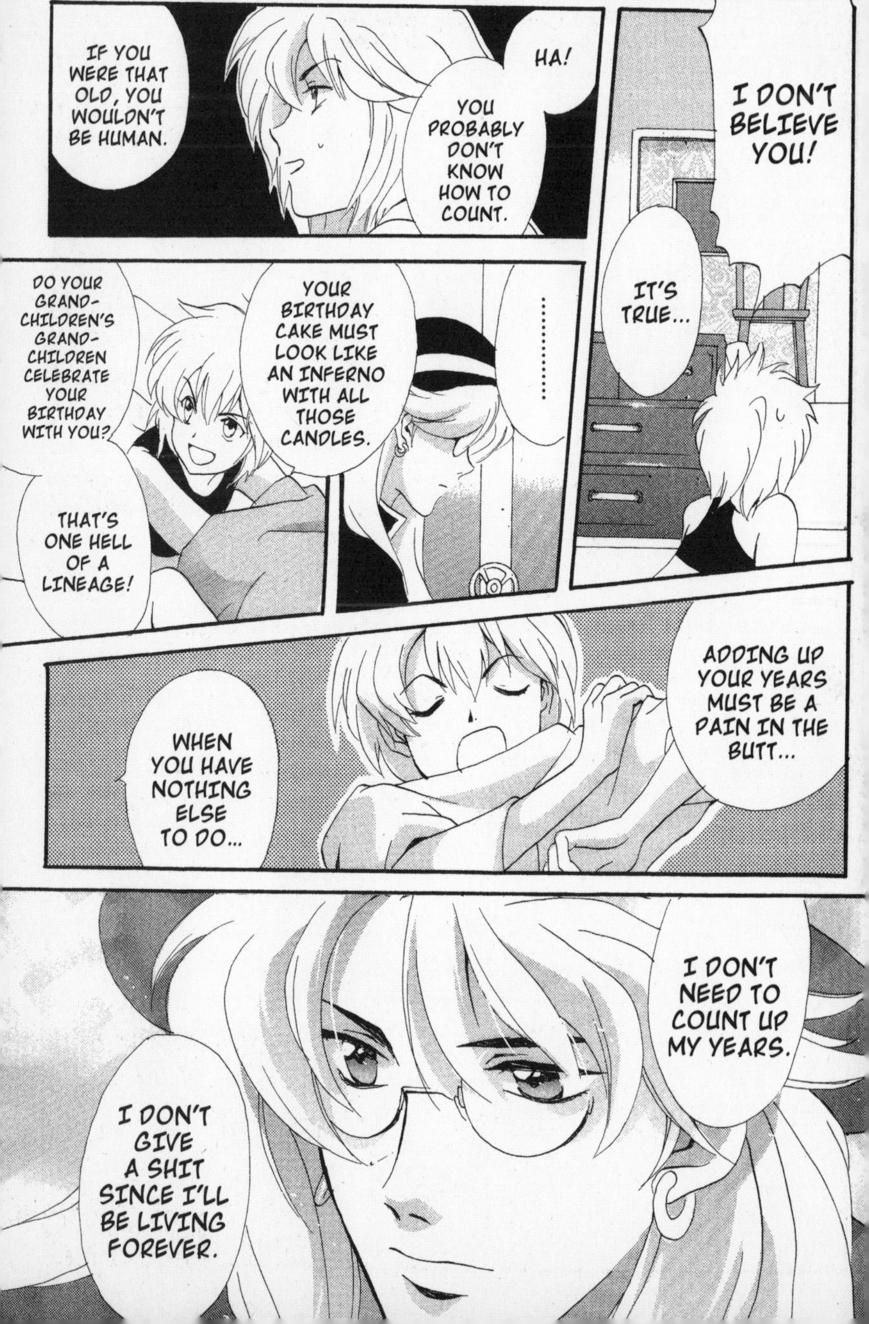
I DON'T BELIEVE YOU!
IT'S TRUE...
HA!
YOU PROBABLY DON'T KNOW HOW TO COUNT.
IF YOU WERE THAT OLD, YOU WOULDN'T BE HUMAN.
......
YOUR BIRTHDAY CAKE MUST LOOK LIKE AN INFERNO WITH ALL THOSE CANDLES.
DO YOUR GRAND-CHILDREN'S GRAND-CHILDREN CELEBRATE YOUR BIRTHDAY WITH YOU?
THAT'S ONE HELL OF A LINEAGE!
ADDING UP YOUR YEARS MUST BE A PAIN IN THE BUTT...
WHEN YOU HAVE NOTHING ELSE TO DO...
I DON'T NEED TO COUNT UP MY YEARS.
I DON'T GIVE A SHIT SINCE I'LL BE LIVING FOREVER.

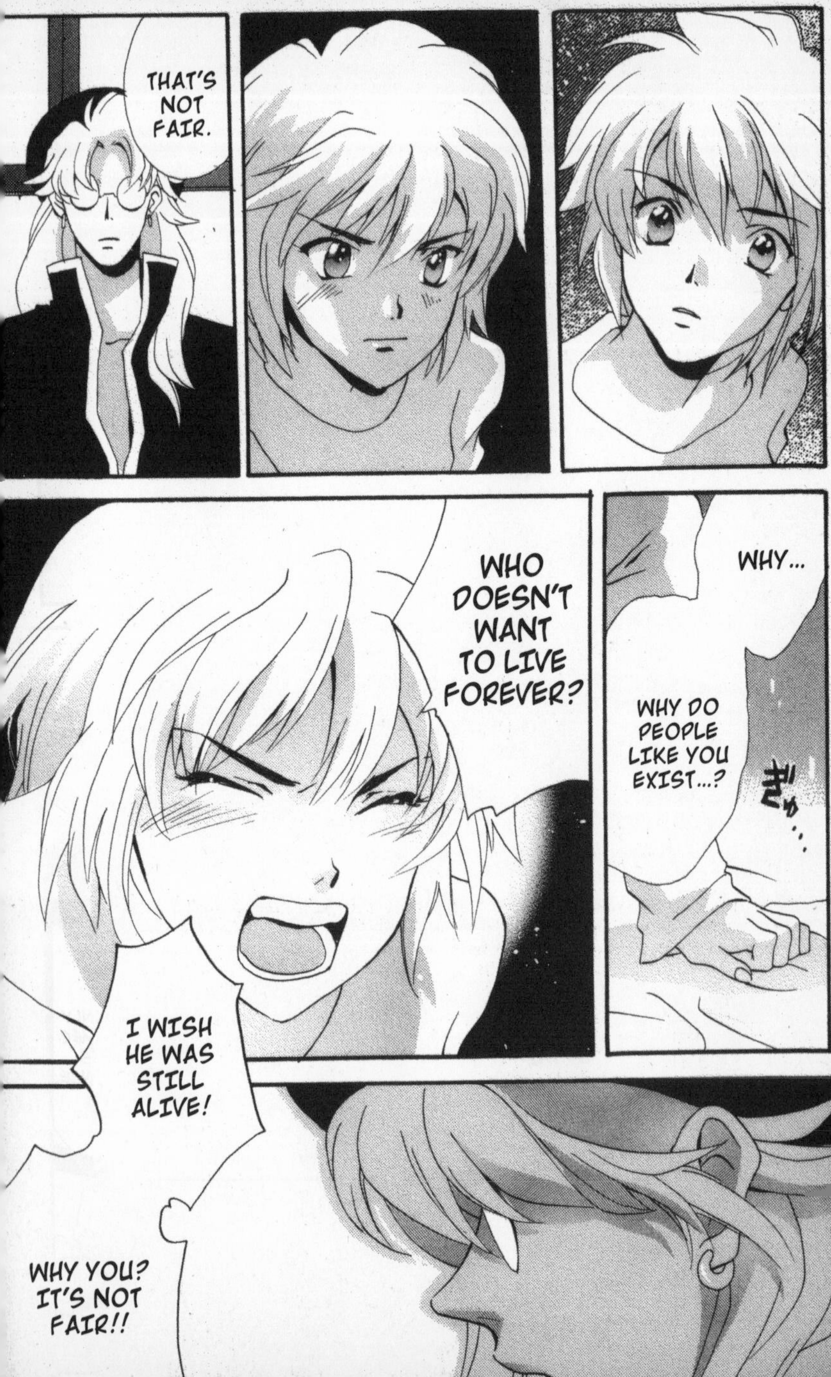
THAT'S NOT FAIR.
WHY...
WHY DO PEOPLE LIKE YOU EXIST...?
ぎゅ...
WHO DOESN'T WANT TO LIVE FOREVER?
I WISH HE WAS STILL ALIVE!
WHY YOU? IT'S NOT FAIR!!

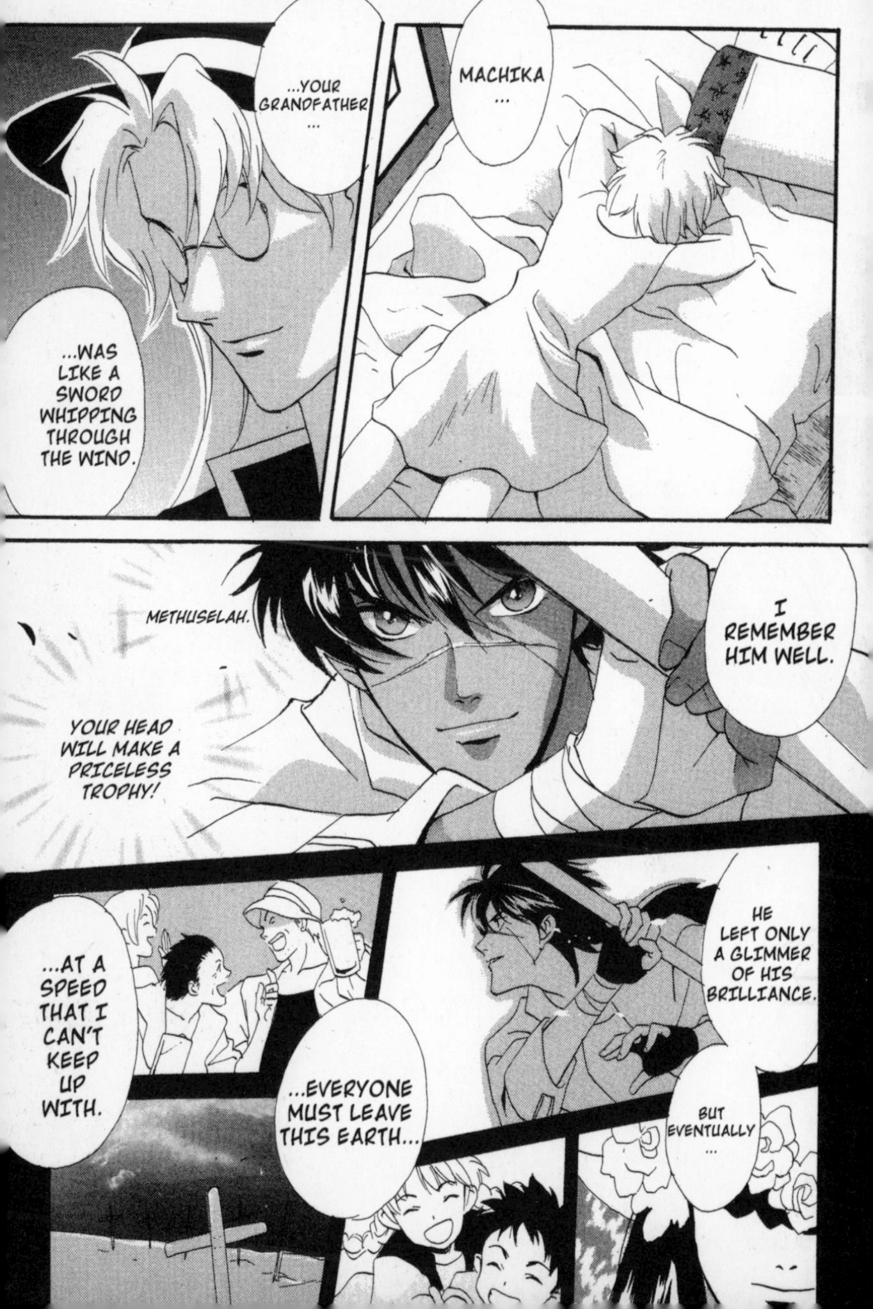
MACHIKA ...
...YOUR GRANDFATHER ...
...WAS LIKE A SWORD WHIPPING THROUGH THE WIND.
I REMEMBER HIM WELL.
METHUSELAH.
YOUR HEAD WILL MAKE A PRICELESS TROPHY!
HE LEFT ONLY A GLIMMER OF HIS BRILLIANCE.
...AT A SPEED THAT I CAN'T KEEP UP WITH.
BUT EVENTUALLY ...
...EVERYONE MUST LEAVE THIS EARTH...

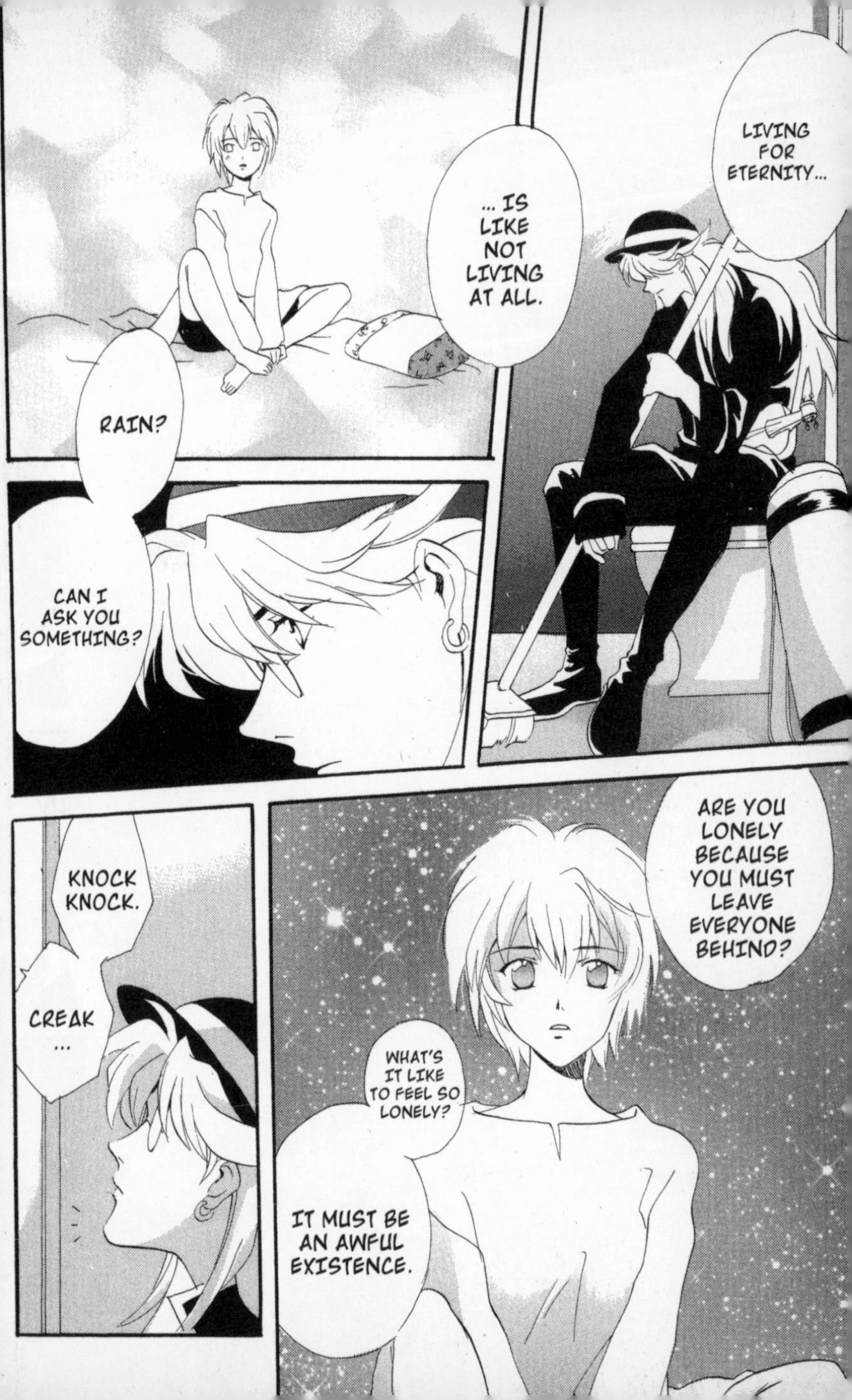
LIVING FOR ETERNITY...
... IS LIKE NOT LIVING AT ALL.
RAIN?
CAN I ASK YOU SOMETHING?
ARE YOU LONELY BECAUSE YOU MUST LEAVE EVERYONE BEHIND?
WHAT'S IT LIKE TO FEEL SO LONELY?
IT MUST BE AN AWFUL EXISTENCE.
KNOCK KNOCK.
CREAK ...

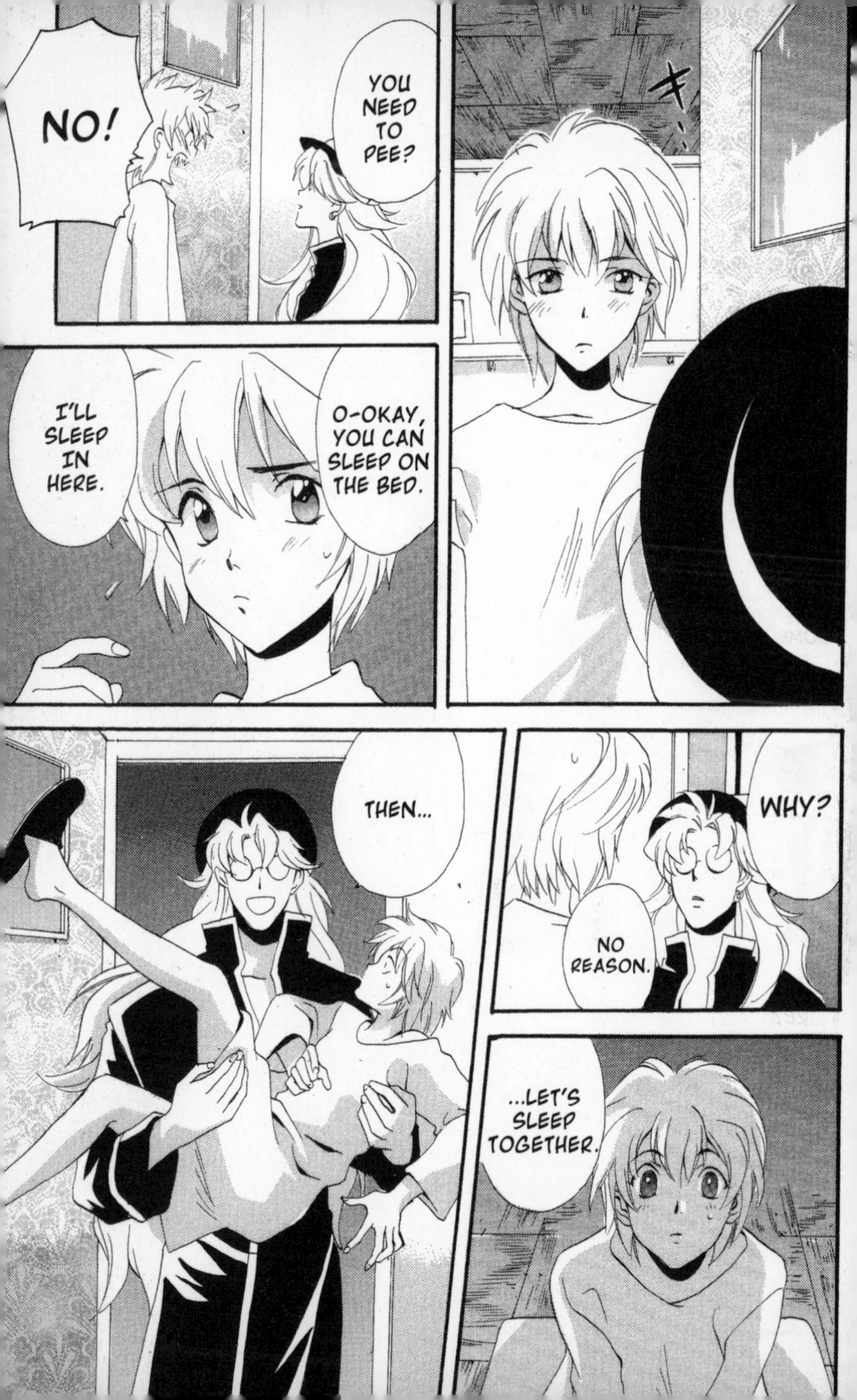
YOU NEED TO PEE?
NO!
O-OKAY, YOU CAN SLEEP ON THE BED.
I'LL SLEEP IN HERE.
WHY?
NO REASON.
...LET'S SLEEP TOGETHER.
THEN...

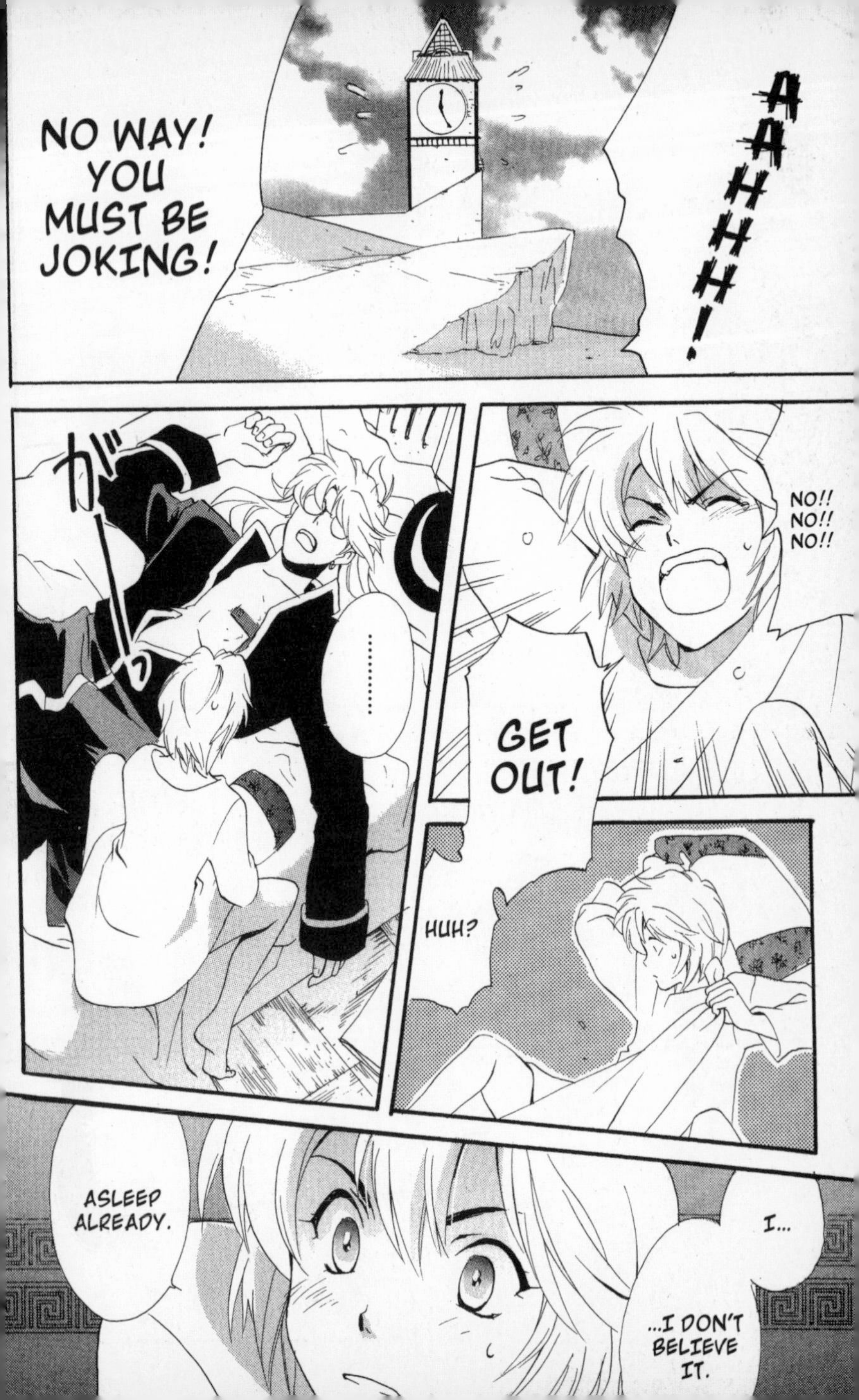
AAHHHH!
NO WAY! YOU MUST BE JOKING!
NO!! NO!! NO!!
GET OUT!
HUH?
が
......
I...
...I DON'T BELIEVE IT.
ASLEEP ALREADY.

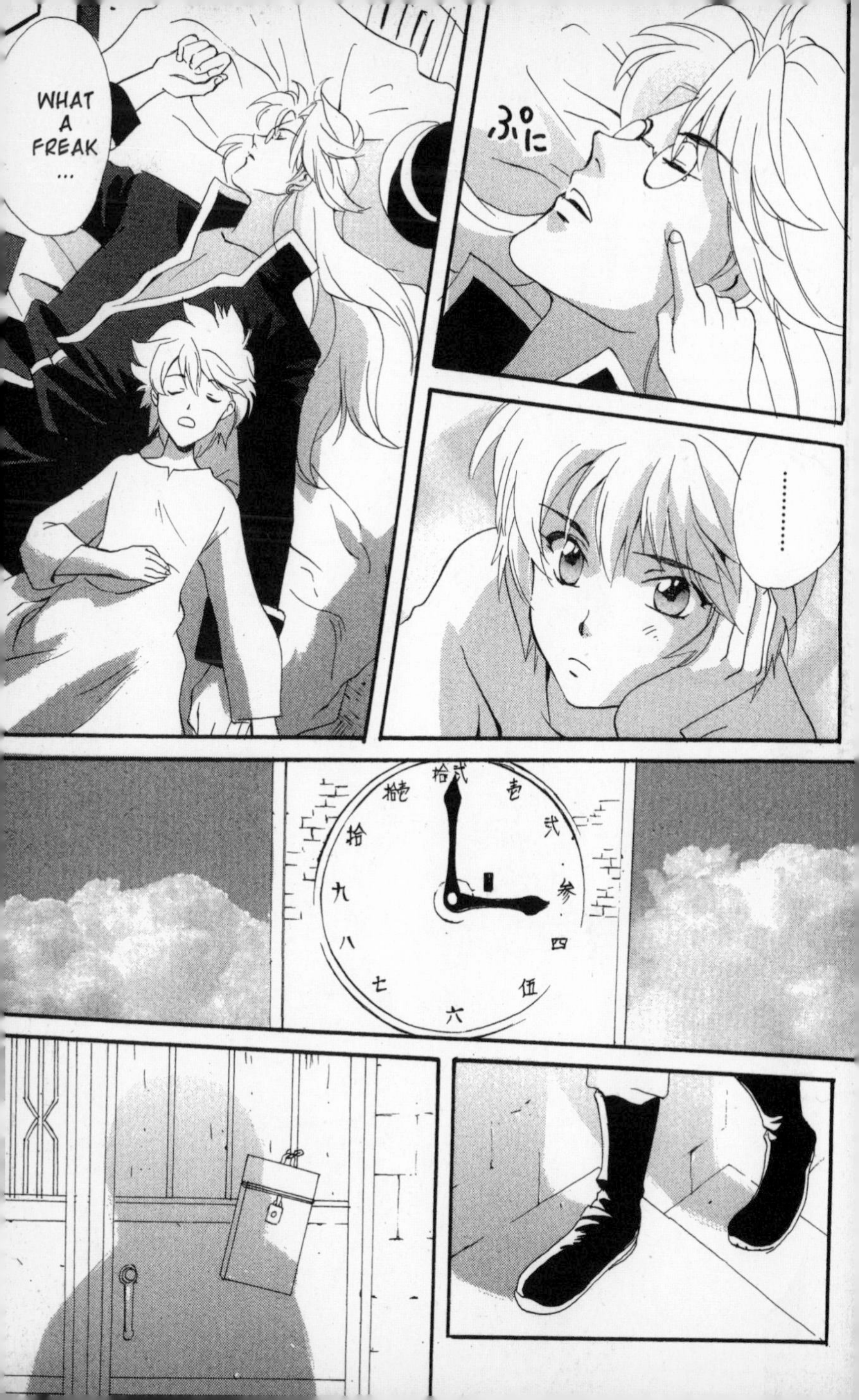
ぷに
......
WHAT A FREAK ...

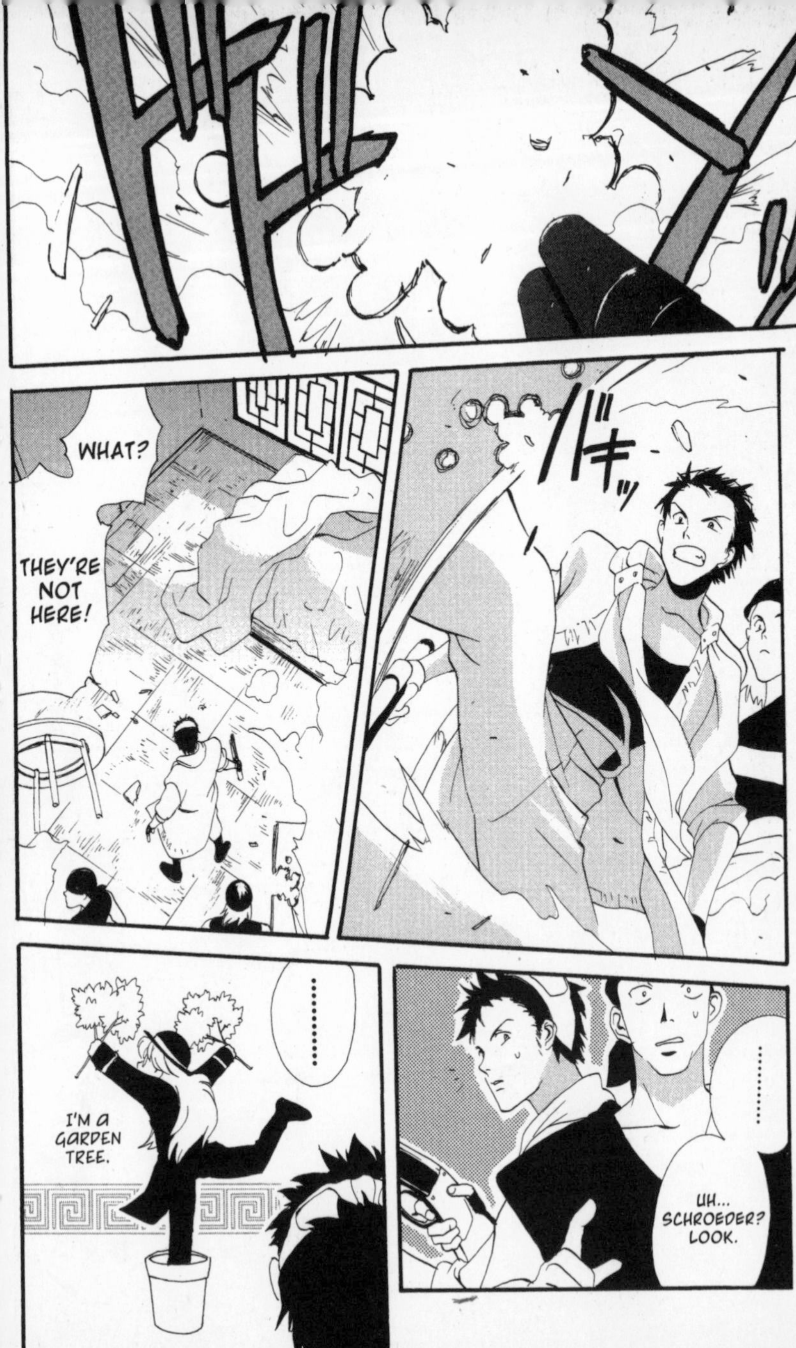
WHAT?
THEY'RE NOT HERE!
......
UH... SCHROEDER? LOOK.
......
I'M A GARDEN TREE.

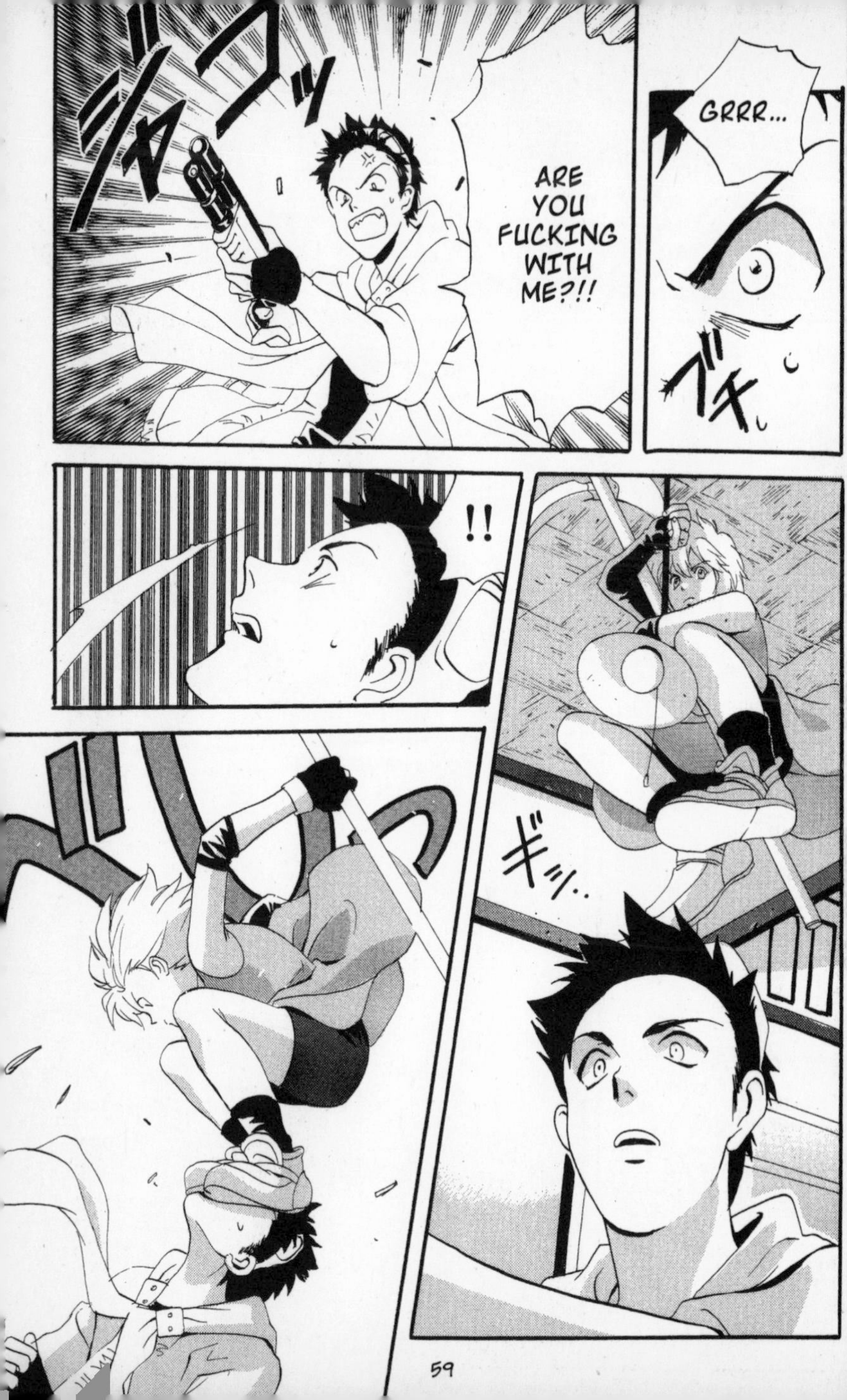
GRRR...
ARE YOU FUCKING WITH ME?!!
!!

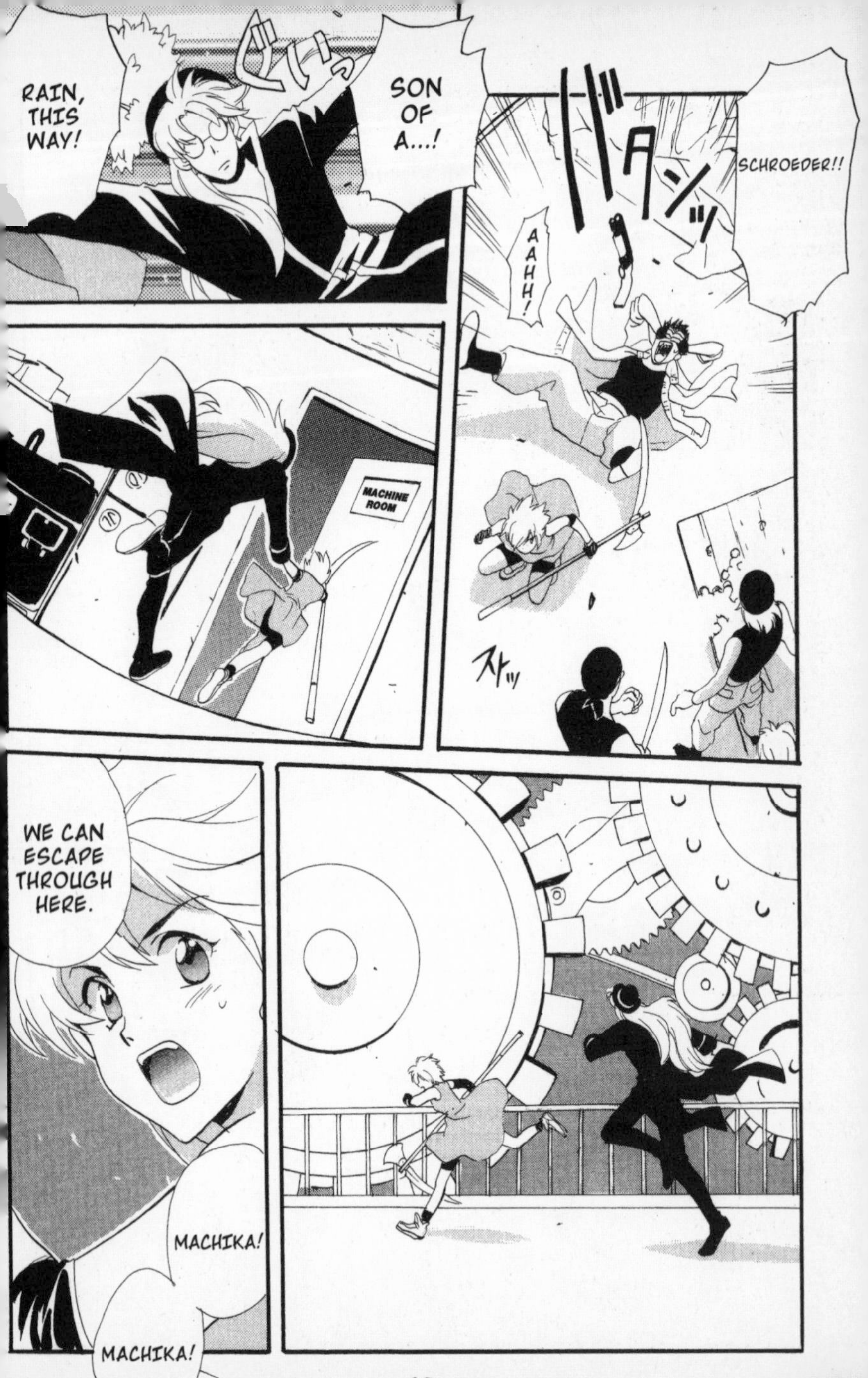
SCHROEDER!!
AAHH!
SON OF A...!
RAIN, THIS WAY!
MACHINE ROOM
WE CAN ESCAPE THROUGH HERE.
MACHIKA!
MACHIKA!

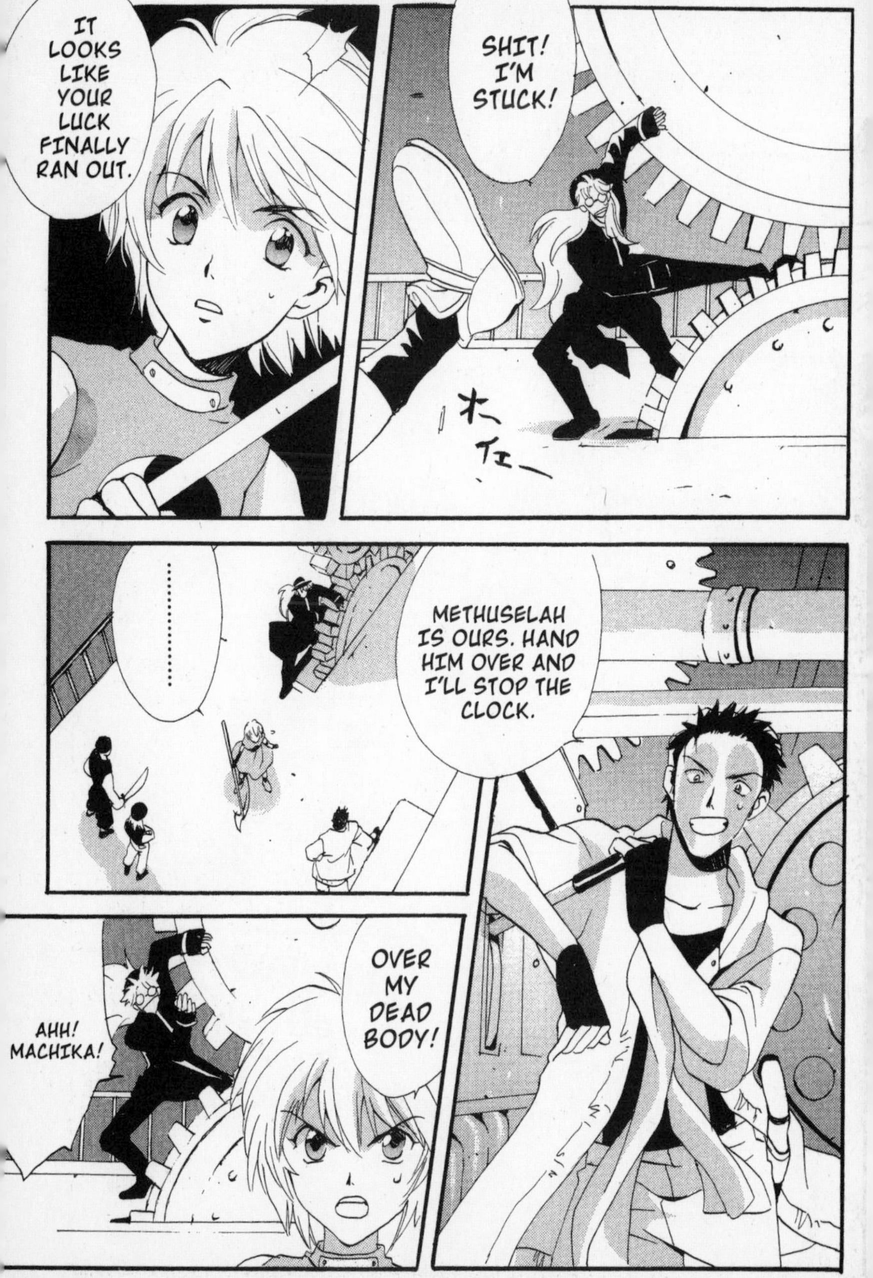
SHIT! I'M STUCK!
IT LOOKS LIKE YOUR LUCK FINALLY RAN OUT.
METHUSELAH IS OURS. HAND HIM OVER AND I'LL STOP THE CLOCK.
......
OVER MY DEAD BODY!
AHH! MACHIKA!

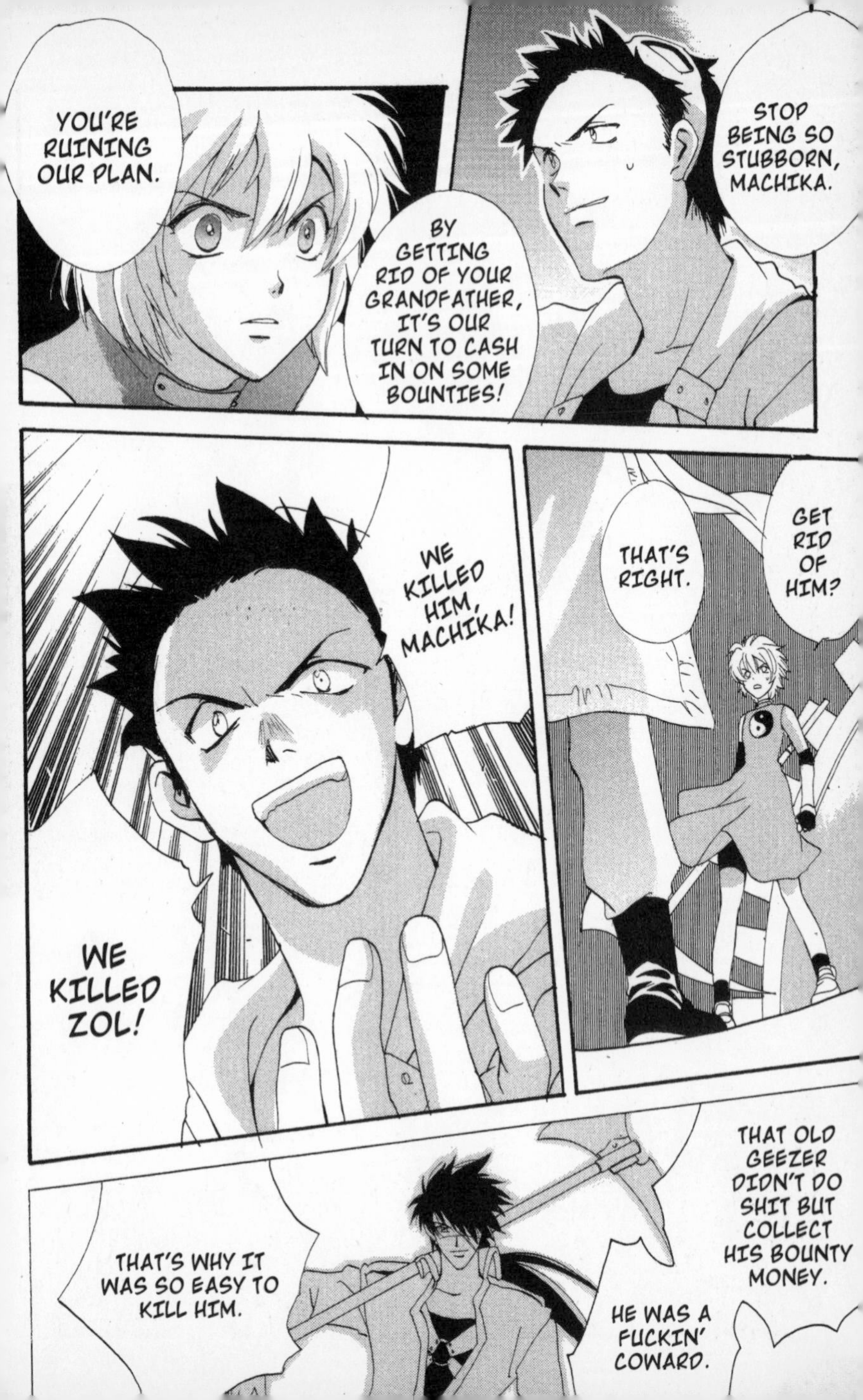
STOP BEING SO STUBBORN, MACHIKA.
YOU'RE RUINING OUR PLAN.
BY GETTING RID OF YOUR GRANDFATHER, IT'S OUR TURN TO CASH IN ON SOME BOUNTIES!
GET RID OF HIM?
THAT'S RIGHT.
WE KILLED HIM, MACHIKA!
WE KILLED ZOL!
THAT OLD GEEZER DIDN'T DO SHIT BUT COLLECT HIS BOUNTY MONEY.
HE WAS A FUCKIN' COWARD.
THAT'S WHY IT WAS SO EASY TO KILL HIM.

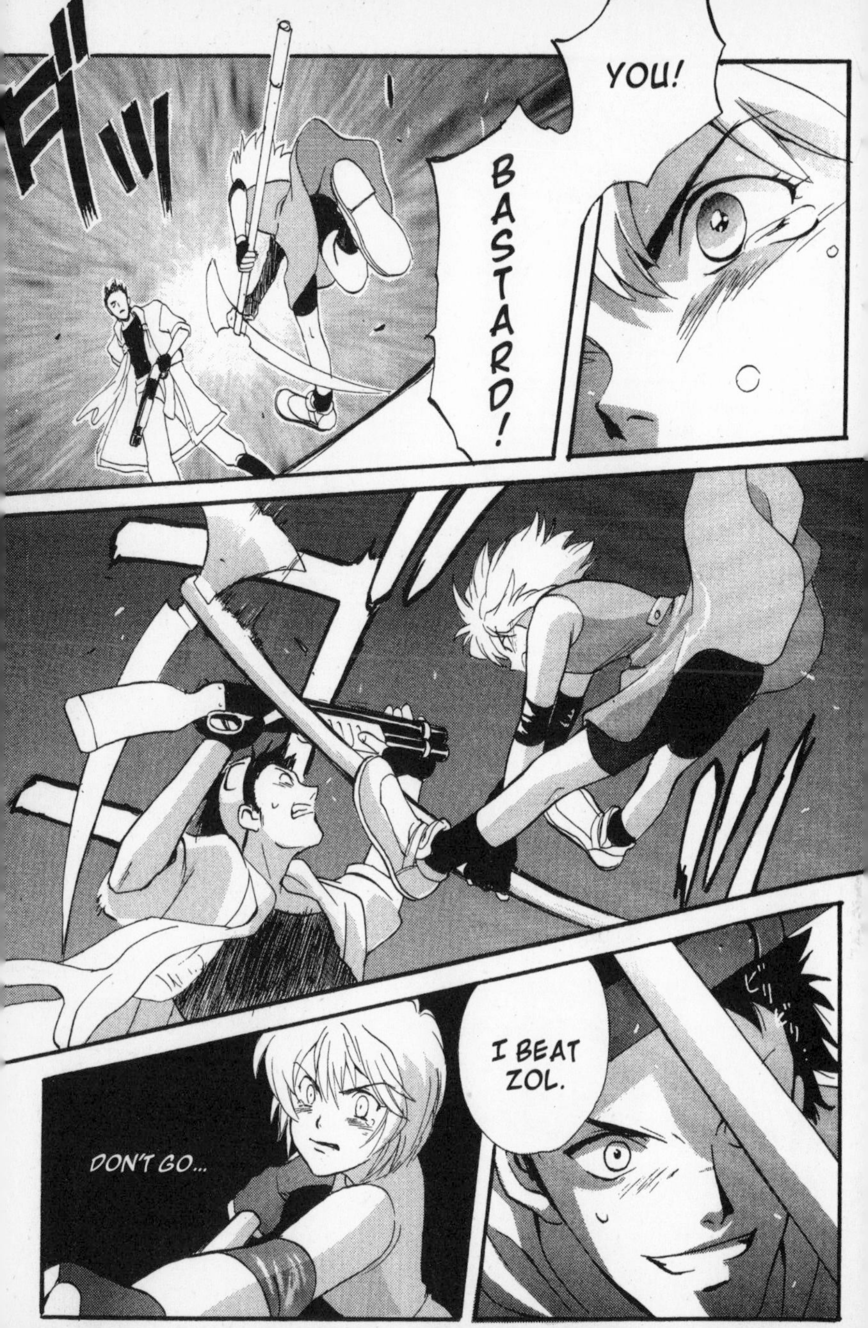

YOU!
BASTARD!
ダッ
I BEAT ZOL.
ビリビリ
DON'T GO...

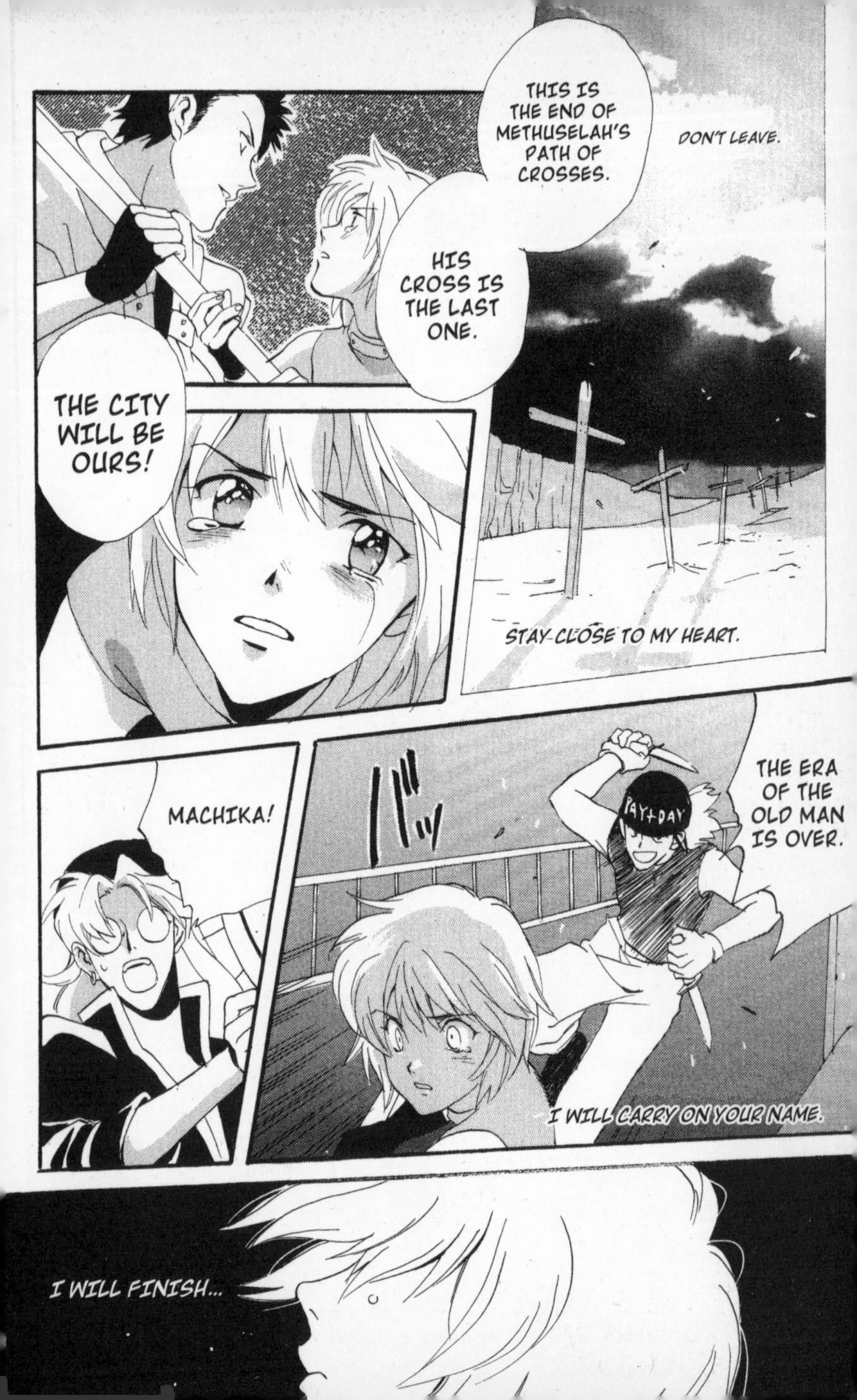
DON'T LEAVE.
STAY-CLOSE TO MY HEART.
THIS IS THE END OF METHUSELAH'S PATH OF CROSSES.
HIS CROSS IS THE LAST ONE.
THE CITY WILL BE OURS!
THE ERA OF THE OLD MAN IS OVER.
ドッ
PAY+DAY
I WILL CARRY ON YOUR NAME.
MACHIKA!
I WILL FINISH...

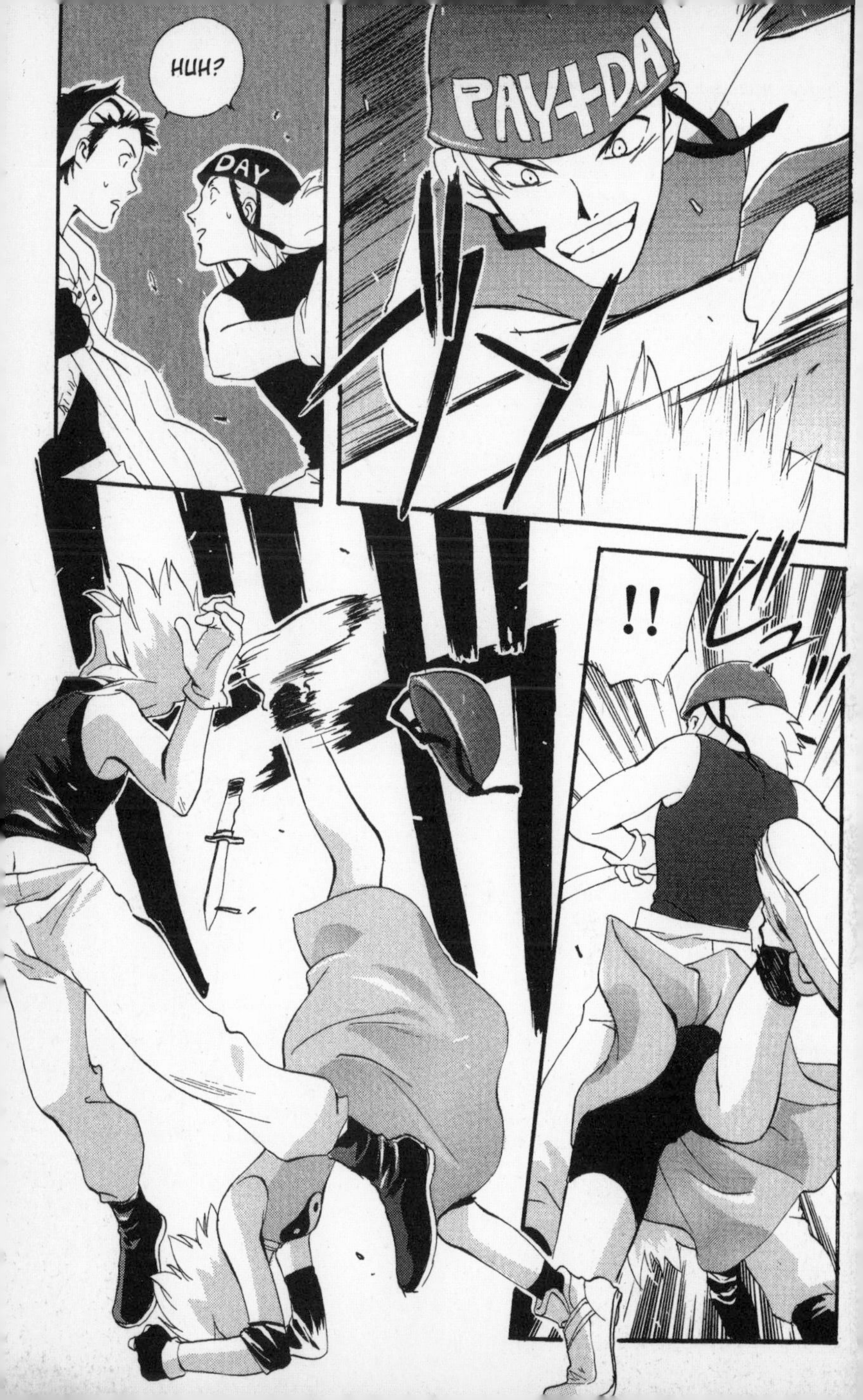
PAY+DAY
DAY
HUH?
!!

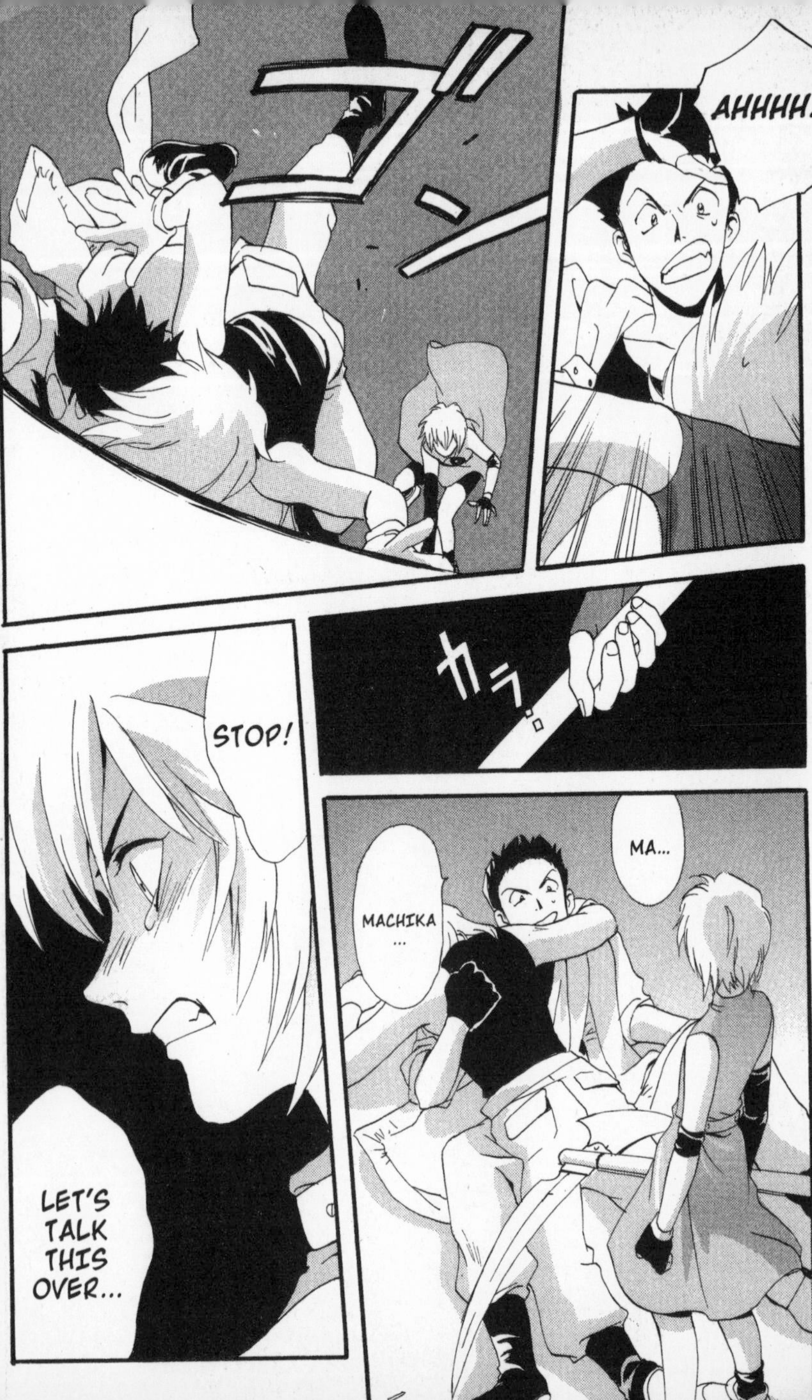
AHHHH!
カラ
MA...
MACHIKA ...
STOP!
LET'S TALK THIS OVER...

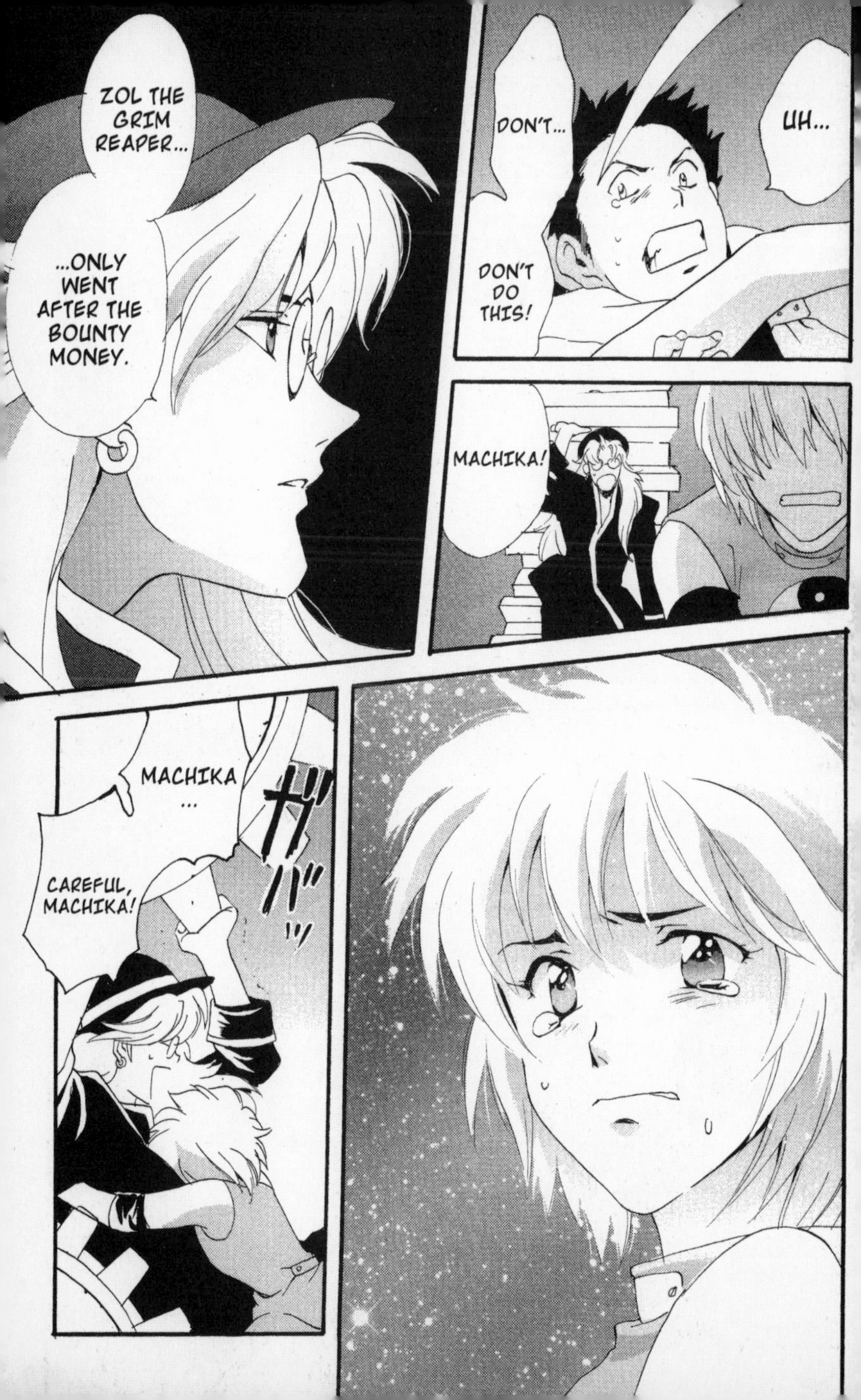
UH...
DON'T...
DON'T DO THIS!
MACHIKA!
ZOL THE GRIM REAPER...
...ONLY WENT AFTER THE BOUNTY MONEY.
MACHIKA ...
ガバッ
CAREFUL, MACHIKA!

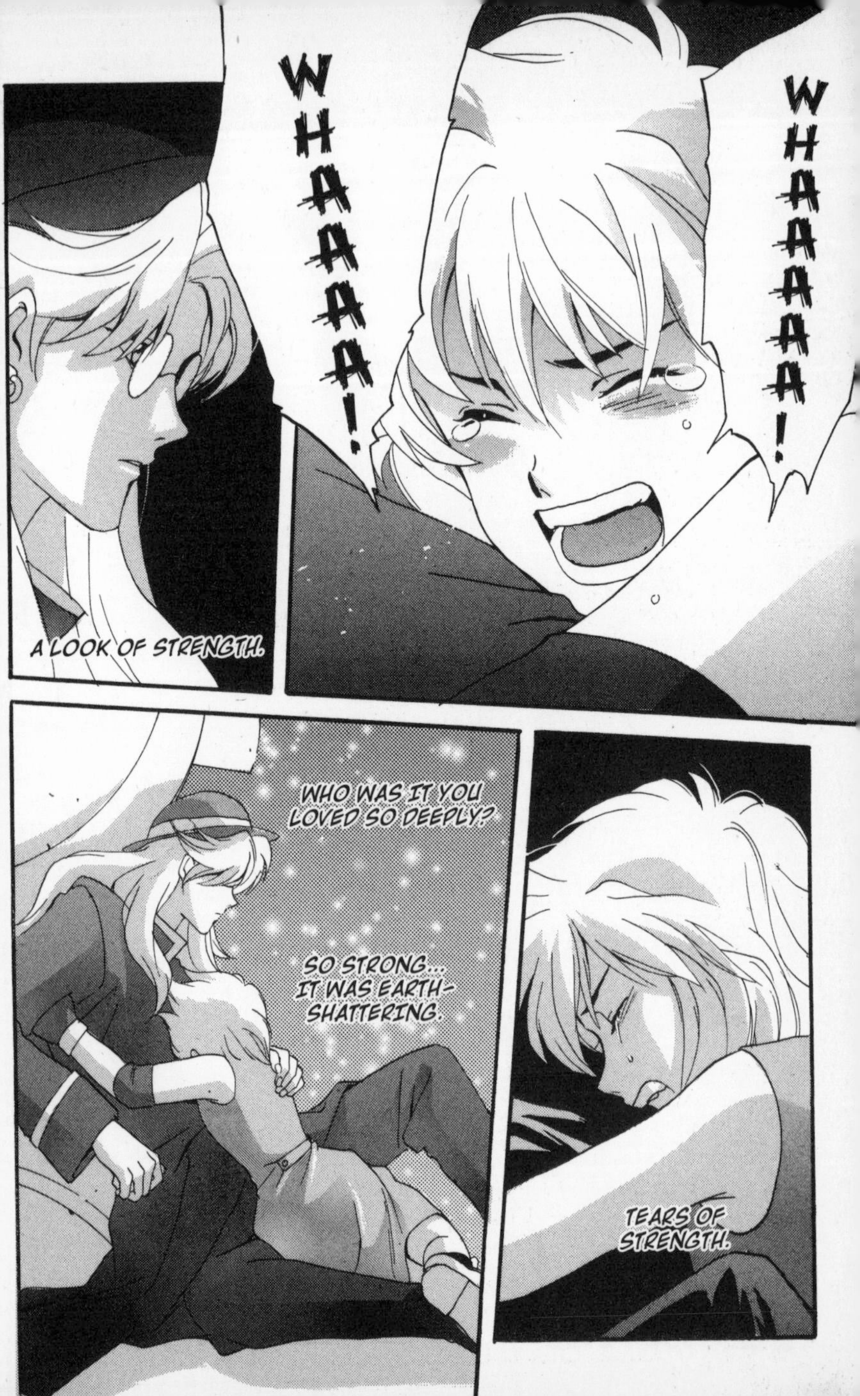
WHAAAAAA!
WHAAAAA!
A LOOK OF STRENGTH.
TEARS OF STRENGTH.
WHO WAS IT YOU LOVED SO DEEPLY?
SO STRONG... IT WAS EARTH-SHATTERING.

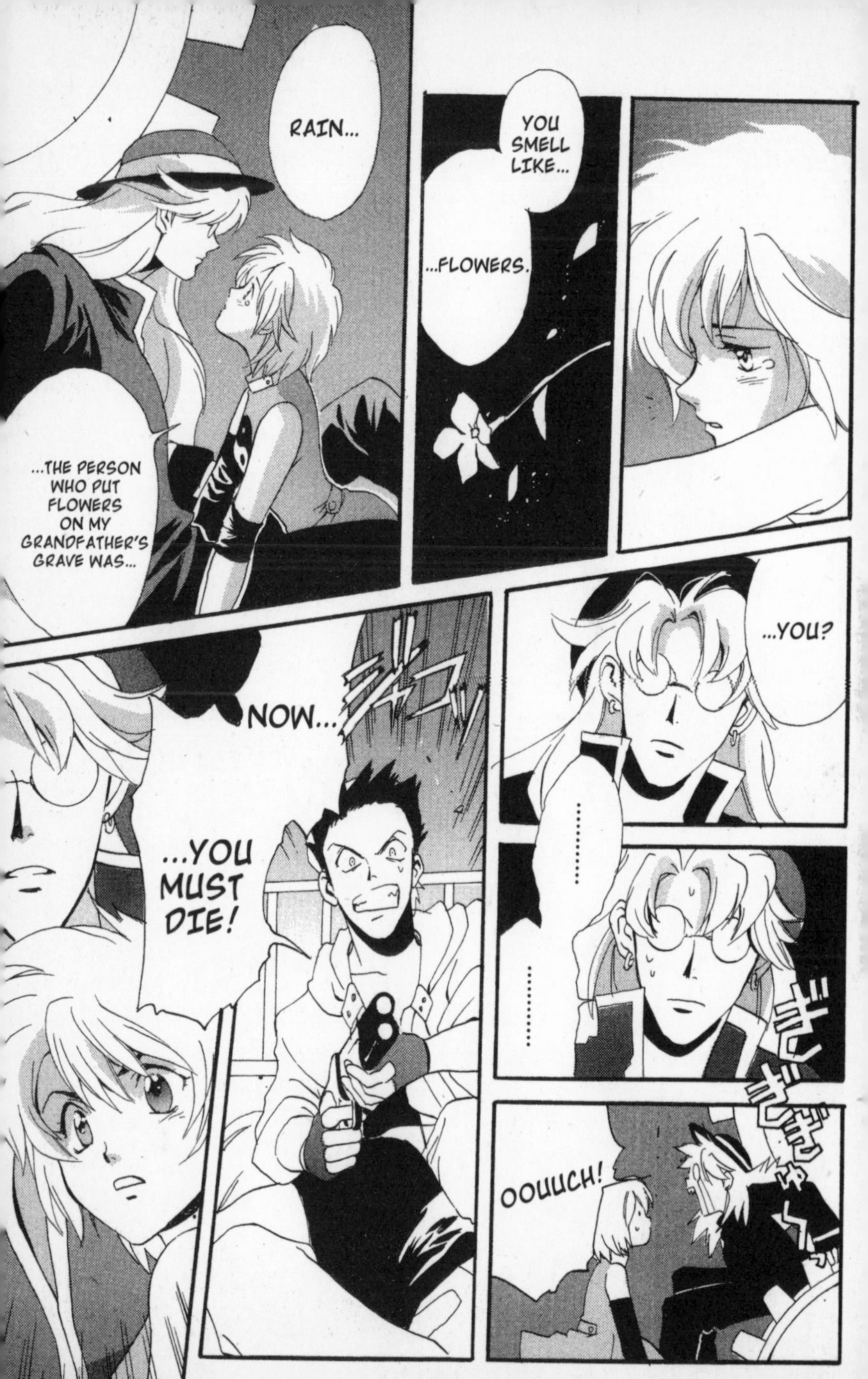
YOU SMELL LIKE...
...FLOWERS.
RAIN...
...THE PERSON WHO PUT FLOWERS ON MY GRANDFATHER'S GRAVE WAS...
...YOU?
OOUUCH!
NOW...
...YOU MUST DIE!

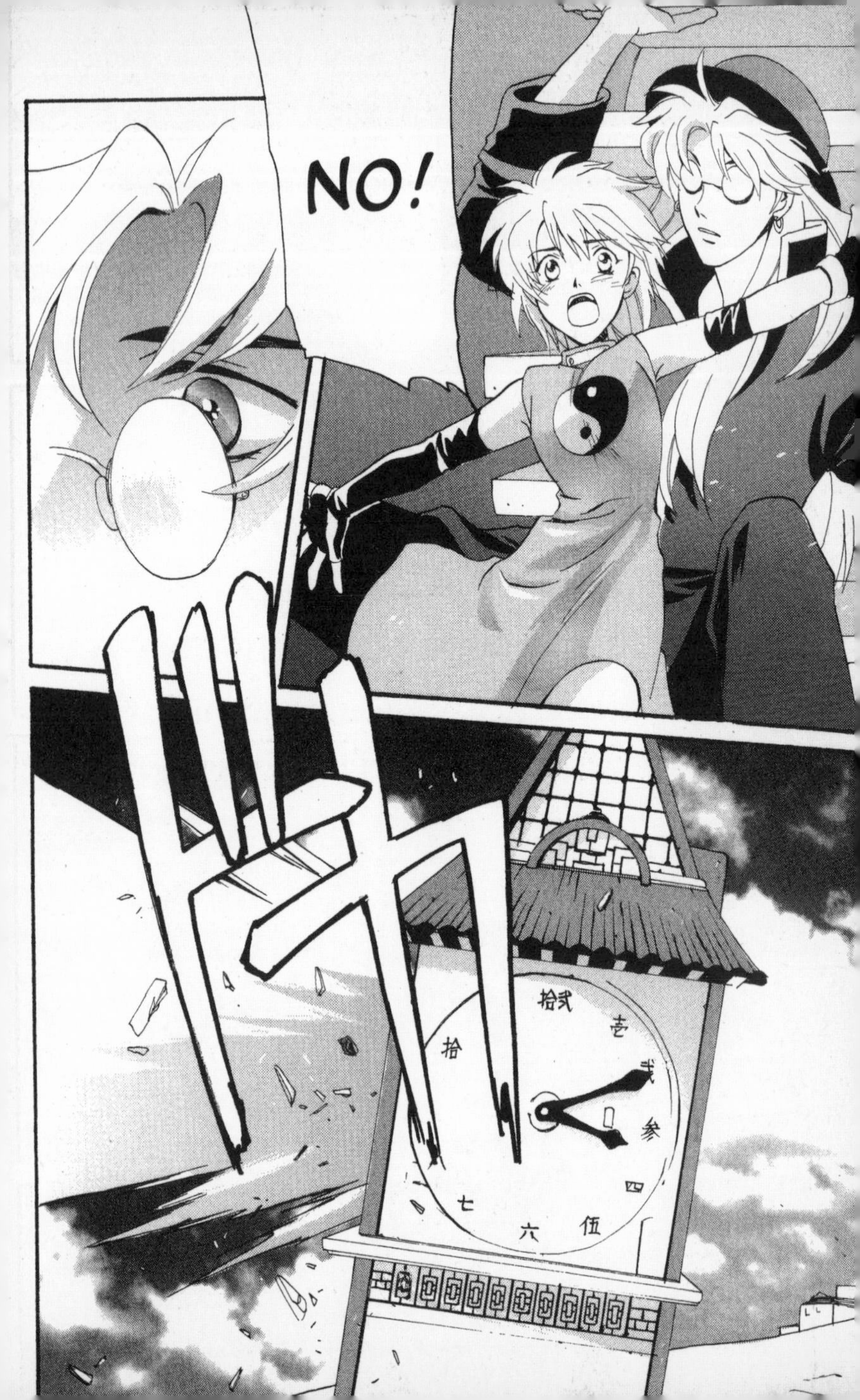
NO!
拾弐
壱
弐
参
四
伍
六
七
拾

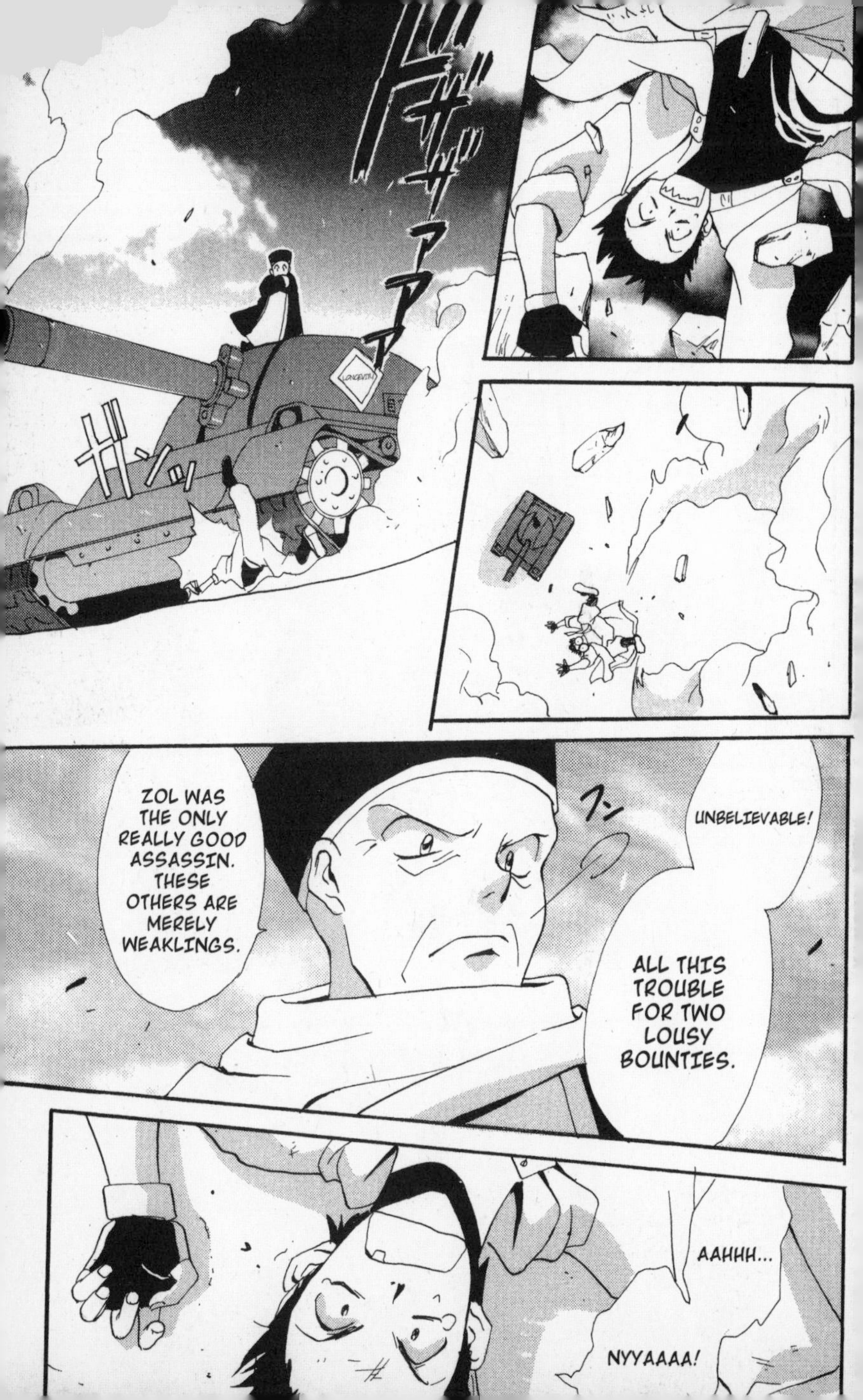
UNBELIEVABLE!
ALL THIS TROUBLE FOR TWO LOUSY BOUNTIES.
ZOL WAS THE ONLY REALLY GOOD ASSASSIN. THESE OTHERS ARE MERELY WEAKLINGS.
AAHHH...
NYYAAAA!

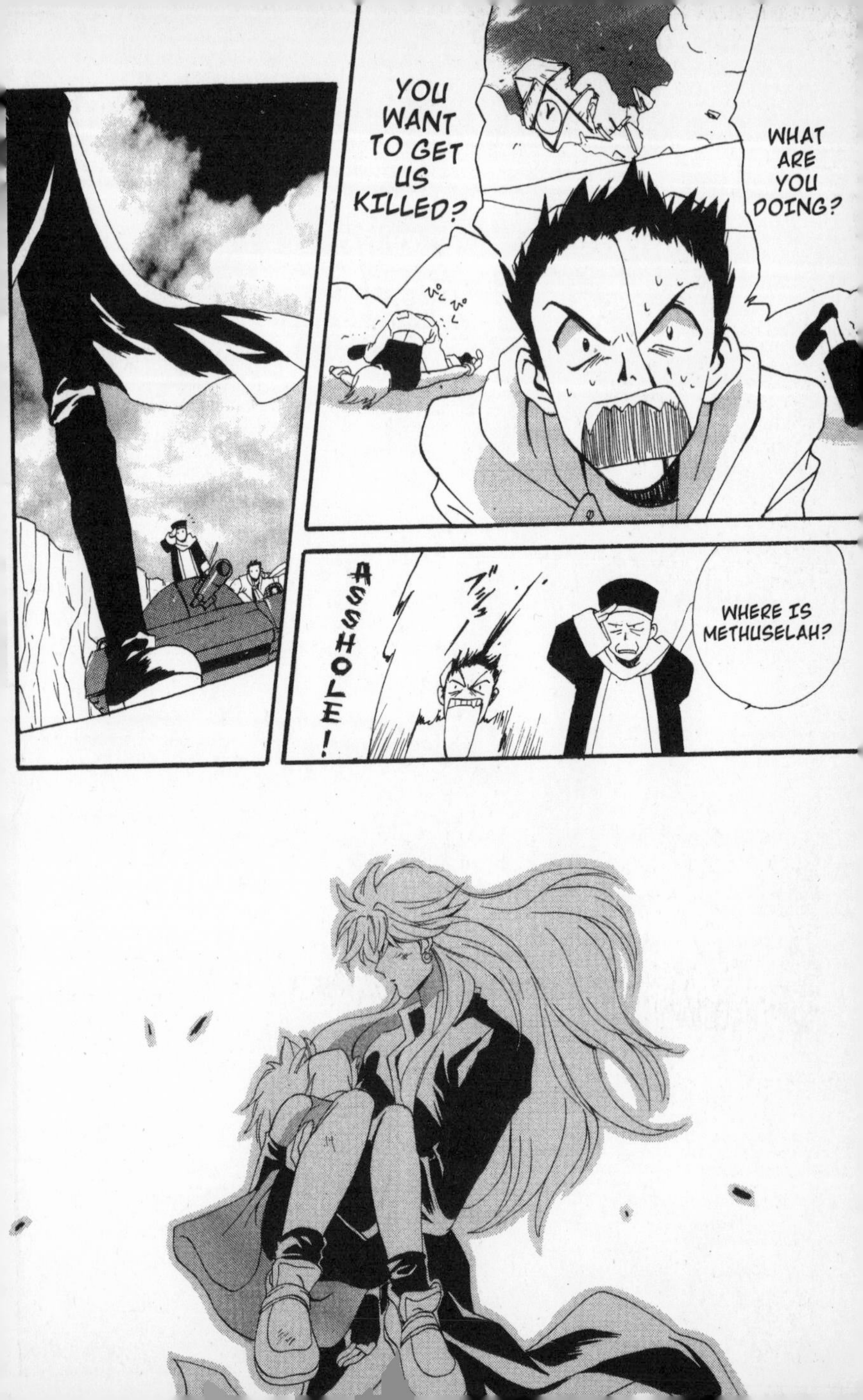
WHAT ARE YOU DOING?
YOU WANT TO GET US KILLED?
WHERE IS METHUSELAH?
ASSHOLE!

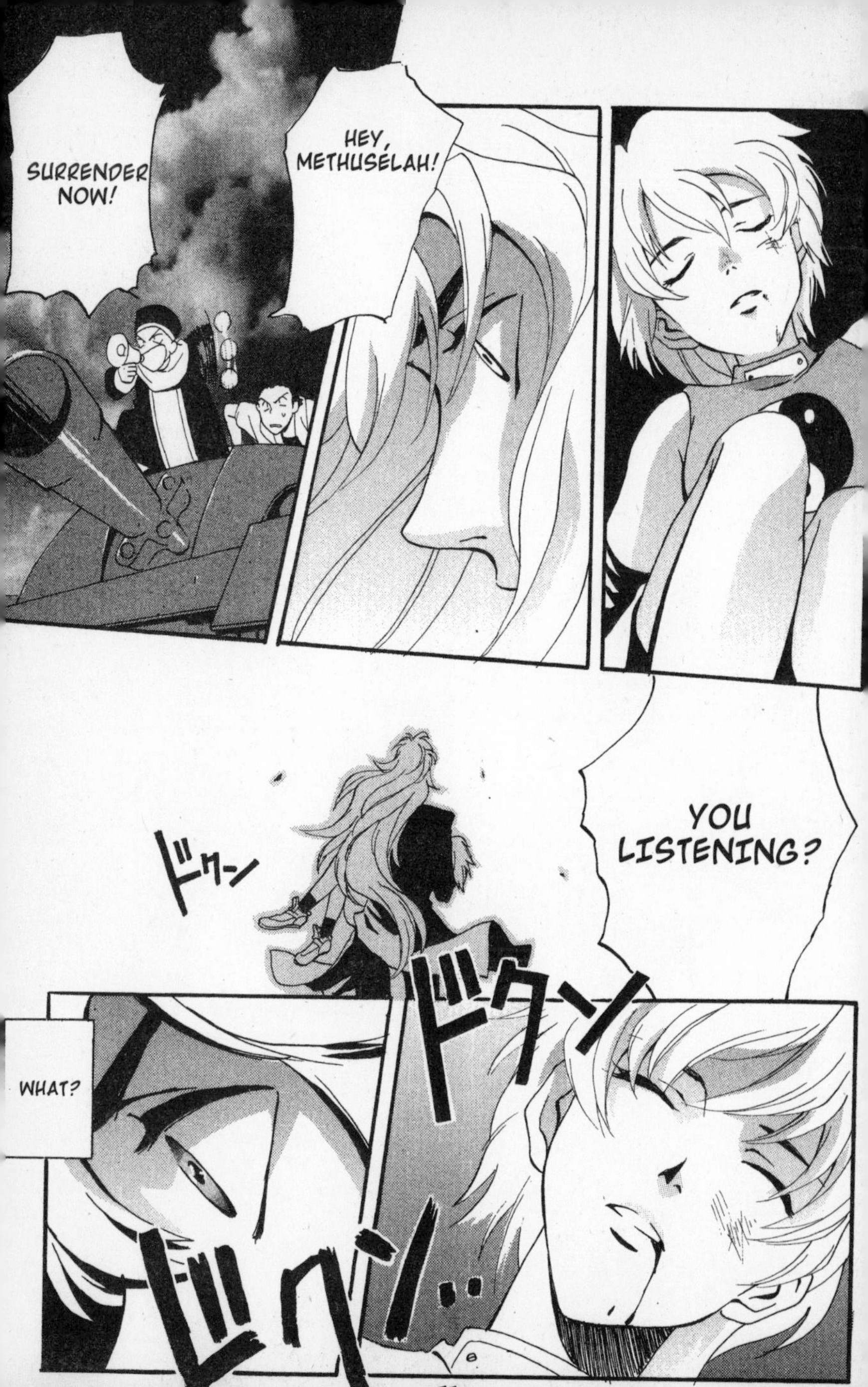
HEY, METHUSÉLAH!
SURRENDER NOW!
YOU LISTENING?
ドクーン
ドクン
WHAT?

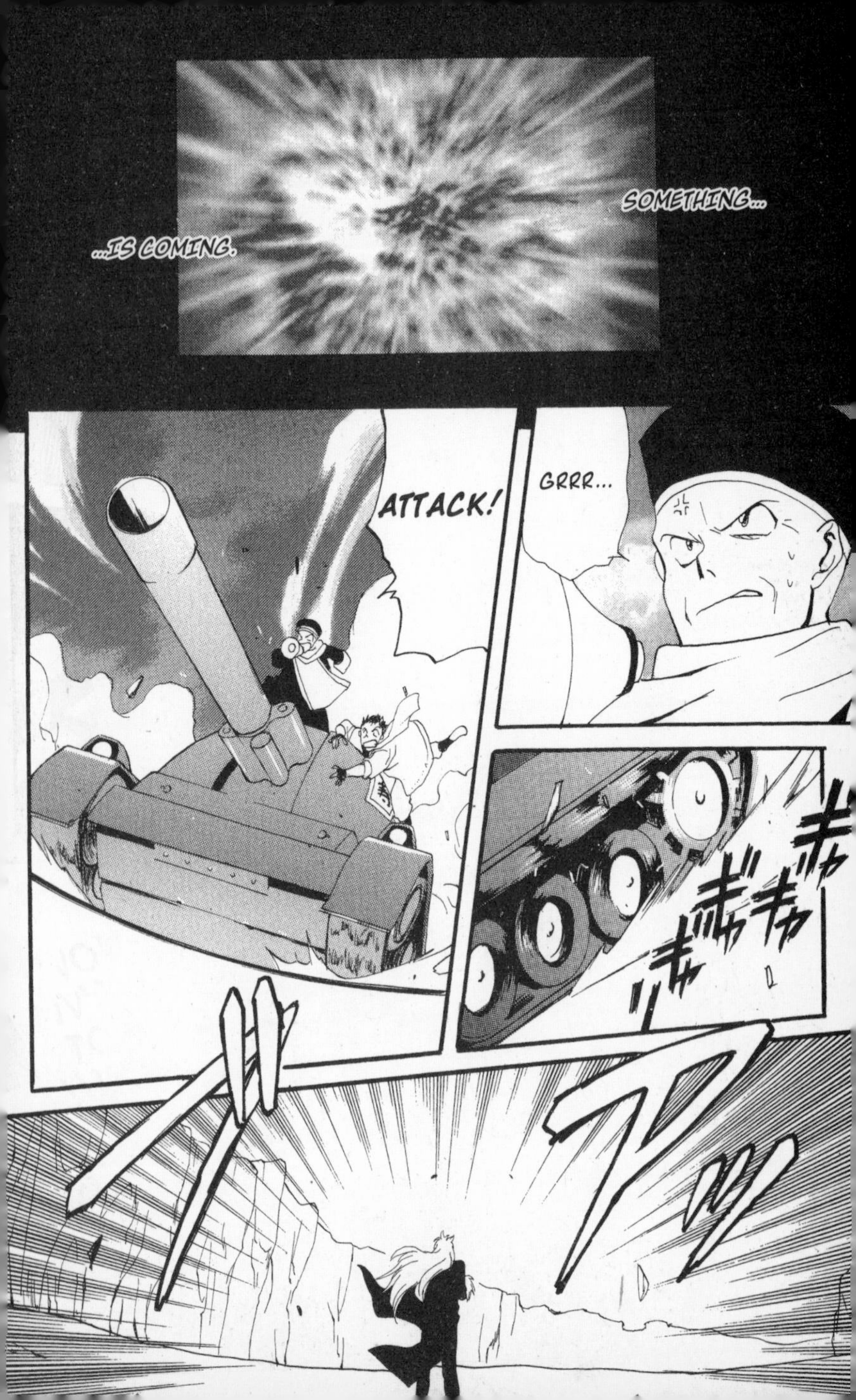
SOMETHING...
...IS COMING.
GRRR...
ATTACK!

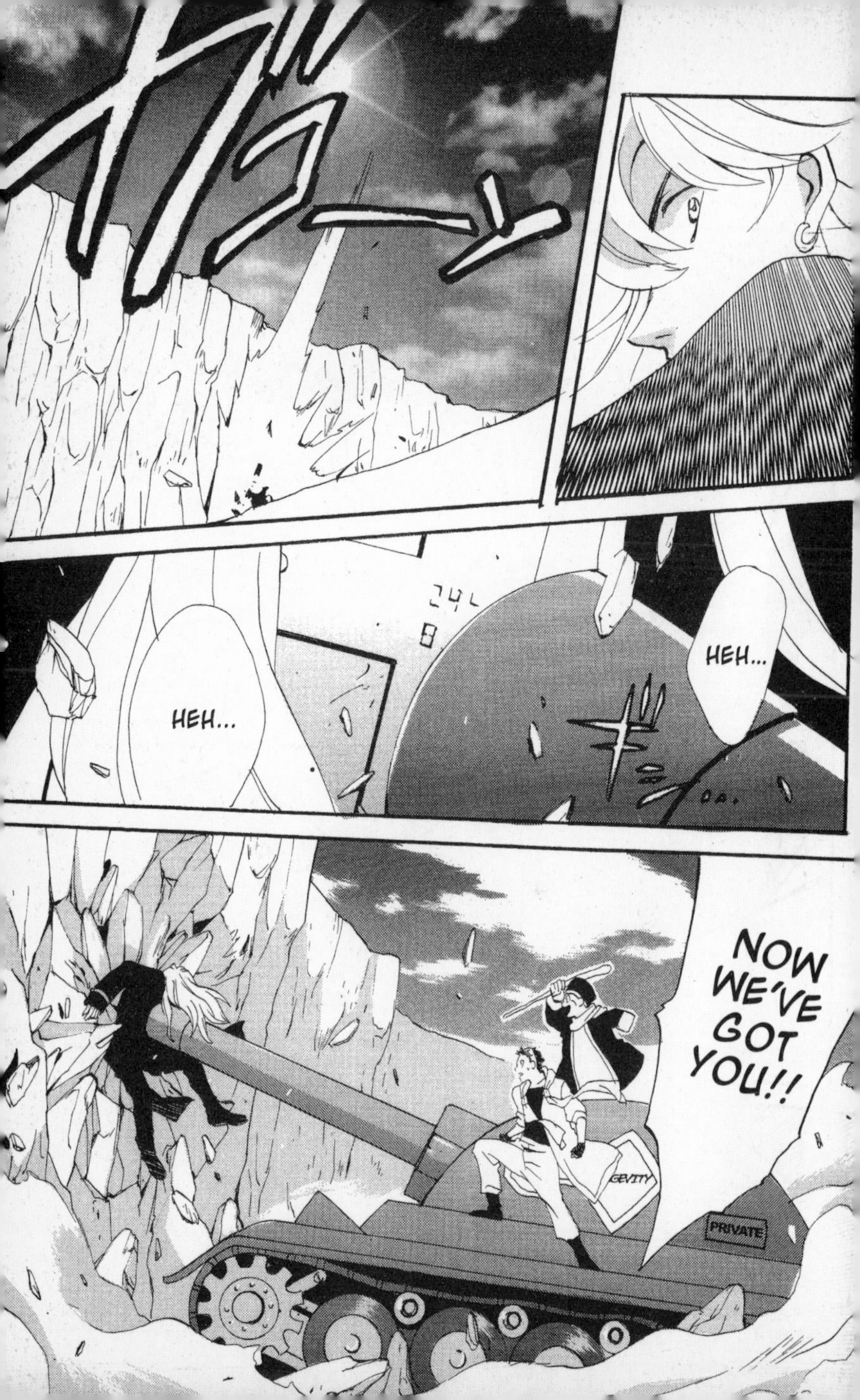
HEH...
HEH...
NOW WE'VE GOT YOU!!
GEVITY
PRIVATE

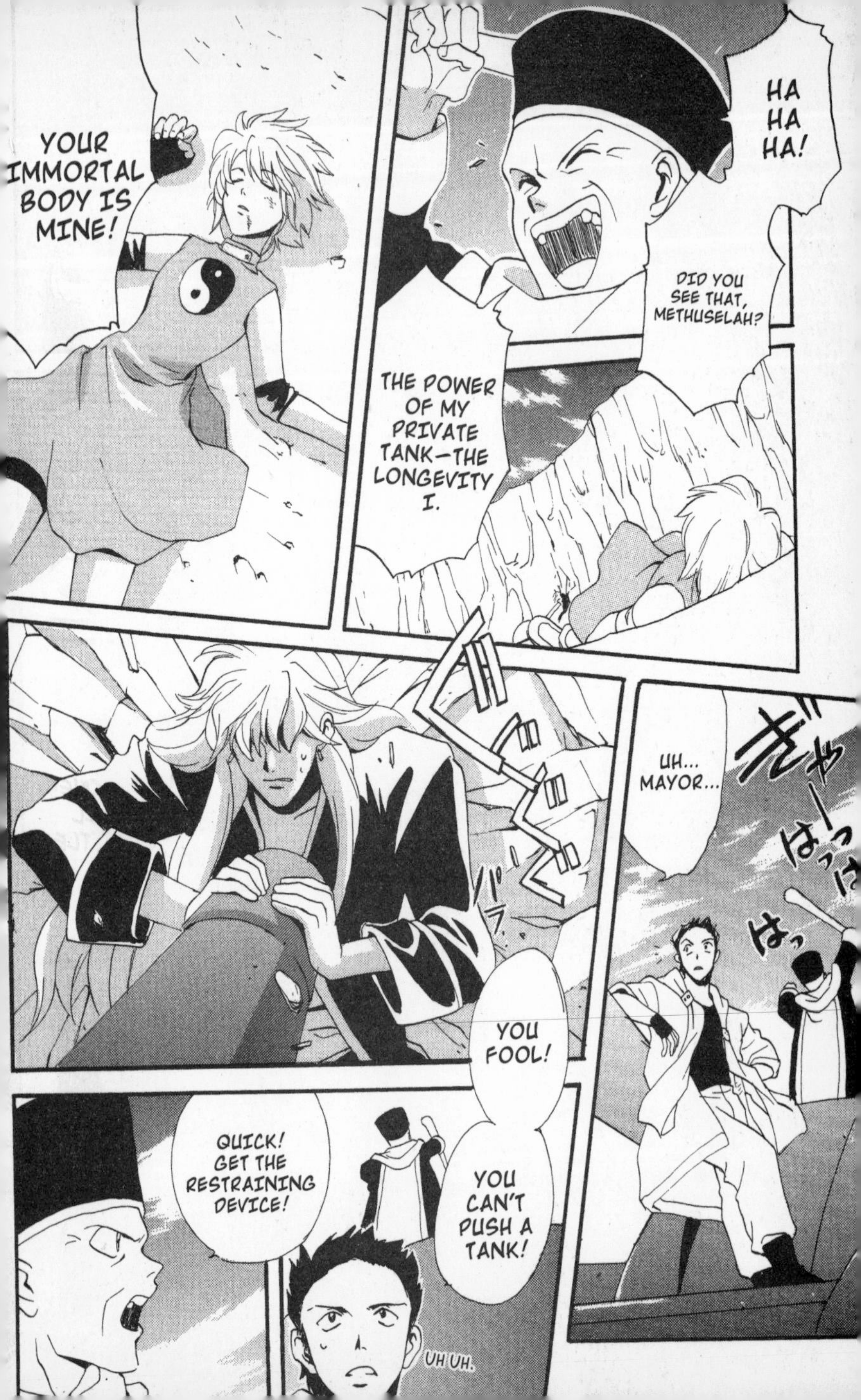
HA HA HA!
DID YOU SEE THAT, METHUSELAH?
THE POWER OF MY PRIVATE TANK—THE LONGEVITY I.
YOUR IMMORTAL BODY IS MINE!
UH... MAYOR...
ぎゃーはっは
はっ
パラ
YOU FOOL!
YOU CAN'T PUSH A TANK!
QUICK! GET THE RESTRAINING DEVICE!
UH UH.

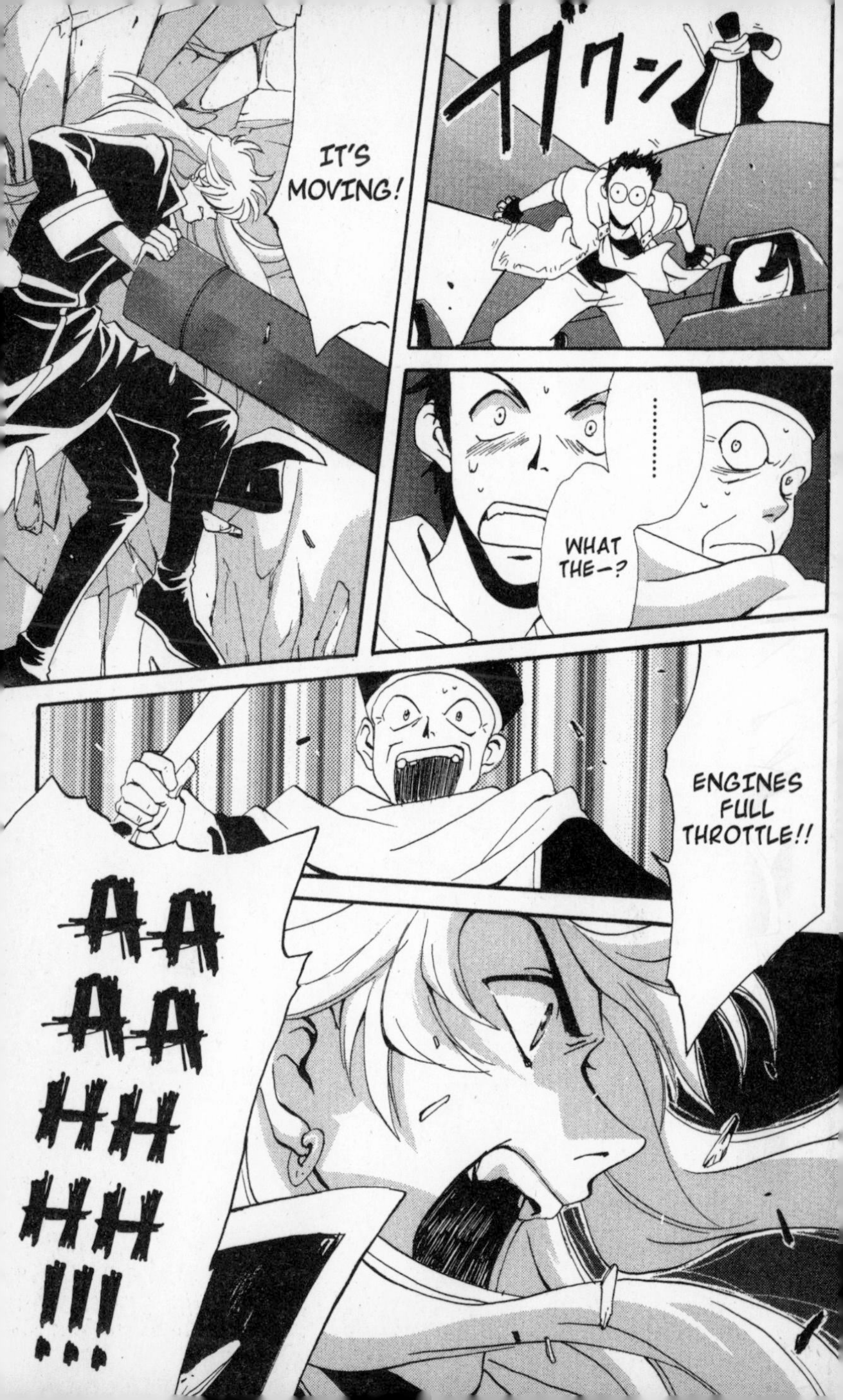
ガクン
......
WHAT THE—?
IT'S MOVING!
ENGINES FULL THROTTLE!!
AAAAHHHH!!!

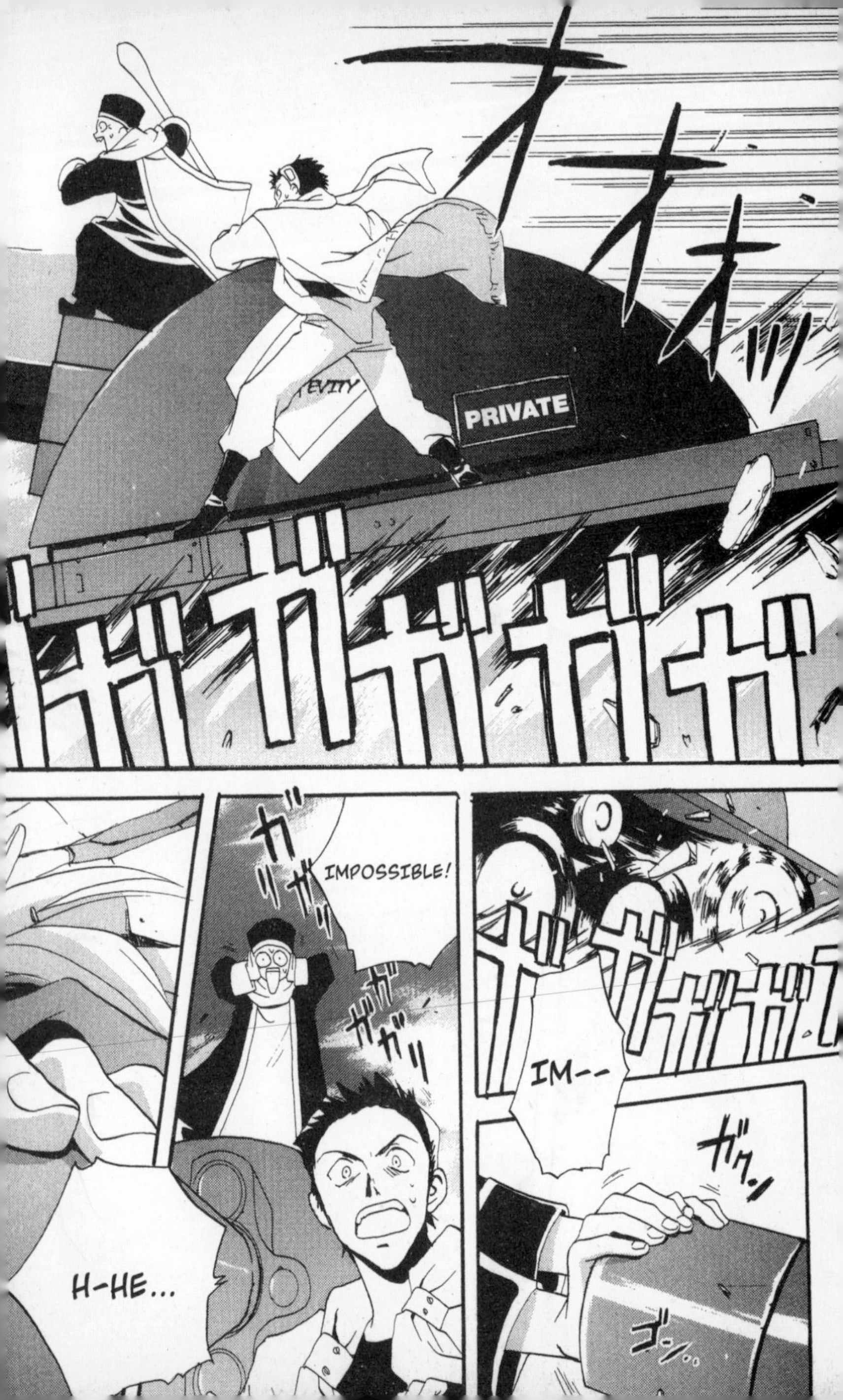
EVITY
PRIVATE
IM--
IMPOSSIBLE!
H-HE...

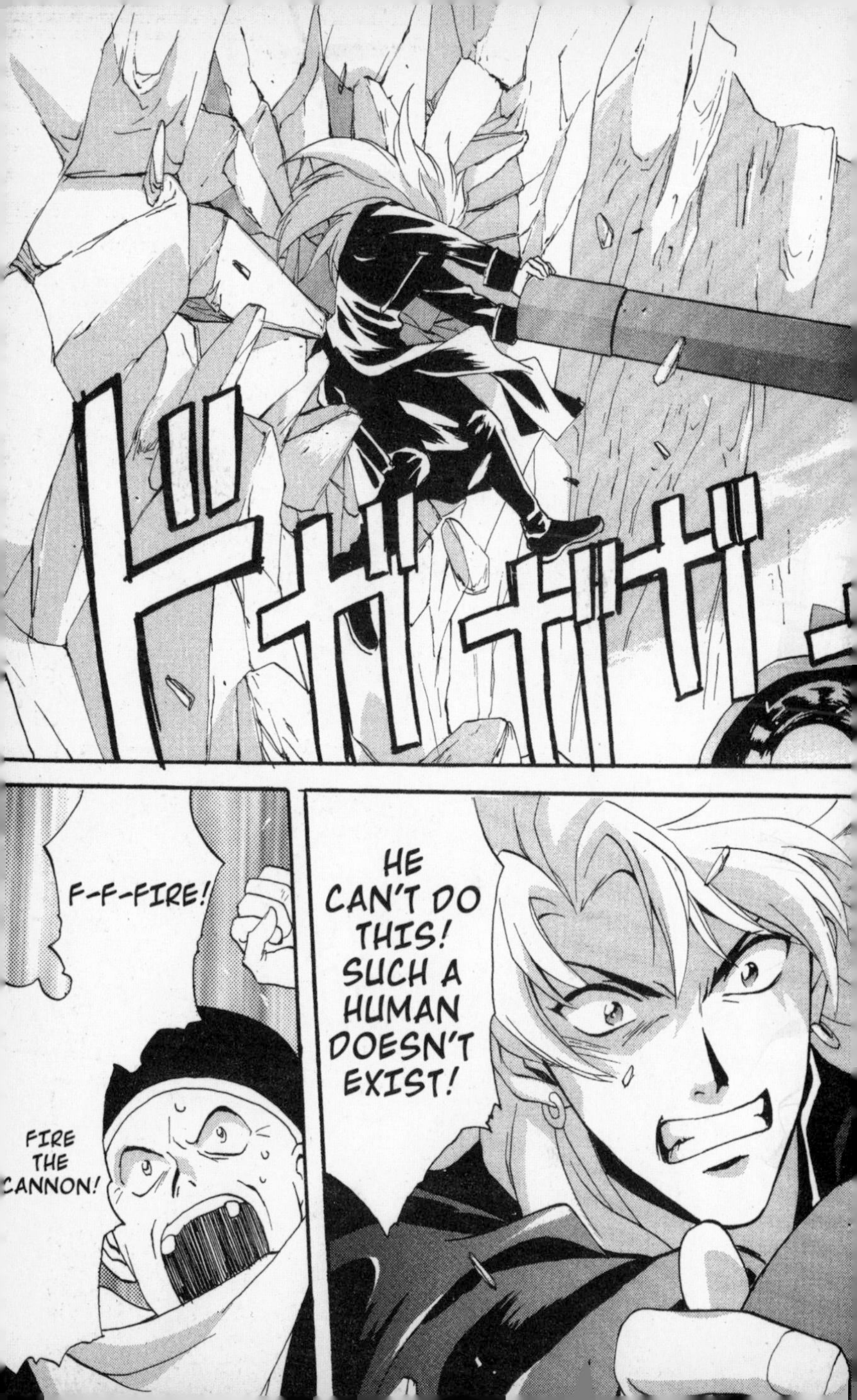
ドガガガ
HE CAN'T DO THIS! SUCH A HUMAN DOESN'T EXIST!
F-F-FIRE!
FIRE THE CANNON!

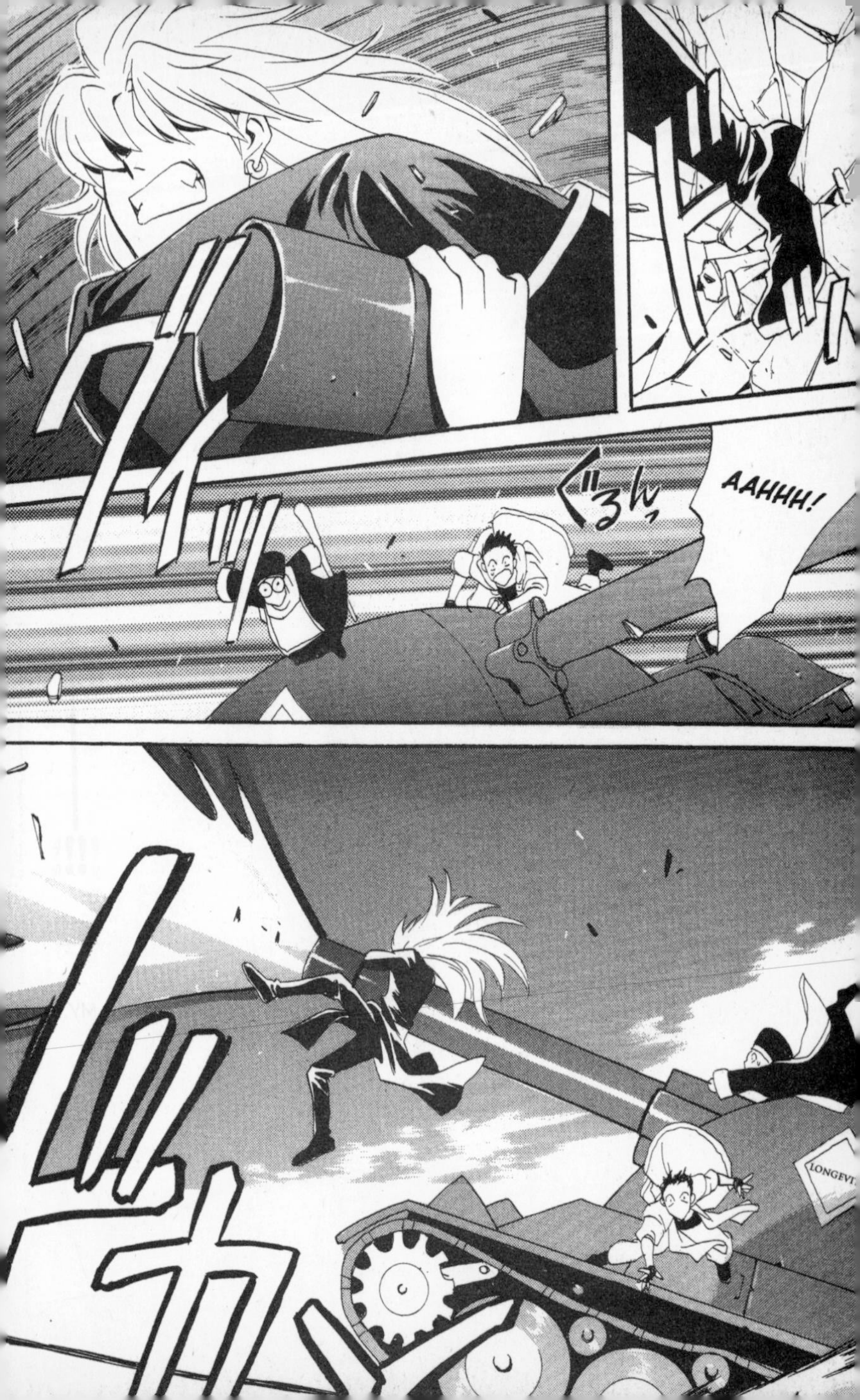
ぐるん
AAHHH!
LONGEVI

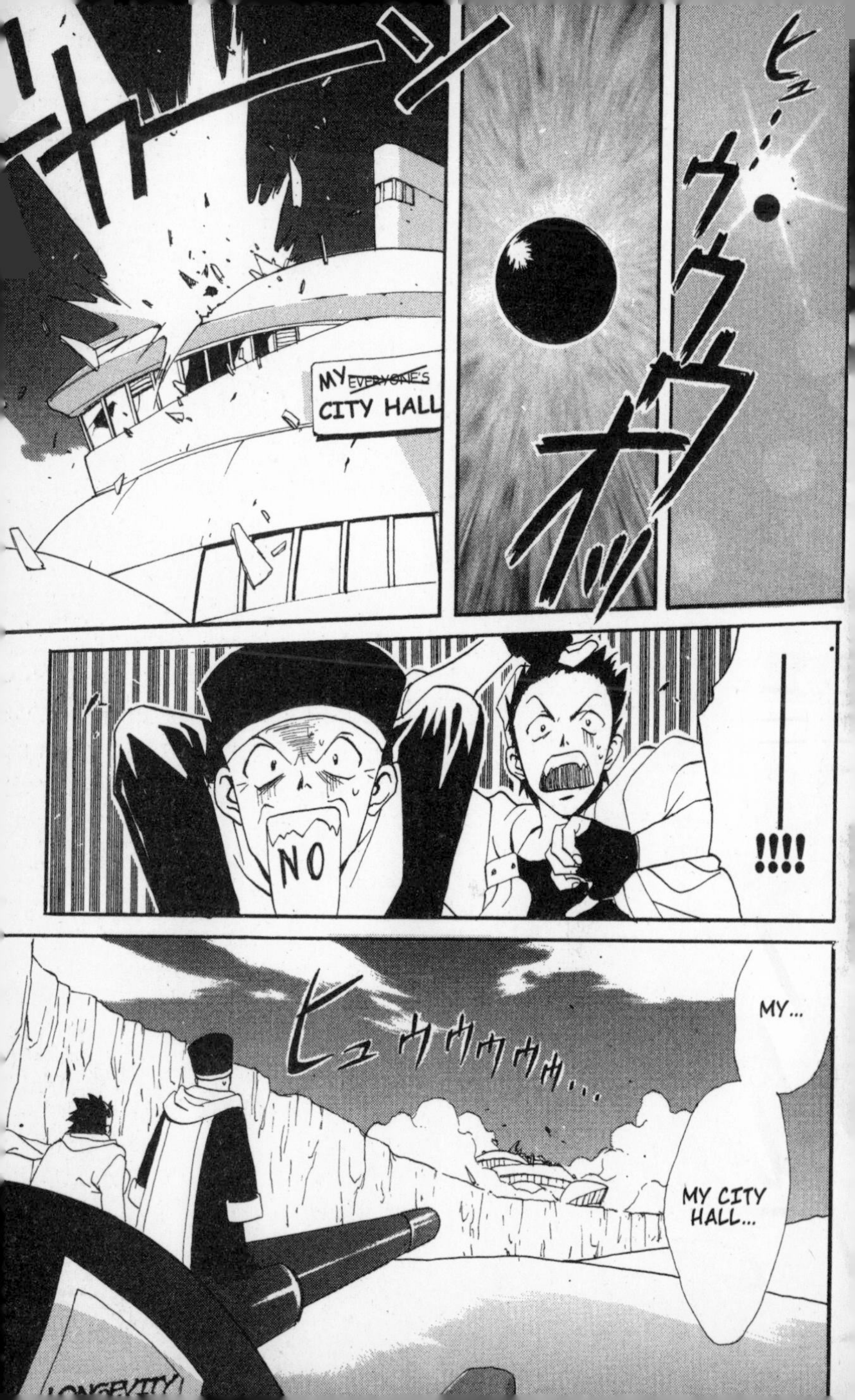

MY ~~EVERYONE'S~~
CITY HALL
NO
!!!!
MY...
MY CITY HALL...
LONGEVITY

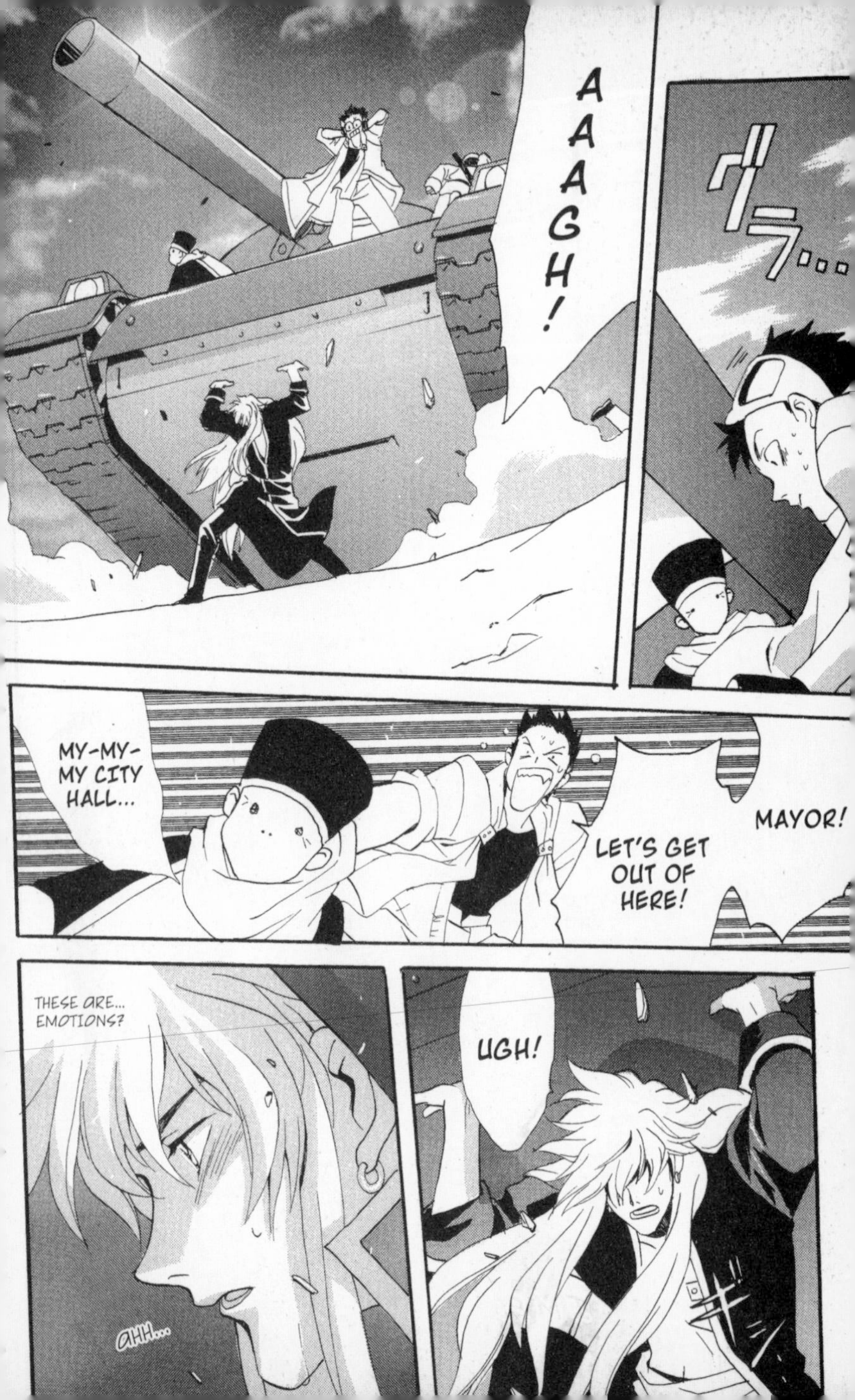

グラ...
AAAAGH!
MAYOR!
LET'S GET OUT OF HERE!
MY-MY-MY CITY HALL...
UGH!
THESE ARE... EMOTIONS?
AHH...

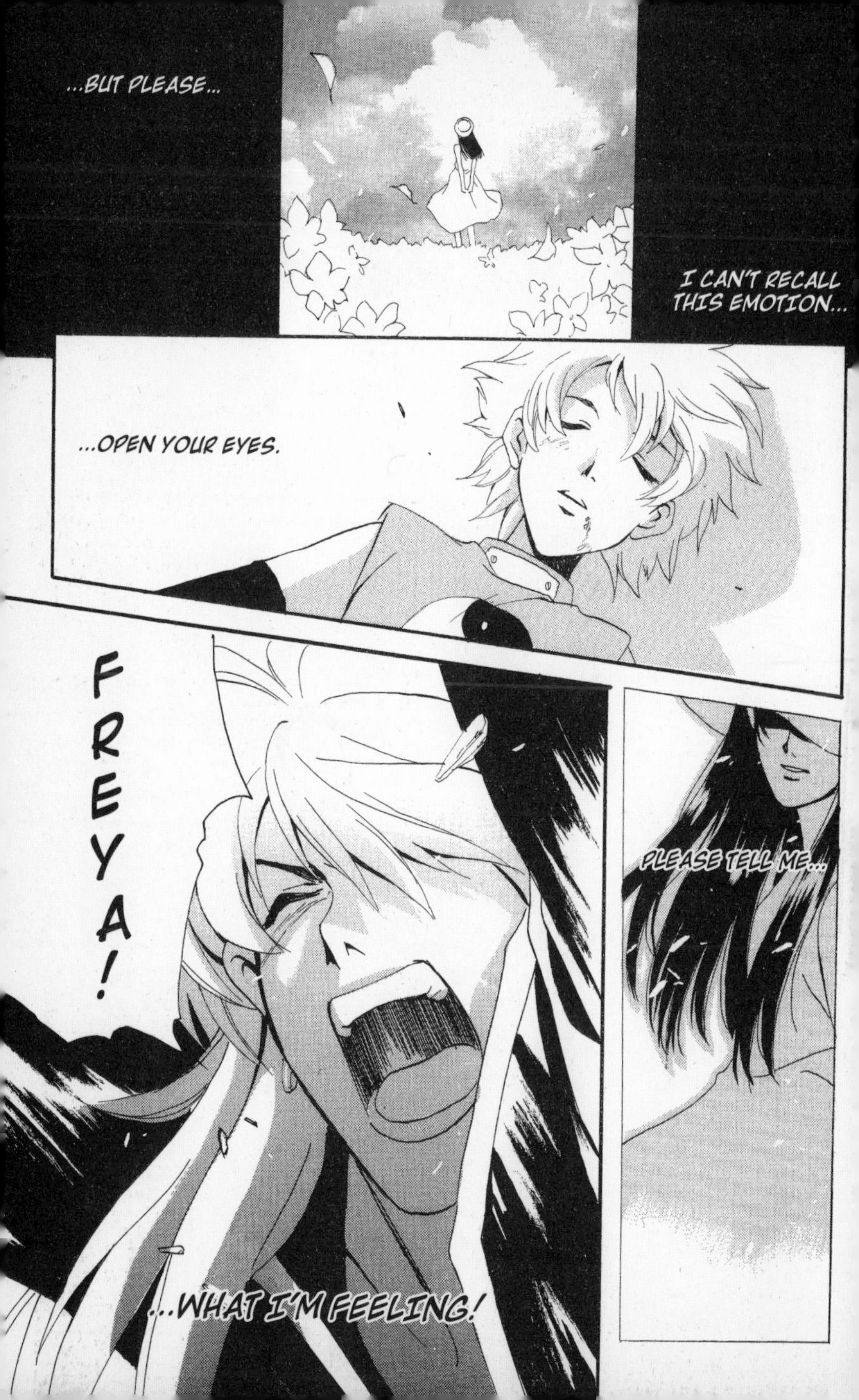
I CAN'T RECALL THIS EMOTION...
...BUT PLEASE...
...OPEN YOUR EYES.
PLEASE TELL ME...
FREYA!
...WHAT I'M FEELING!

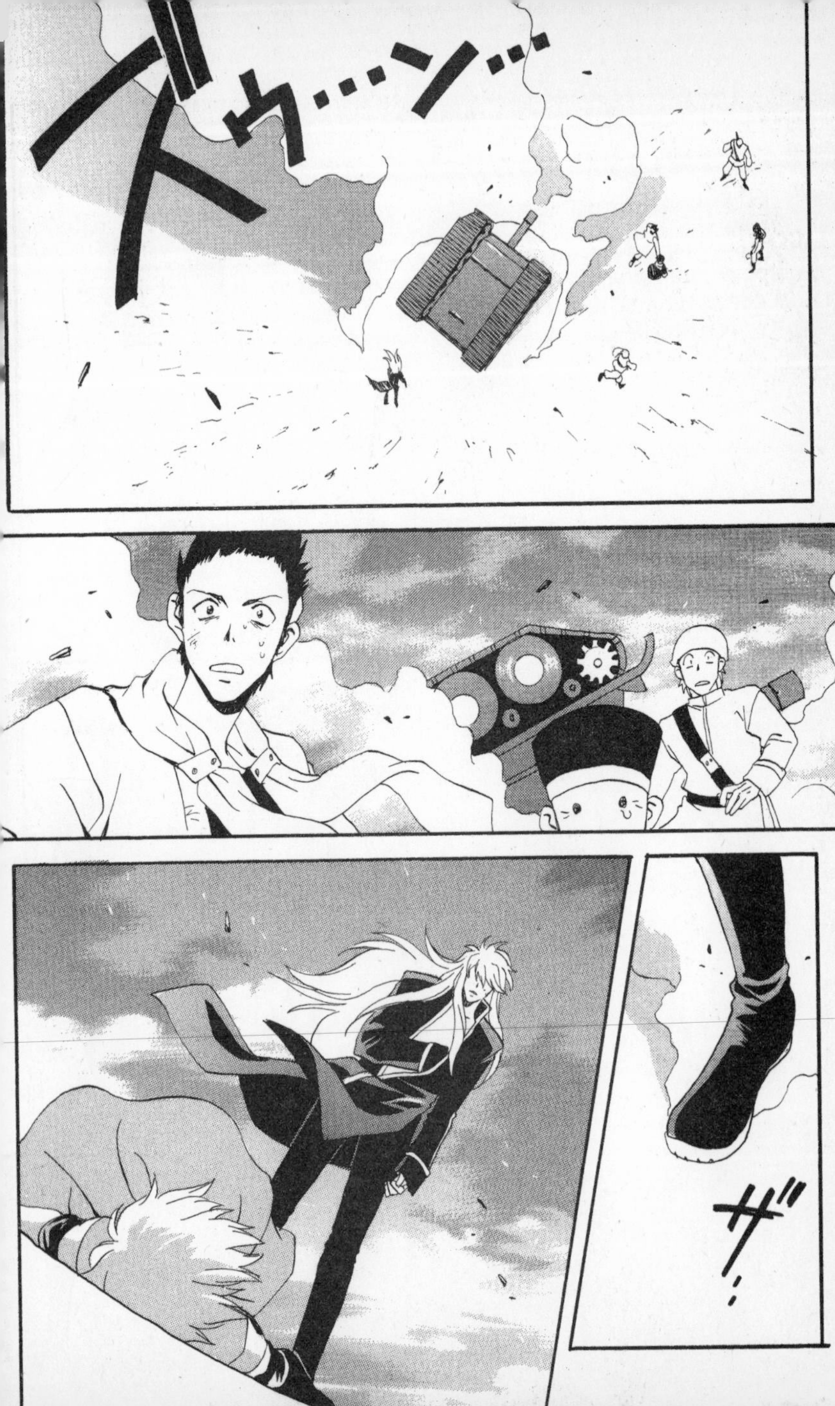
ズゥ…ン…
ザ

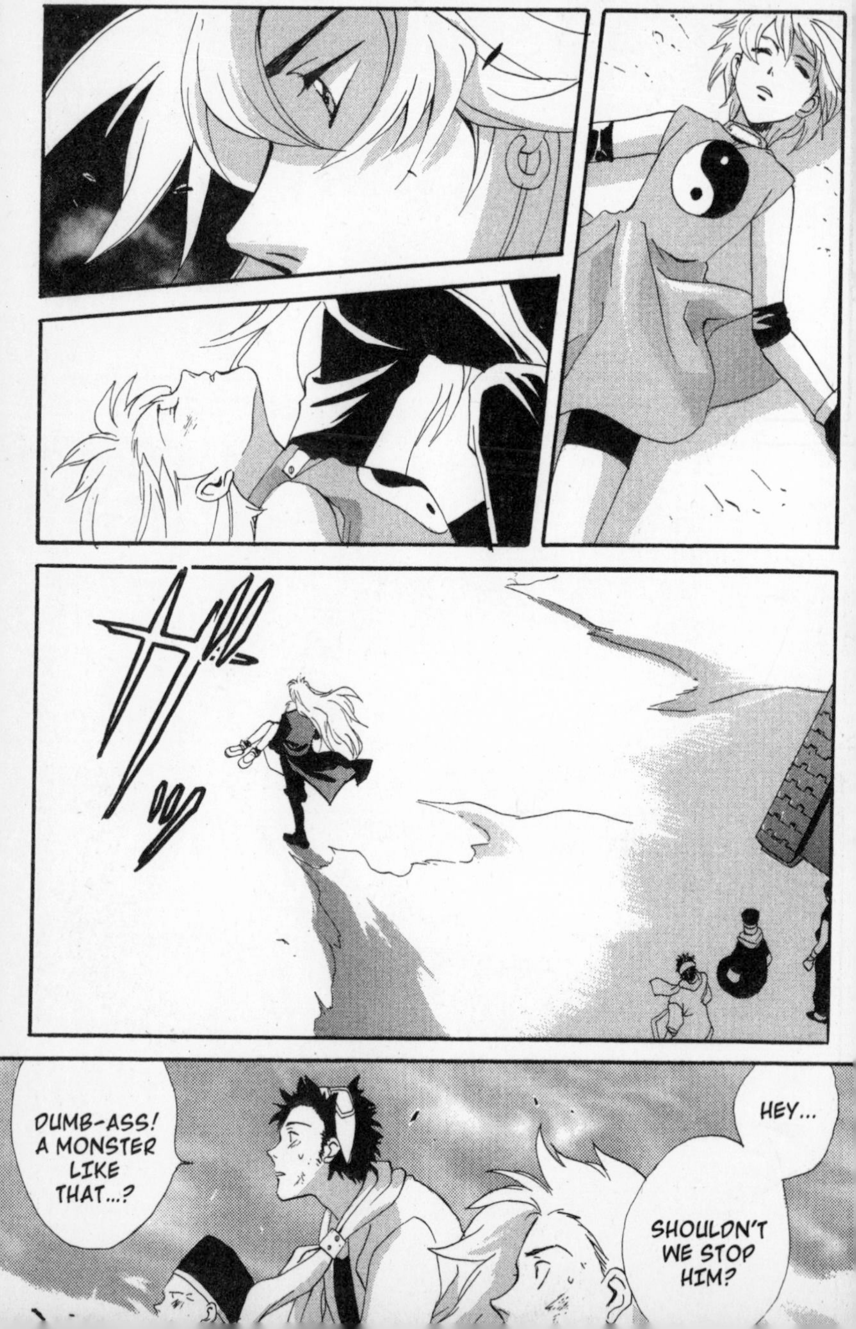
HEY...
SHOULDN'T WE STOP HIM?
DUMB-ASS! A MONSTER LIKE THAT...?

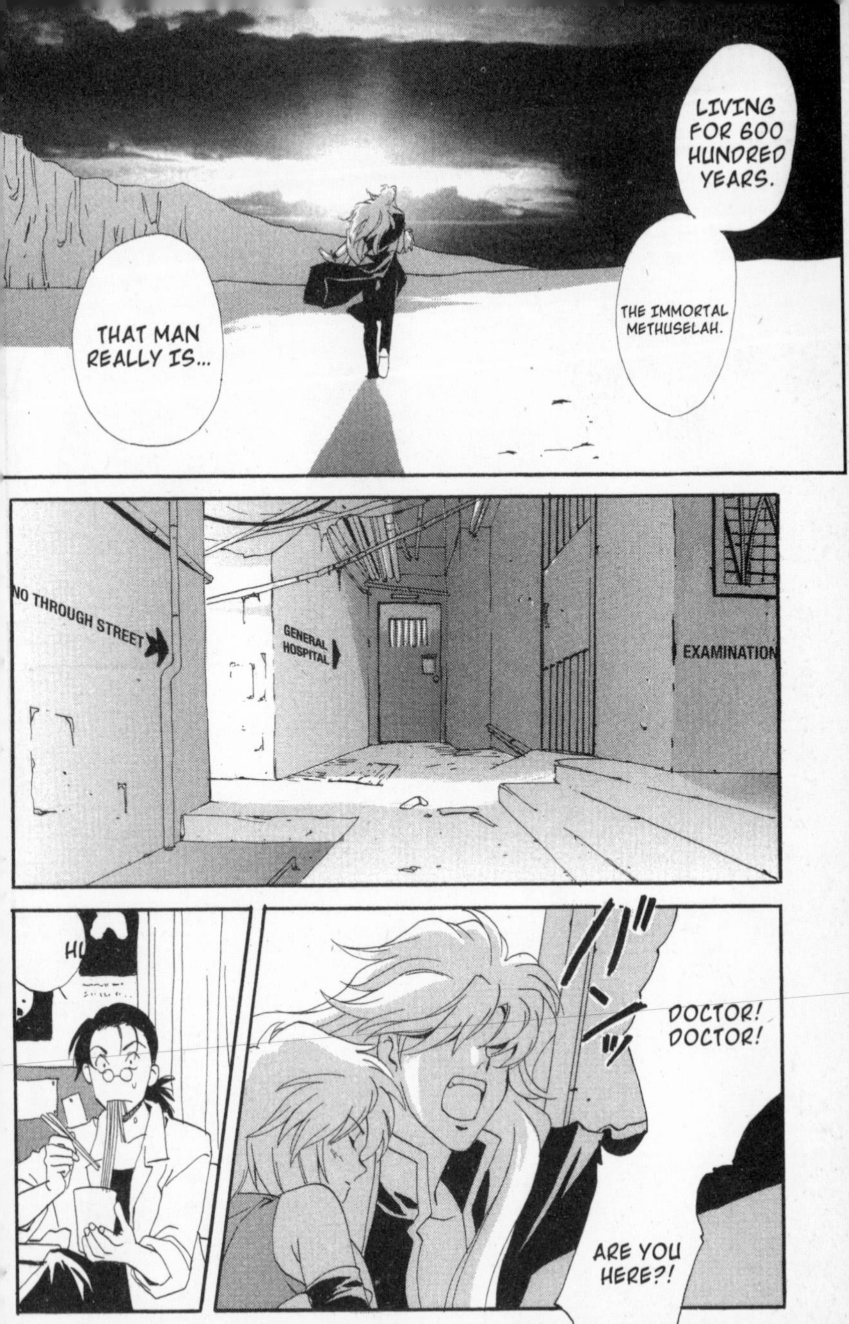
LIVING FOR 600 HUNDRED YEARS.
THE IMMORTAL METHUSELAH.
THAT MAN REALLY IS...
EXAMINATION
GENERAL HOSPITAL
NO THROUGH STREET
DOCTOR! DOCTOR!
ARE YOU HERE?!
HU

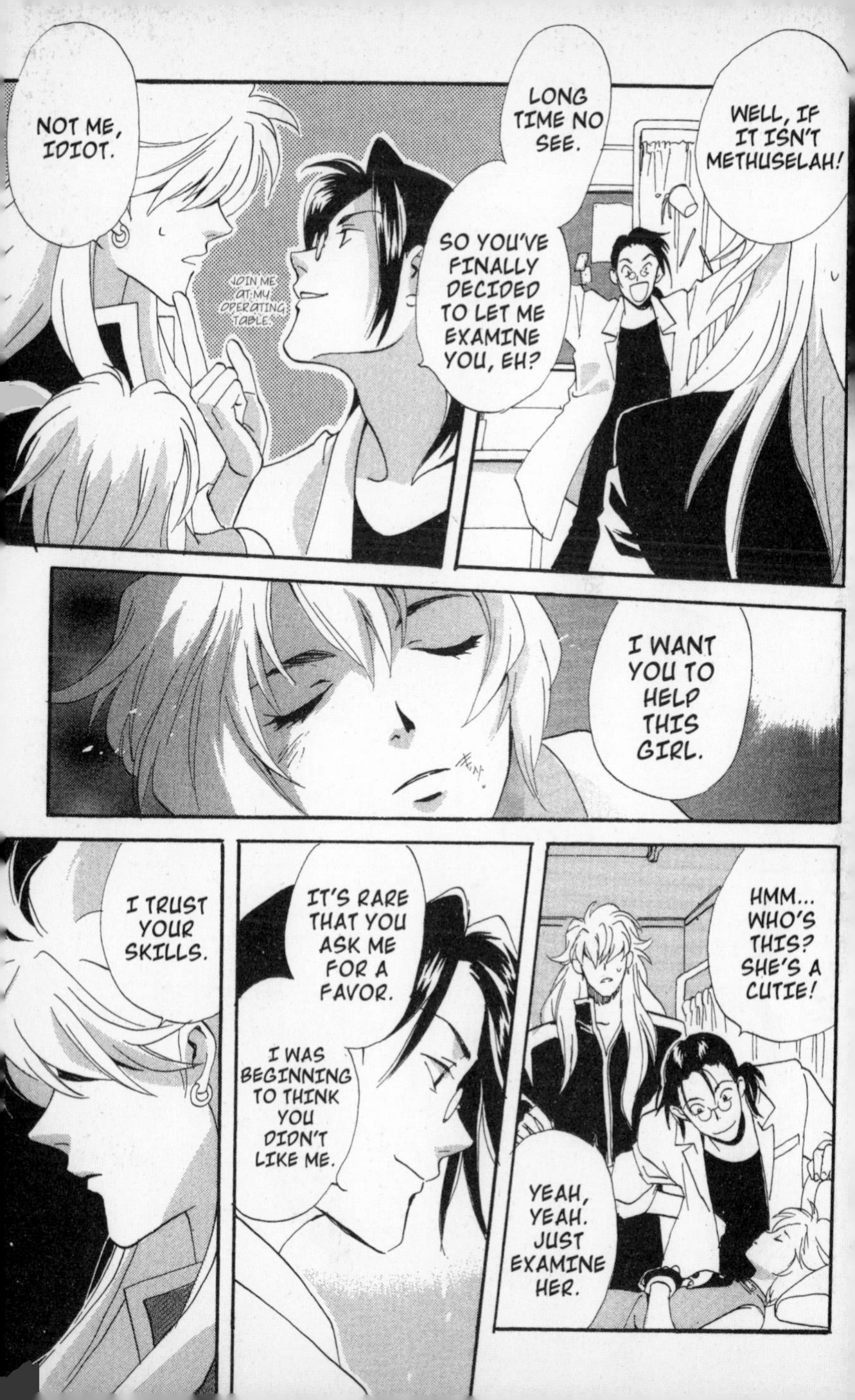
WELL, IF IT ISN'T METHUSELAH!
LONG TIME NO SEE.
SO YOU'VE FINALLY DECIDED TO LET ME EXAMINE YOU, EH?
JOIN ME AT MY OPERATING TABLE.
NOT ME, IDIOT.
I WANT YOU TO HELP THIS GIRL.
HMM... WHO'S THIS? SHE'S A CUTIE!
YEAH, YEAH. JUST EXAMINE HER.
IT'S RARE THAT YOU ASK ME FOR A FAVOR.
I WAS BEGINNING TO THINK YOU DIDN'T LIKE ME.
I TRUST YOUR SKILLS.

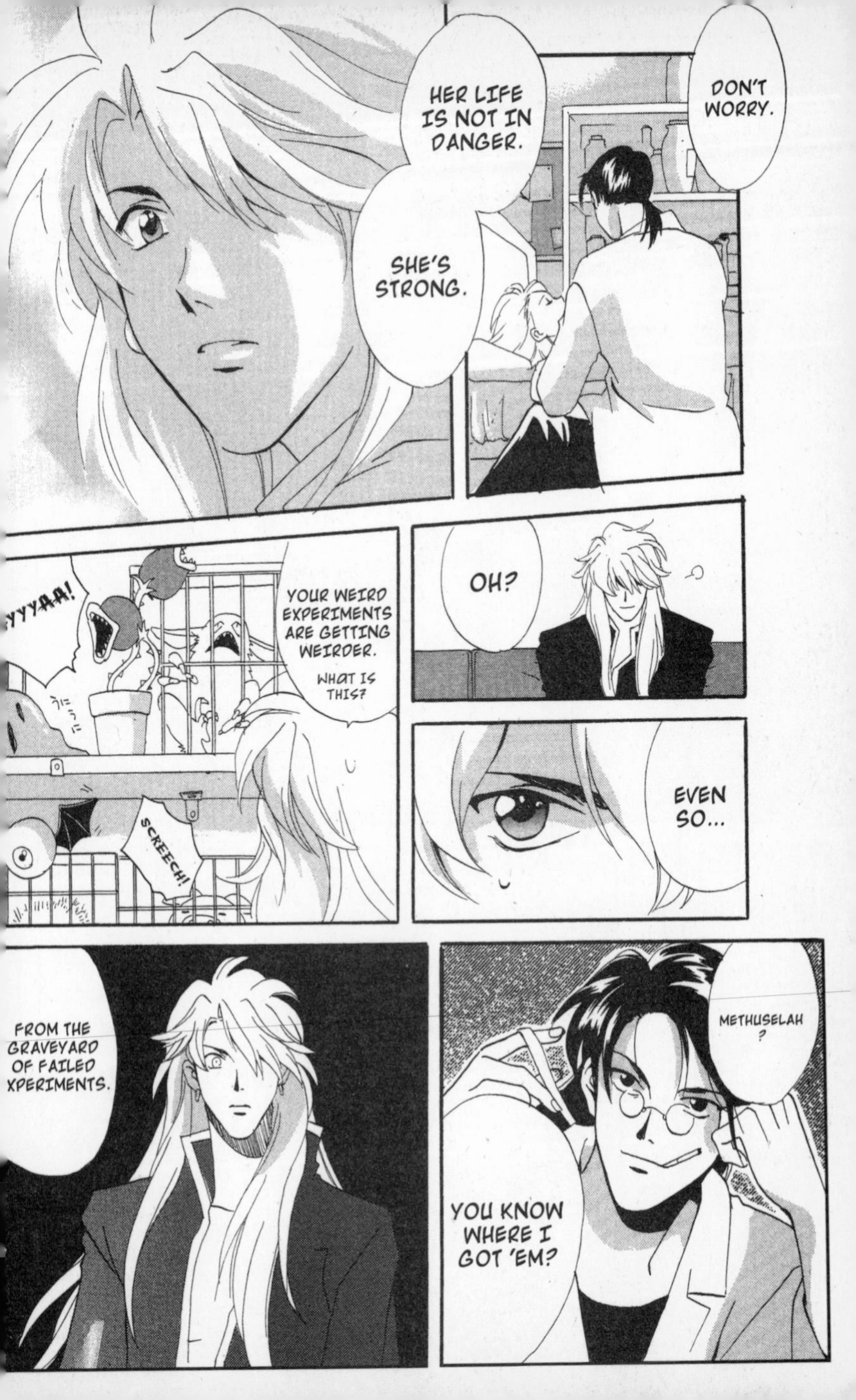
DON'T WORRY.
HER LIFE IS NOT IN DANGER.
SHE'S STRONG.
OH?
EVEN SO...
YOUR WEIRD EXPERIMENTS ARE GETTING WEIRDER.
WHAT IS THIS?
YYYAA!
SCREECH!
METHUSELAH?
YOU KNOW WHERE I GOT 'EM?
FROM THE GRAVEYARD OF FAILED XPERIMENTS.

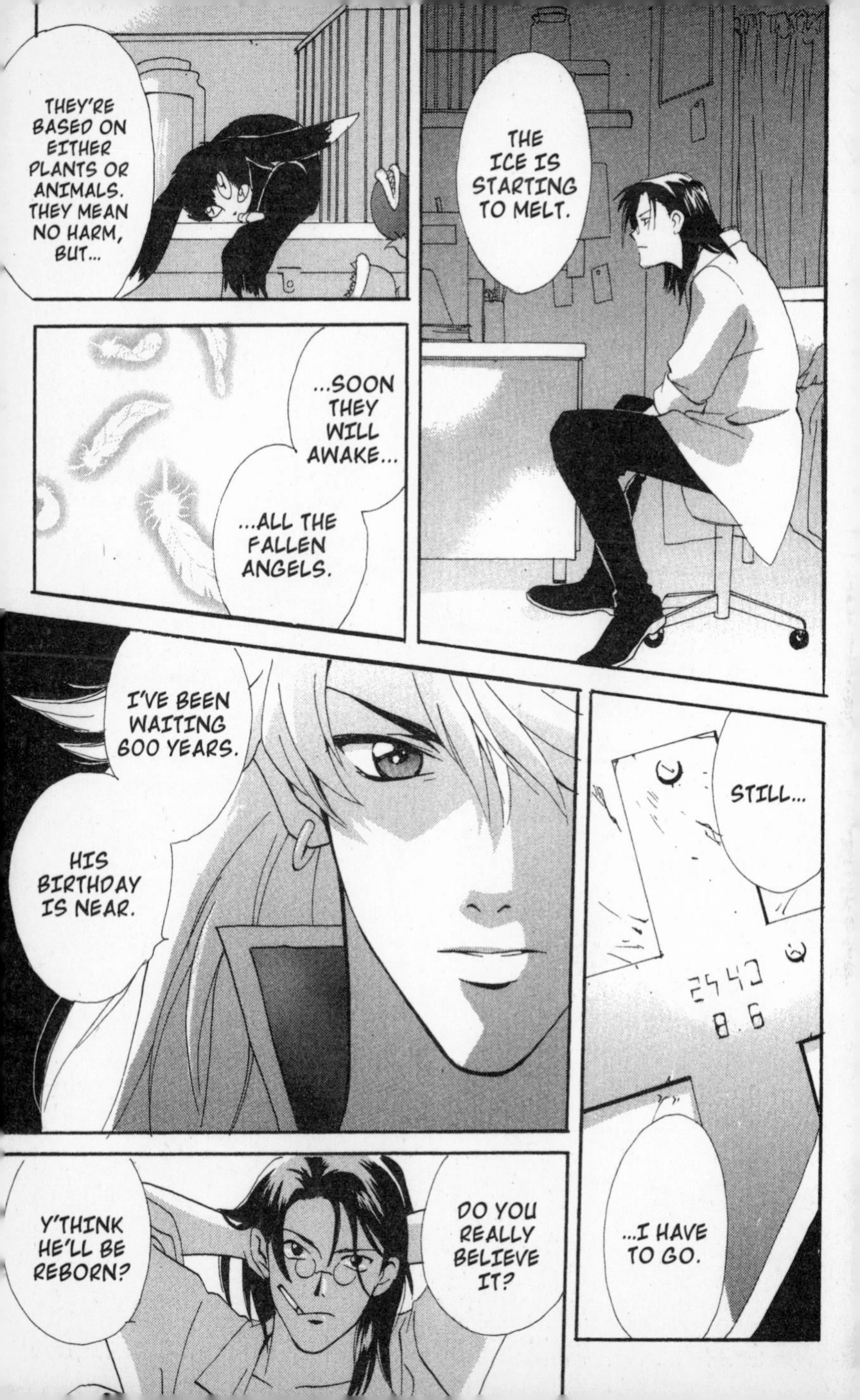
THE ICE IS STARTING TO MELT.
THEY'RE BASED ON EITHER PLANTS OR ANIMALS. THEY MEAN NO HARM, BUT...
...SOON THEY WILL AWAKE...
...ALL THE FALLEN ANGELS.
STILL...
...I HAVE TO GO.
I'VE BEEN WAITING 600 YEARS.
HIS BIRTHDAY IS NEAR.
DO YOU REALLY BELIEVE IT?
Y'THINK HE'LL BE REBORN?

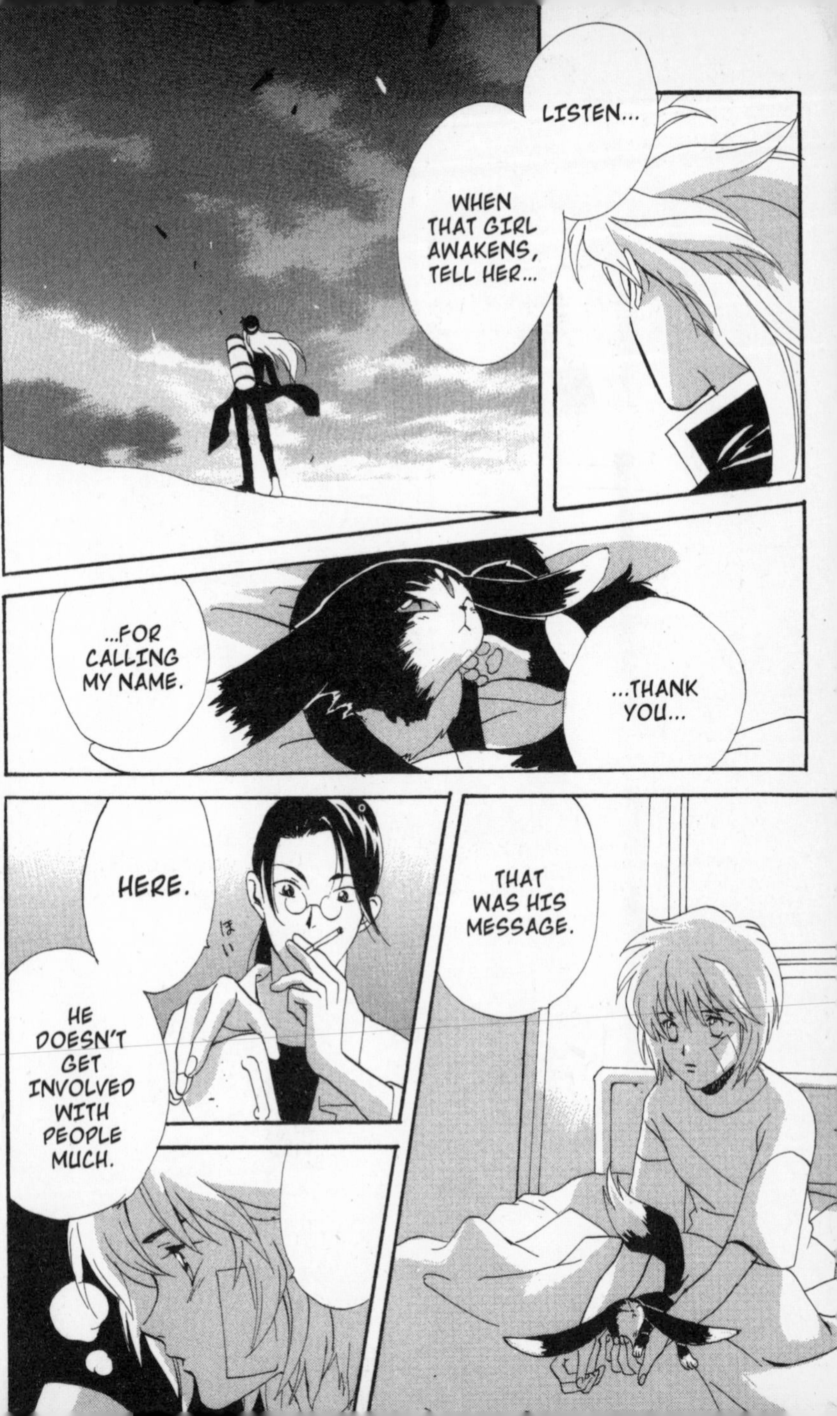
LISTEN...
WHEN THAT GIRL AWAKENS, TELL HER...
...THANK YOU...
...FOR CALLING MY NAME.
THAT WAS HIS MESSAGE.
HERE.
はい
HE DOESN'T GET INVOLVED WITH PEOPLE MUCH.

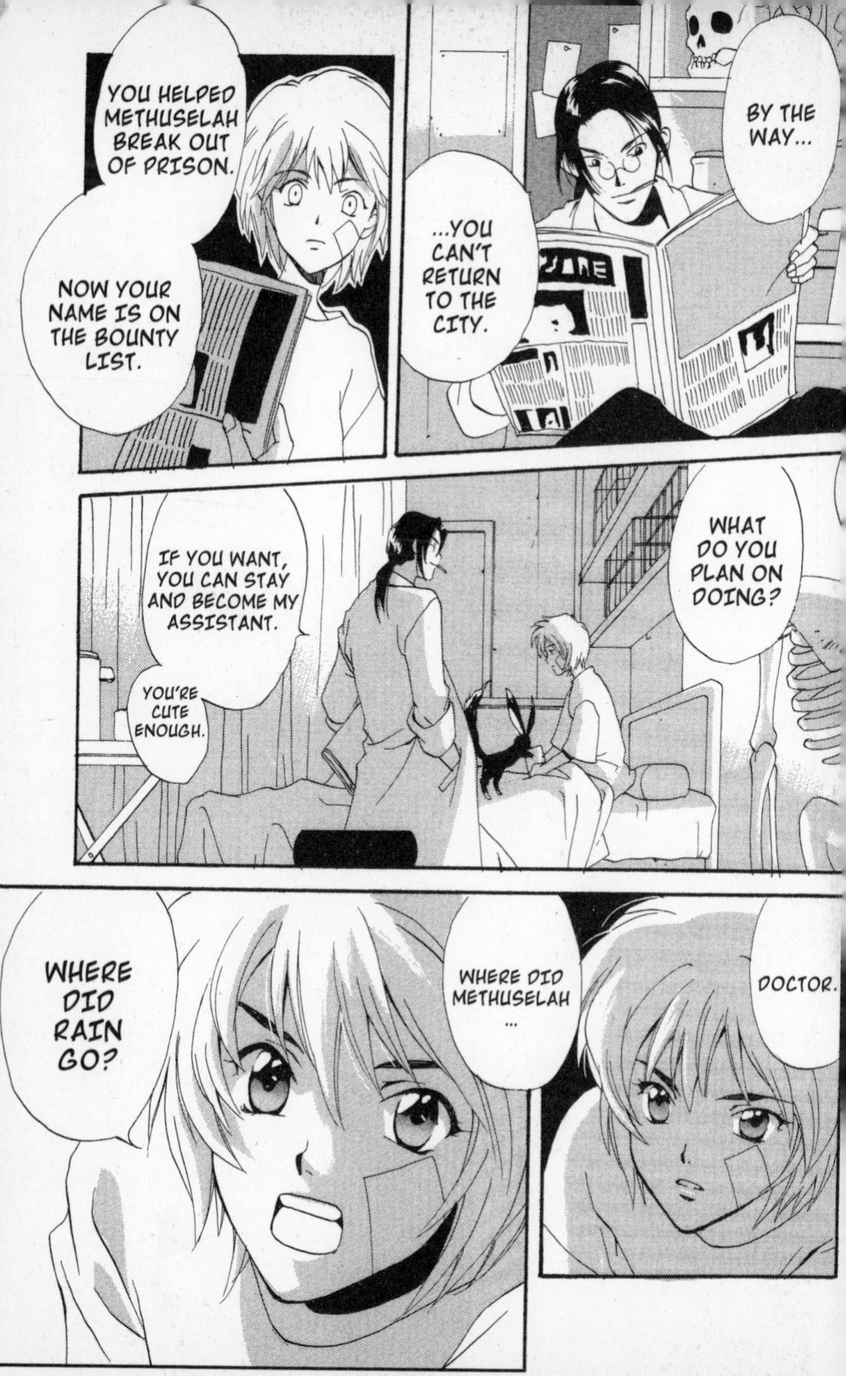

BY THE WAY...
...YOU CAN'T RETURN TO THE CITY.
YOU HELPED METHUSELAH BREAK OUT OF PRISON.
NOW YOUR NAME IS ON THE BOUNTY LIST.
WHAT DO YOU PLAN ON DOING?
IF YOU WANT, YOU CAN STAY AND BECOME MY ASSISTANT.
YOU'RE CUTE ENOUGH.
DOCTOR.
WHERE DID METHUSELAH ...
WHERE DID RAIN GO?

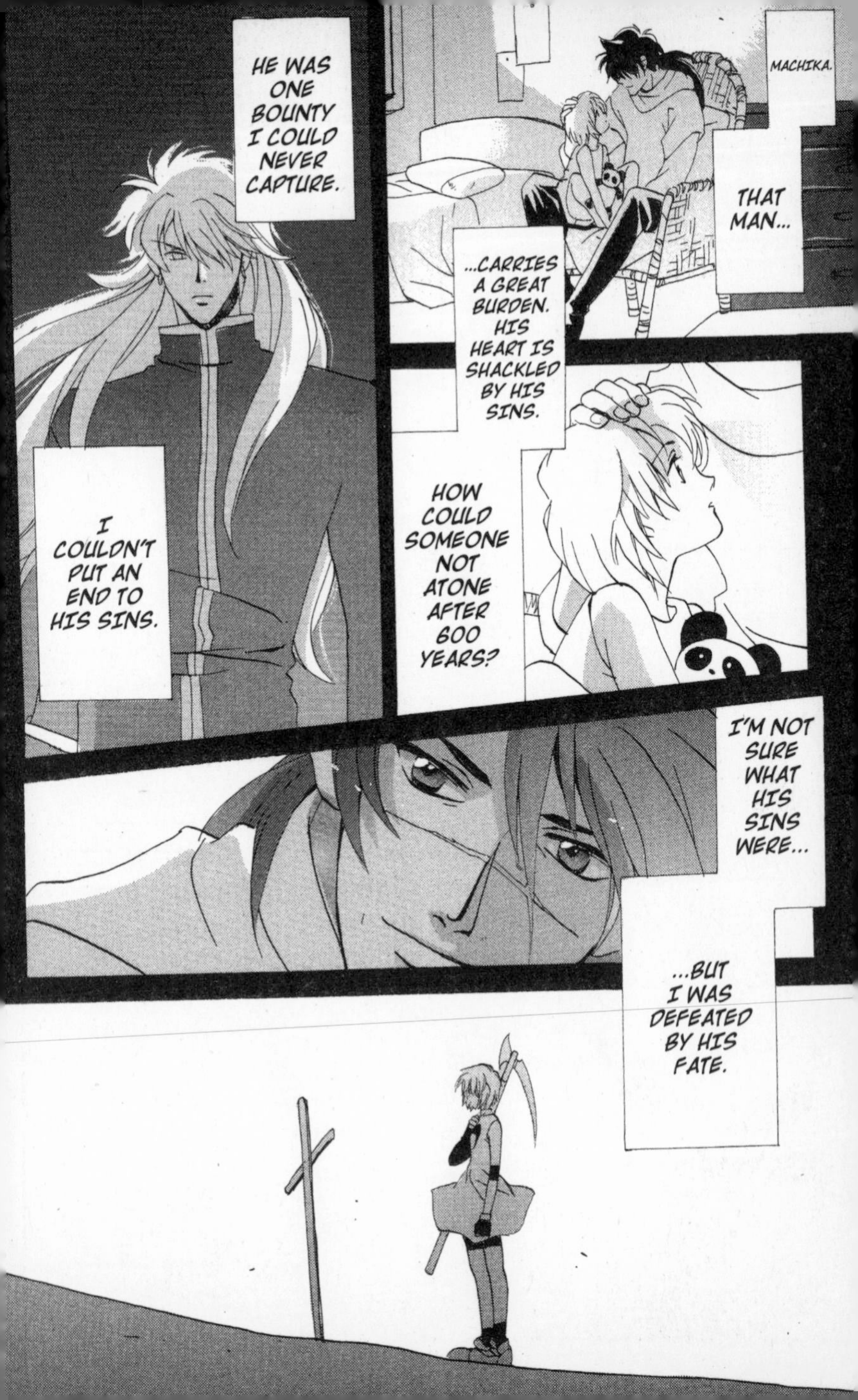
MACHIKA.
THAT MAN...
...CARRIES A GREAT BURDEN. HIS HEART IS SHACKLED BY HIS SINS.
HOW COULD SOMEONE NOT ATONE AFTER 600 YEARS?
HE WAS ONE BOUNTY I COULD NEVER CAPTURE.
I COULDN'T PUT AN END TO HIS SINS.
I'M NOT SURE WHAT HIS SINS WERE...
...BUT I WAS DEFEATED BY HIS FATE.

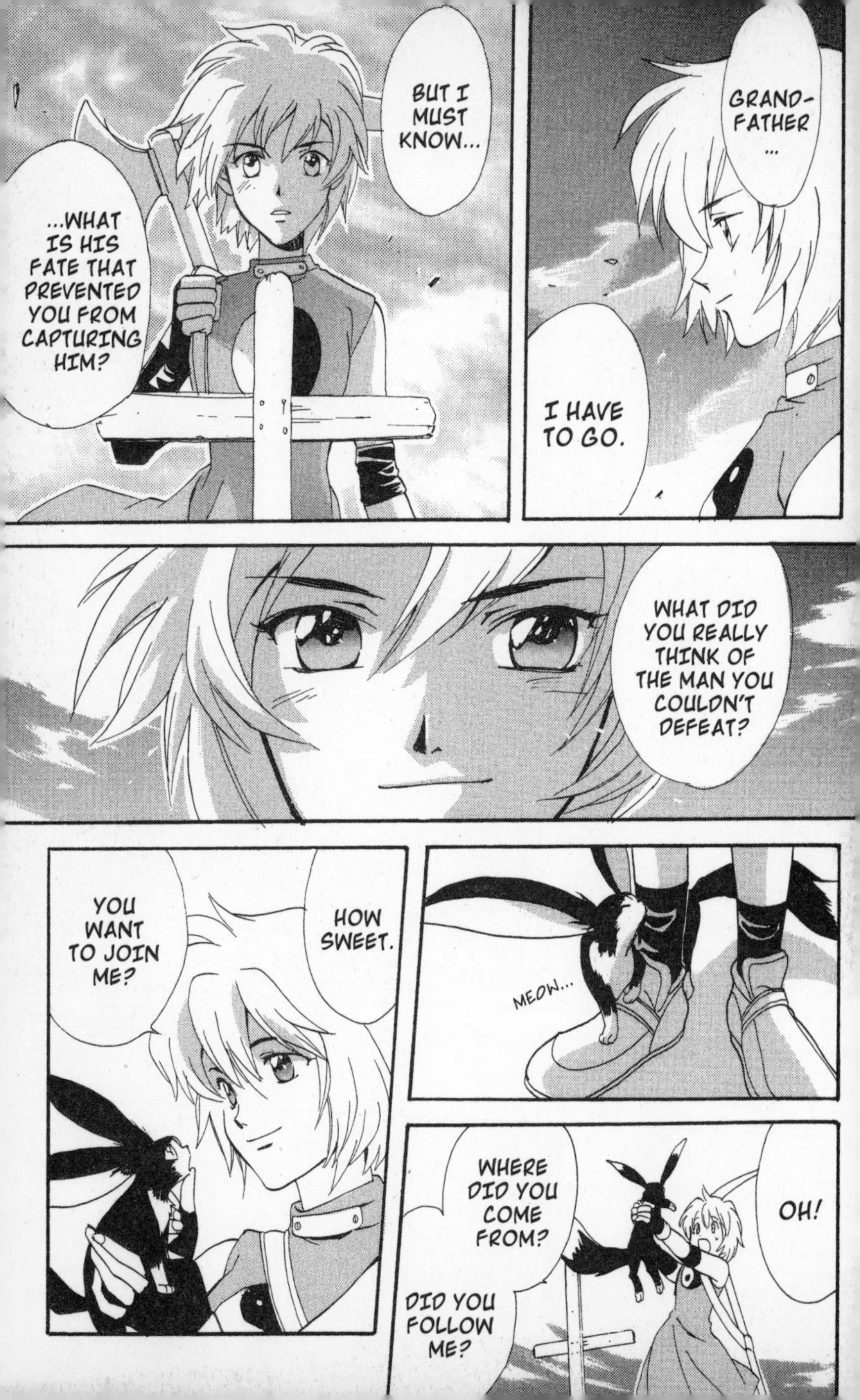
GRAND-FATHER ...
I HAVE TO GO.
BUT I MUST KNOW...
...WHAT IS HIS FATE THAT PREVENTED YOU FROM CAPTURING HIM?
WHAT DID YOU REALLY THINK OF THE MAN YOU COULDN'T DEFEAT?
MEOW...
OH!
WHERE DID YOU COME FROM?
DID YOU FOLLOW ME?
HOW SWEET.
YOU WANT TO JOIN ME?

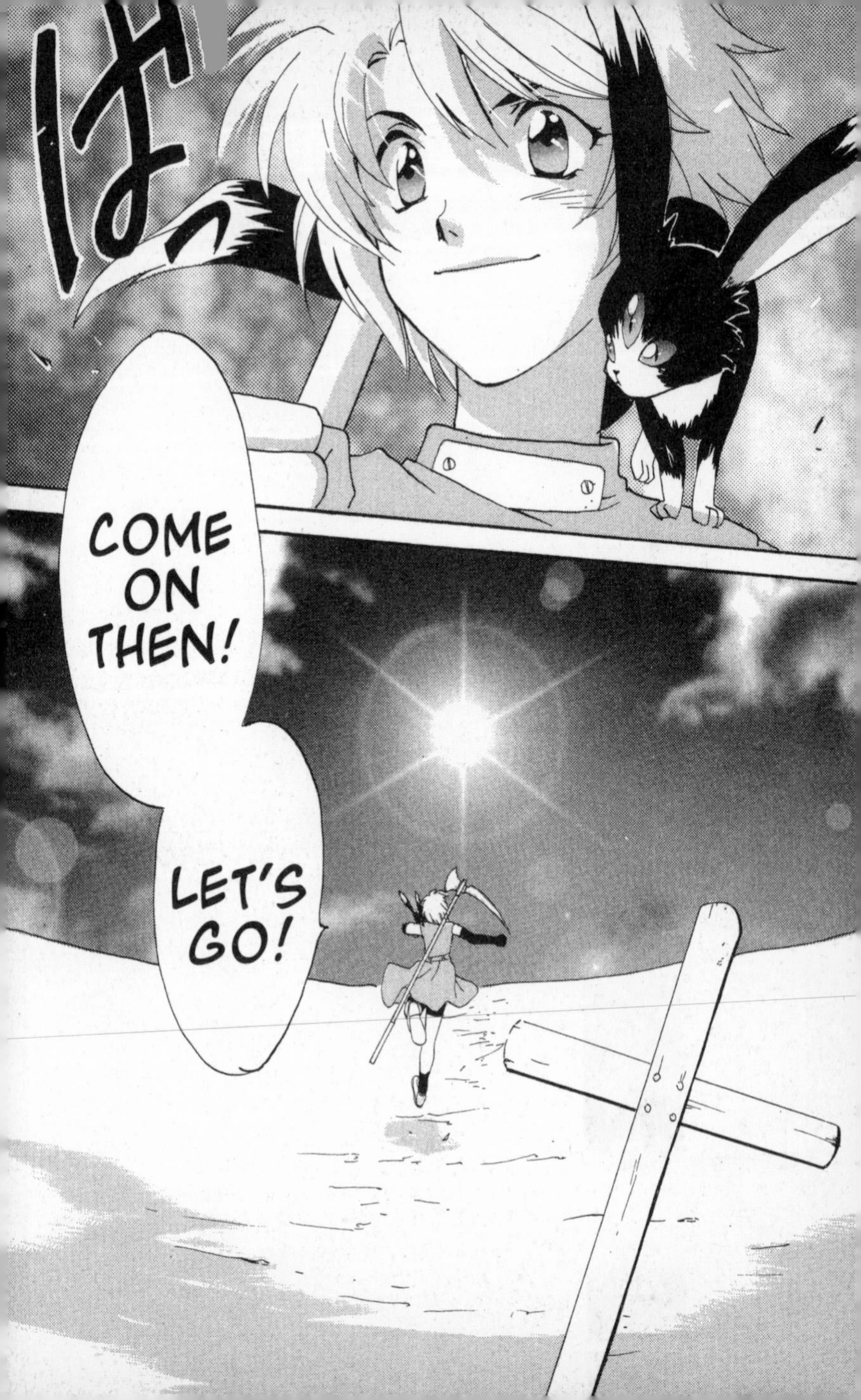
ぱっ
COME ON THEN!
LET'S GO!

RAIN JEWLITT

AGE : 624
HEIGHT : 194CM
BLOOD TYPE : ?

COMMAND
FIGHT
REVENGE
FLEE

LV: 92
OFFENSE
STRENGTH: 22-279
(changes)
DEFENSE
STRENGTH: 83
SPEED: 49
WIT: 51
LUCK: 3

EQUIPMENT
WEAPON: VIOLIN / OFFENSE STRENGTH + 0
(confuses enemy)
ARMOR: VESTMENT / DEFENSE STRENGTH + 12
ACCESSORY: IRON CROSS /
RETURNS ALL STATUS TO NORMAL

DEATHBLOW TECHNIQUE COMMAND

NICE SCREW UP   ⬅➡➡Ⓟ

SUDDENLY FALLS   ⬇⬇

TANK THROW   ⬅↙⬇↘➡Ⓟ+Ⓖ

THERE IS NO USE GOING TO A HIGHER LEVEL. HIS PLAN OF ATTACK IS TO
CONFUSE HIS OPPONENTS AND THEN FLEE FROM THE CHAOS. ONCE HE'S
CAUGHT, THE STORY..., THE STORY WON'T PROGRESS!

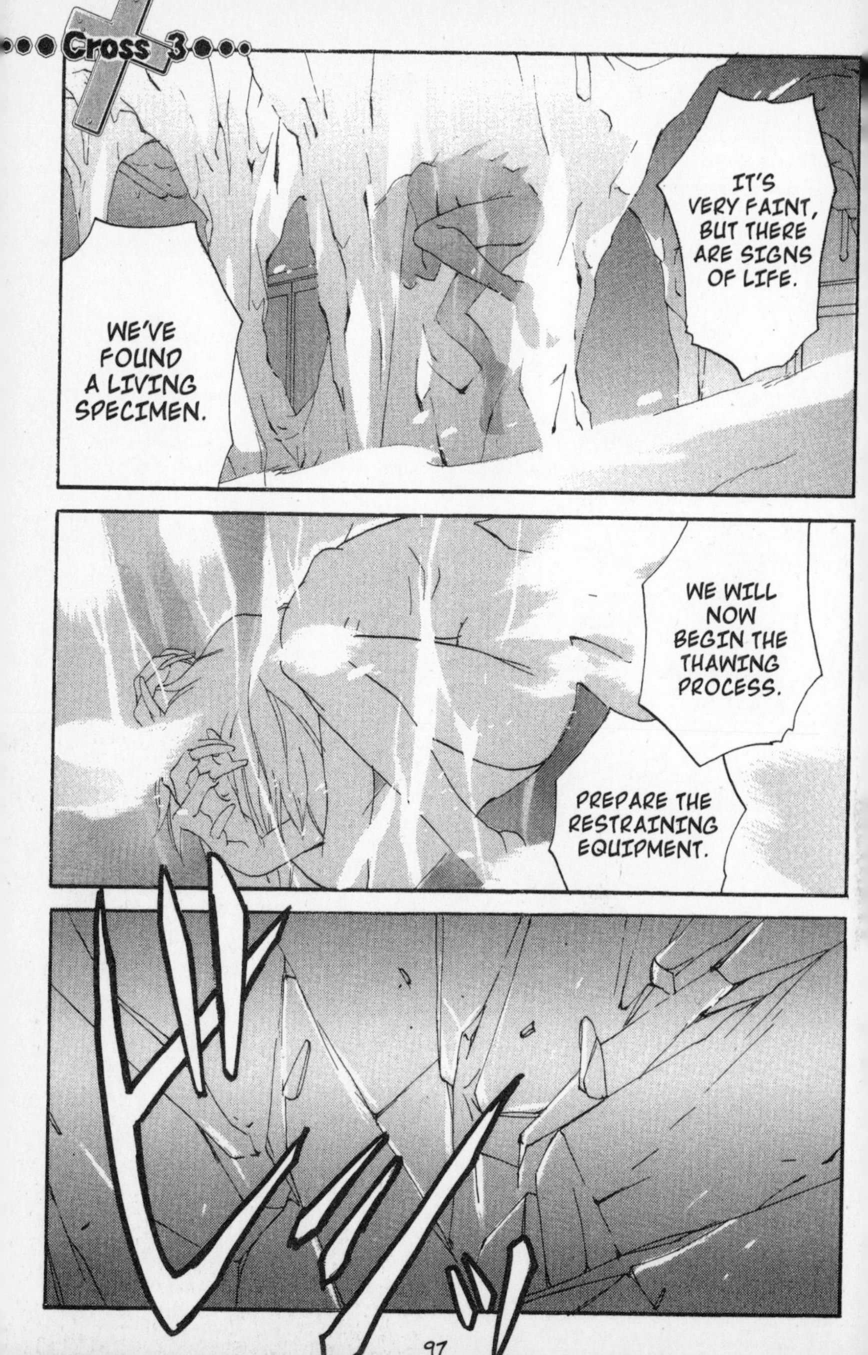
Cross 3
IT'S VERY FAINT, BUT THERE ARE SIGNS OF LIFE.
WE'VE FOUND A LIVING SPECIMEN.
WE WILL NOW BEGIN THE THAWING PROCESS.
PREPARE THE RESTRAINING EQUIPMENT.

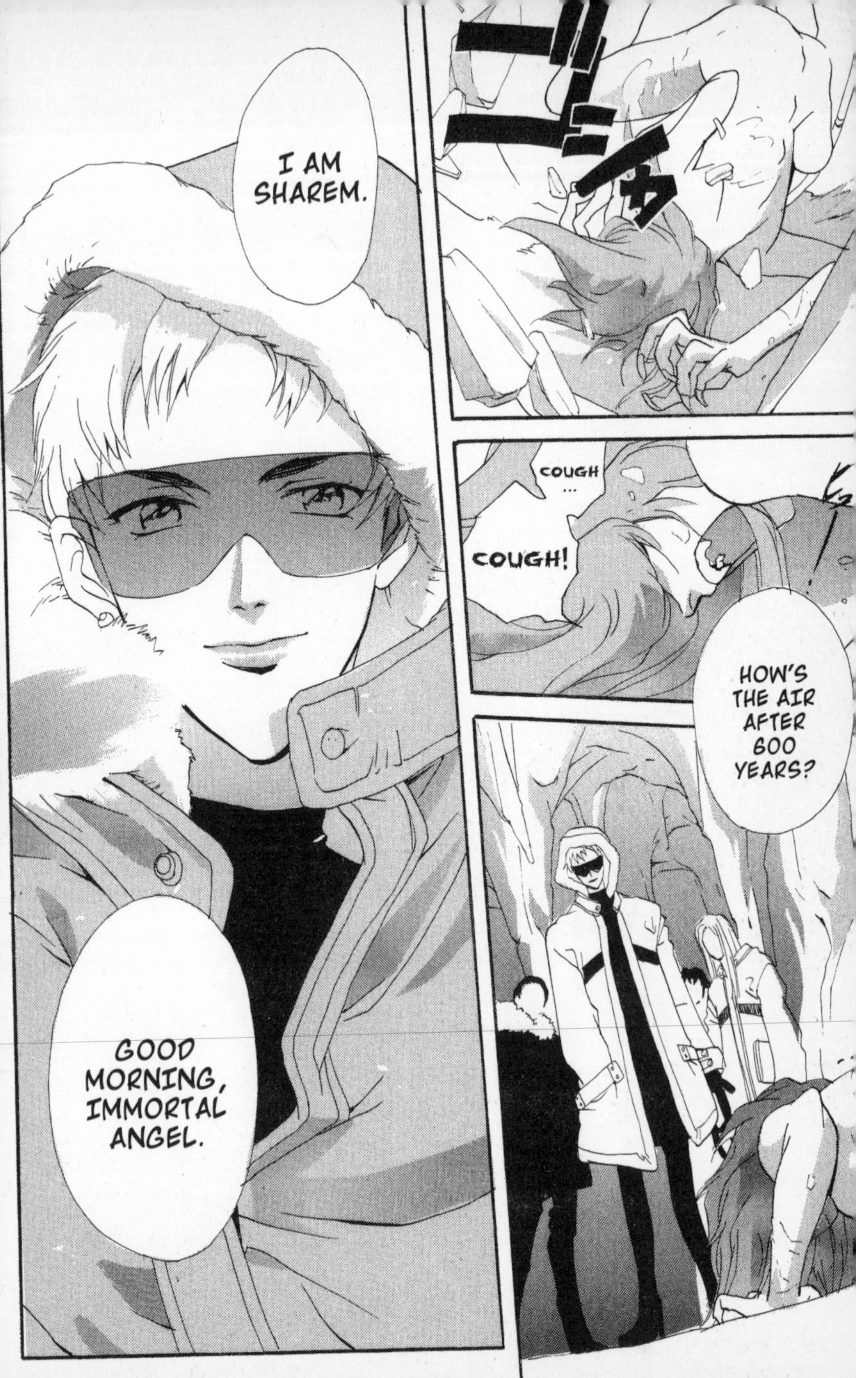
COUGH ...
COUGH!
HOW'S THE AIR AFTER 600 YEARS?
I AM SHAREM.
GOOD MORNING, IMMORTAL ANGEL.

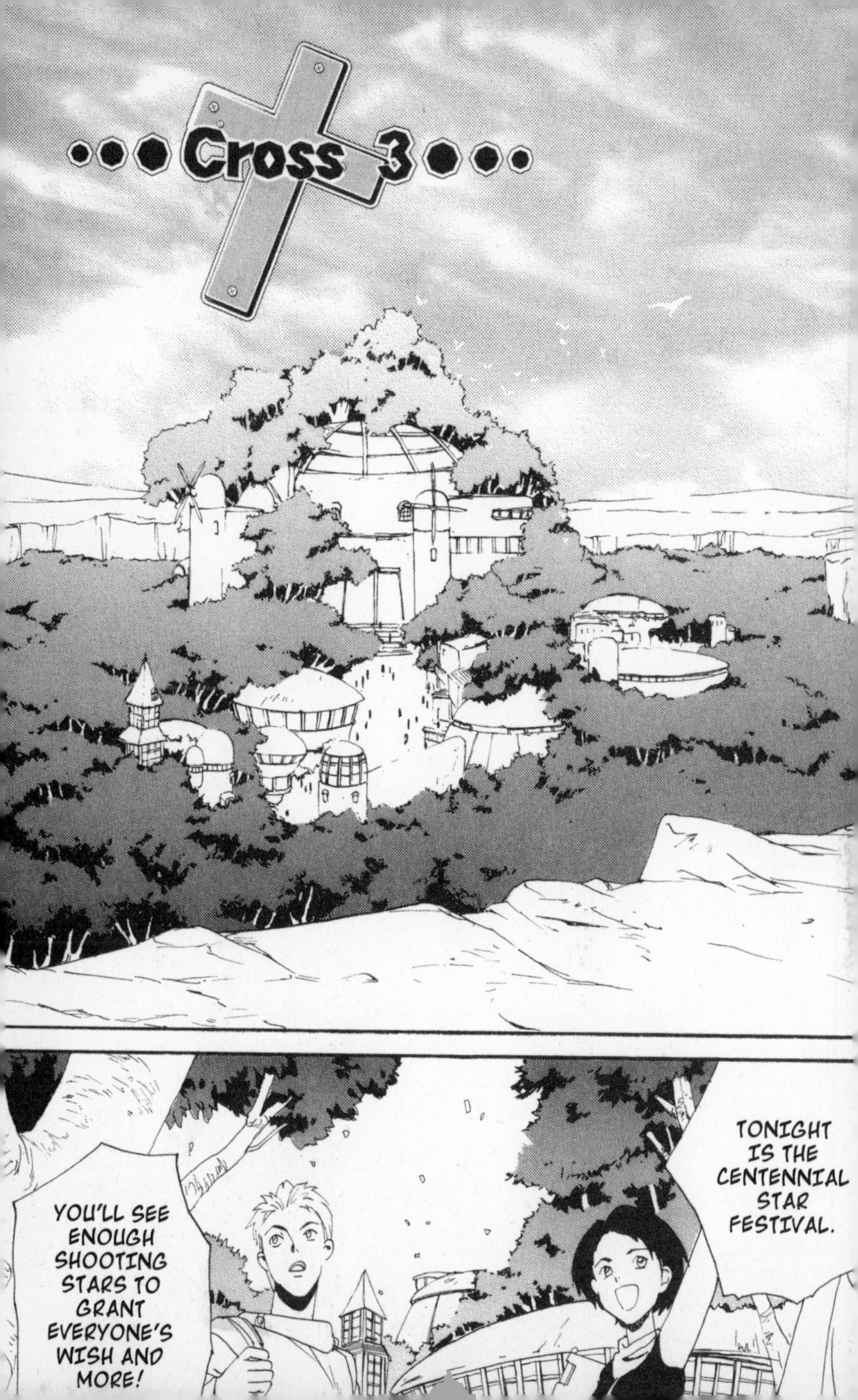
Cross 3
TONIGHT IS THE CENTENNIAL STAR FESTIVAL.
YOU'LL SEE ENOUGH SHOOTING STARS TO GRANT EVERYONE'S WISH AND MORE!

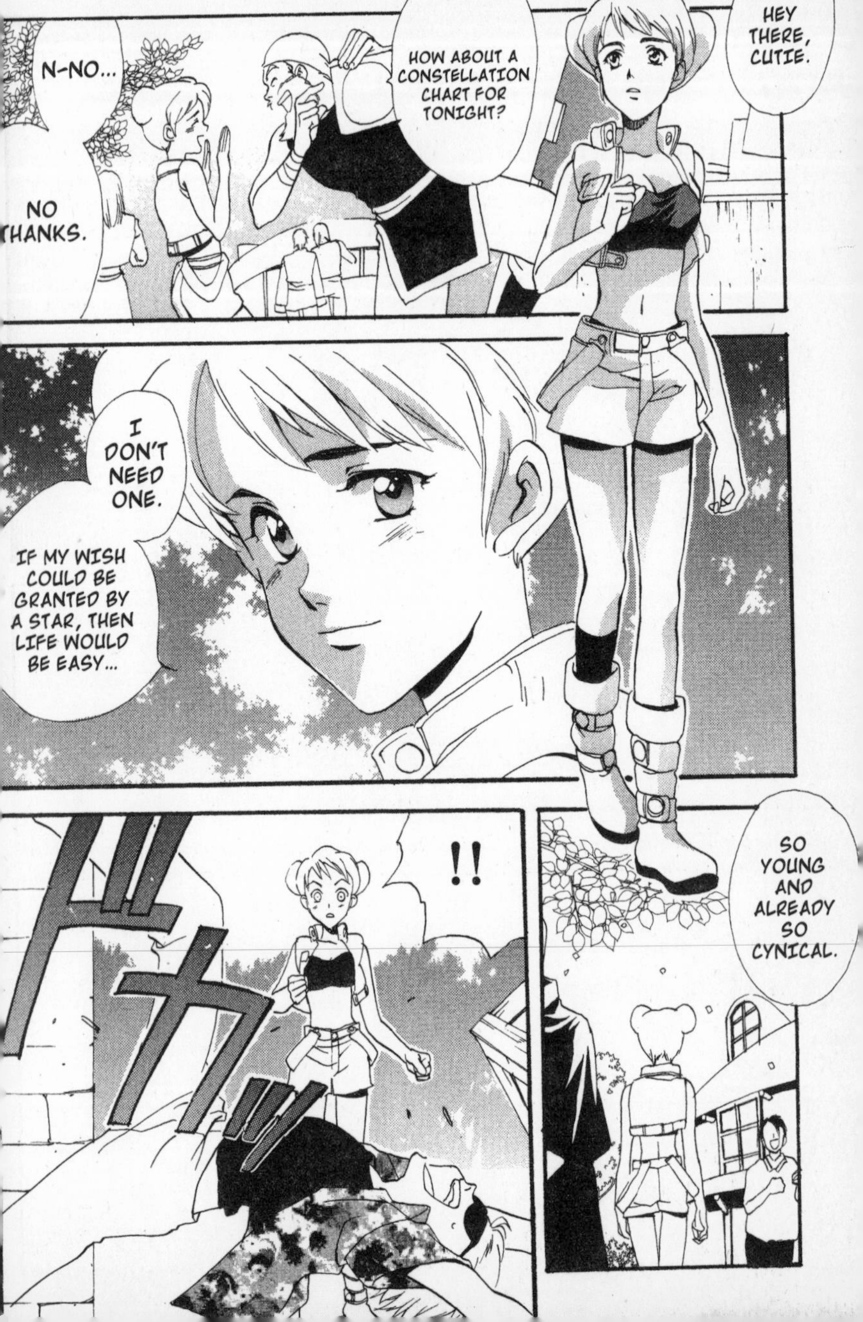
HEY THERE, CUTIE.
HOW ABOUT A CONSTELLATION CHART FOR TONIGHT?
N-NO...
NO THANKS.
I DON'T NEED ONE.
IF MY WISH COULD BE GRANTED BY A STAR, THEN LIFE WOULD BE EASY...
SO YOUNG AND ALREADY SO CYNICAL.
!!
ドカッ

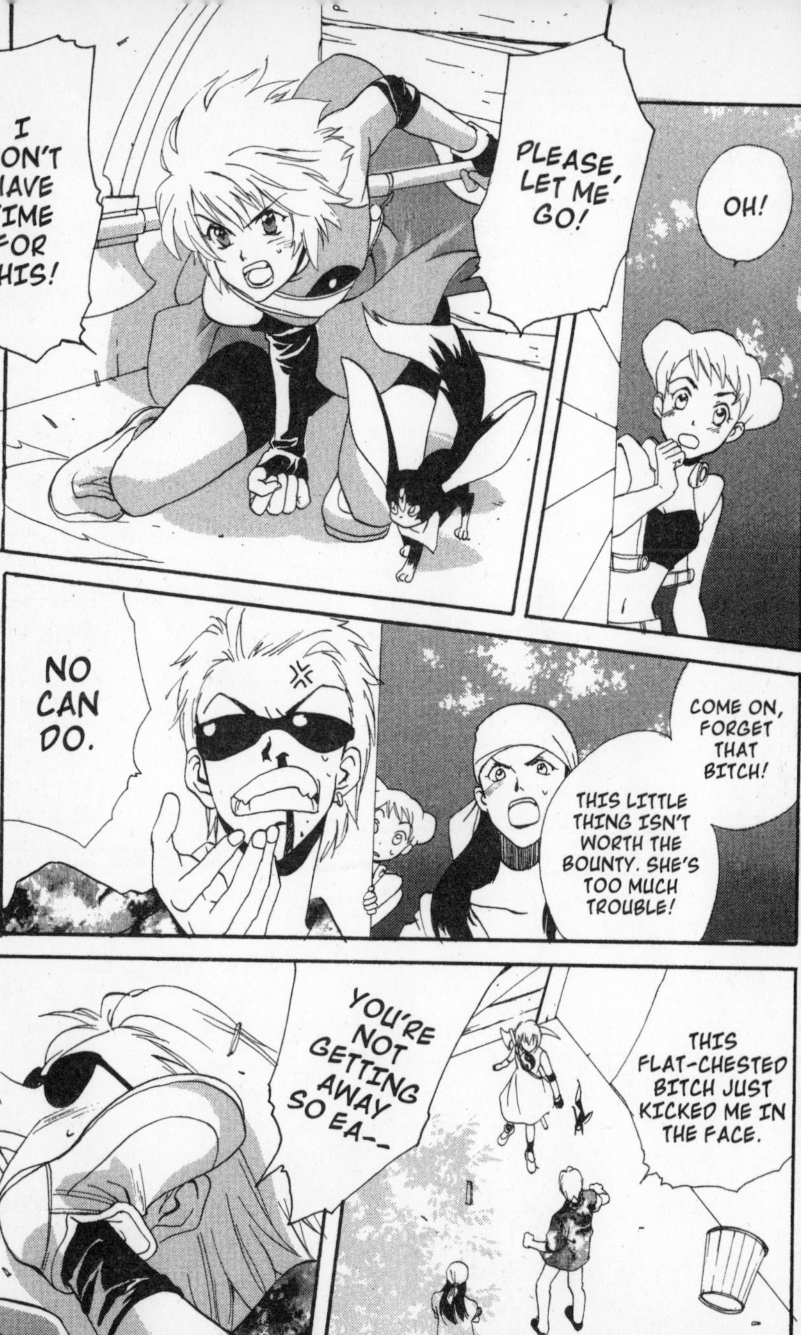
OH!
PLEASE, LET ME GO!
I DON'T HAVE TIME FOR THIS!
COME ON, FORGET THAT BITCH!
THIS LITTLE THING ISN'T WORTH THE BOUNTY. SHE'S TOO MUCH TROUBLE!
NO CAN DO.
THIS FLAT-CHESTED BITCH JUST KICKED ME IN THE FACE.
YOU'RE NOT GETTING AWAY SO EA--

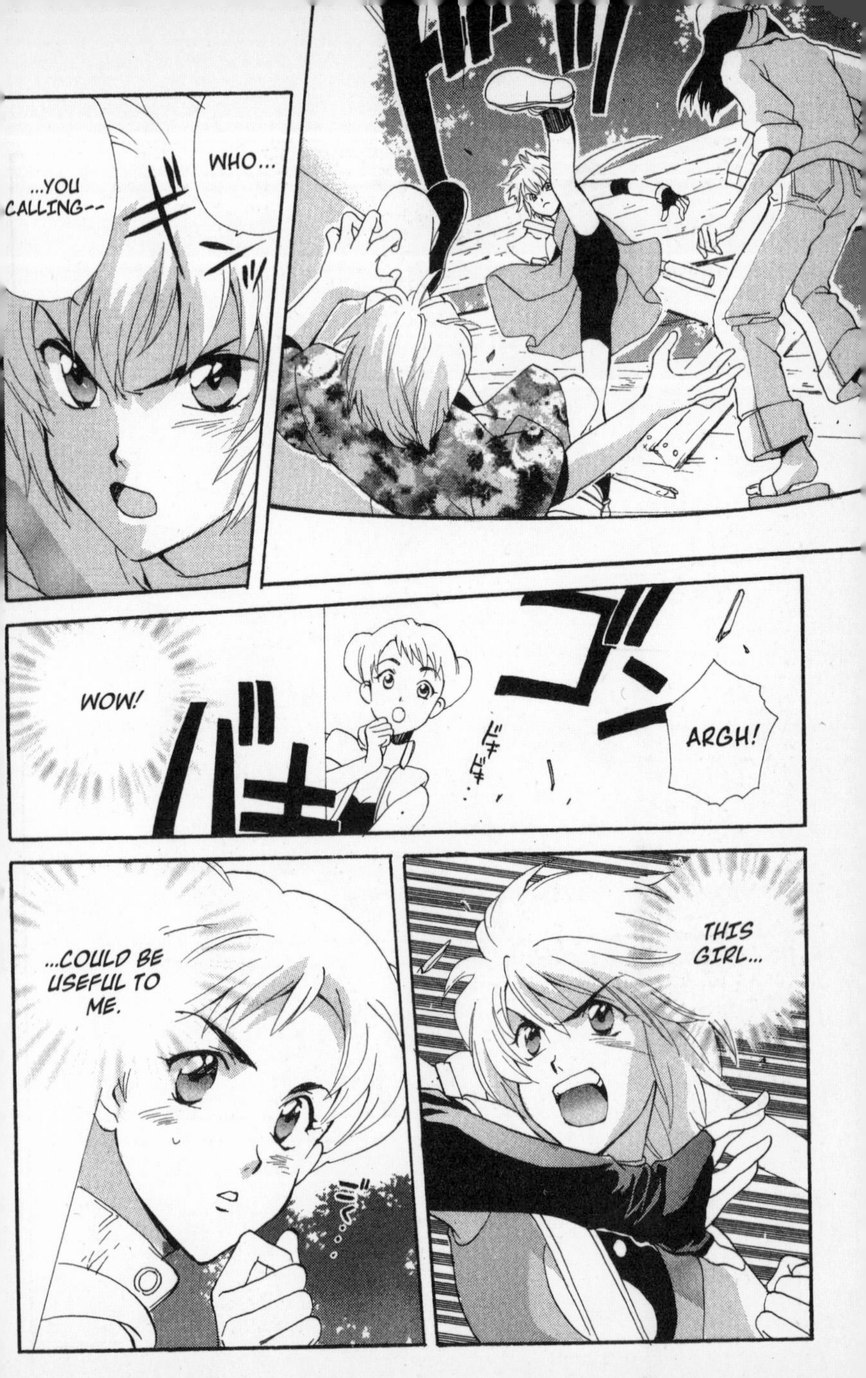
WHO...
...YOU CALLING--
ARGH!
WOW!
THIS GIRL...
...COULD BE USEFUL TO ME.

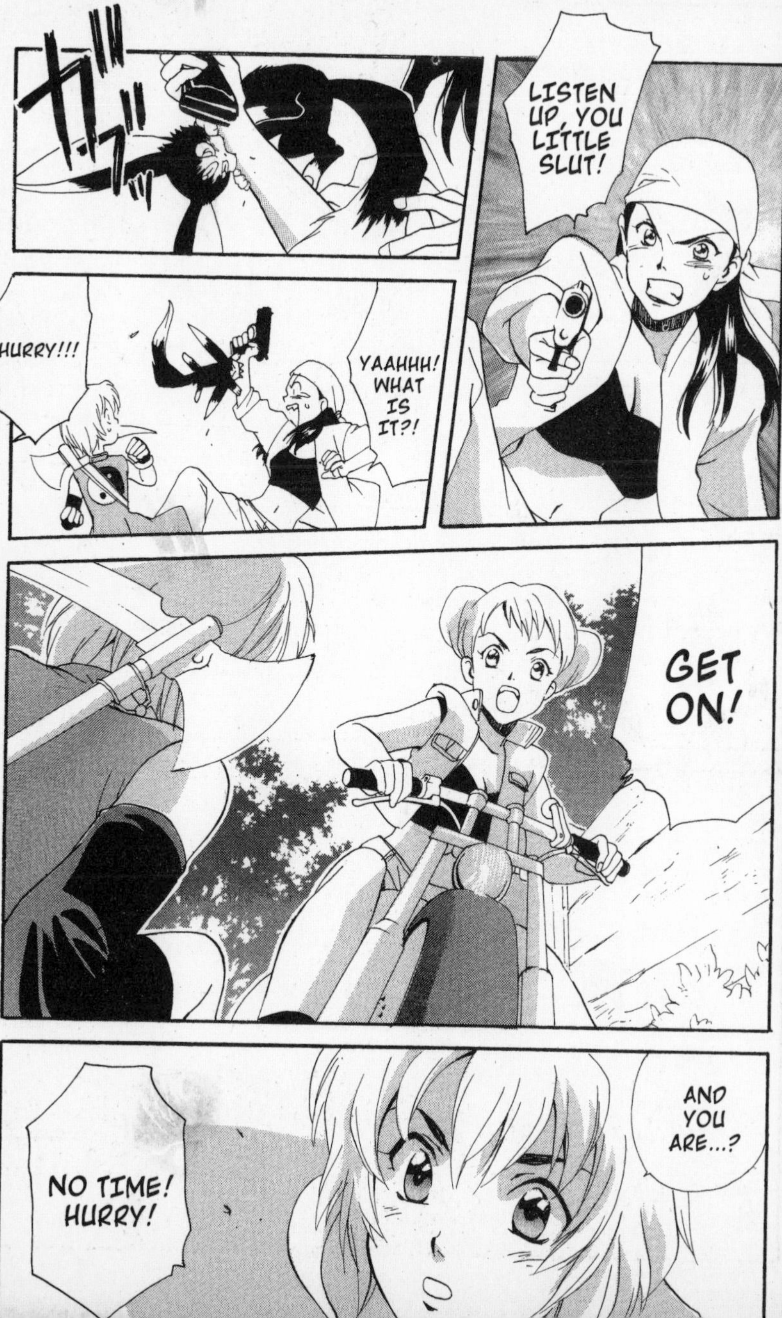
LISTEN UP, YOU LITTLE SLUT!
YAAHHH! WHAT IS IT?!
HURRY!!!
GET ON!
AND YOU ARE...?
NO TIME! HURRY!

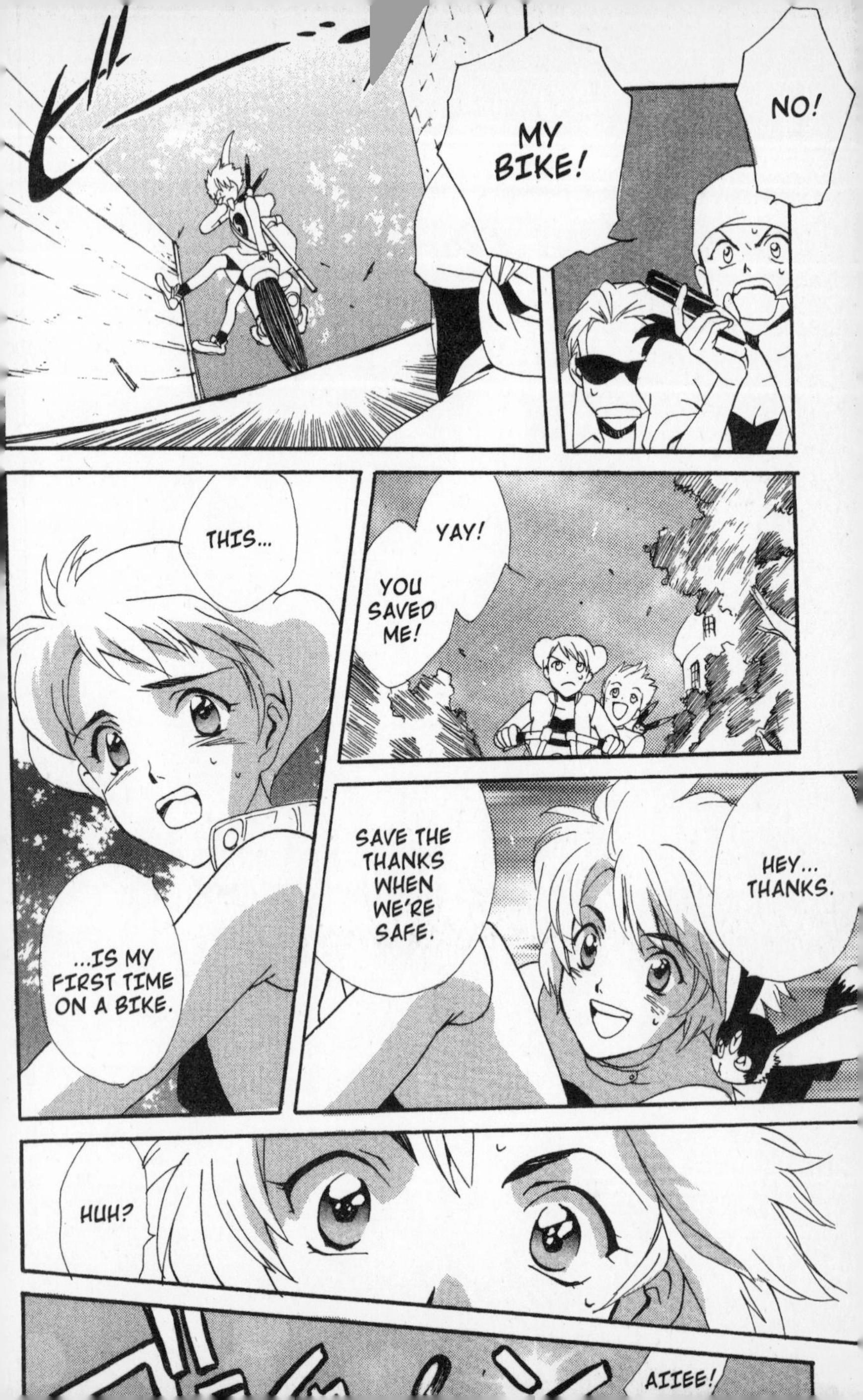
NO!
MY BIKE!
YAY!
YOU SAVED ME!
HEY... THANKS.
SAVE THE THANKS WHEN WE'RE SAFE.
THIS...
...IS MY FIRST TIME ON A BIKE.
HUH?
AIIEE!

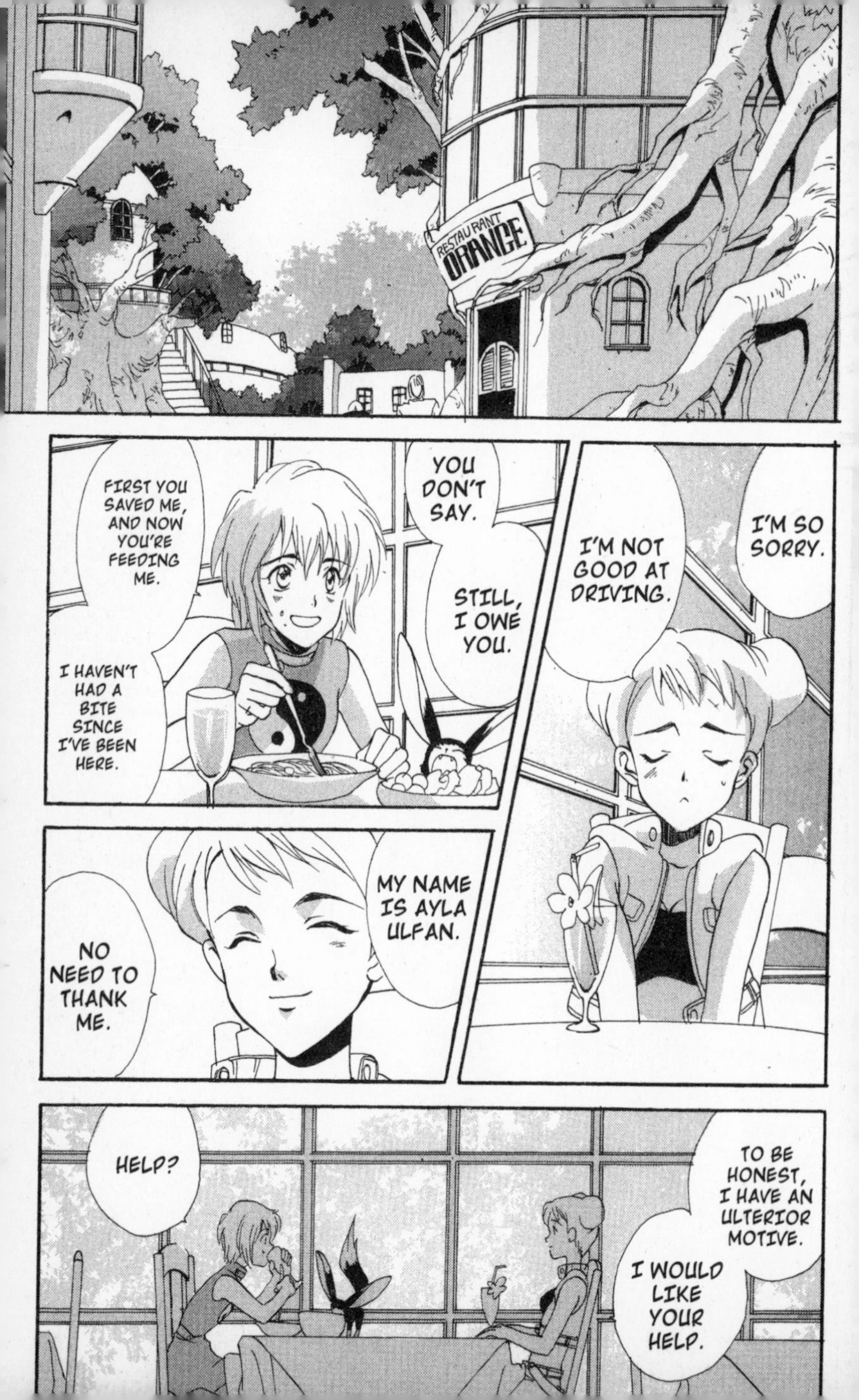
RESTAURANT ORANGE
I'M SO SORRY.
I'M NOT GOOD AT DRIVING.
YOU DON'T SAY.
STILL, I OWE YOU.
FIRST YOU SAVED ME, AND NOW YOU'RE FEEDING ME.
I HAVEN'T HAD A BITE SINCE I'VE BEEN HERE.
MY NAME IS AYLA ULFAN.
NO NEED TO THANK ME.
TO BE HONEST, I HAVE AN ULTERIOR MOTIVE.
I WOULD LIKE YOUR HELP.
HELP?

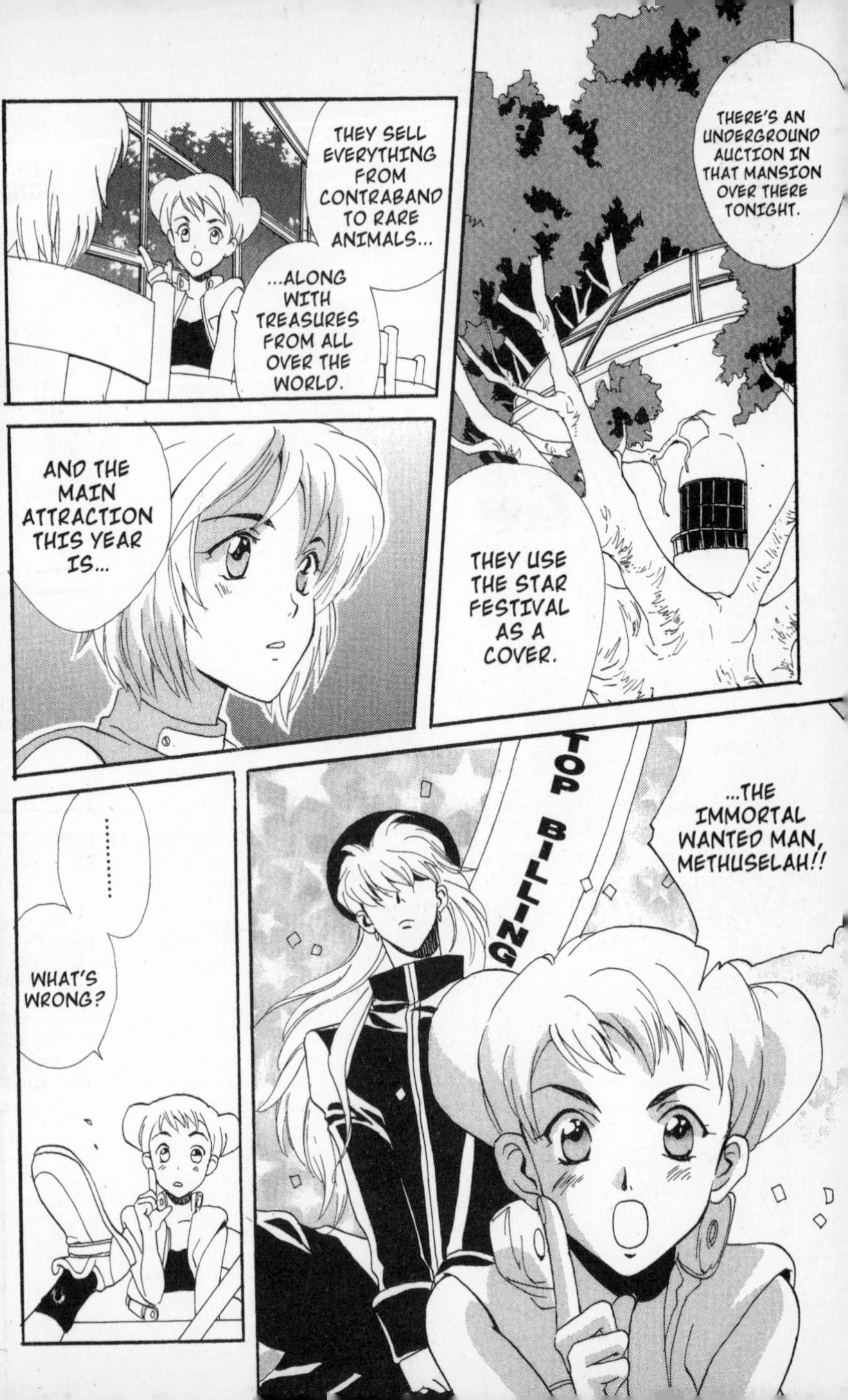
THERE'S AN UNDERGROUND AUCTION IN THAT MANSION OVER THERE TONIGHT.
THEY USE THE STAR FESTIVAL AS A COVER.
THEY SELL EVERYTHING FROM CONTRABAND TO RARE ANIMALS...
...ALONG WITH TREASURES FROM ALL OVER THE WORLD.
AND THE MAIN ATTRACTION THIS YEAR IS...
...THE IMMORTAL WANTED MAN, METHUSELAH!!
TOP BILLING
....
WHAT'S WRONG?

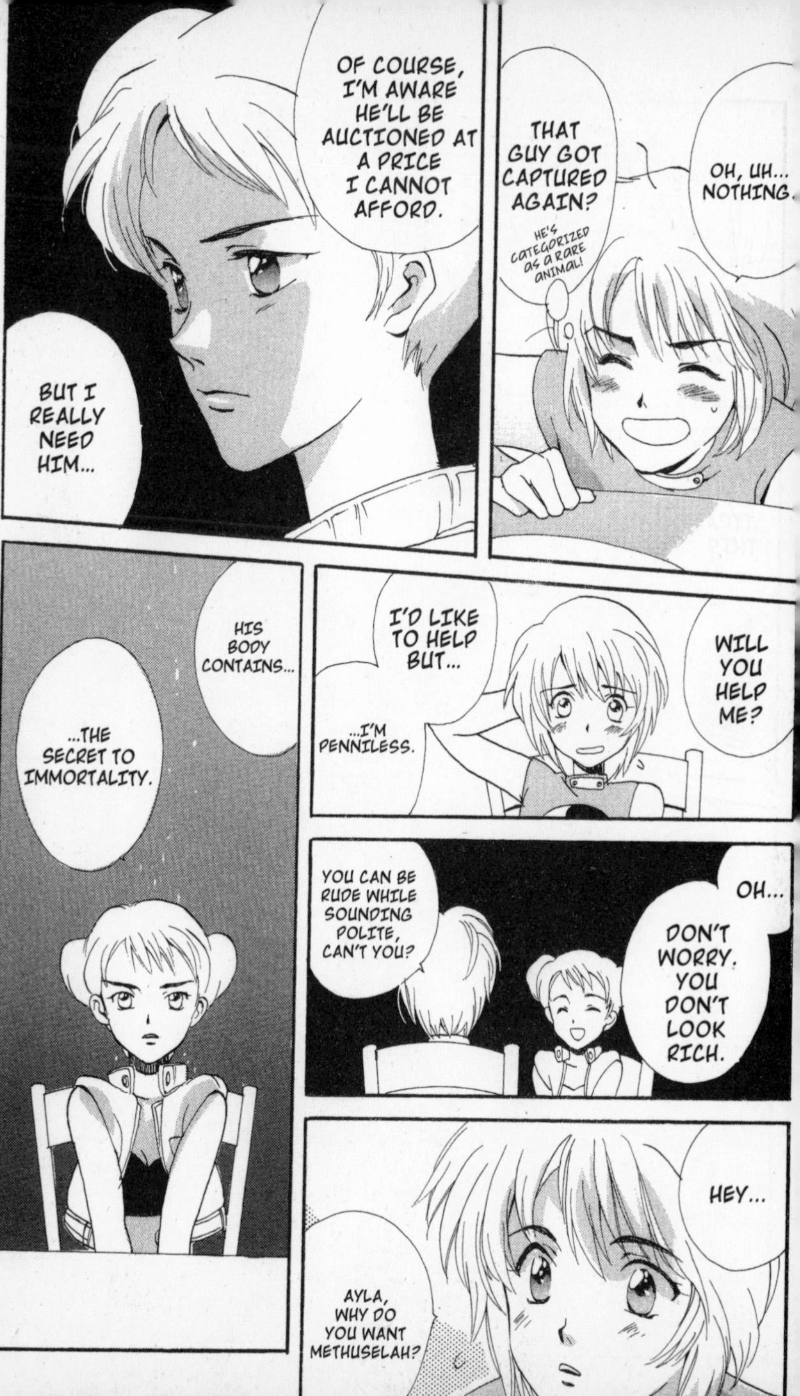
THAT GUY GOT CAPTURED AGAIN?
HE'S CATEGORIZED AS A RARE ANIMAL!
OH, UH... NOTHING.
OF COURSE, I'M AWARE HE'LL BE AUCTIONED AT A PRICE I CANNOT AFFORD.
BUT I REALLY NEED HIM...
WILL YOU HELP ME?
I'D LIKE TO HELP BUT...
...I'M PENNILESS.
OH...
DON'T WORRY. YOU DON'T LOOK RICH.
YOU CAN BE RUDE WHILE SOUNDING POLITE, CAN'T YOU?
HEY...
AYLA, WHY DO YOU WANT METHUSELAH?
HIS BODY CONTAINS...
...THE SECRET TO IMMORTALITY.

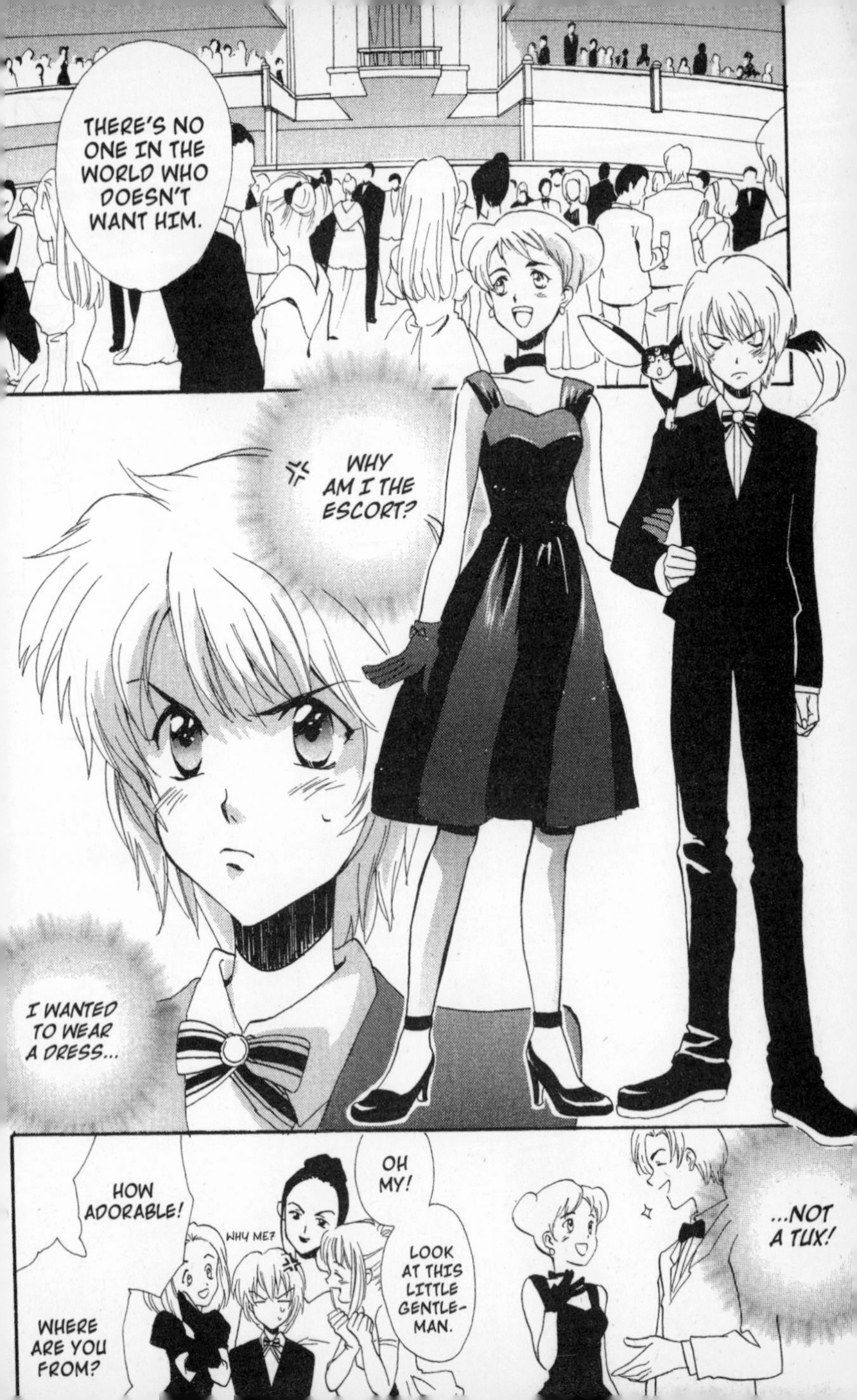
THERE'S NO ONE IN THE WORLD WHO DOESN'T WANT HIM.
WHY AM I THE ESCORT?
I WANTED TO WEAR A DRESS...
...NOT A TUX!
OH MY!
HOW ADORABLE!
LOOK AT THIS LITTLE GENTLE-MAN.
WHY ME?
WHERE ARE YOU FROM?

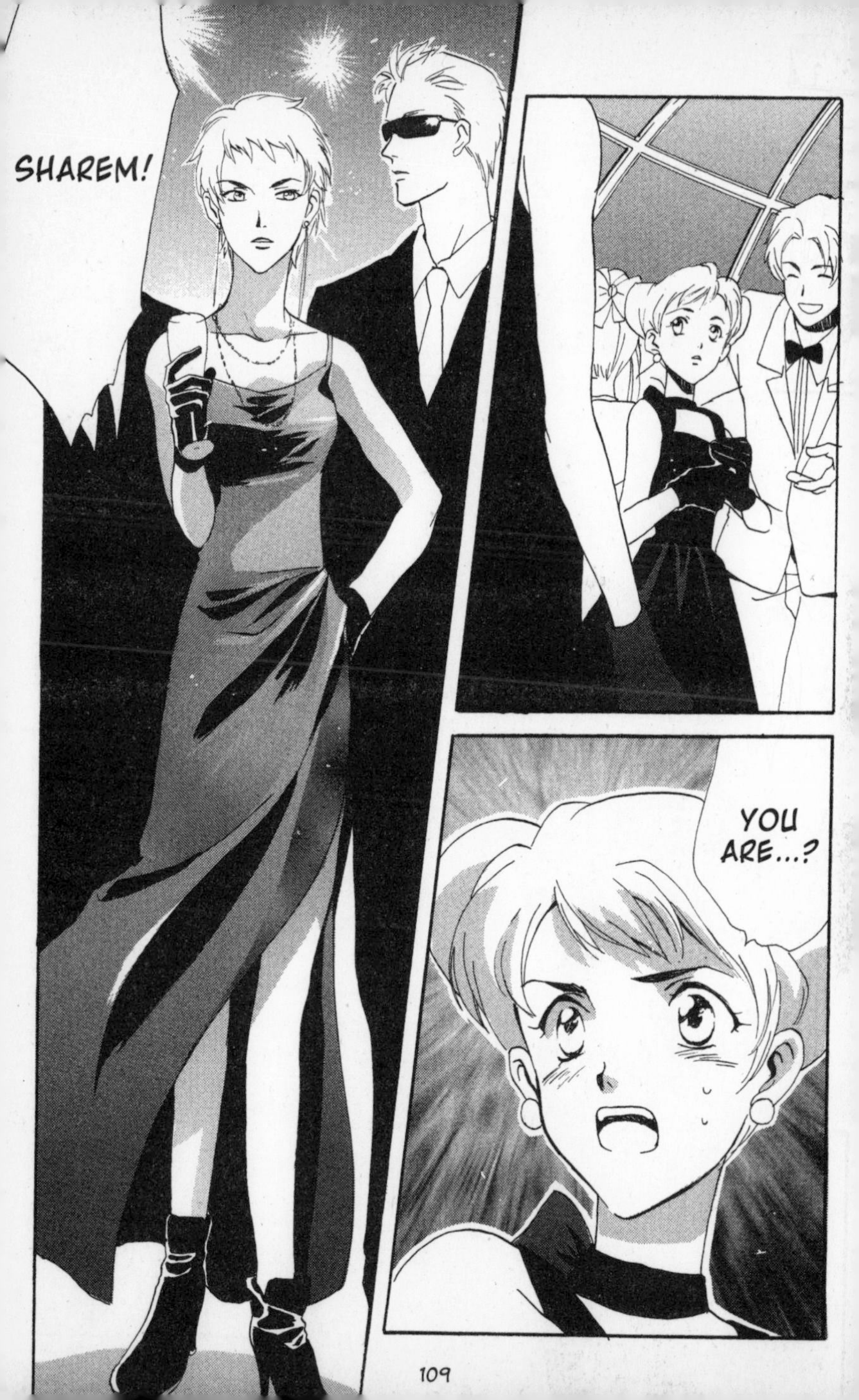
YOU ARE...?
SHAREM!

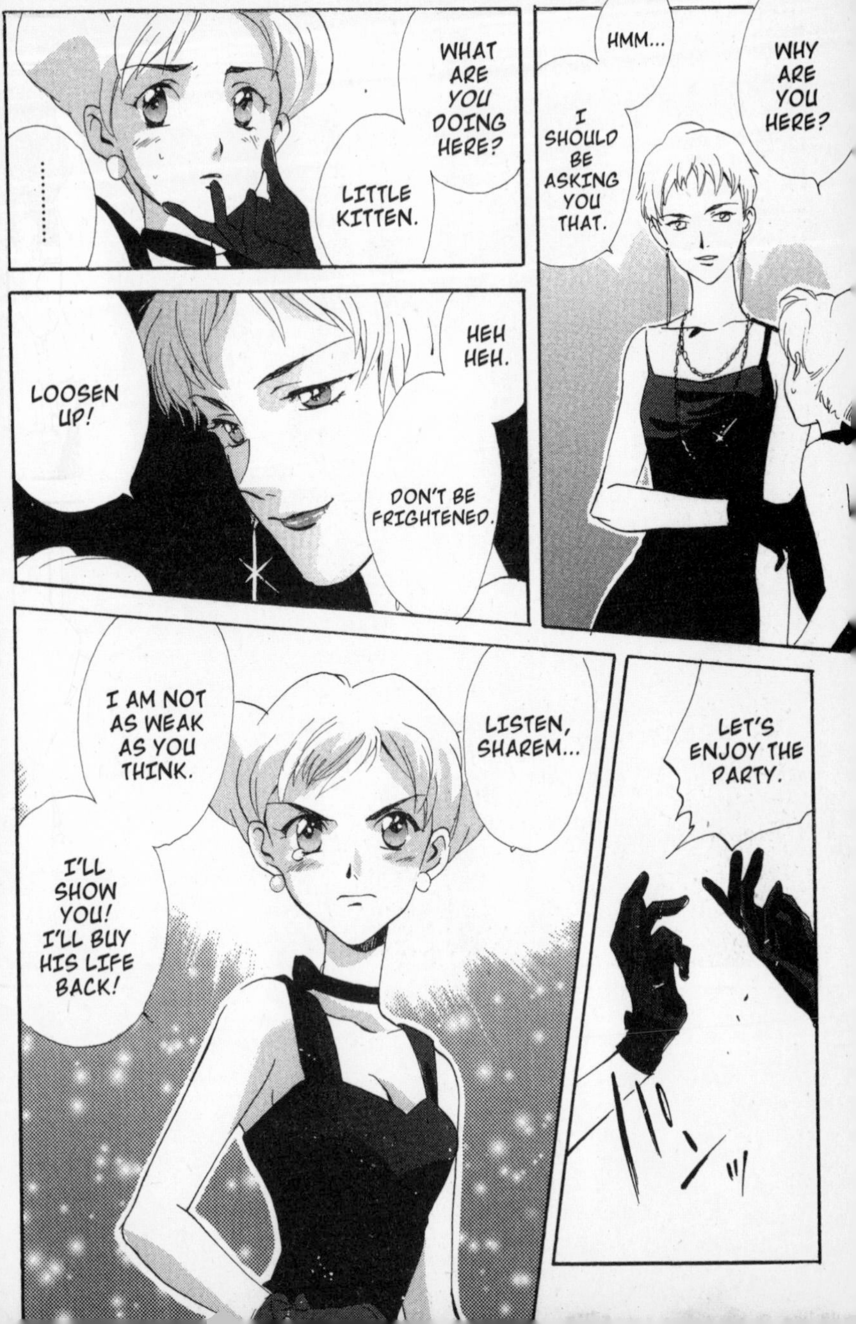
WHY ARE YOU HERE?
HMM...
I SHOULD BE ASKING YOU THAT.
WHAT ARE YOU DOING HERE?
LITTLE KITTEN.
......
HEH HEH.
DON'T BE FRIGHTENED.
LOOSEN UP!
LET'S ENJOY THE PARTY.
LISTEN, SHAREM...
I AM NOT AS WEAK AS YOU THINK.
I'LL SHOW YOU! I'LL BUY HIS LIFE BACK!

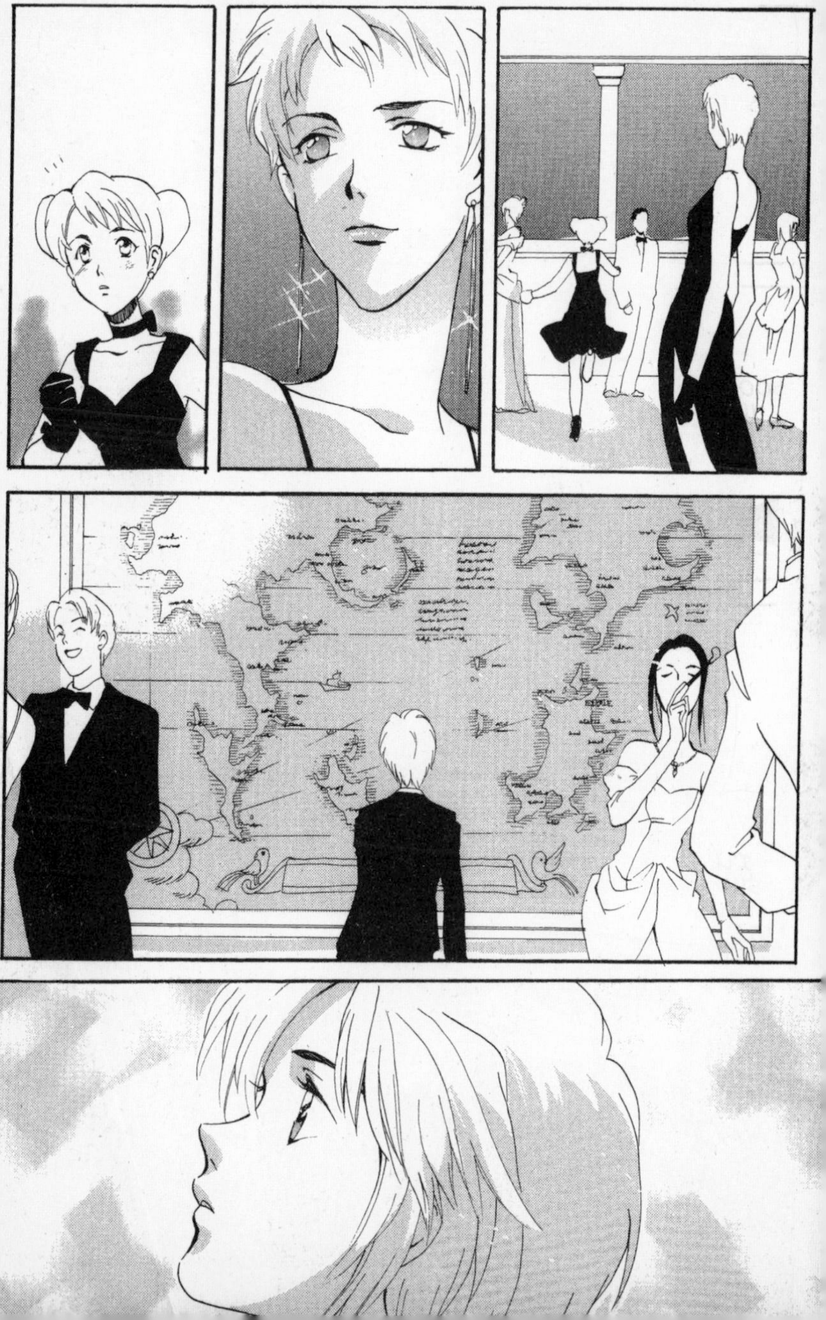

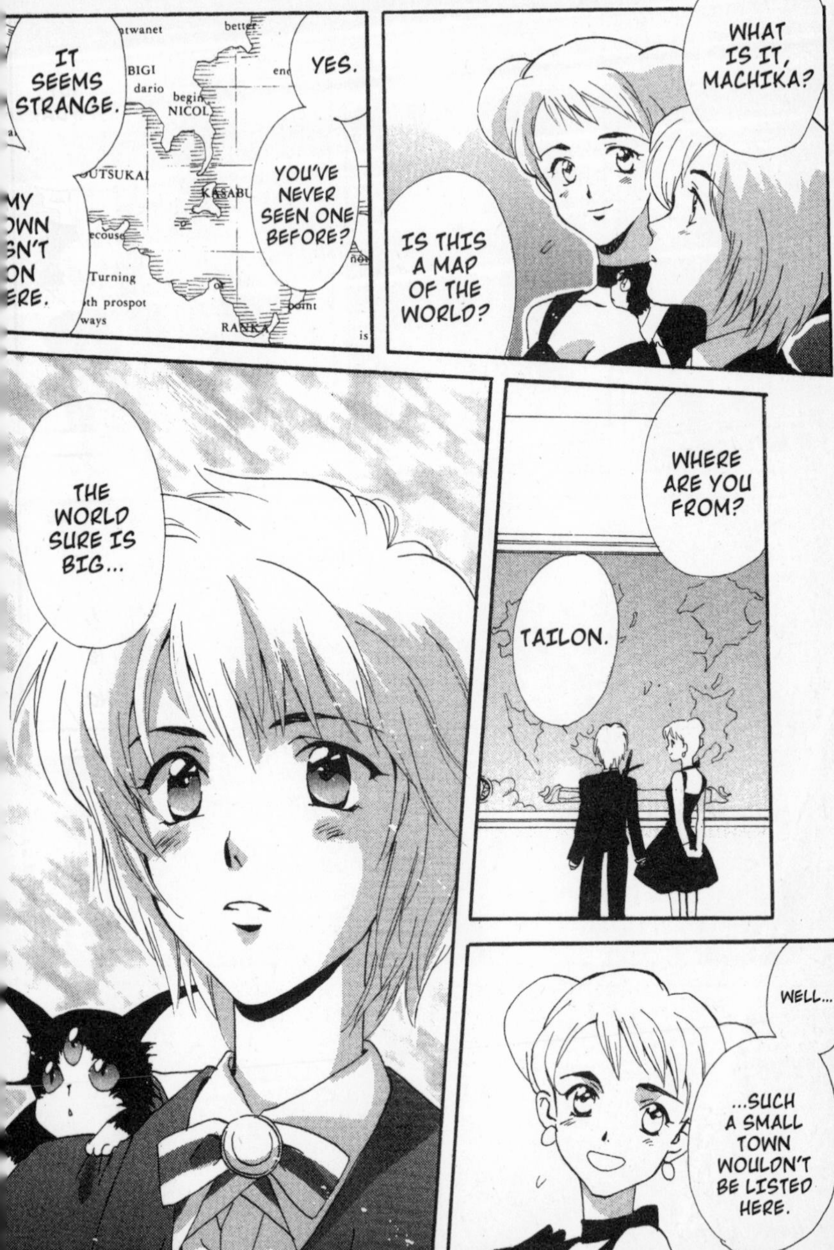
WHAT IS IT, MACHIKA?
IS THIS A MAP OF THE WORLD?
YES.
YOU'VE NEVER SEEN ONE BEFORE?
IT SEEMS STRANGE.
MY
OWN
SN'T
ON
ERE.
better
BIGI
dario
begin
NICOL
KASABU
Turning
ways
RANKA
point
WHERE ARE YOU FROM?
TAILON.
WELL...
...SUCH A SMALL TOWN WOULDN'T BE LISTED HERE.
THE WORLD SURE IS BIG...

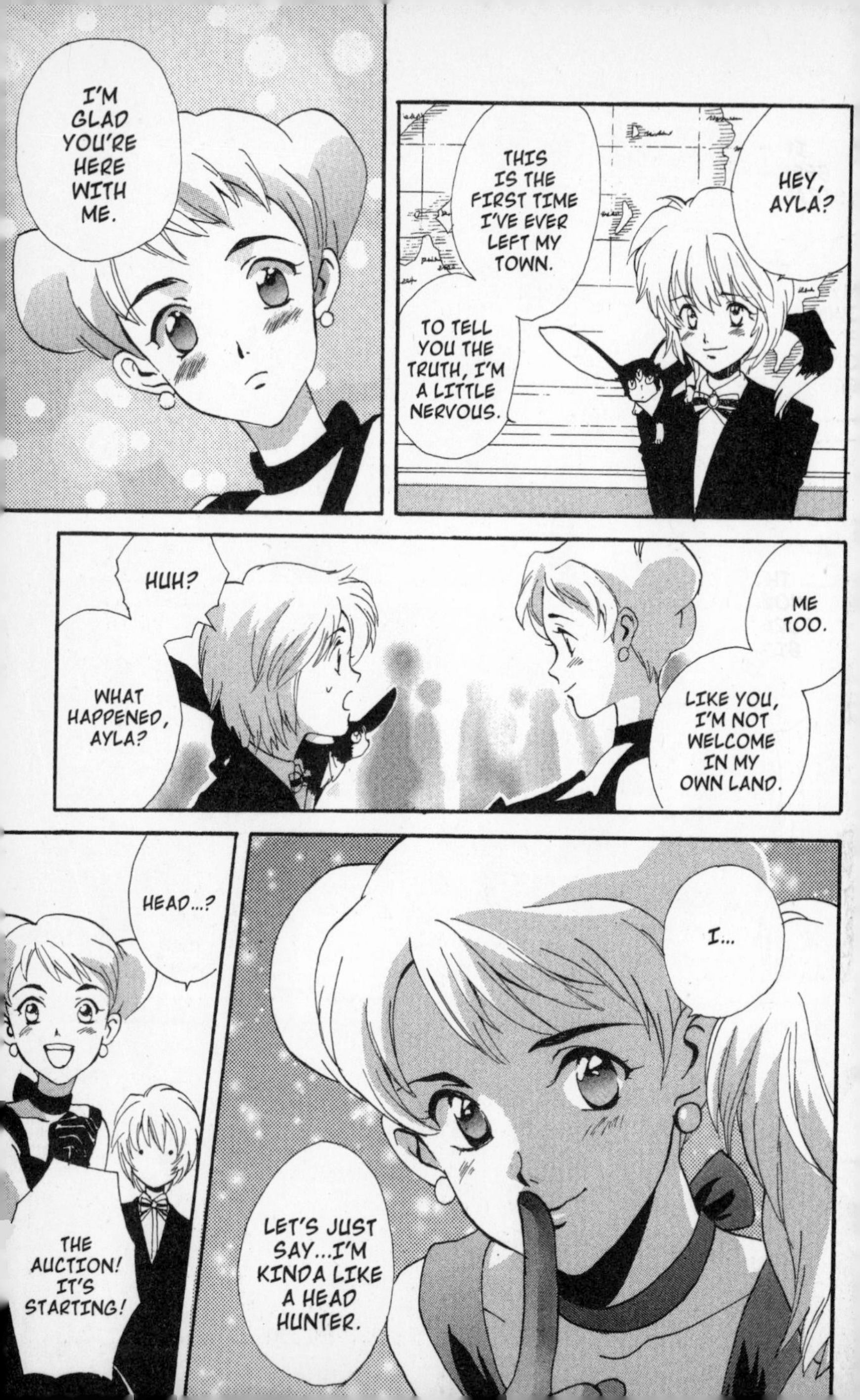
HEY, AYLA?
THIS IS THE FIRST TIME I'VE EVER LEFT MY TOWN.
TO TELL YOU THE TRUTH, I'M A LITTLE NERVOUS.
I'M GLAD YOU'RE HERE WITH ME.
ME TOO.
LIKE YOU, I'M NOT WELCOME IN MY OWN LAND.
HUH?
WHAT HAPPENED, AYLA?
I...
LET'S JUST SAY...I'M KINDA LIKE A HEAD HUNTER.
HEAD...?
THE AUCTION! IT'S STARTING!

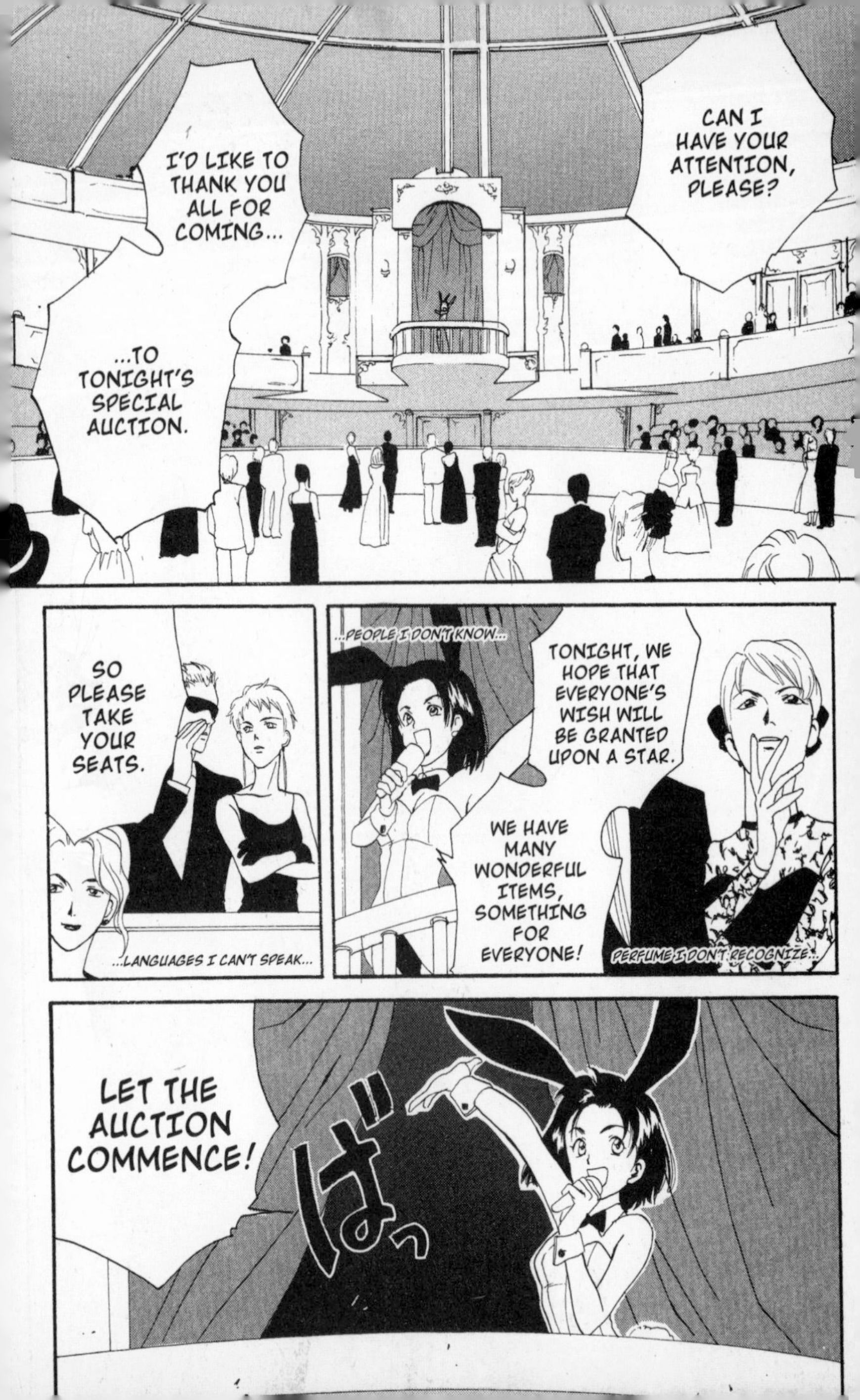
CAN I HAVE YOUR ATTENTION, PLEASE?
I'D LIKE TO THANK YOU ALL FOR COMING...
...TO TONIGHT'S SPECIAL AUCTION.
TONIGHT, WE HOPE THAT EVERYONE'S WISH WILL BE GRANTED UPON A STAR.
...PEOPLE I DON'T KNOW...
WE HAVE MANY WONDERFUL ITEMS, SOMETHING FOR EVERYONE!
PERFUME I DON'T RECOGNIZE...
SO PLEASE TAKE YOUR SEATS.
...LANGUAGES I CAN'T SPEAK...
ばっ
LET THE AUCTION COMMENCE!

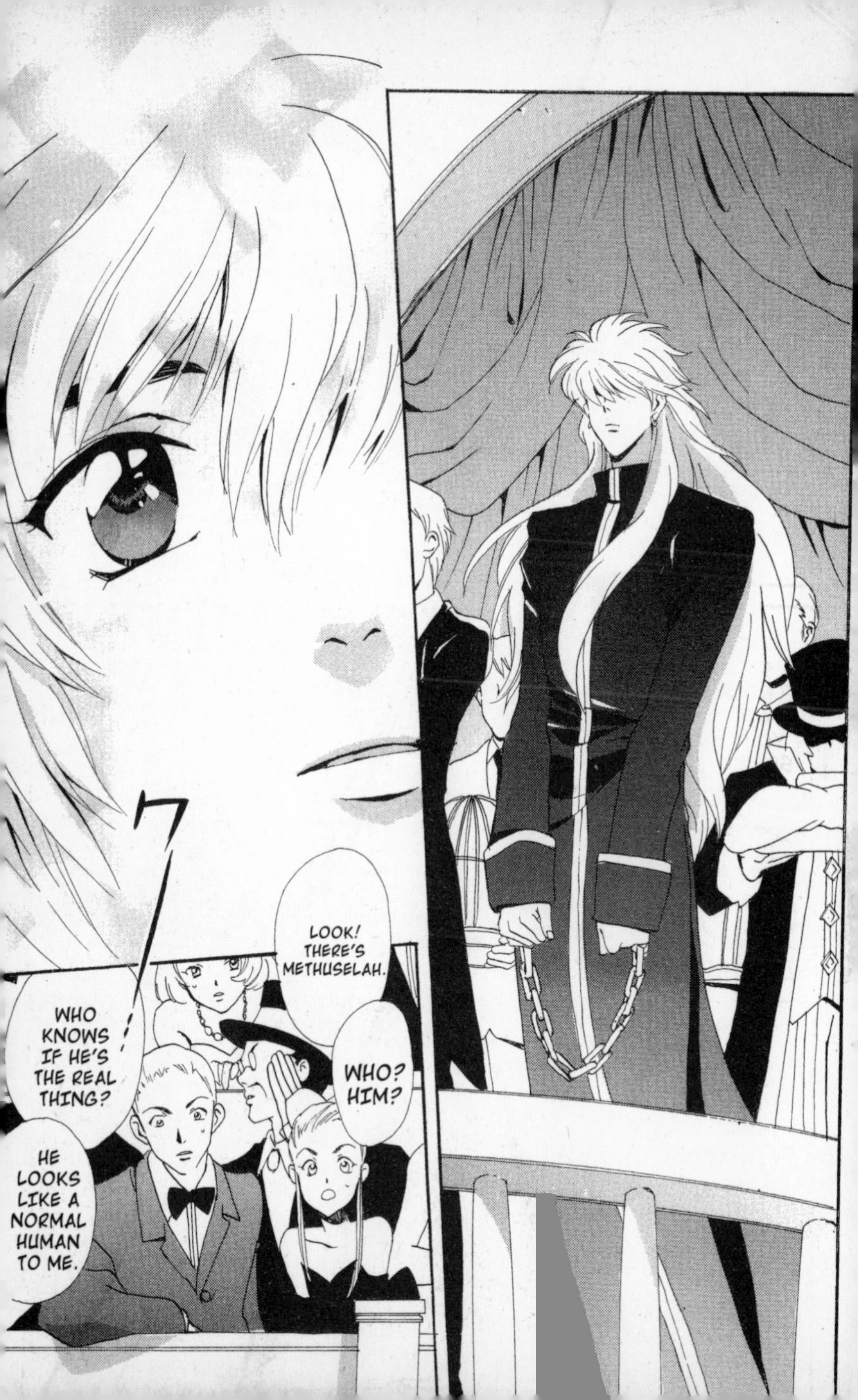
LOOK! THERE'S METHUSELAH.
WHO? HIM?
WHO KNOWS IF HE'S THE REAL THING?
HE LOOKS LIKE A NORMAL HUMAN TO ME.

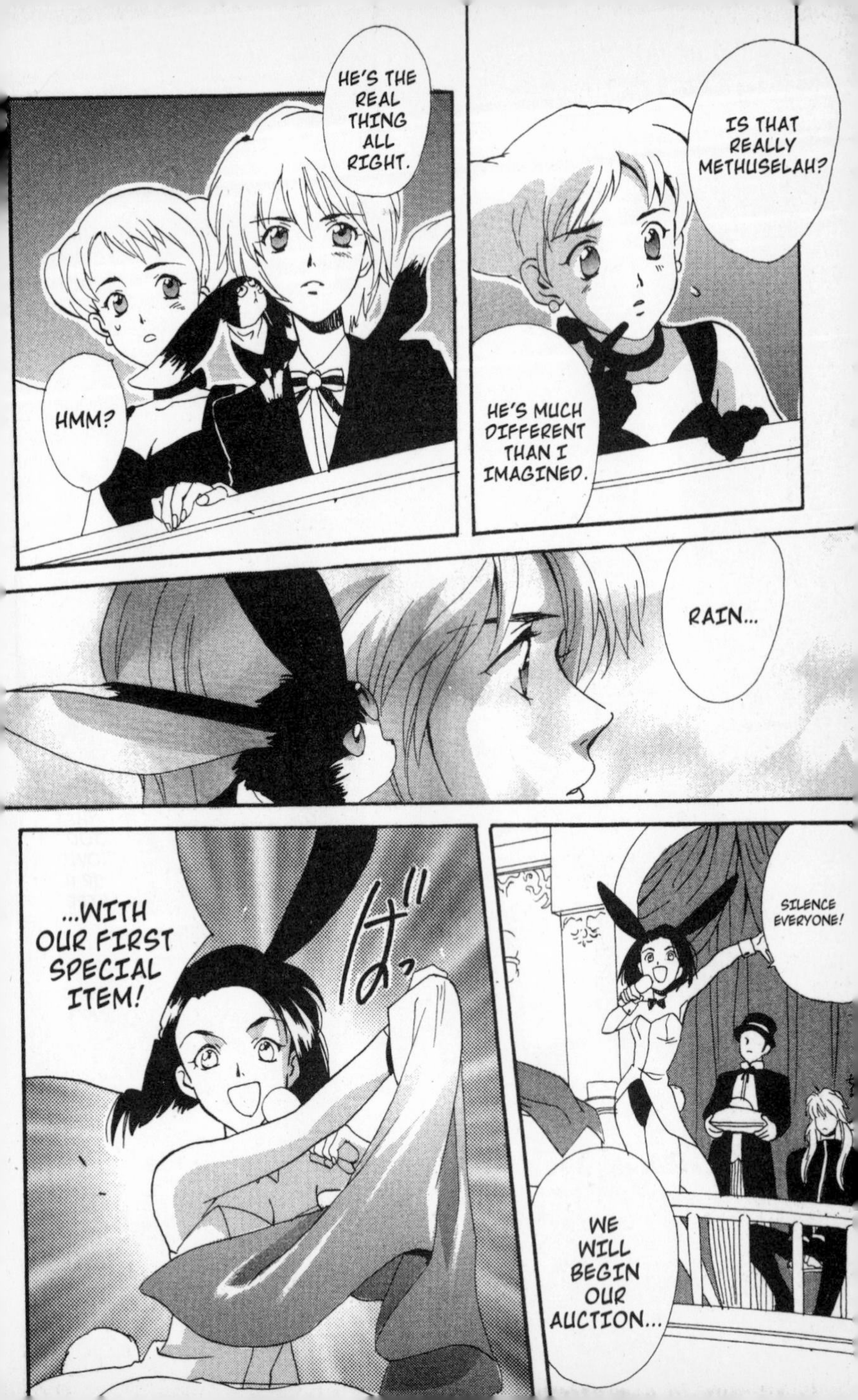
IS THAT REALLY METHUSELAH?
HE'S MUCH DIFFERENT THAN I IMAGINED.
HE'S THE REAL THING ALL RIGHT.
HMM?
RAIN...
SILENCE EVERYONE!
WE WILL BEGIN OUR AUCTION...
...WITH OUR FIRST SPECIAL ITEM!
ばっ

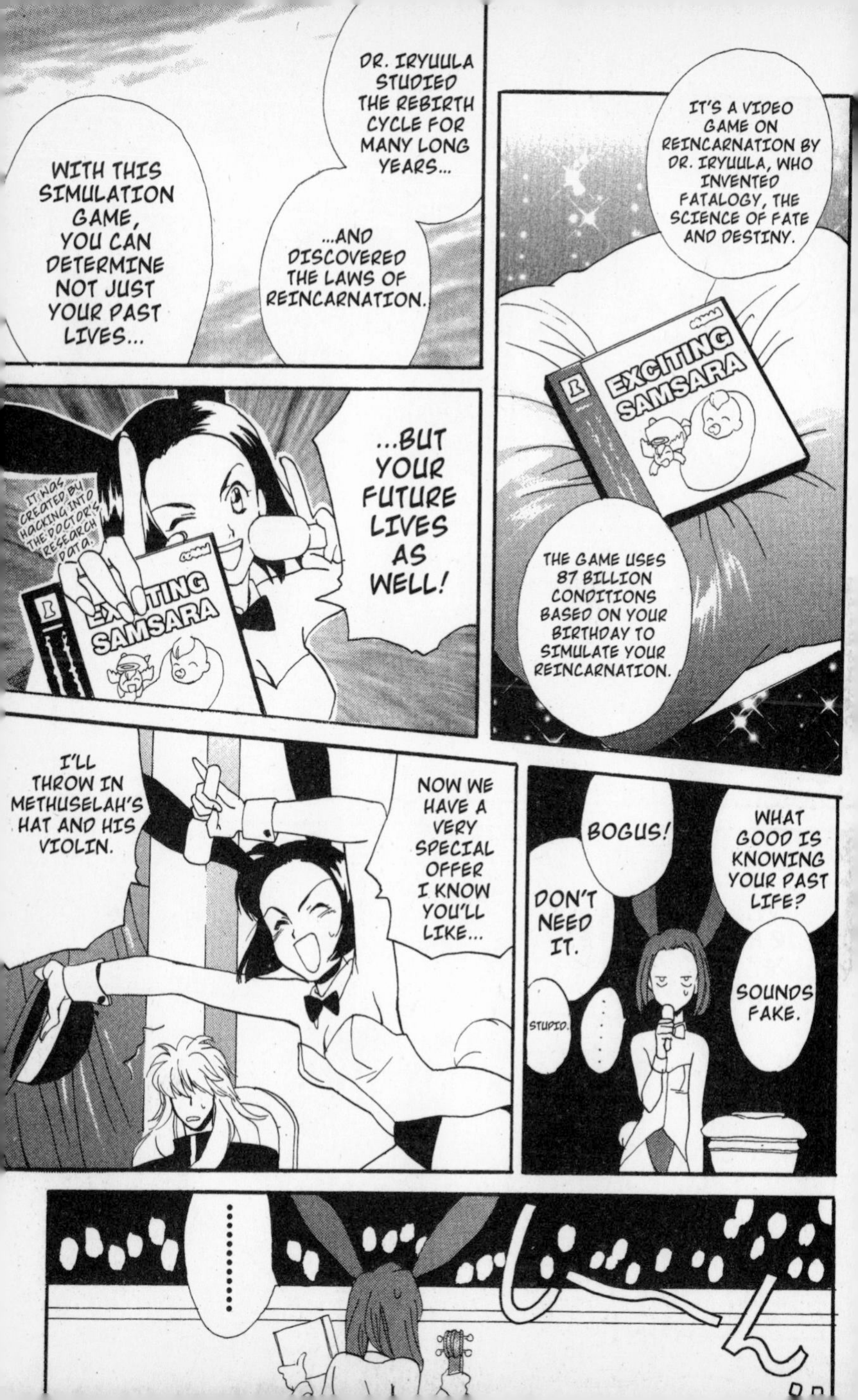
IT'S A VIDEO GAME ON REINCARNATION BY DR. IRYUULA, WHO INVENTED FATALOGY, THE SCIENCE OF FATE AND DESTINY.
EXCITING SAMSARA
THE GAME USES 87 BILLION CONDITIONS BASED ON YOUR BIRTHDAY TO SIMULATE YOUR REINCARNATION.
DR. IRYUULA STUDIED THE REBIRTH CYCLE FOR MANY LONG YEARS...
...AND DISCOVERED THE LAWS OF REINCARNATION.
WITH THIS SIMULATION GAME, YOU CAN DETERMINE NOT JUST YOUR PAST LIVES...
...BUT YOUR FUTURE LIVES AS WELL!
IT WAS CREATED BY HACKING INTO THE DOCTOR'S RESEARCH DATA.
EXCITING SAMSARA
WHAT GOOD IS KNOWING YOUR PAST LIFE?
BOGUS!
DON'T NEED IT.
SOUNDS FAKE.
......
STUPID.
NOW WE HAVE A VERY SPECIAL OFFER I KNOW YOU'LL LIKE...
I'LL THROW IN METHUSELAH'S HAT AND HIS VIOLIN.
....

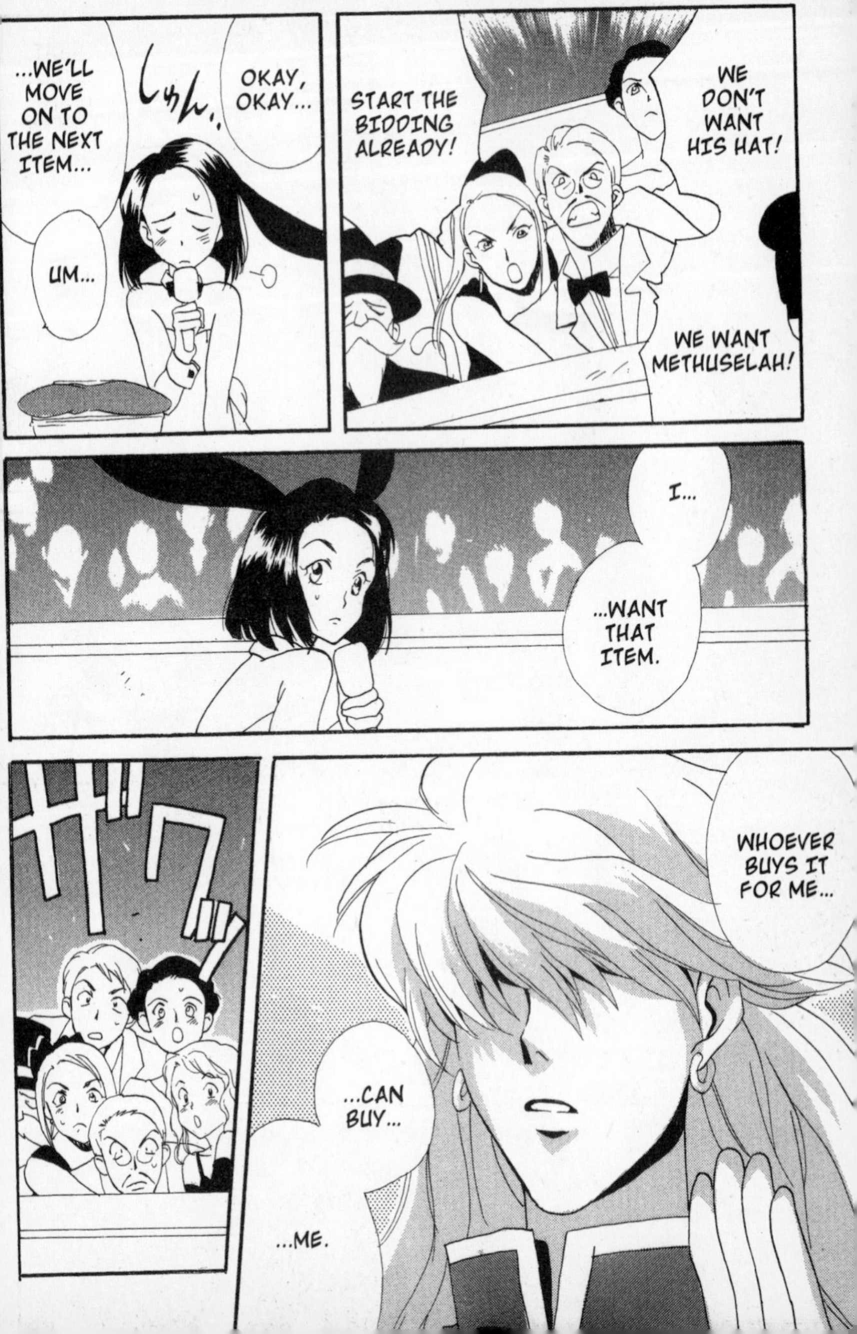
WE DON'T WANT HIS HAT!
START THE BIDDING ALREADY!
WE WANT METHUSELAH!
OKAY, OKAY...
しゅん..
...WE'LL MOVE ON TO THE NEXT ITEM...
UM...
I...
...WANT THAT ITEM.
WHOEVER BUYS IT FOR ME...
...CAN BUY...
...ME.
ザワッ

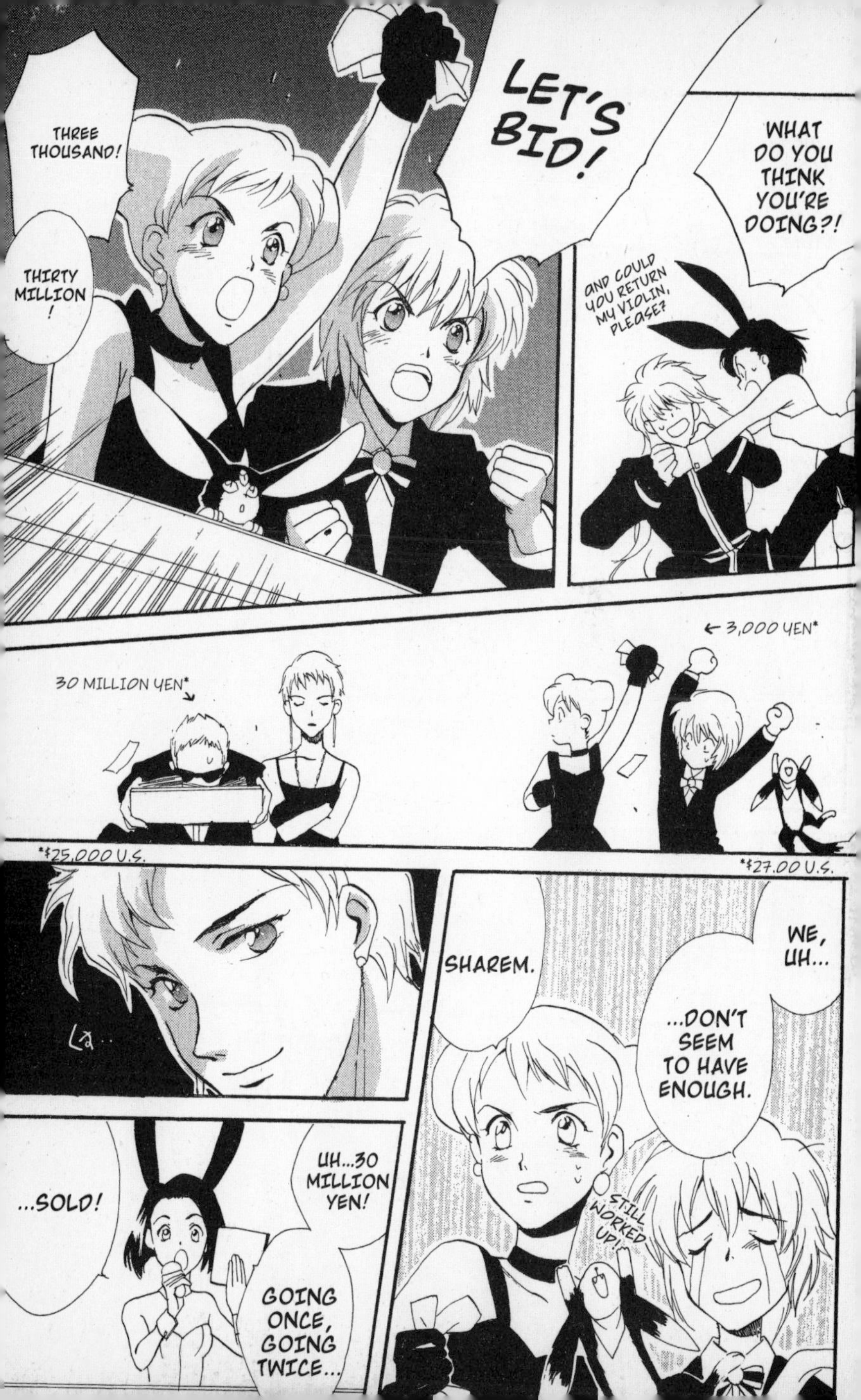
WHAT DO YOU THINK YOU'RE DOING?!
AND COULD YOU RETURN MY VIOLIN, PLEASE?
LET'S BID!
THREE THOUSAND!
THIRTY MILLION!
← 3,000 YEN*
30 MILLION YEN*
*$27.00 U.S.
*$25,000 U.S.
WE, UH...
...DON'T SEEM TO HAVE ENOUGH.
SHAREM.
STILL WORKED UP!
UH...30 MILLION YEN!
GOING ONCE, GOING TWICE...
...SOLD!

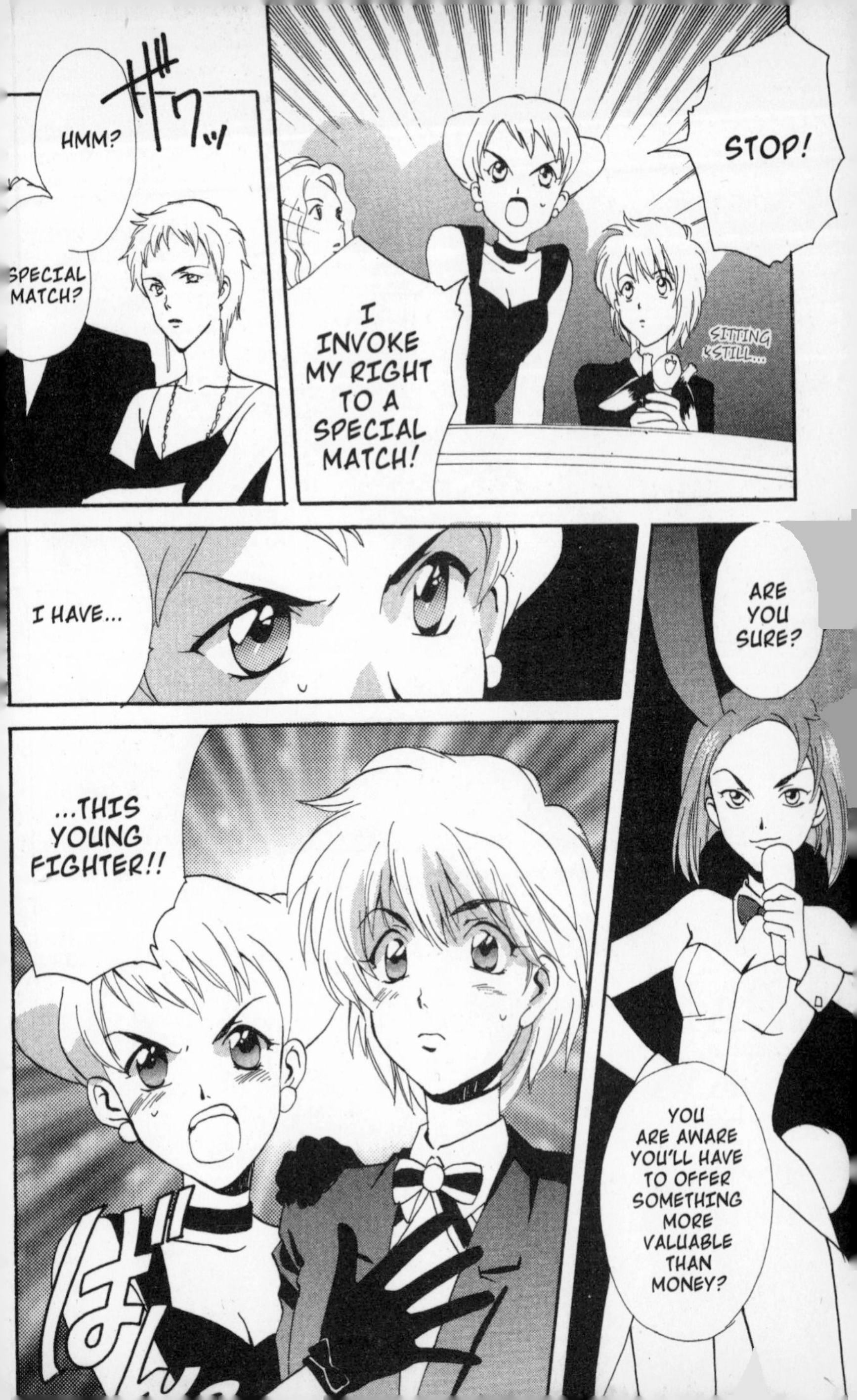
STOP!
SITTING STILL...
I INVOKE MY RIGHT TO A SPECIAL MATCH!
ザワッ
HMM?
SPECIAL MATCH?
ARE YOU SURE?
YOU ARE AWARE YOU'LL HAVE TO OFFER SOMETHING MORE VALUABLE THAN MONEY?
I HAVE...
...THIS YOUNG FIGHTER!!

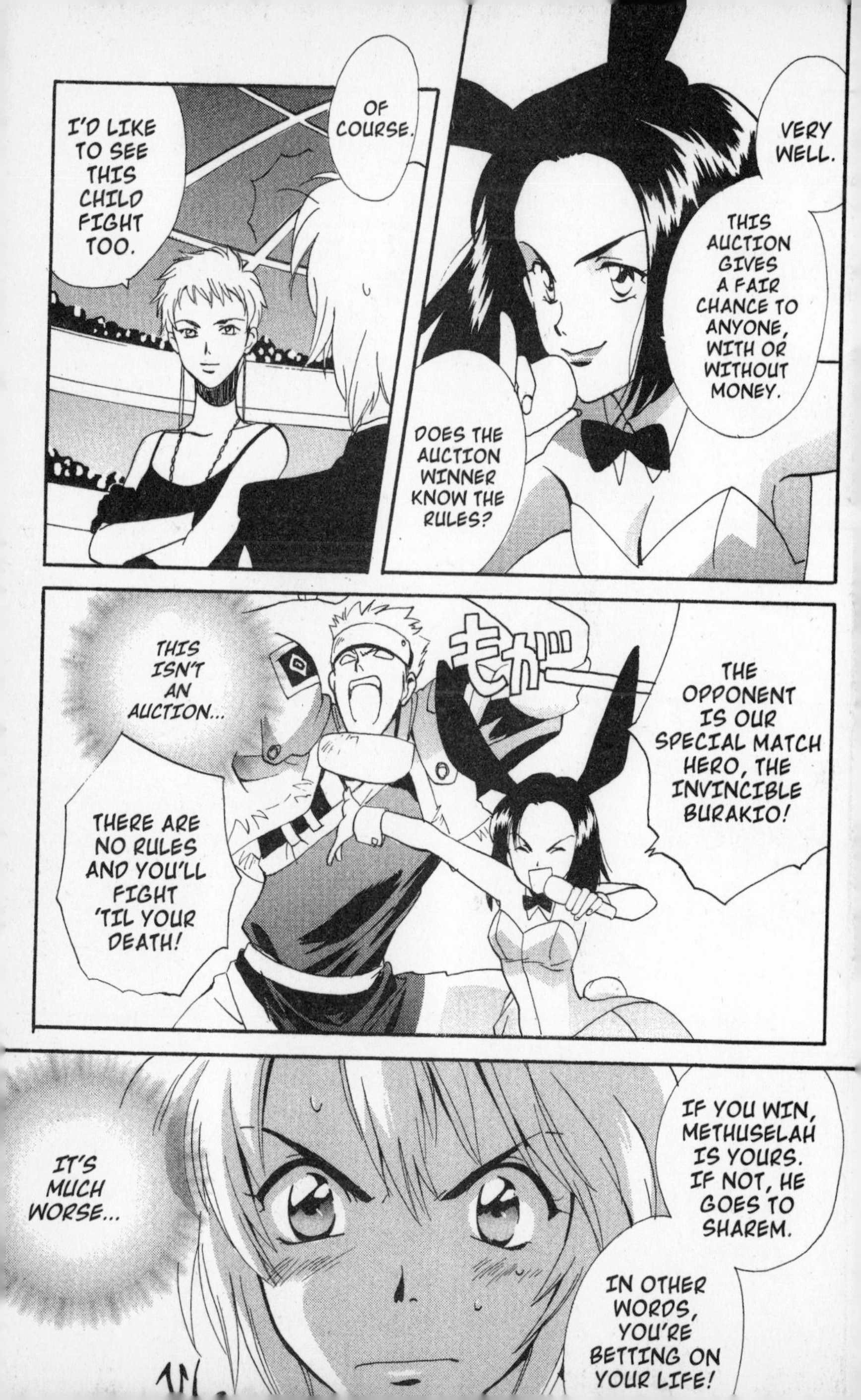
I'D LIKE TO SEE THIS CHILD FIGHT TOO.
OF COURSE.
VERY WELL.
THIS AUCTION GIVES A FAIR CHANCE TO ANYONE, WITH OR WITHOUT MONEY.
DOES THE AUCTION WINNER KNOW THE RULES?
THIS ISN'T AN AUCTION...
THERE ARE NO RULES AND YOU'LL FIGHT 'TIL YOUR DEATH!
もが
THE OPPONENT IS OUR SPECIAL MATCH HERO, THE INVINCIBLE BURAKIO!
IT'S MUCH WORSE...
IF YOU WIN, METHUSELAH IS YOURS. IF NOT, HE GOES TO SHAREM.
IN OTHER WORDS, YOU'RE BETTING ON YOUR LIFE!

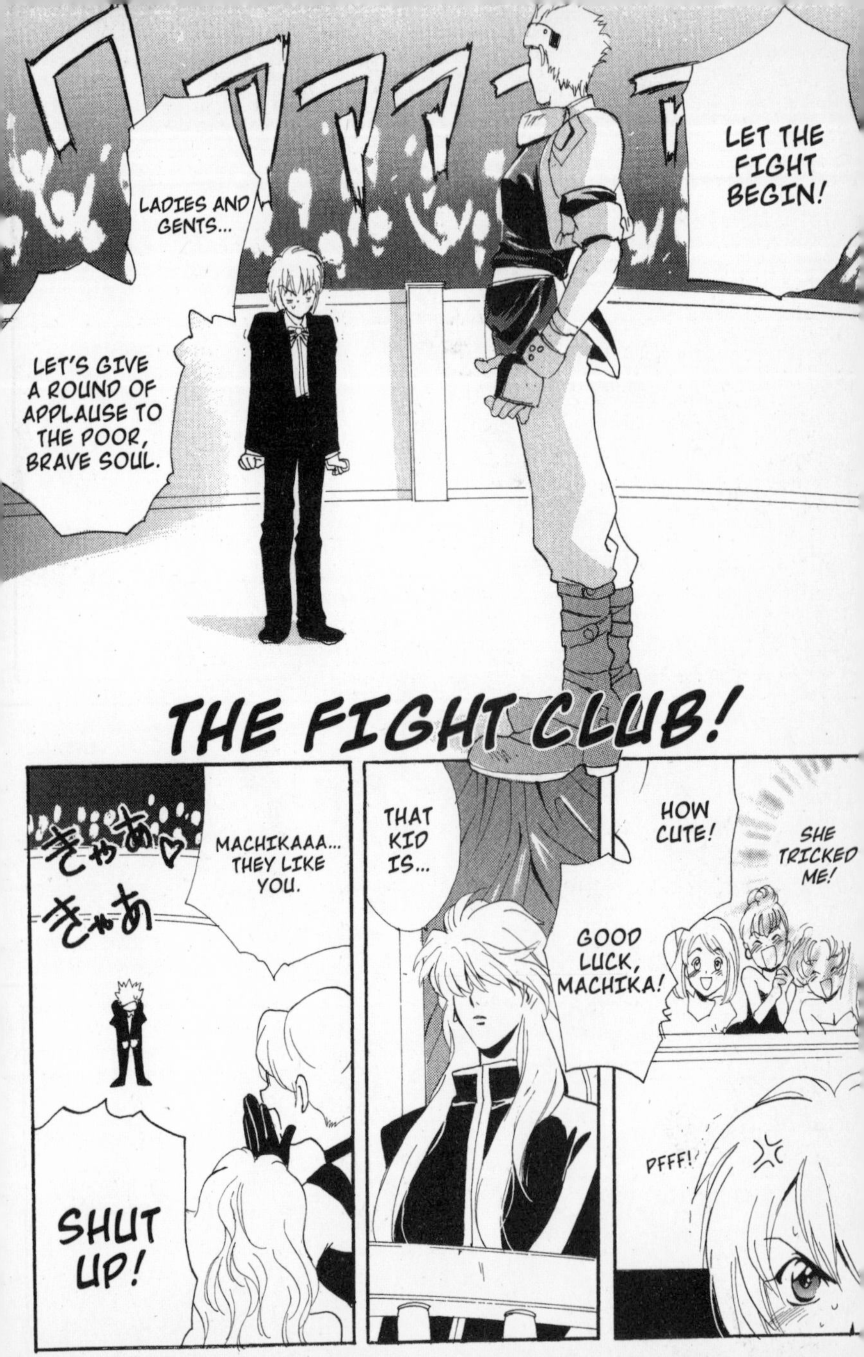
ワァァァー
LET THE FIGHT BEGIN!
LADIES AND GENTS...
LET'S GIVE A ROUND OF APPLAUSE TO THE POOR, BRAVE SOUL.
THE FIGHT CLUB!
SHE TRICKED ME!
HOW CUTE!
GOOD LUCK, MACHIKA!
PFFF!
THAT KID IS...
MACHIKAAA... THEY LIKE YOU.
きゃあ♡
きゃあ
SHUT UP!

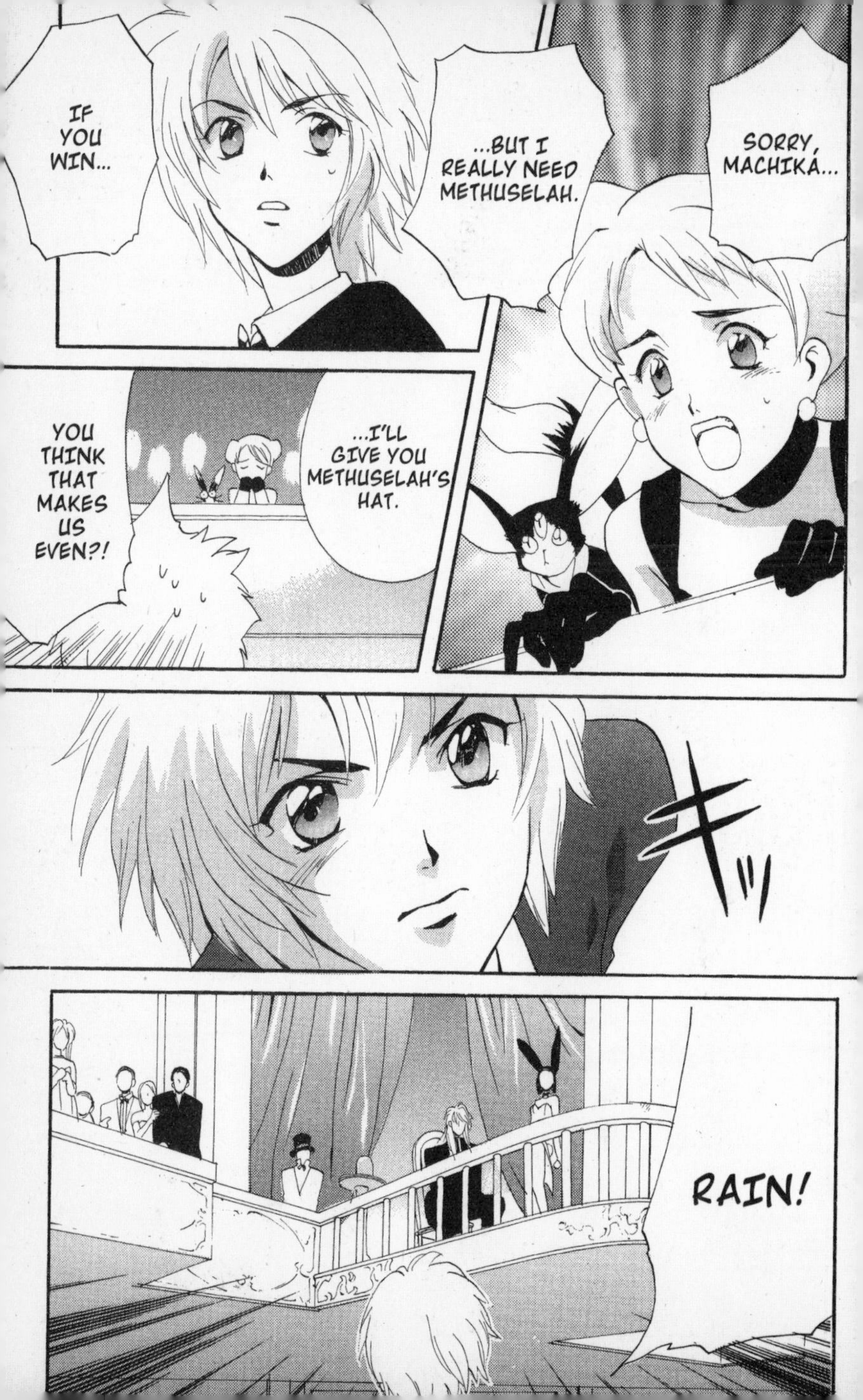
SORRY, MACHIKA...
...BUT I REALLY NEED METHUSELAH.
IF YOU WIN...
...I'LL GIVE YOU METHUSELAH'S HAT.
YOU THINK THAT MAKES US EVEN?!
キッ
RAIN!

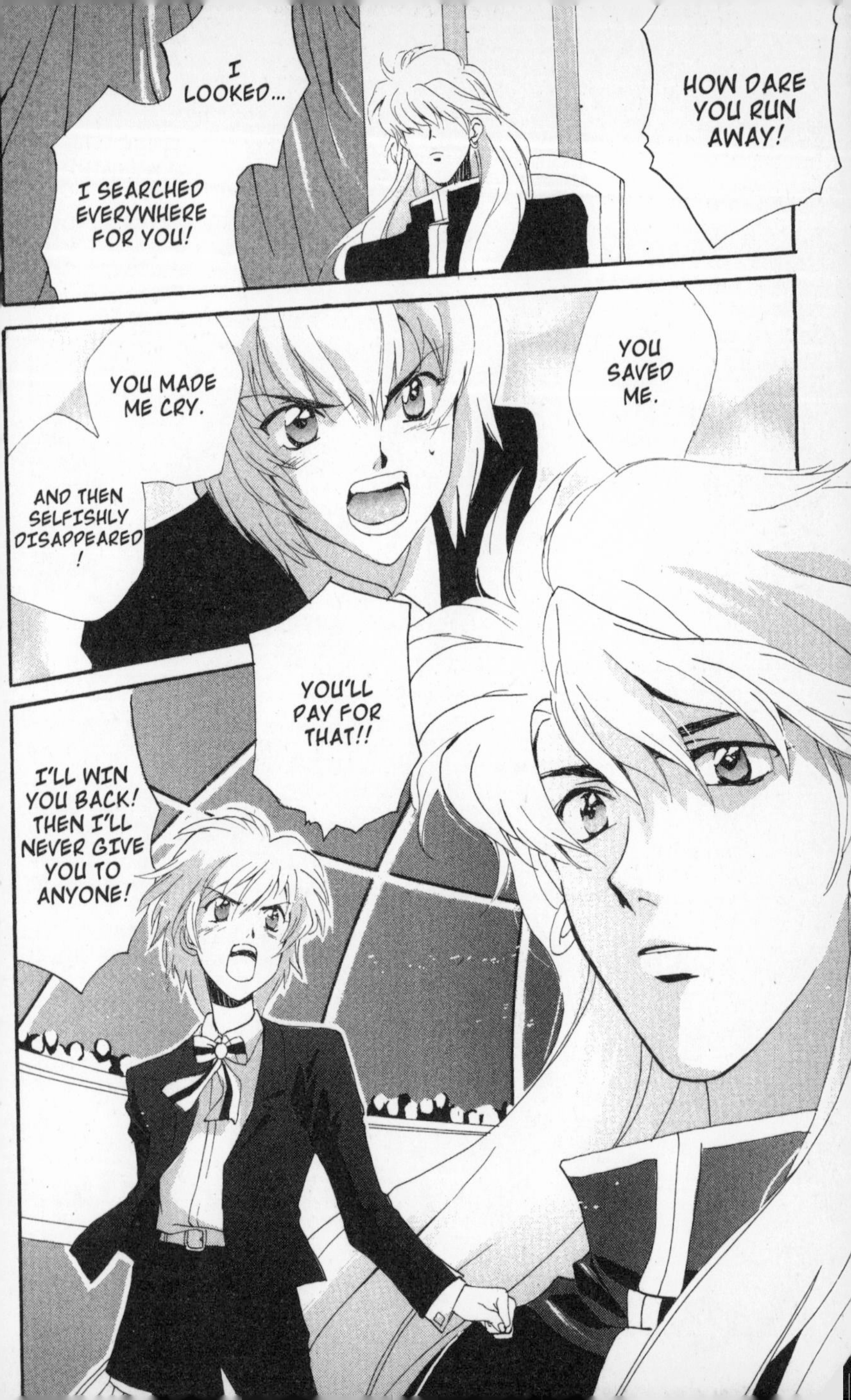
HOW DARE YOU RUN AWAY!
I LOOKED...
I SEARCHED EVERYWHERE FOR YOU!
YOU SAVED ME.
YOU MADE ME CRY.
AND THEN SELFISHLY DISAPPEARED!
YOU'LL PAY FOR THAT!!
I'LL WIN YOU BACK! THEN I'LL NEVER GIVE YOU TO ANYONE!

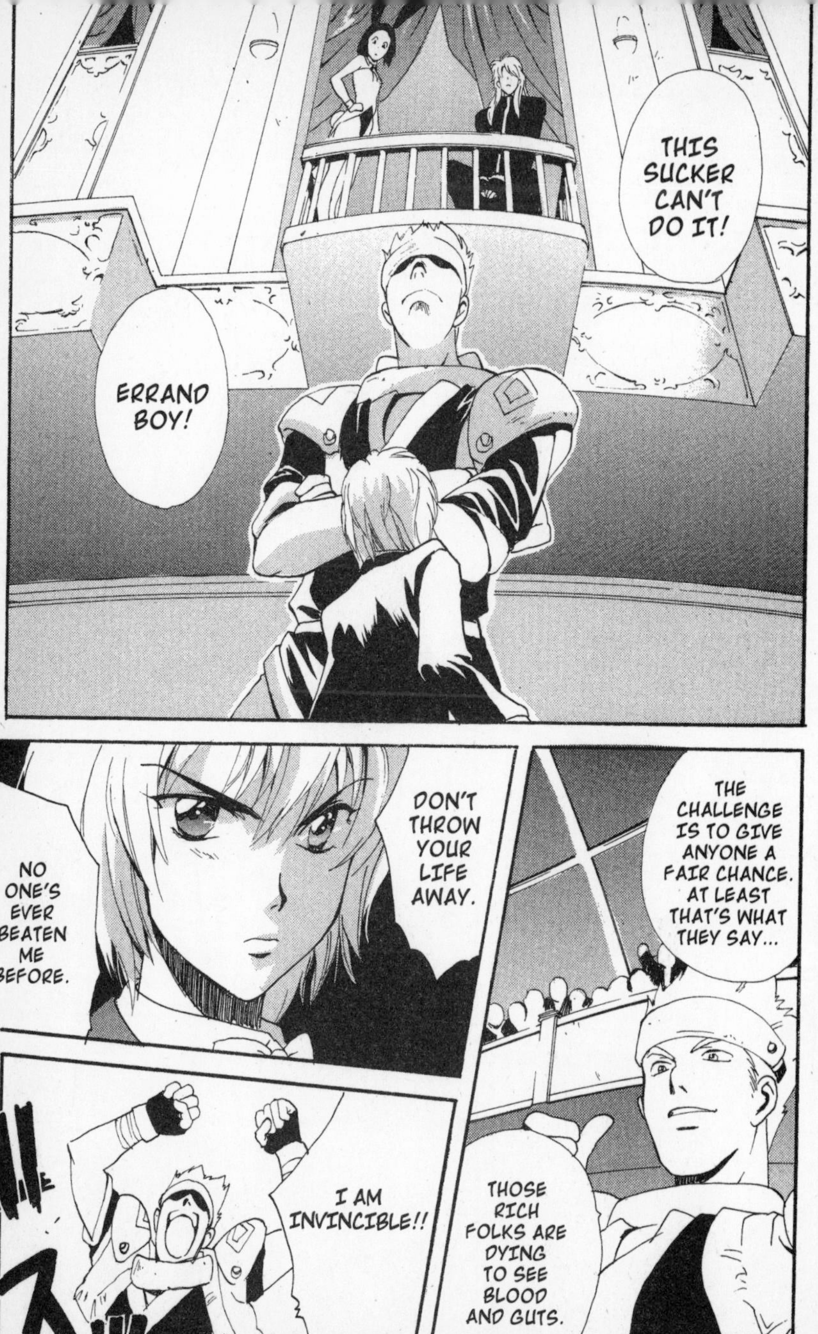
THIS SUCKER CAN'T DO IT!
ERRAND BOY!
THE CHALLENGE IS TO GIVE ANYONE A FAIR CHANCE. AT LEAST THAT'S WHAT THEY SAY...
THOSE RICH FOLKS ARE DYING TO SEE BLOOD AND GUTS.
DON'T THROW YOUR LIFE AWAY.
NO ONE'S EVER BEATEN ME BEFORE.
I AM INVINCIBLE!!

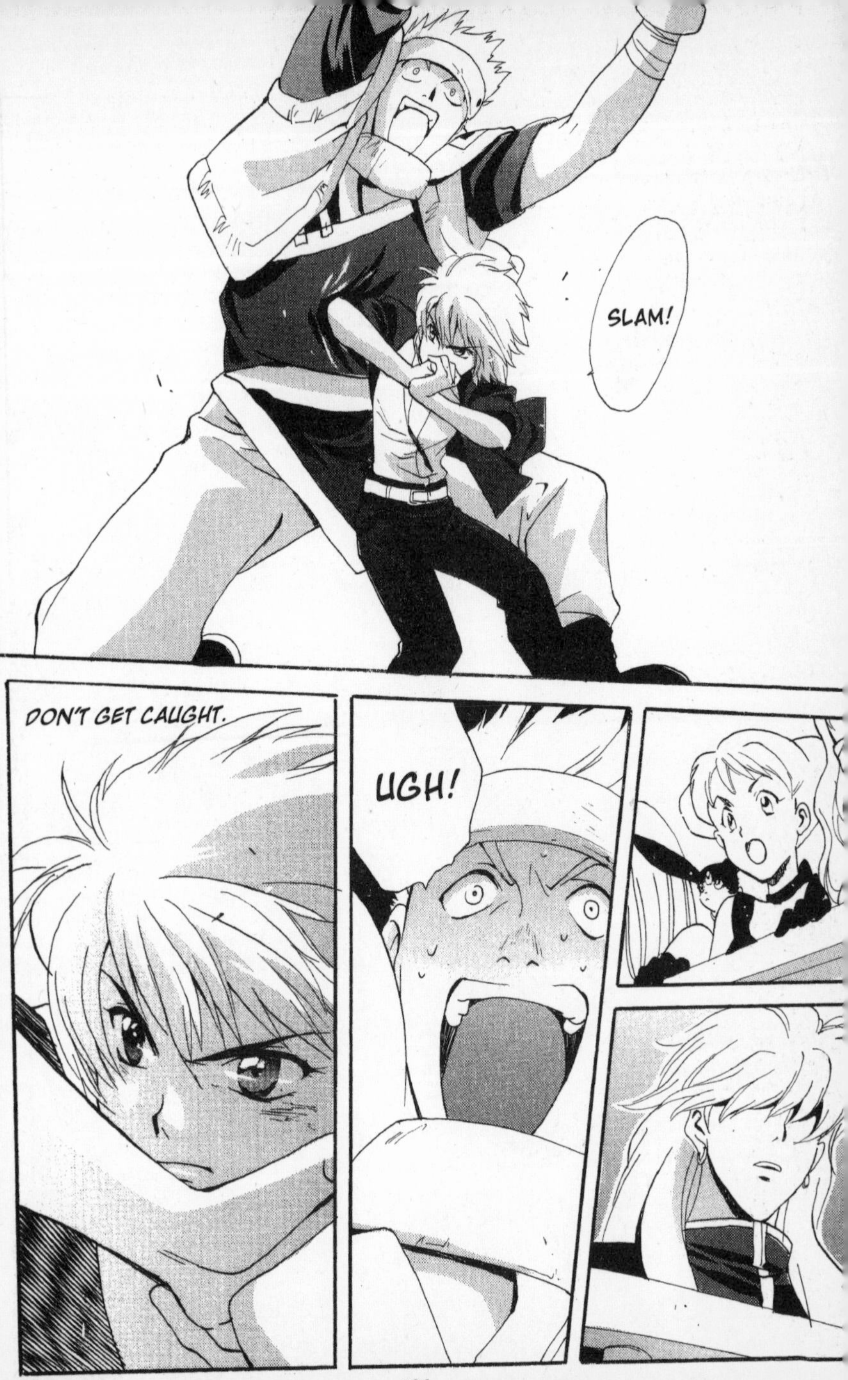
SLAM!
UGH!
DON'T GET CAUGHT.

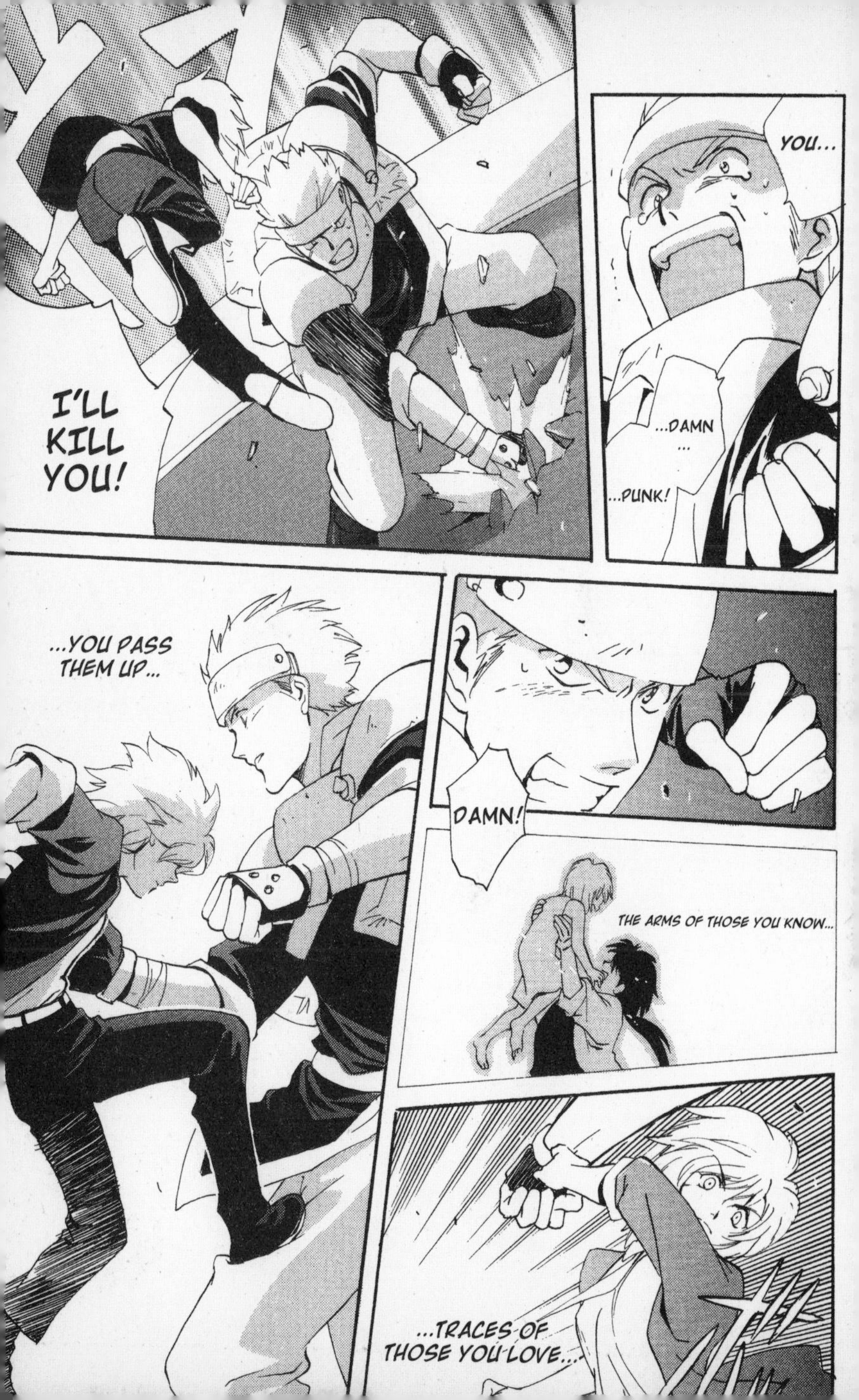
YOU...
...DAMN
...
...PUNK!
I'LL KILL YOU!
DAMN!
THE ARMS OF THOSE YOU KNOW...
...TRACES OF THOSE YOU LOVE...
...YOU PASS THEM UP...

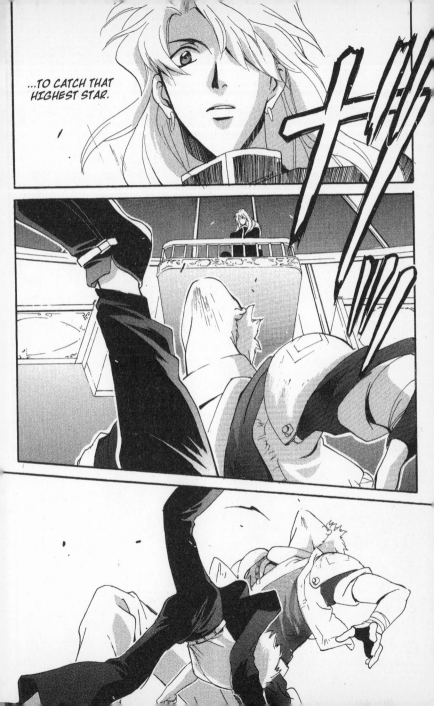

...TO CATCH THAT
HIGHEST STAR.

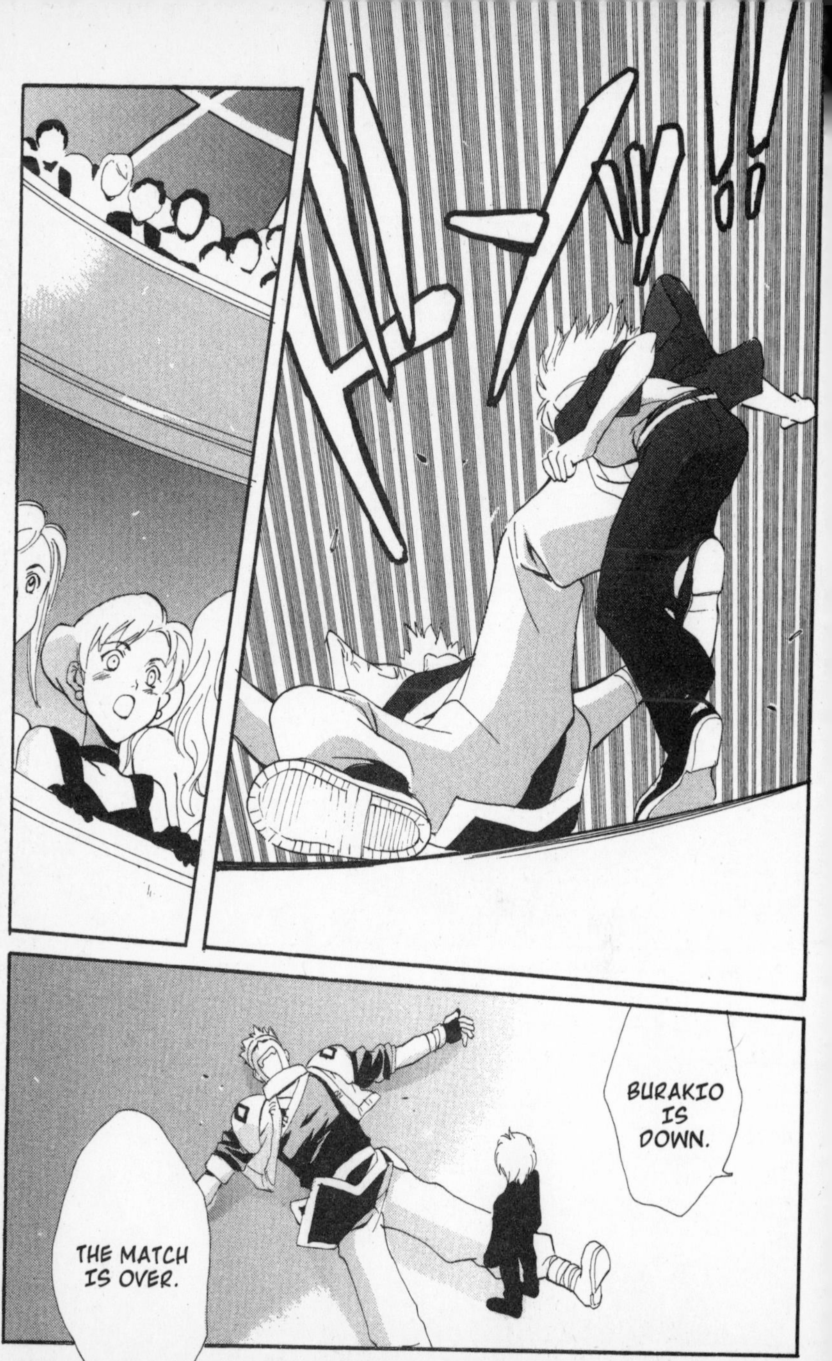
BURAKIO IS DOWN.
THE MATCH IS OVER.

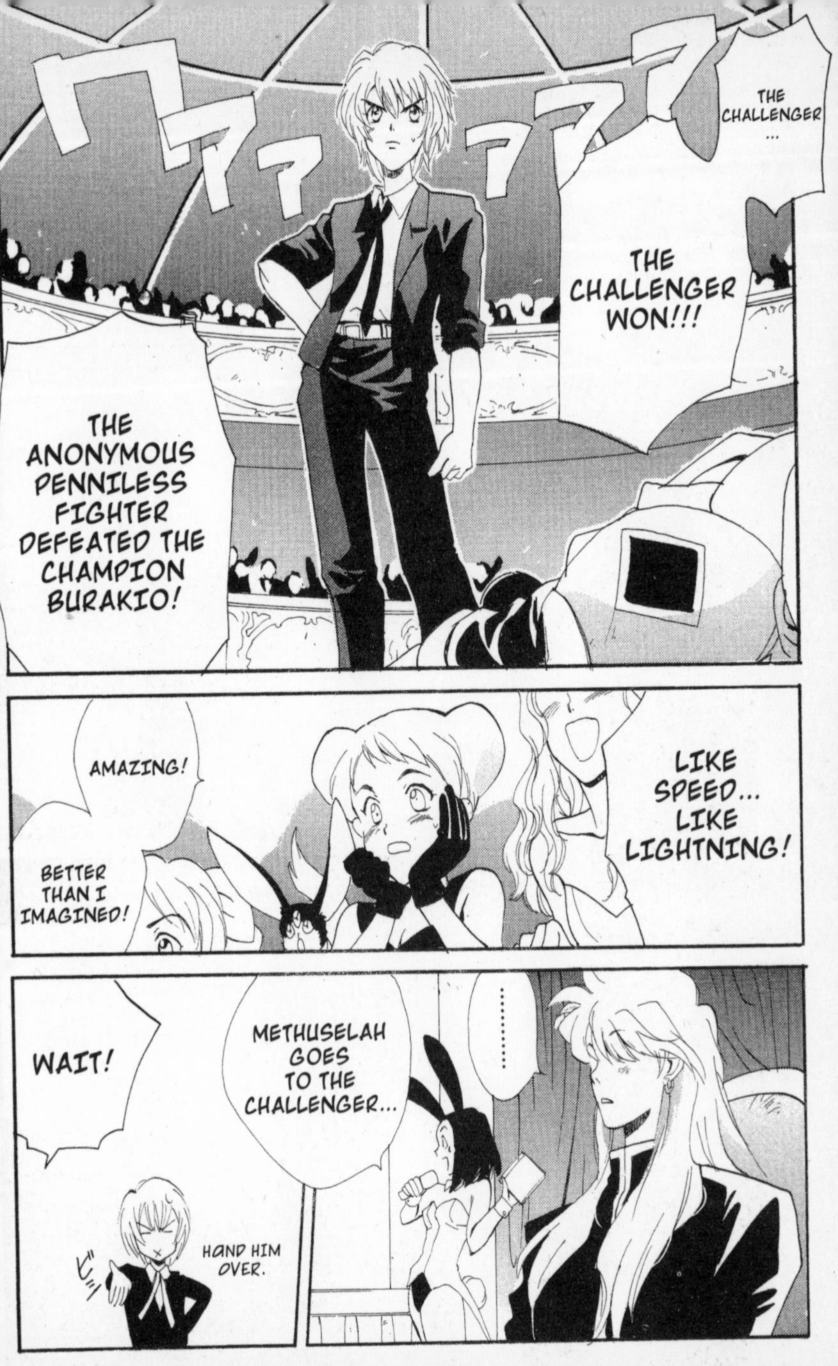
ワアアアアア
THE CHALLENGER ...
THE CHALLENGER WON!!!
THE ANONYMOUS PENNILESS FIGHTER DEFEATED THE CHAMPION BURAKIO!
LIKE SPEED... LIKE LIGHTNING!
AMAZING!
BETTER THAN I IMAGINED!
......
METHUSELAH GOES TO THE CHALLENGER...
WAIT!
HAND HIM OVER.

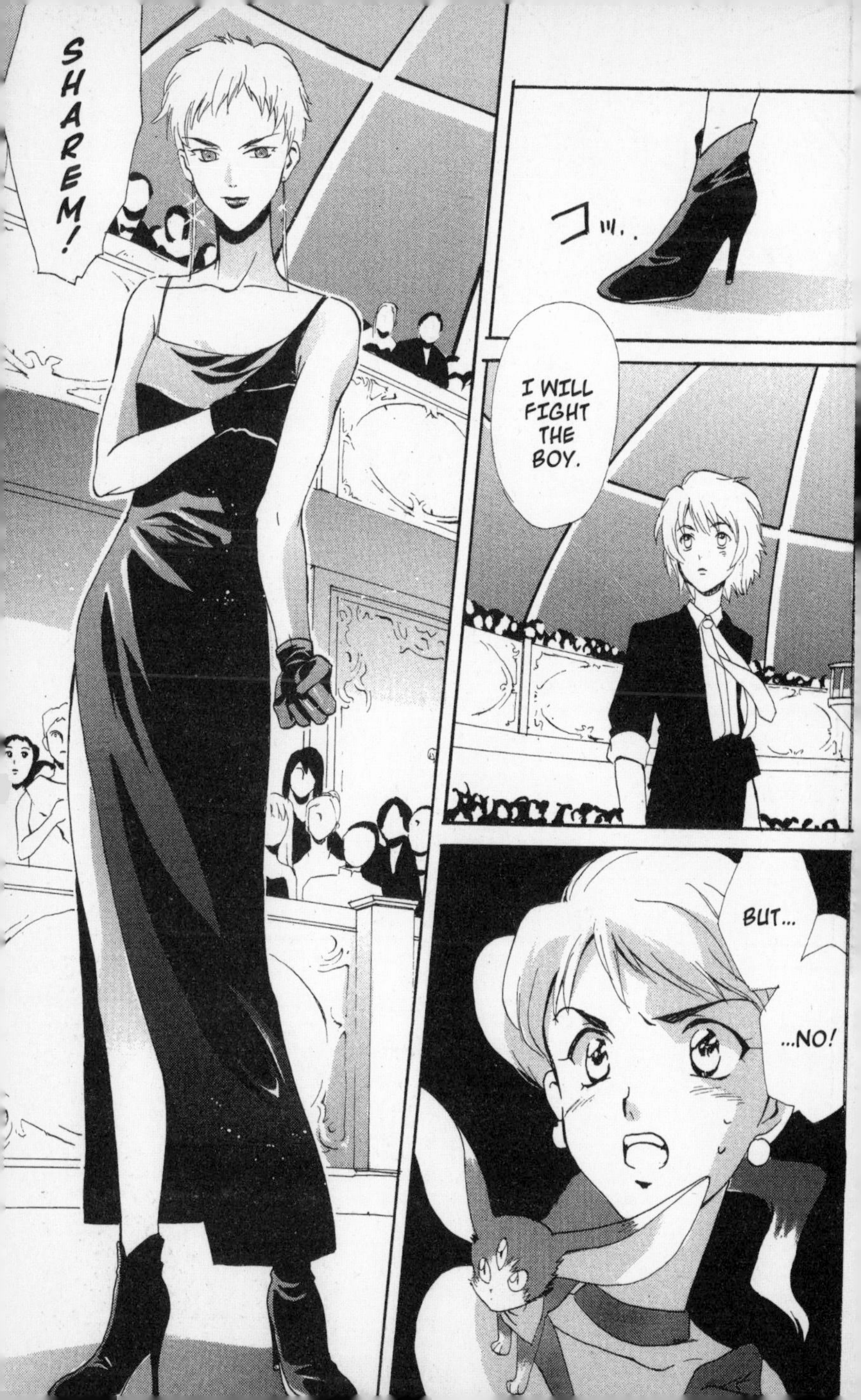
コッ..
I WILL FIGHT THE BOY.
BUT...
...NO!
SHAREM!

BLACK-MARKET DOCTOR

AGE : 34
HEIGHT : 181CM
BLOOD TYPE : B

COMMAND
SNEER
MEDICAL EXAM
EMERGENCY OPERATION

LV: 62
HP: 604/604
OFFENSE
STRENGTH: 33
DEFENSE
STRENGTH: 48
SPEED: 32
WIT: 98
LUCK: 52

EQUIPMENT
WEAPON: SURGICAL KNIFE /
        OFFENSE STRENGTH + 18
ARMOR: WHITE COAT /
       DEFENSE STRENGTH + 13
ACCESSORY: TRUTH SERUM /
           FORCES OPPONENT TO
           REVEAL THE TRUTH

DEATHBLOW TECHNIQUE COMMAND

ANESTHESIA   ⇨Ⓟ

DISSECTION   ⇩⇨Ⓟ+Ⓖ

DEATH SENTENCE (from squat position) Ⓟ+Ⓚ

SINCE THERE IS NO "FIGHT" COMMAND THERE IS
NO WAY FOR HIM TO FIGHT. SCATTER THEM WITH
STRANGENESS UNTIL THE OPPONENT RUNS AWAY.

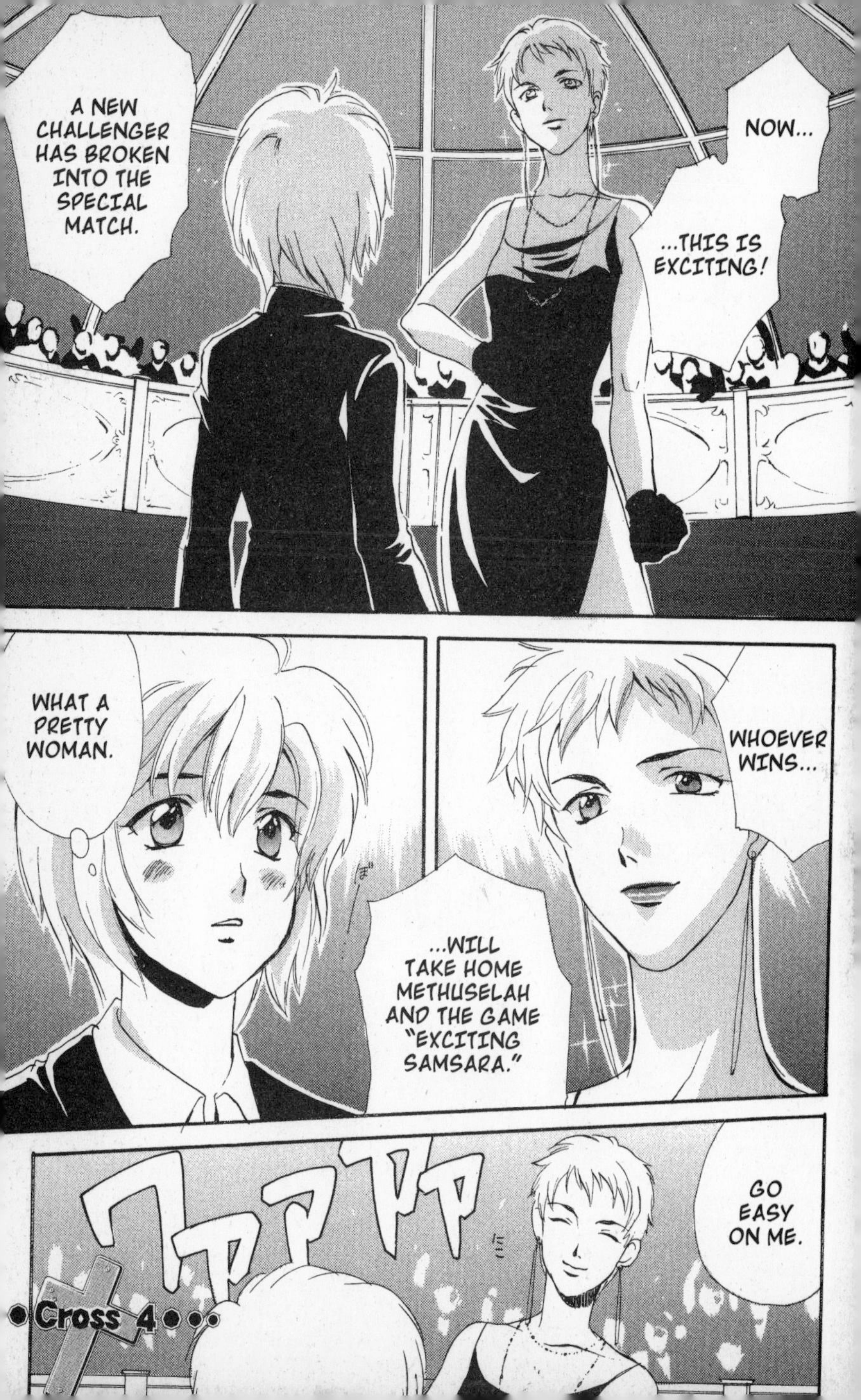
NOW...
...THIS IS EXCITING!
A NEW CHALLENGER HAS BROKEN INTO THE SPECIAL MATCH.
WHOEVER WINS...
...WILL TAKE HOME METHUSELAH AND THE GAME "EXCITING SAMSARA."
WHAT A PRETTY WOMAN.
GO EASY ON ME.
Cross 4

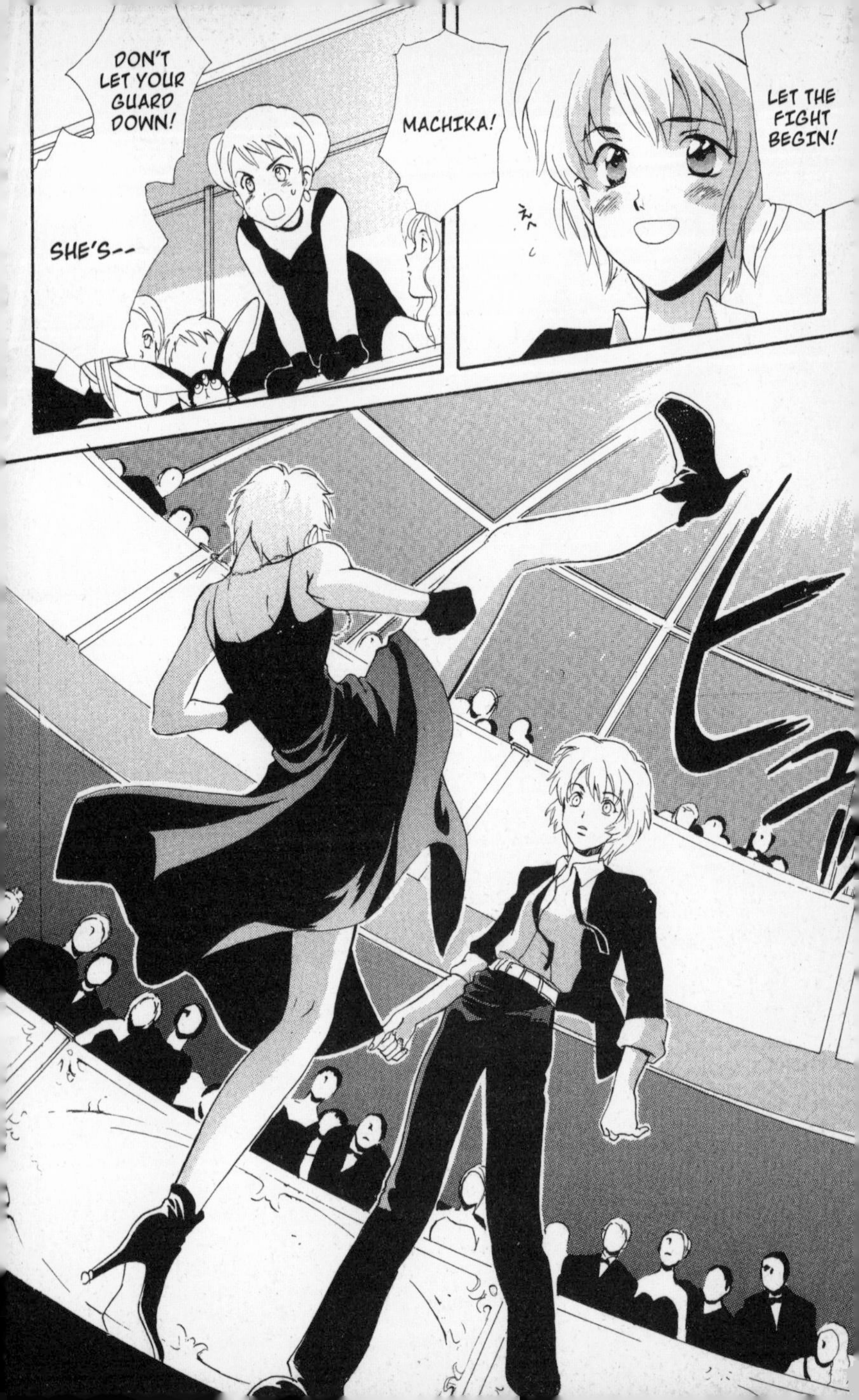
LET THE FIGHT BEGIN!
MACHIKA!
DON'T LET YOUR GUARD DOWN!
SHE'S--

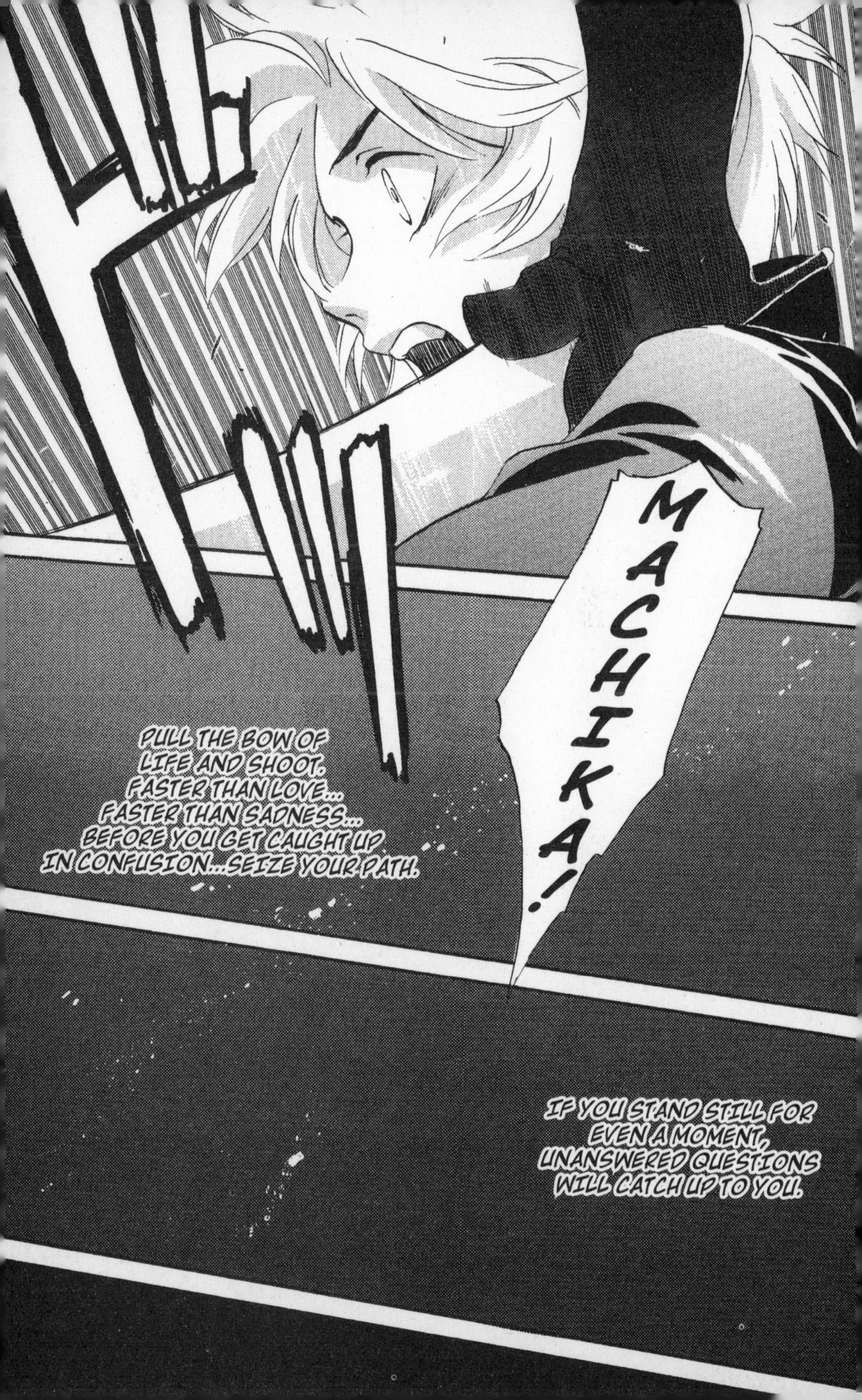
MACHIKA!
PULL THE BOW OF LIFE AND SHOOT. FASTER THAN LOVE... FASTER THAN SADNESS... BEFORE YOU GET CAUGHT UP IN CONFUSION...SEIZE YOUR PATH.
IF YOU STAND STILL FOR EVEN A MOMENT, UNANSWERED QUESTIONS WILL CATCH UP TO YOU.

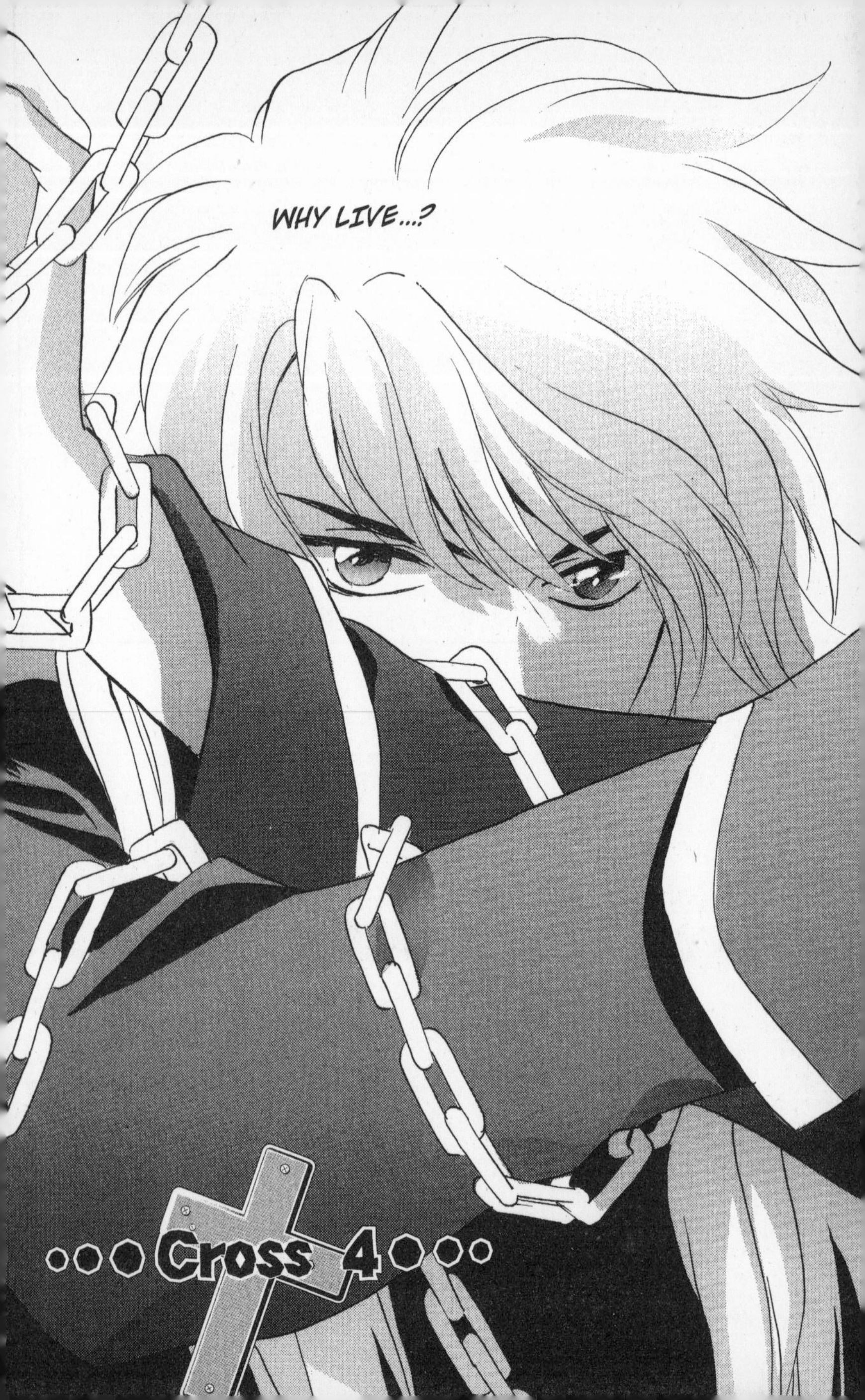
WHY LIVE...?
Cross 4

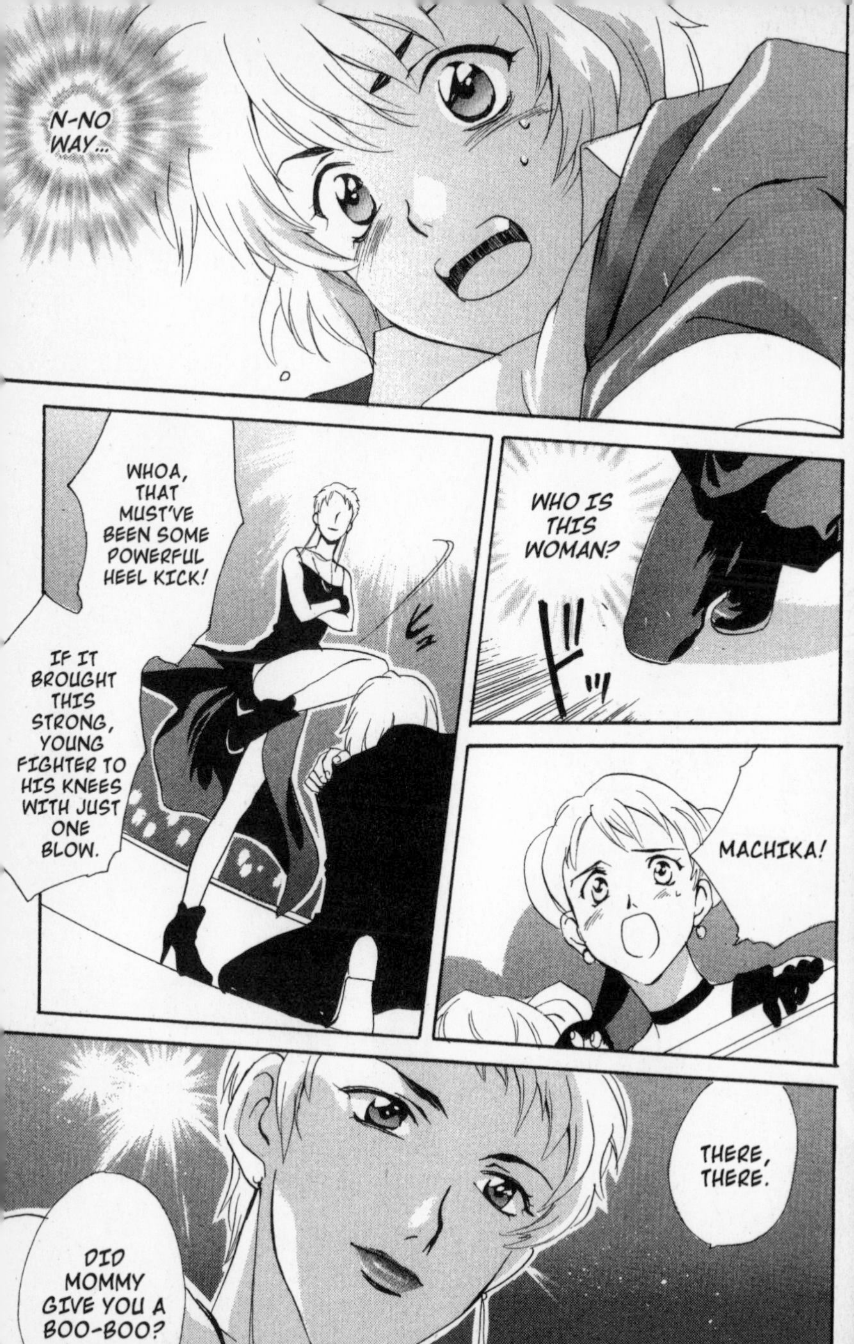
N-NO WAY...
WHO IS THIS WOMAN?
ドッ
MACHIKA!
WHOA, THAT MUST'VE BEEN SOME POWERFUL HEEL KICK!
IF IT BROUGHT THIS STRONG, YOUNG FIGHTER TO HIS KNEES WITH JUST ONE BLOW.
THERE, THERE.
DID MOMMY GIVE YOU A BOO-BOO?

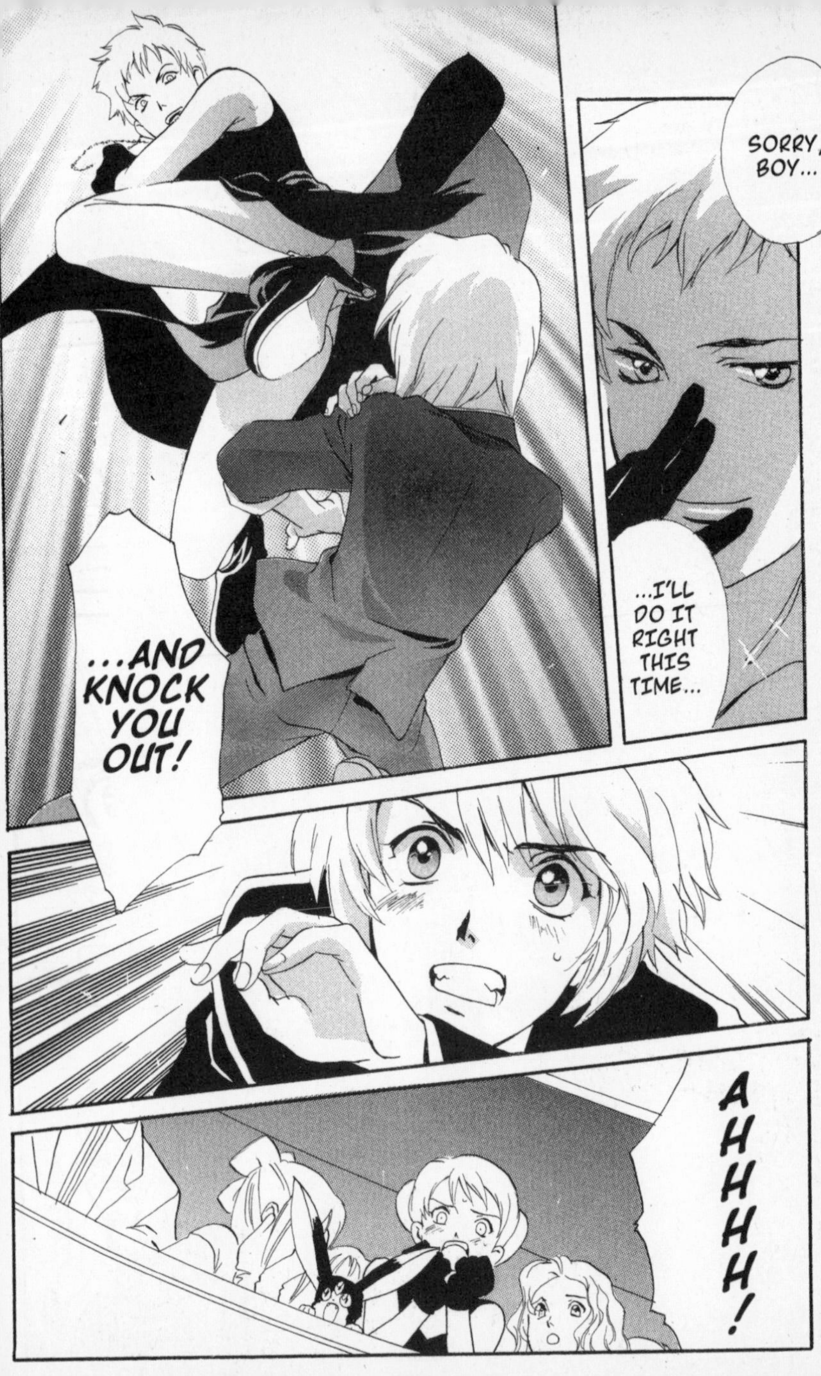
SORRY, BOY...
...I'LL DO IT RIGHT THIS TIME...
...AND KNOCK YOU OUT!
AHHHH!

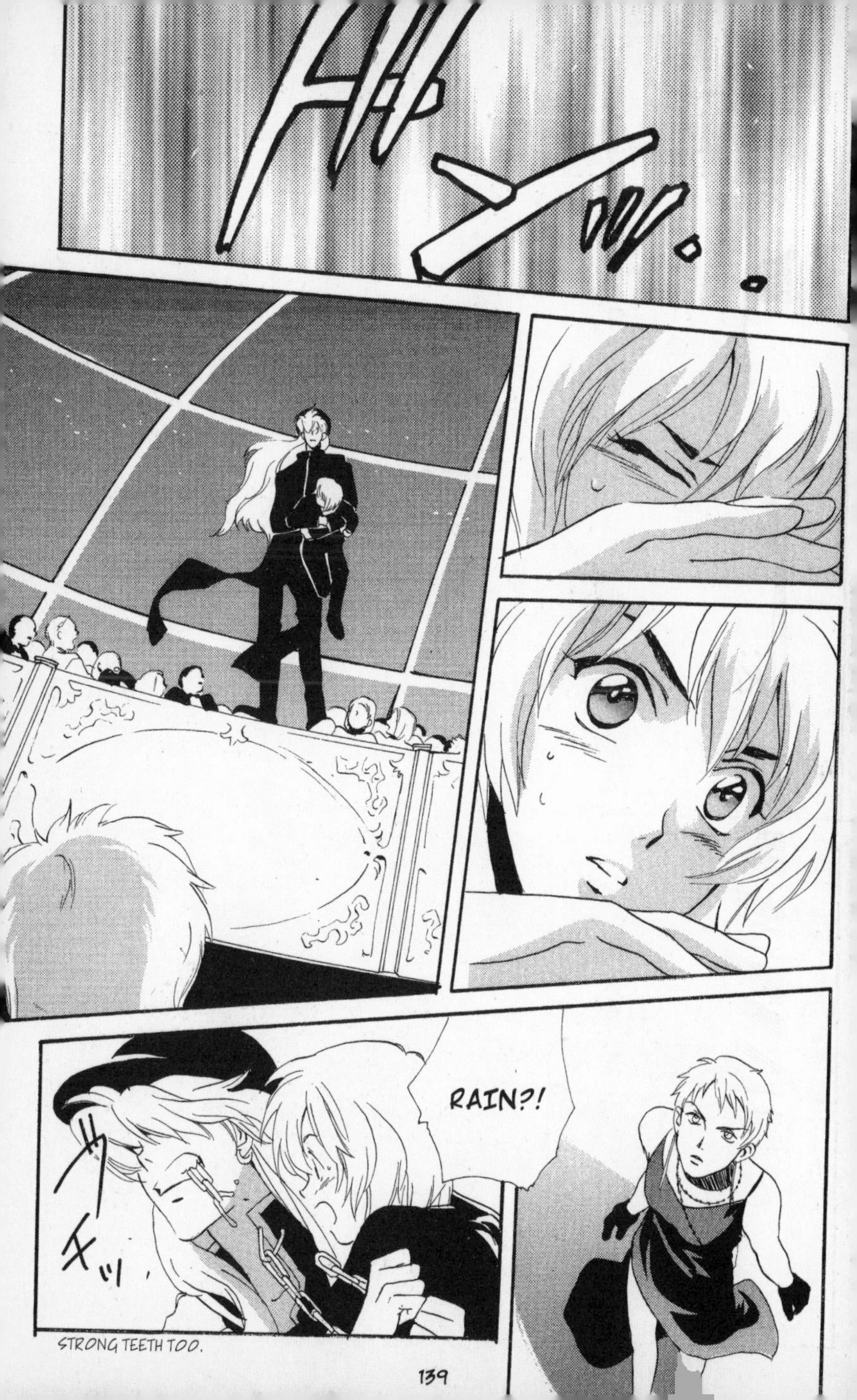
RAIN?!

STRONG TEETH TOO.

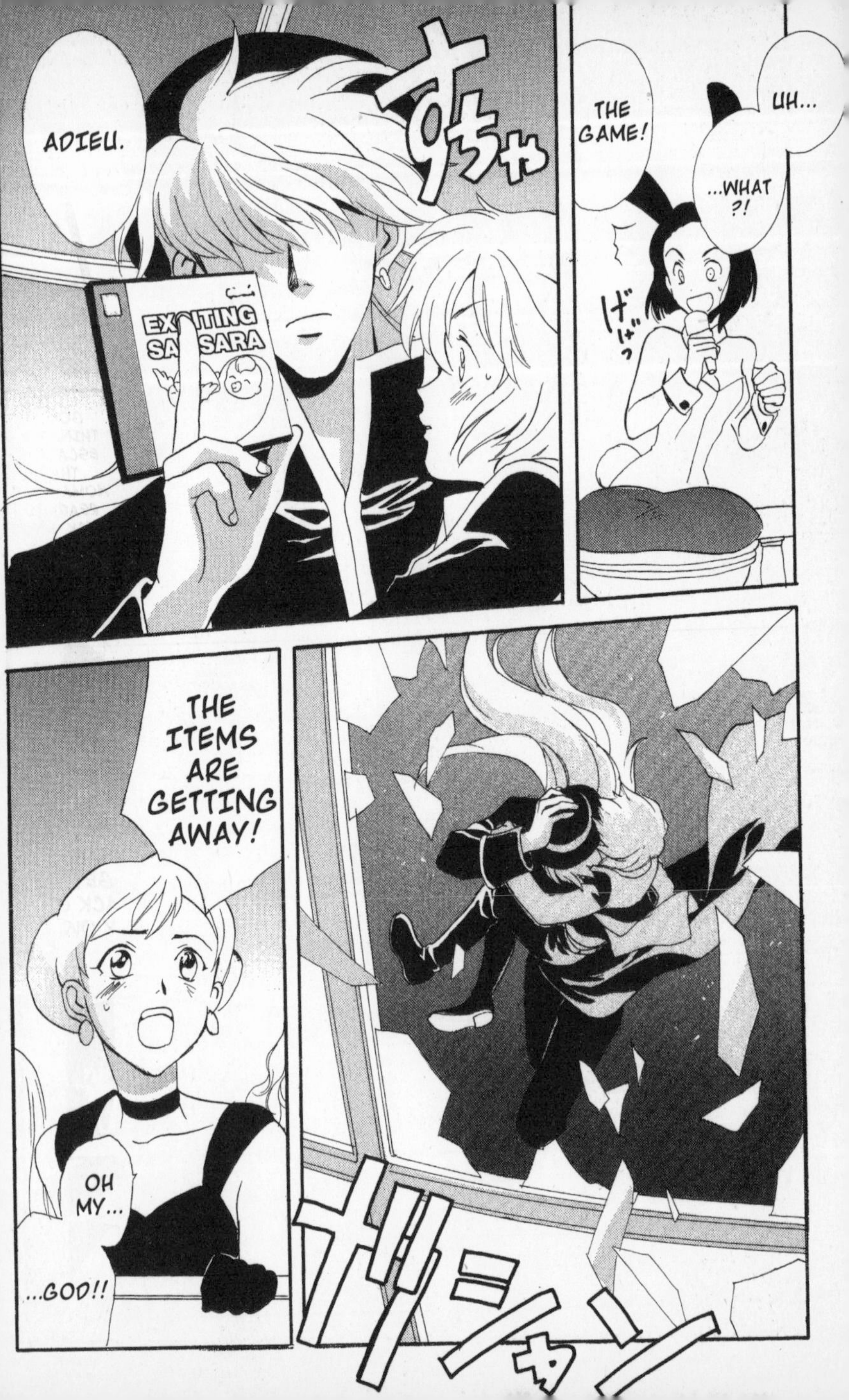
UH...
THE GAME!
...WHAT?!
げげっ
すちゃ
ADIEU.
THE ITEMS ARE GETTING AWAY!
OH MY...
...GOD!!
ガシャン

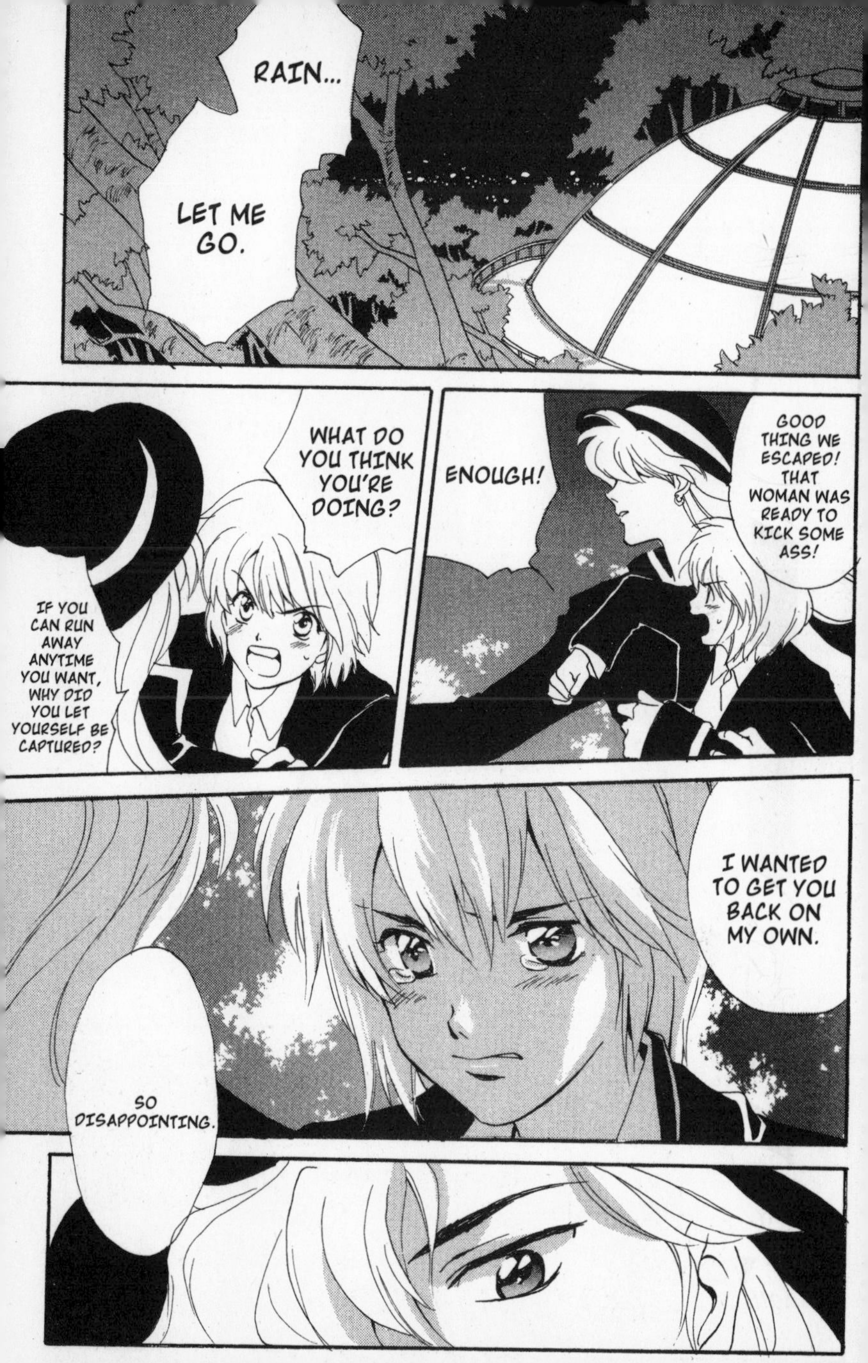
RAIN...
LET ME GO.
GOOD THING WE ESCAPED! THAT WOMAN WAS READY TO KICK SOME ASS!
ENOUGH!
WHAT DO YOU THINK YOU'RE DOING?
IF YOU CAN RUN AWAY ANYTIME YOU WANT, WHY DID YOU LET YOURSELF BE CAPTURED?
I WANTED TO GET YOU BACK ON MY OWN.
SO DISAPPOINTING.

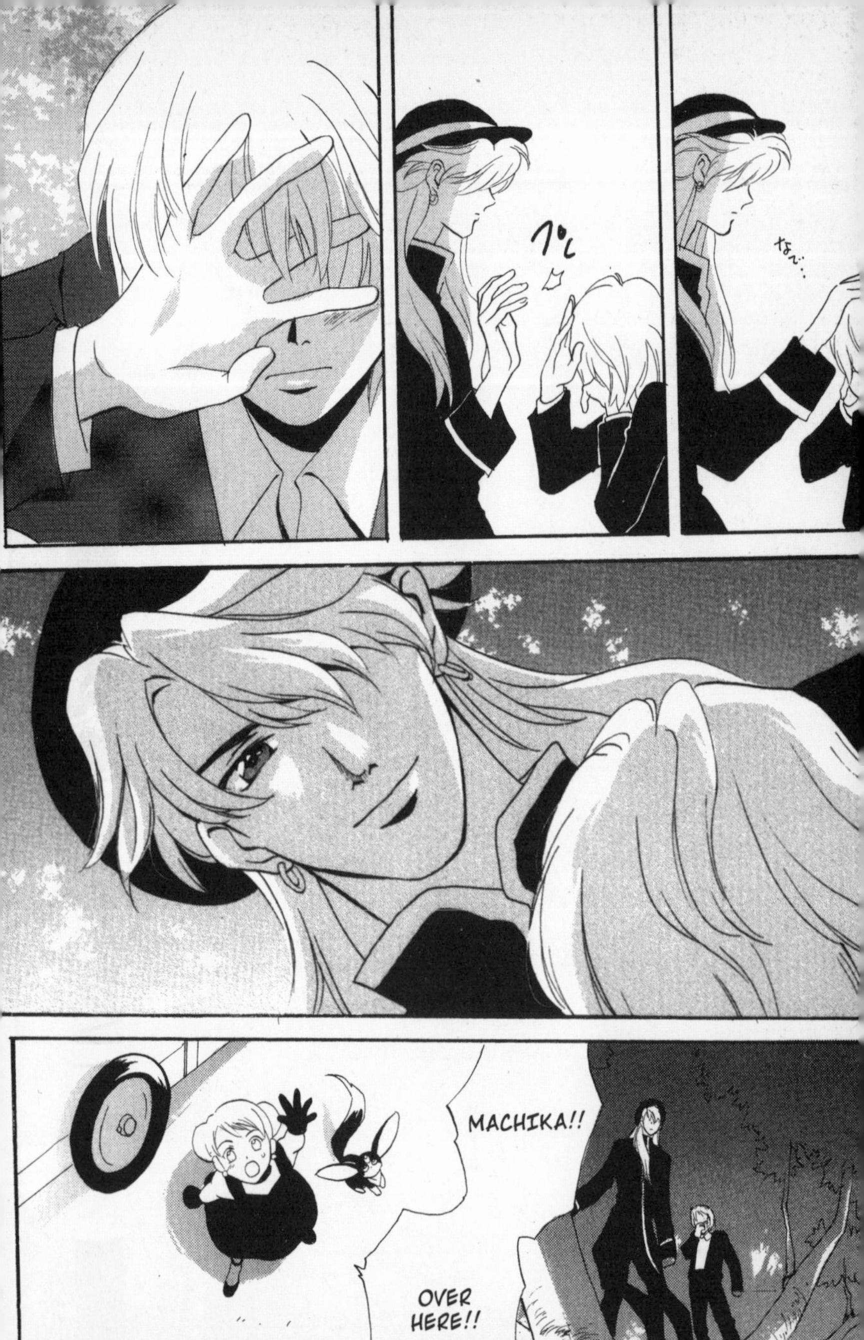
MACHIKA!!
OVER HERE!!

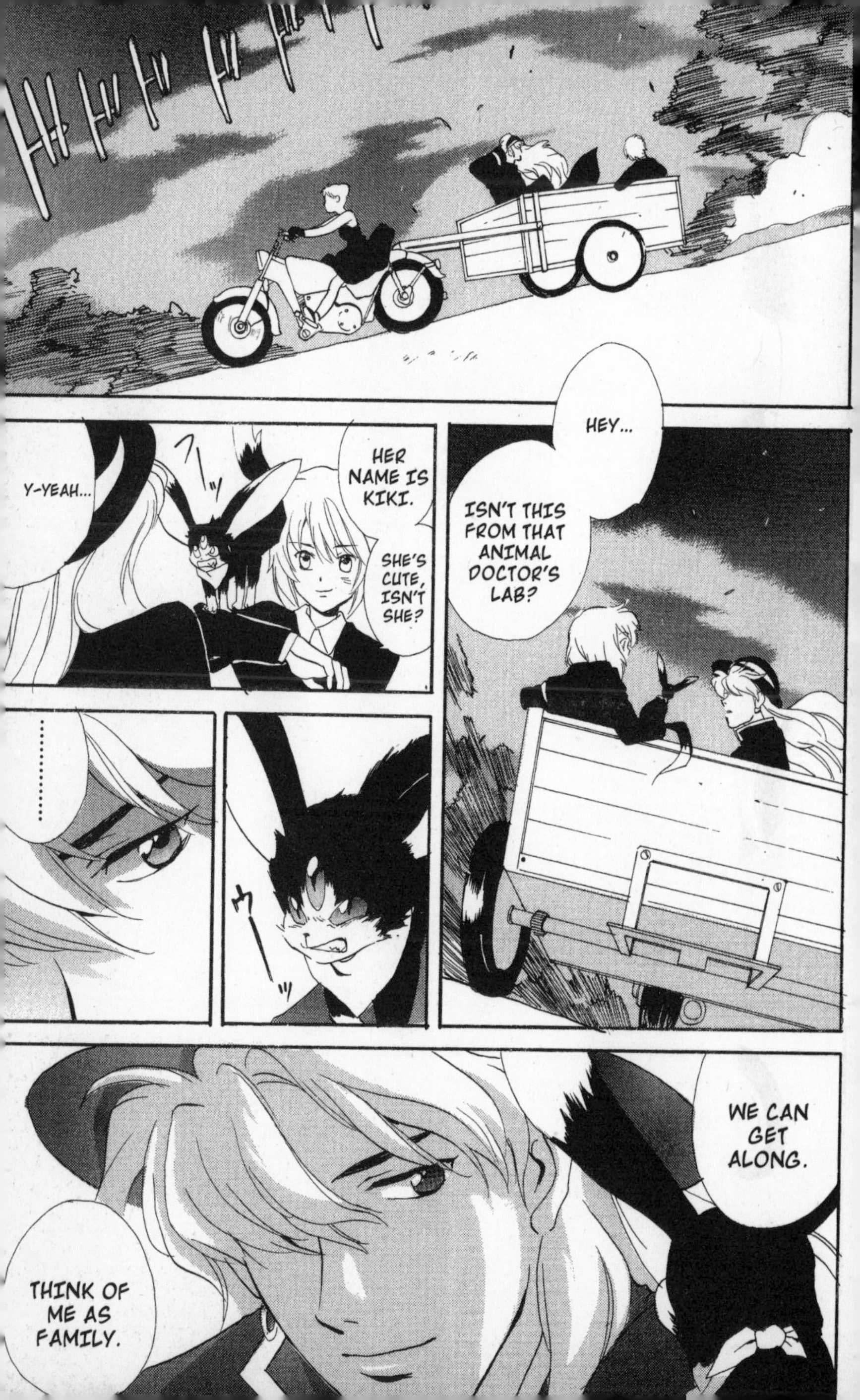
HEY...
ISN'T THIS FROM THAT ANIMAL DOCTOR'S LAB?
HER NAME IS KIKI.
SHE'S CUTE, ISN'T SHE?
Y-YEAH...
......
WE CAN GET ALONG.
THINK OF ME AS FAMILY.

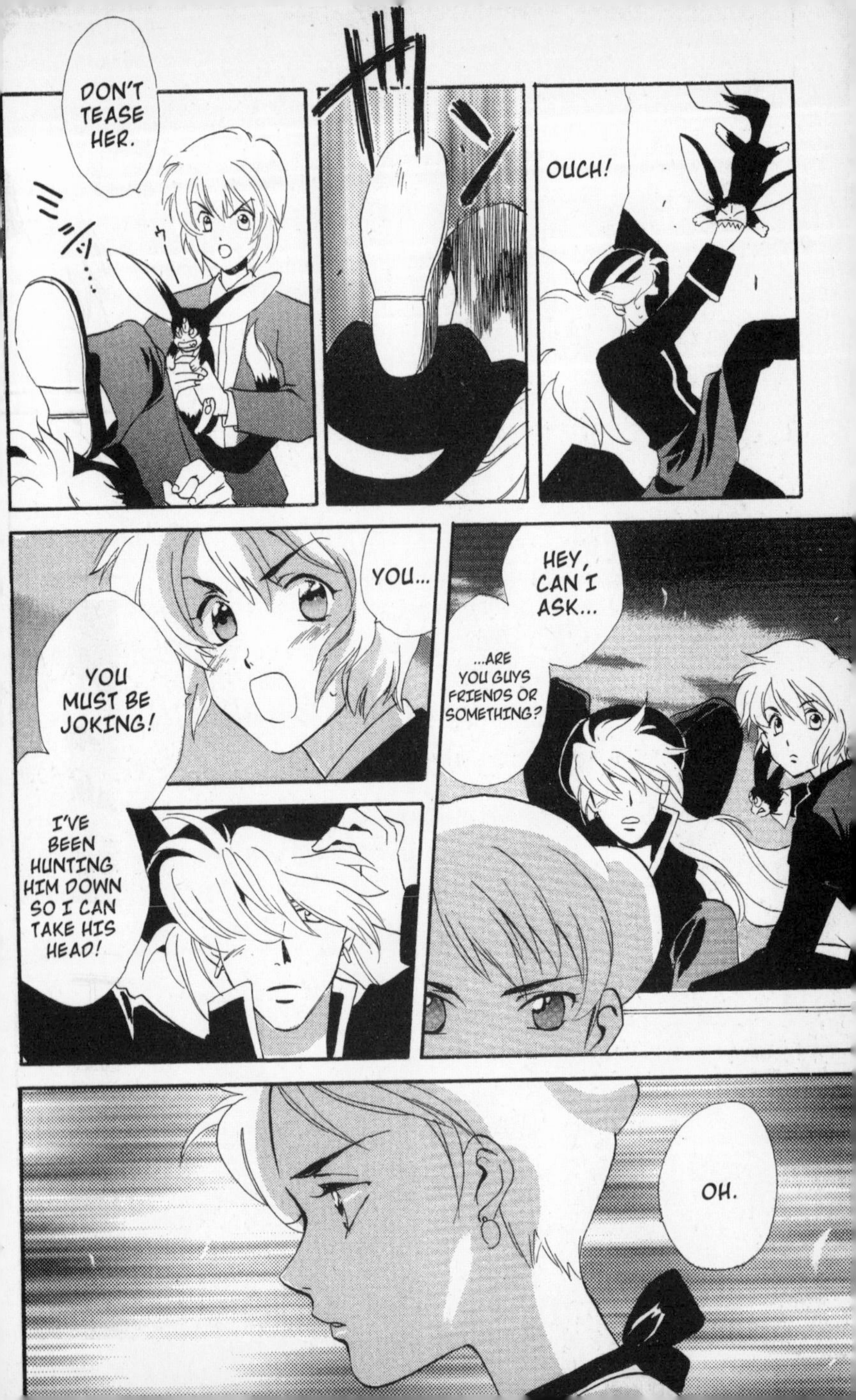
OUCH!
DON'T TEASE HER.
HEY, CAN I ASK...
...ARE YOU GUYS FRIENDS OR SOMETHING?
YOU...
YOU MUST BE JOKING!
I'VE BEEN HUNTING HIM DOWN SO I CAN TAKE HIS HEAD!
OH.

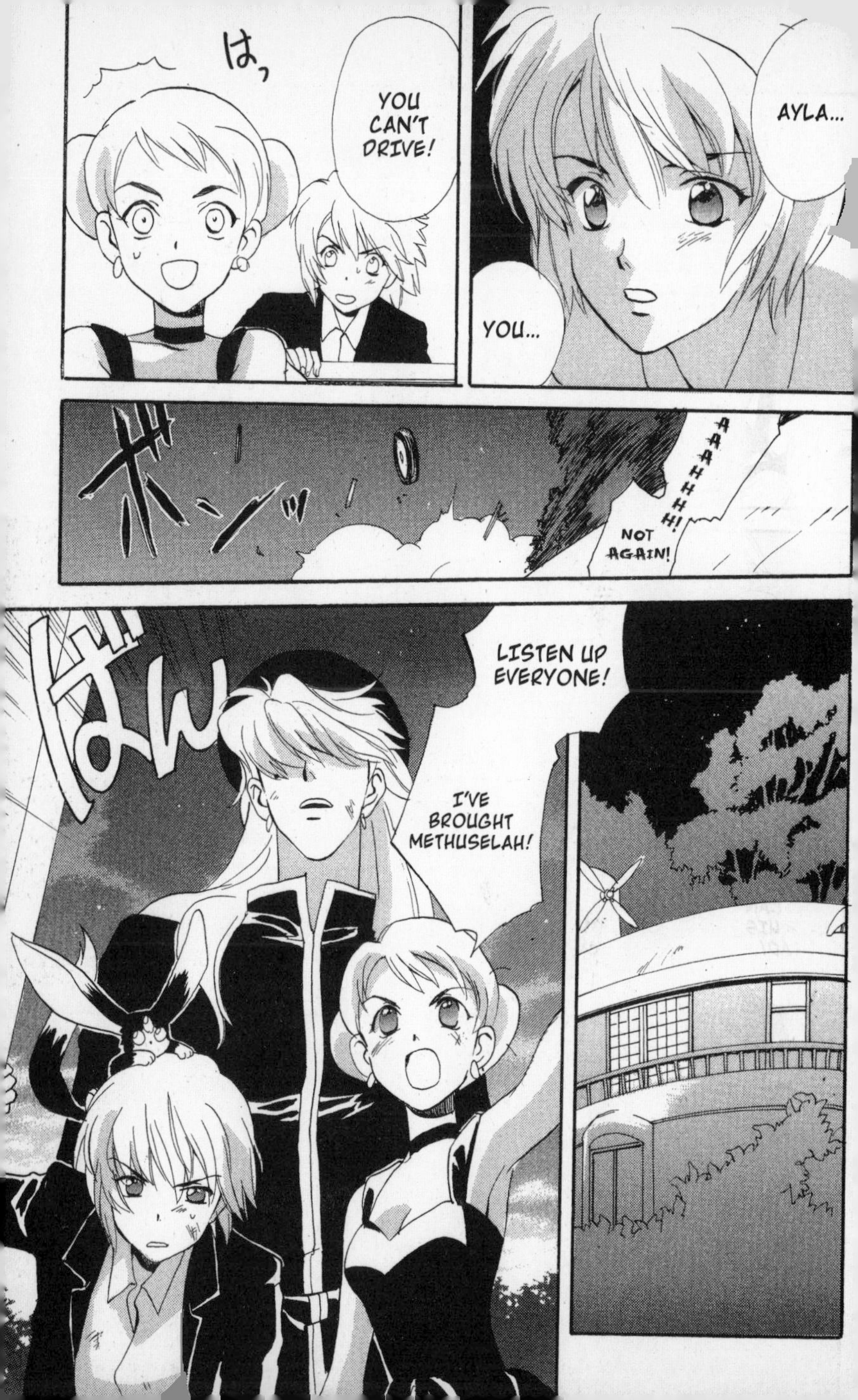
AYLA...
YOU...
YOU CAN'T DRIVE!
はっ
AAAAHHHHHH!
NOT AGAIN!
ボンッ
LISTEN UP EVERYONE!
I'VE BROUGHT METHUSELAH!
ばん

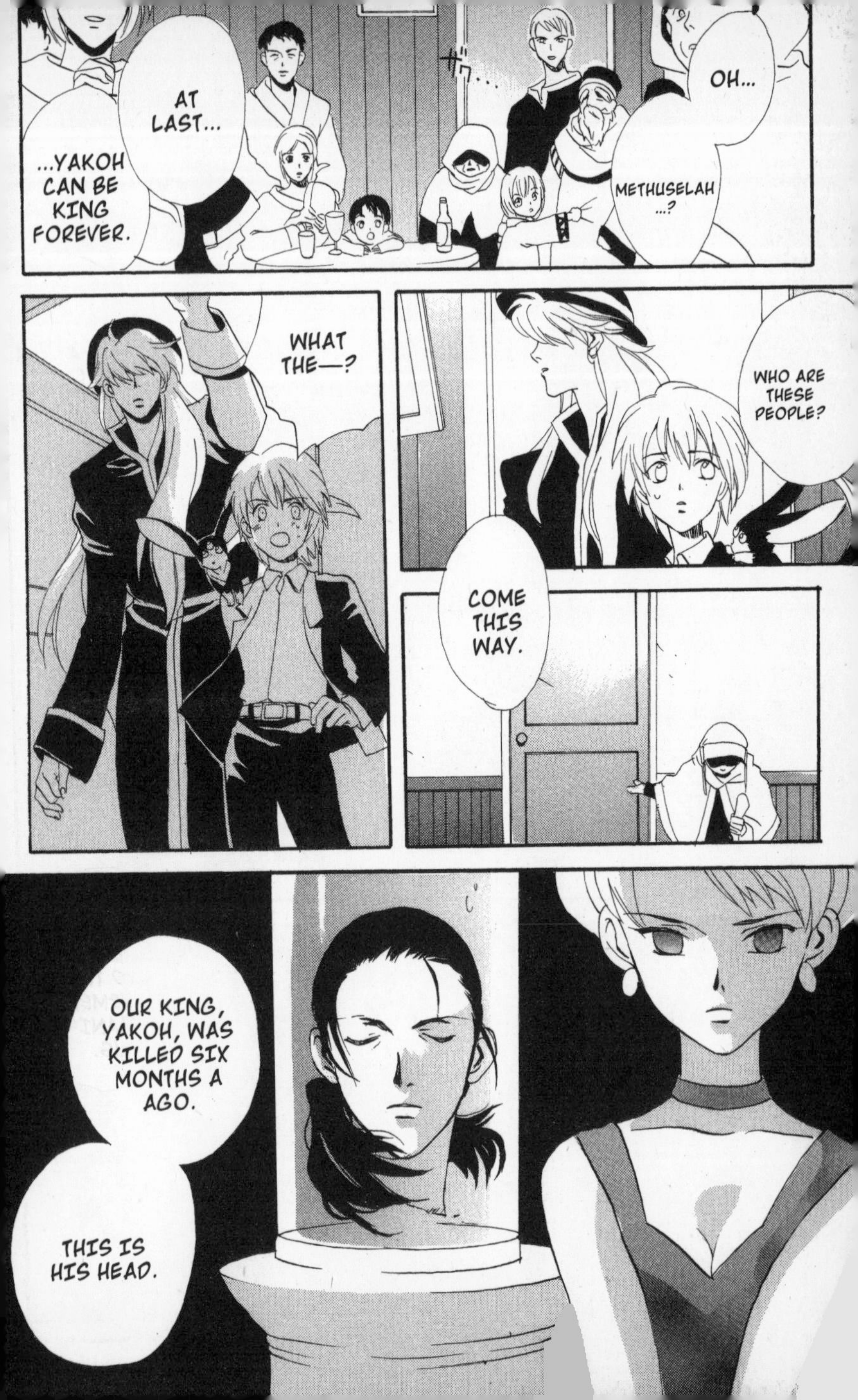
OH...
METHUSELAH...?
AT LAST...
...YAKOH CAN BE KING FOREVER.
WHO ARE THESE PEOPLE?
COME THIS WAY.
WHAT THE—?
OUR KING, YAKOH, WAS KILLED SIX MONTHS A AGO.
THIS IS HIS HEAD.

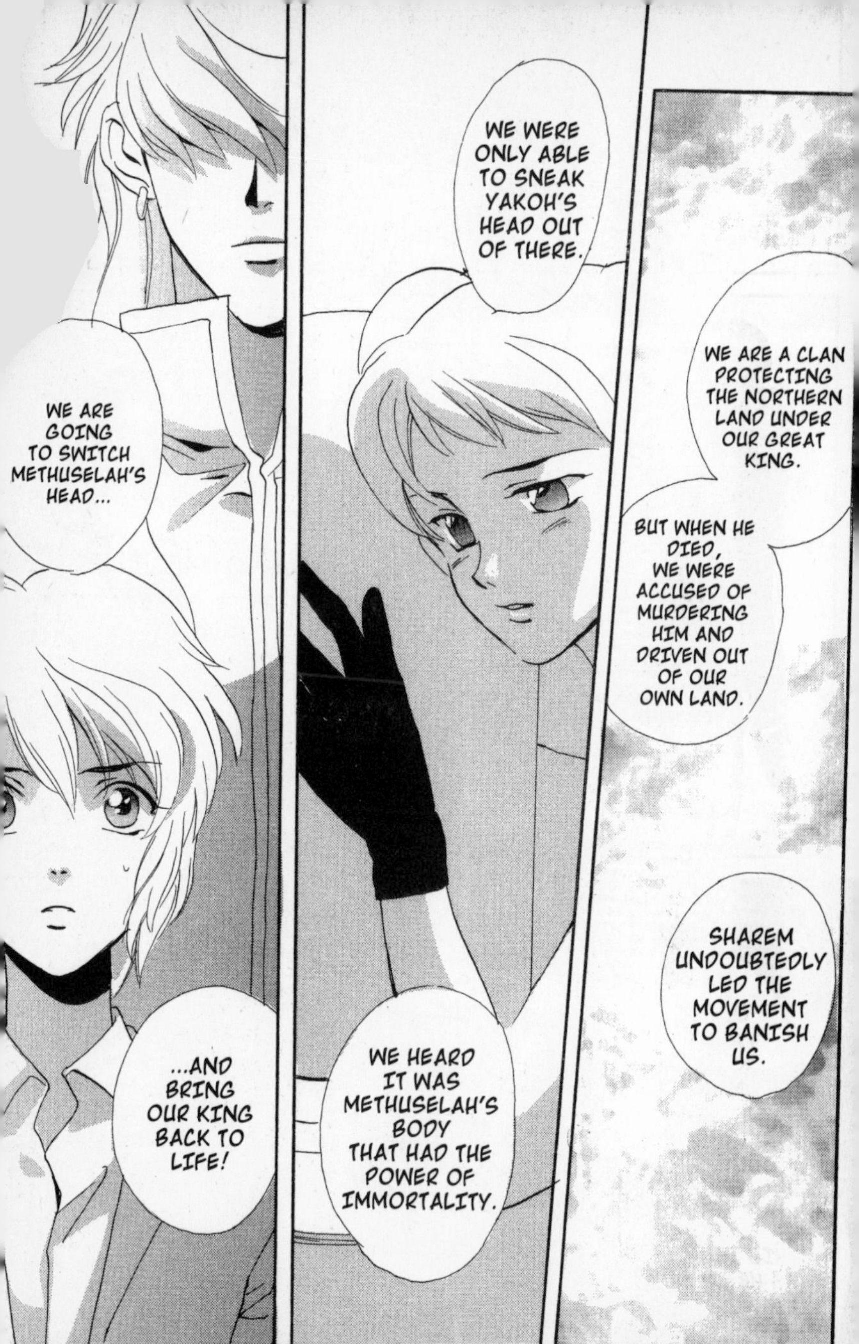
WE ARE A CLAN PROTECTING THE NORTHERN LAND UNDER OUR GREAT KING.
BUT WHEN HE DIED, WE WERE ACCUSED OF MURDERING HIM AND DRIVEN OUT OF OUR OWN LAND.
SHAREM UNDOUBTEDLY LED THE MOVEMENT TO BANISH US.
WE WERE ONLY ABLE TO SNEAK YAKOH'S HEAD OUT OF THERE.
WE HEARD IT WAS METHUSELAH'S BODY THAT HAD THE POWER OF IMMORTALITY.
WE ARE GOING TO SWITCH METHUSELAH'S HEAD...
...AND BRING OUR KING BACK TO LIFE!

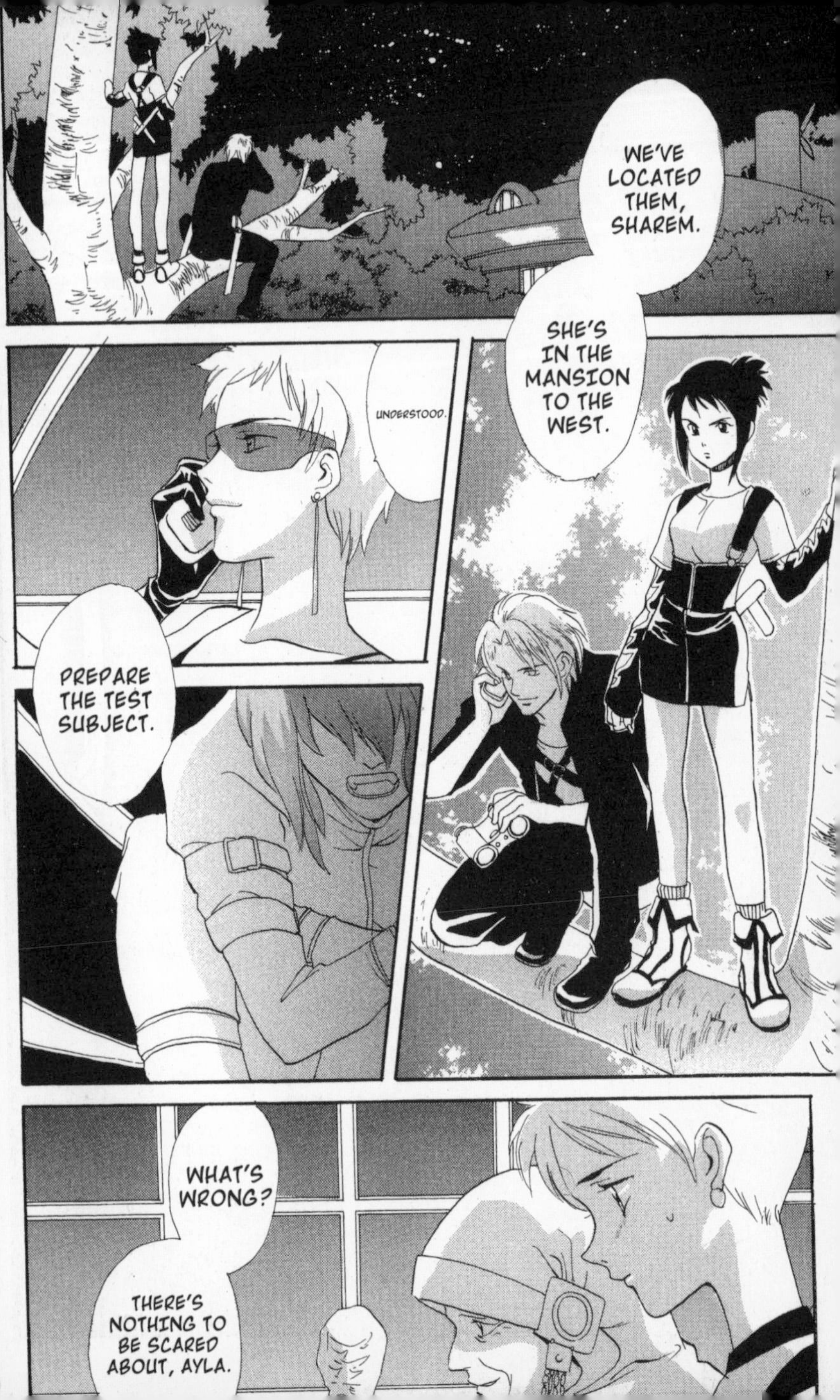
WE'VE LOCATED THEM, SHAREM.
SHE'S IN THE MANSION TO THE WEST.
UNDERSTOOD.
PREPARE THE TEST SUBJECT.
WHAT'S WRONG?
THERE'S NOTHING TO BE SCARED ABOUT, AYLA.

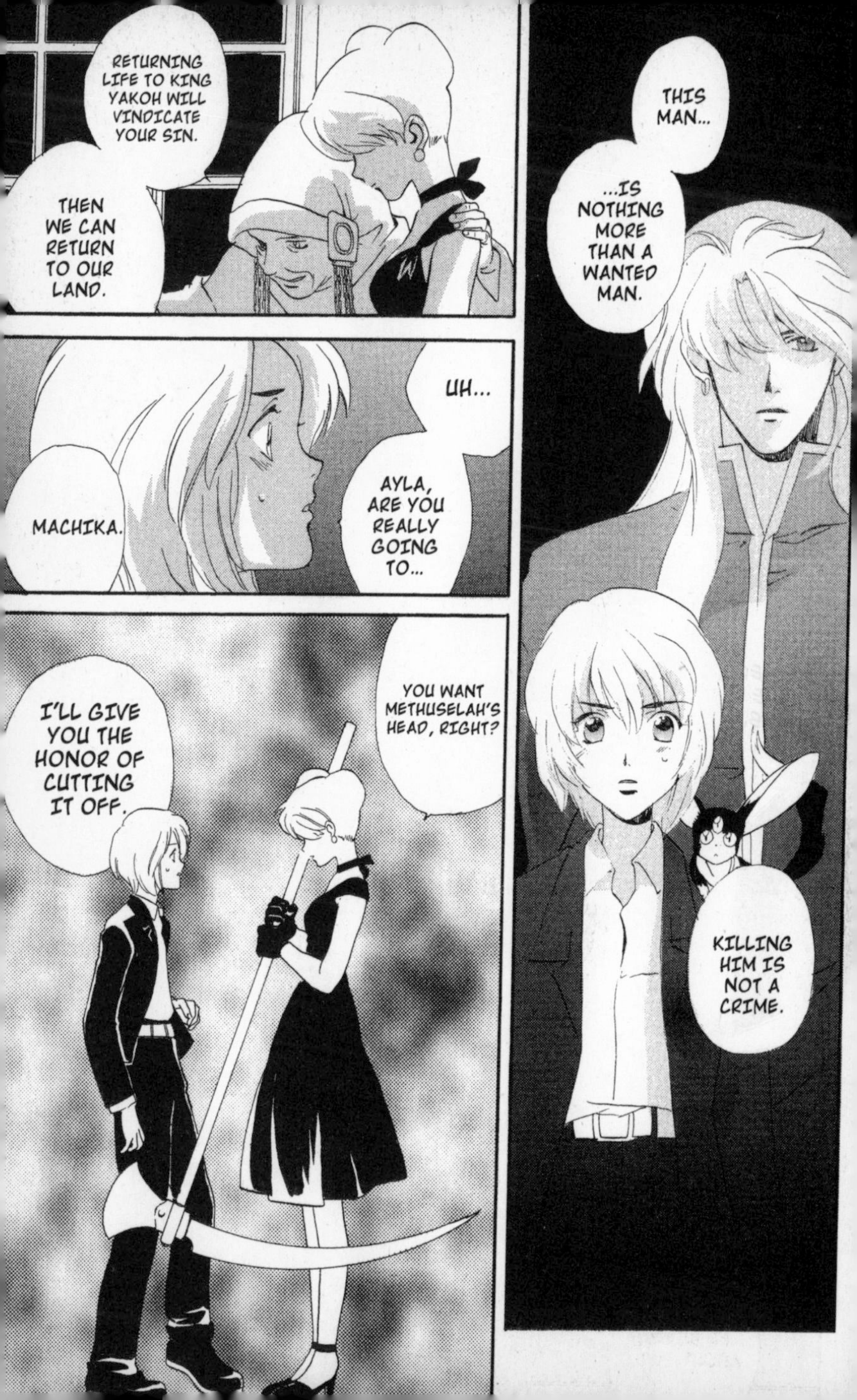
THIS MAN...
...IS NOTHING MORE THAN A WANTED MAN.
KILLING HIM IS NOT A CRIME.
RETURNING LIFE TO KING YAKOH WILL VINDICATE YOUR SIN.
THEN WE CAN RETURN TO OUR LAND.
UH...
AYLA, ARE YOU REALLY GOING TO...
MACHIKA.
YOU WANT METHUSELAH'S HEAD, RIGHT?
I'LL GIVE YOU THE HONOR OF CUTTING IT OFF.

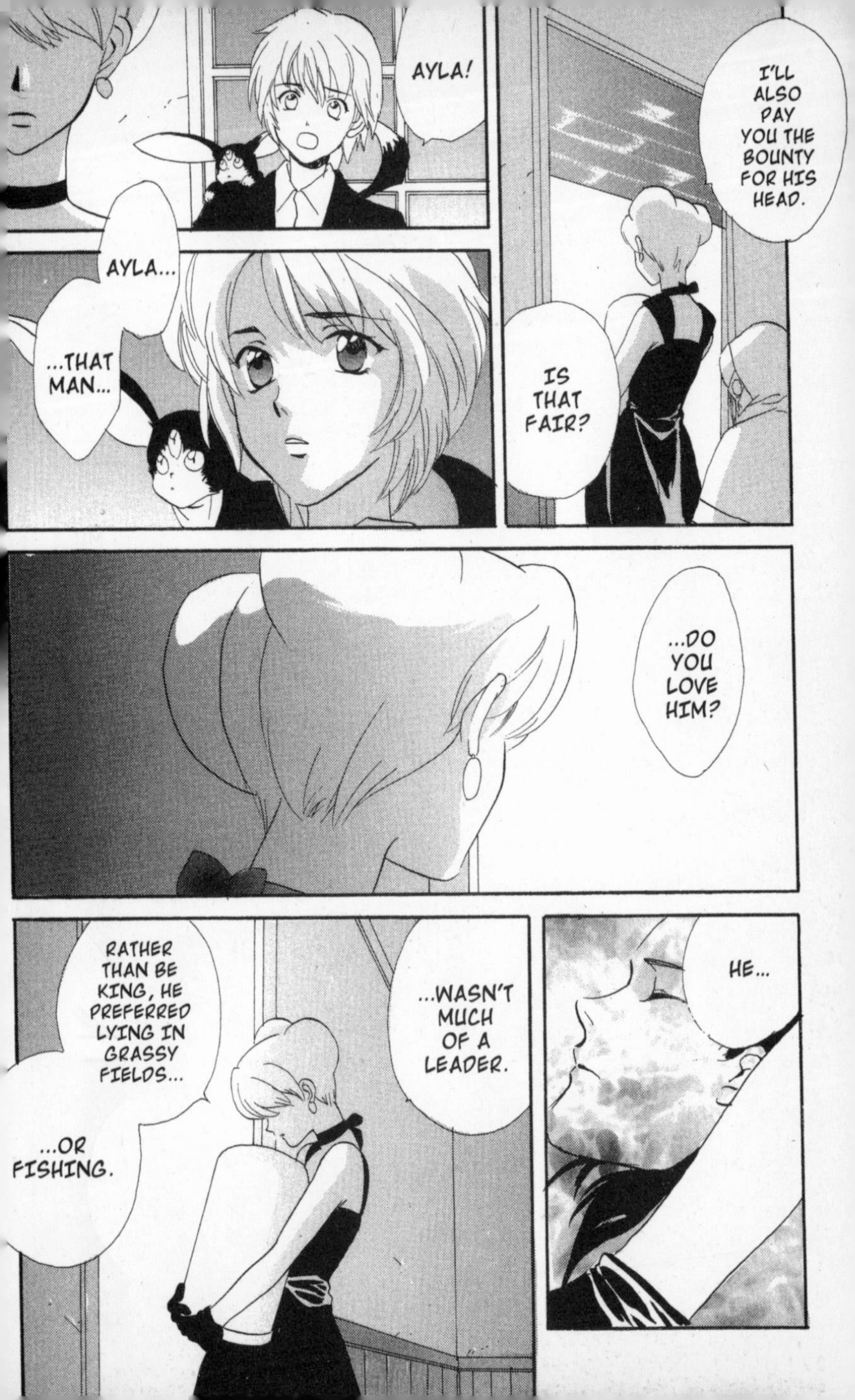
I'LL ALSO PAY YOU THE BOUNTY FOR HIS HEAD.
IS THAT FAIR?
AYLA!
AYLA...
...THAT MAN...
...DO YOU LOVE HIM?
HE...
...WASN'T MUCH OF A LEADER.
RATHER THAN BE KING, HE PREFERRED LYING IN GRASSY FIELDS...
...OR FISHING.

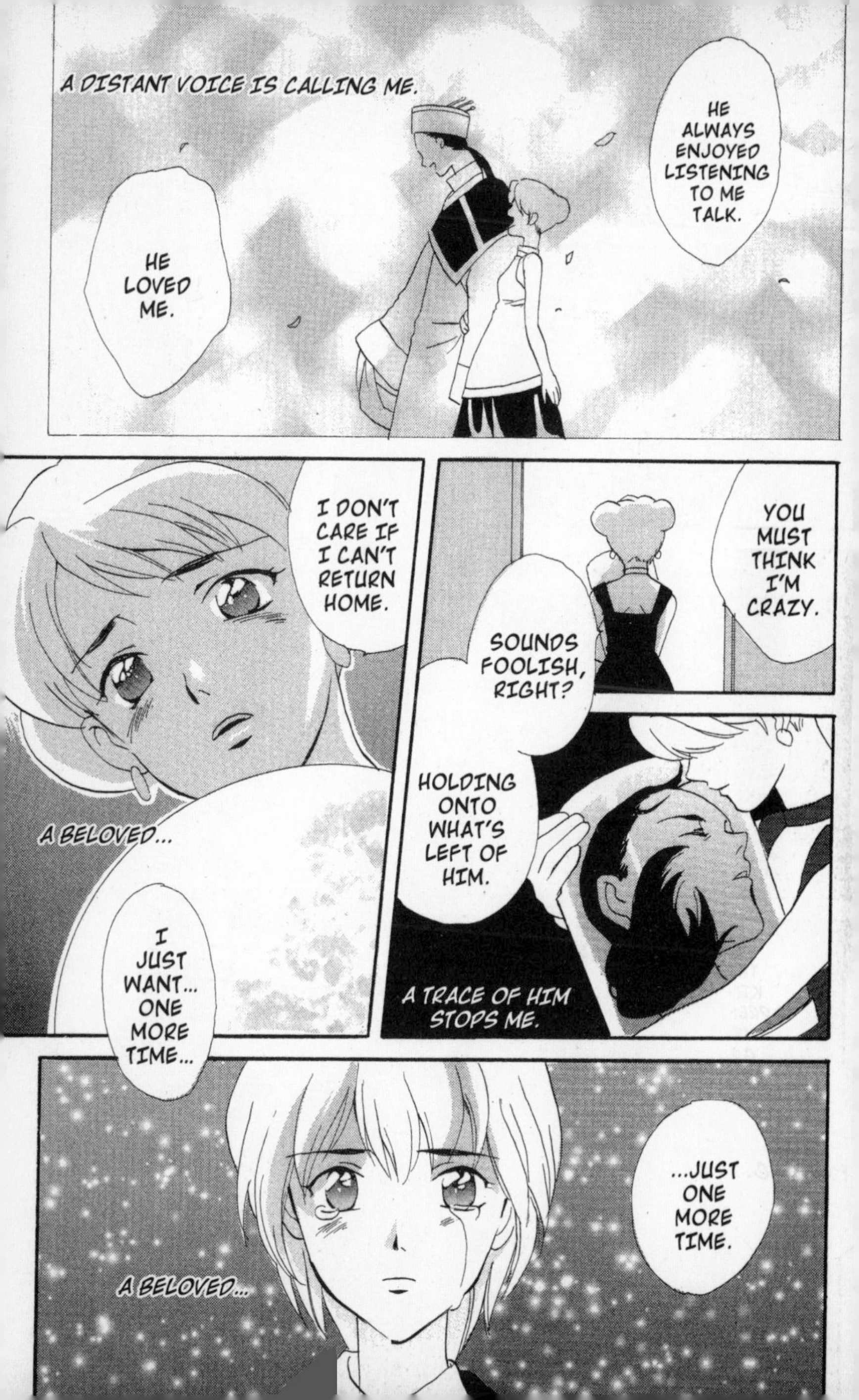
HE ALWAYS ENJOYED LISTENING TO ME TALK.
A DISTANT VOICE IS CALLING ME.
HE LOVED ME.
YOU MUST THINK I'M CRAZY.
SOUNDS FOOLISH, RIGHT?
HOLDING ONTO WHAT'S LEFT OF HIM.
A TRACE OF HIM STOPS ME.
I DON'T CARE IF I CAN'T RETURN HOME.
A BELOVED...
I JUST WANT... ONE MORE TIME...
...JUST ONE MORE TIME.
A BELOVED...

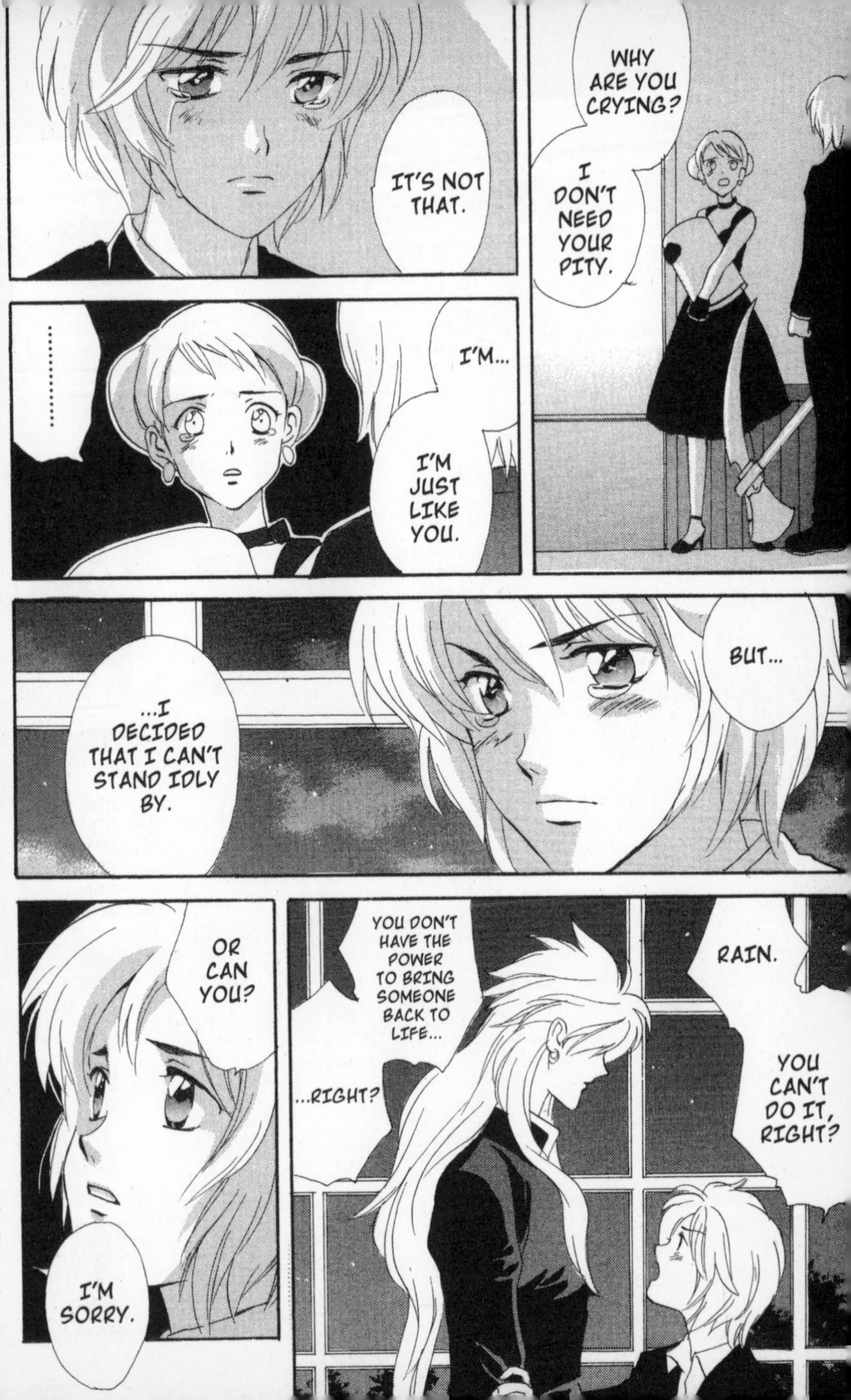
WHY ARE YOU CRYING?
I DON'T NEED YOUR PITY.
IT'S NOT THAT.
....
I'M...
I'M JUST LIKE YOU.
BUT...
...I DECIDED THAT I CAN'T STAND IDLY BY.
RAIN.
YOU DON'T HAVE THE POWER TO BRING SOMEONE BACK TO LIFE...
YOU CAN'T DO IT, RIGHT?
...RIGHT?
OR CAN YOU?
I'M SORRY.

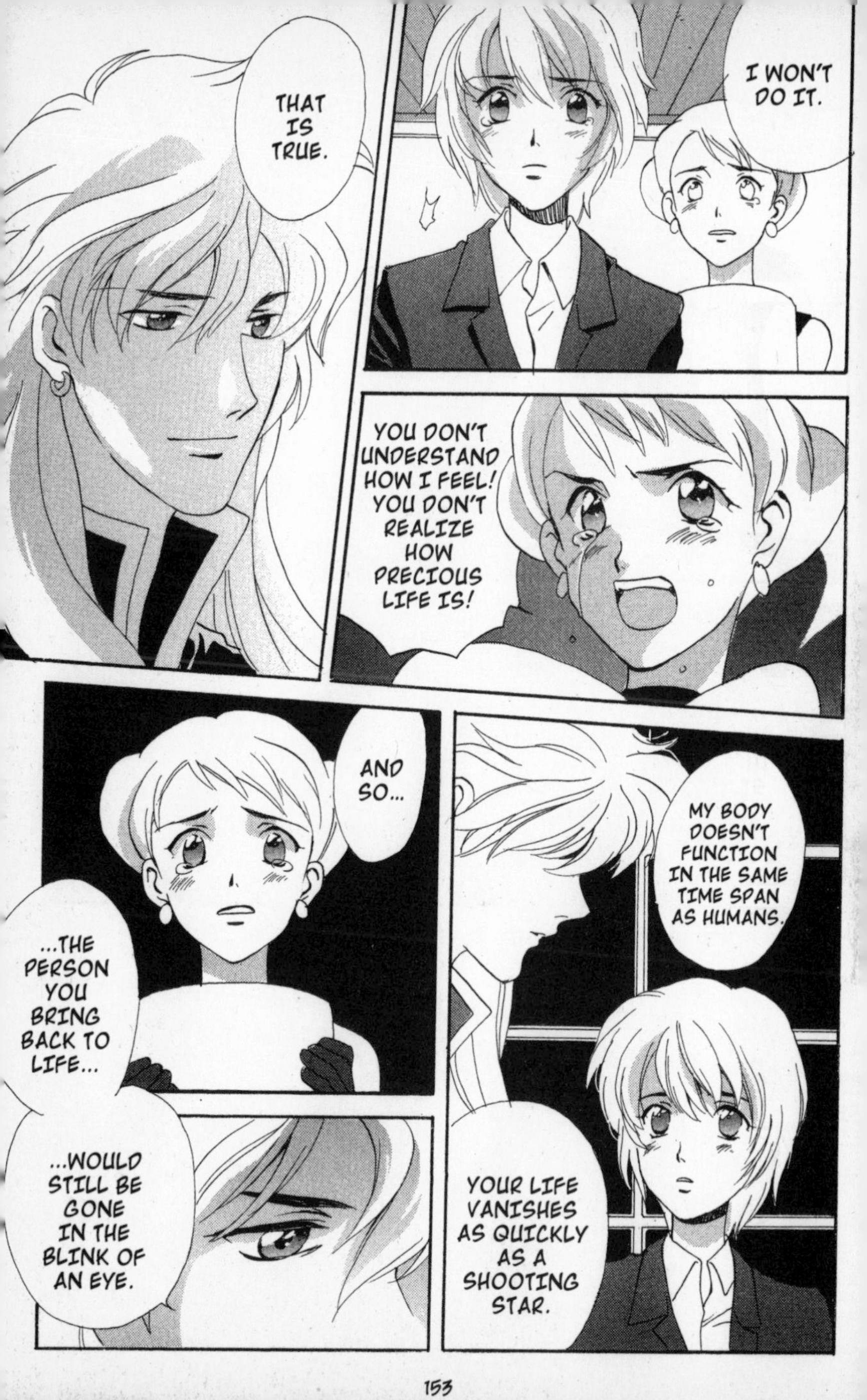
I WON'T DO IT.
YOU DON'T UNDERSTAND HOW I FEEL! YOU DON'T REALIZE HOW PRECIOUS LIFE IS!
THAT IS TRUE.
MY BODY DOESN'T FUNCTION IN THE SAME TIME SPAN AS HUMANS.
YOUR LIFE VANISHES AS QUICKLY AS A SHOOTING STAR.
AND SO...
...THE PERSON YOU BRING BACK TO LIFE...
...WOULD STILL BE GONE IN THE BLINK OF AN EYE.

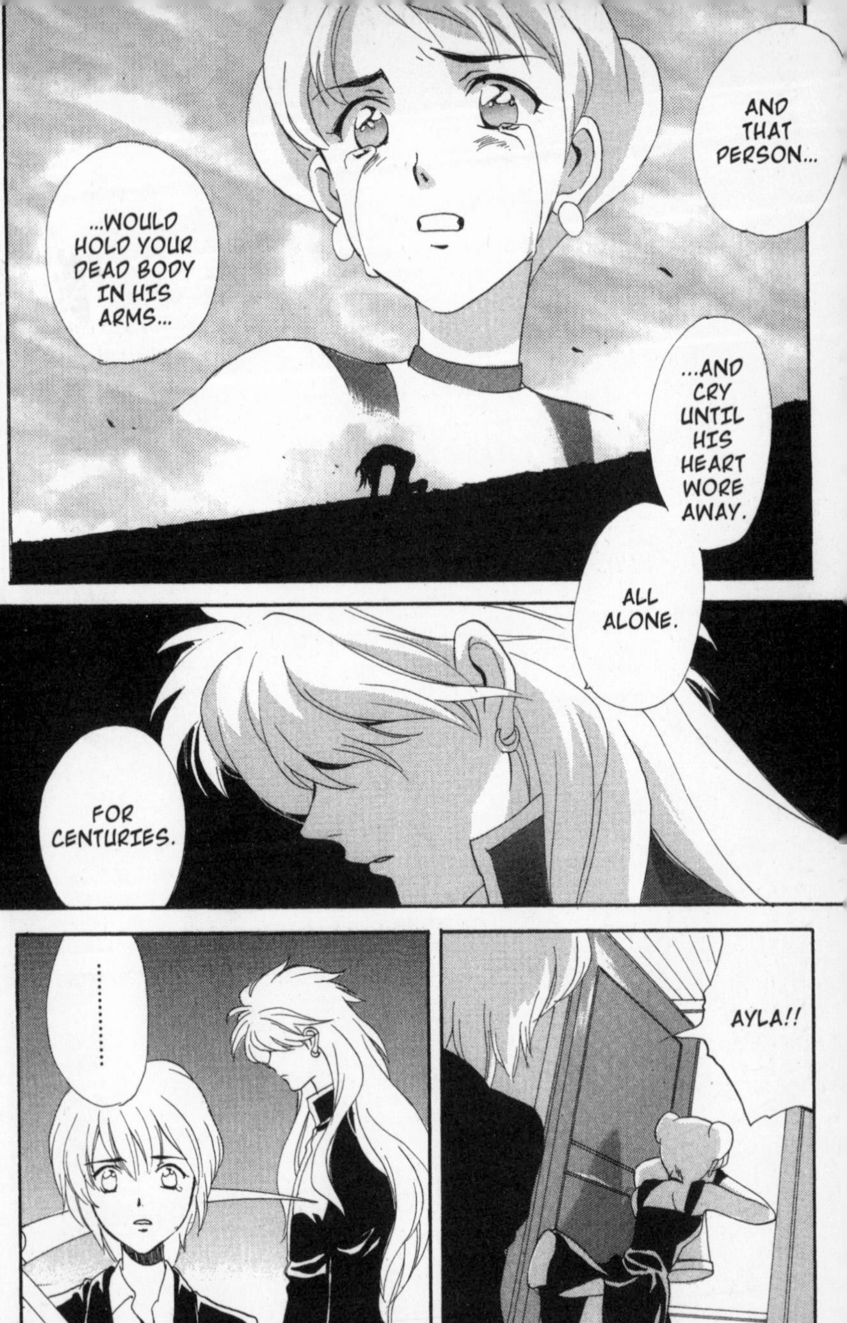
AND THAT PERSON...
...WOULD HOLD YOUR DEAD BODY IN HIS ARMS...
...AND CRY UNTIL HIS HEART WORE AWAY.
ALL ALONE.
FOR CENTURIES.
AYLA!!
....

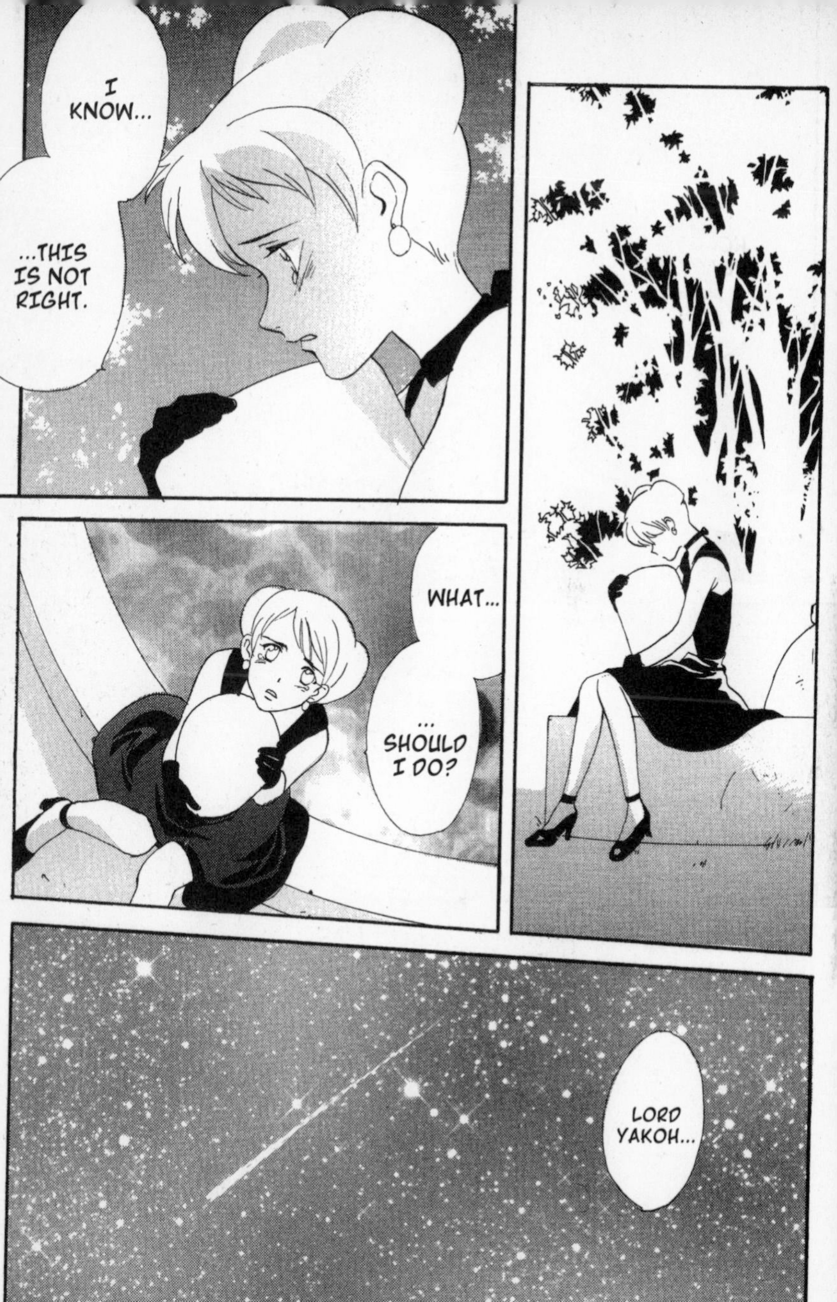
I KNOW...
...THIS IS NOT RIGHT.
WHAT...
...SHOULD I DO?
LORD YAKOH...

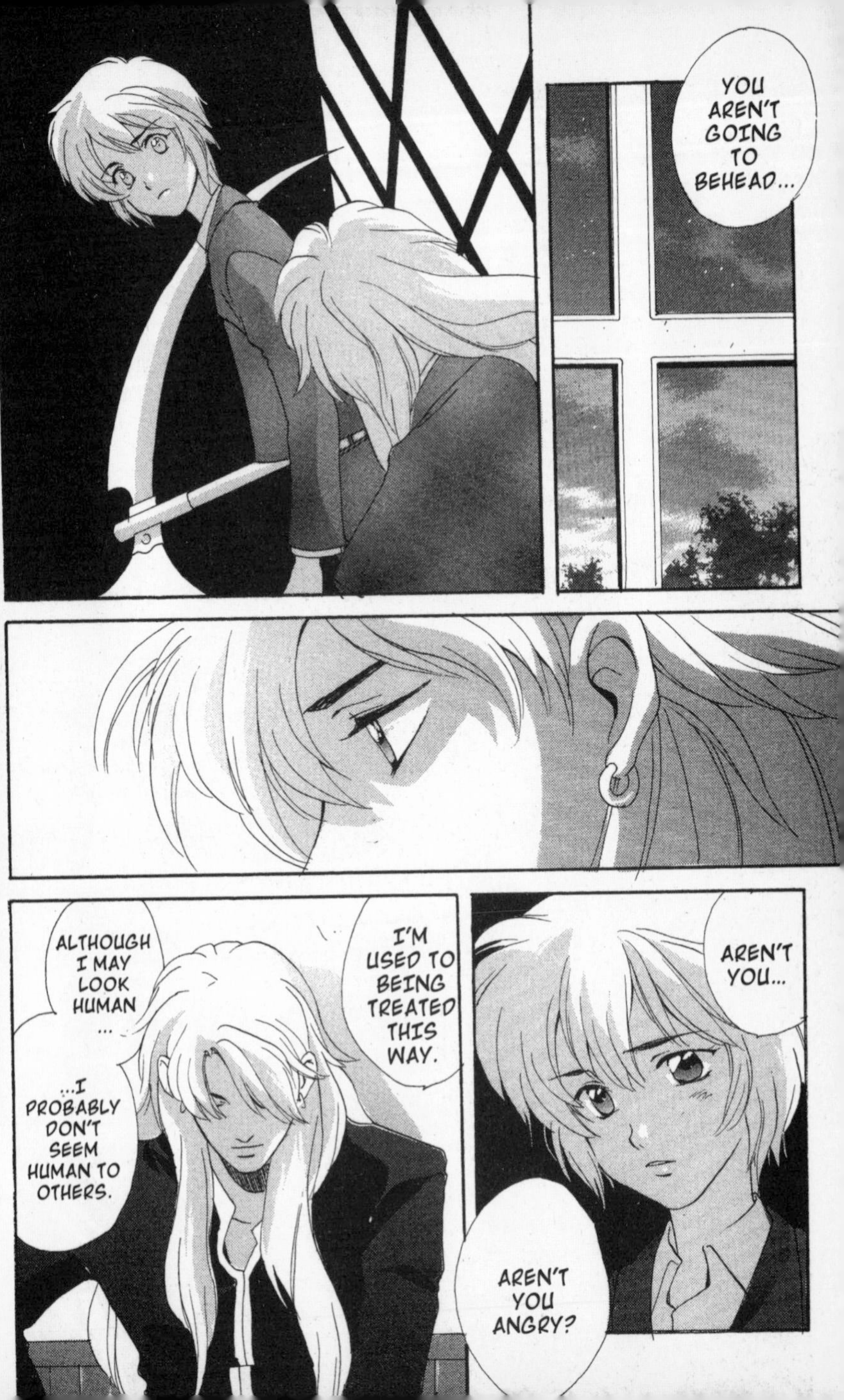
YOU AREN'T GOING TO BEHEAD...
AREN'T YOU...
AREN'T YOU ANGRY?
I'M USED TO BEING TREATED THIS WAY.
ALTHOUGH I MAY LOOK HUMAN ...
...I PROBABLY DON'T SEEM HUMAN TO OTHERS.

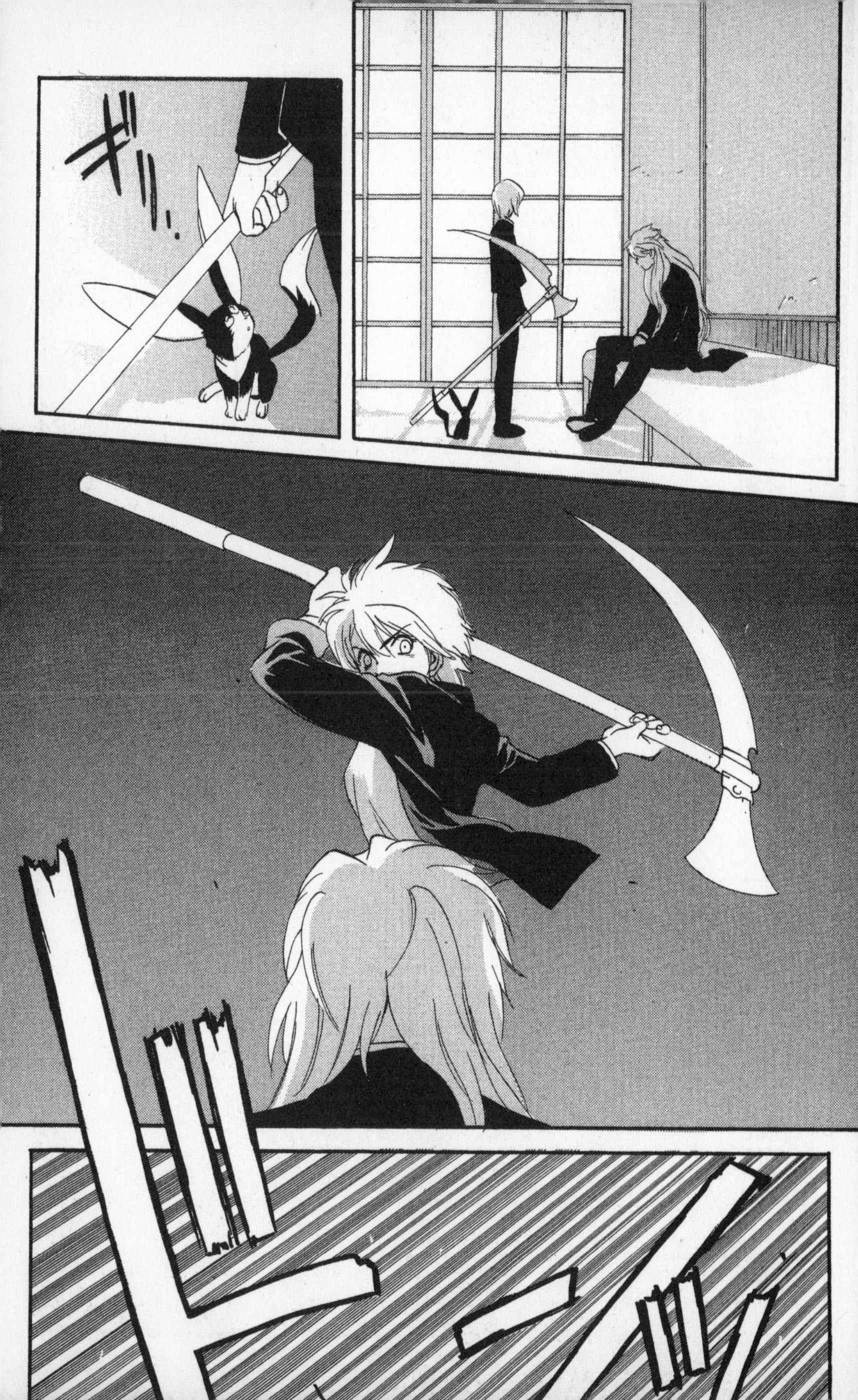
ギリ..

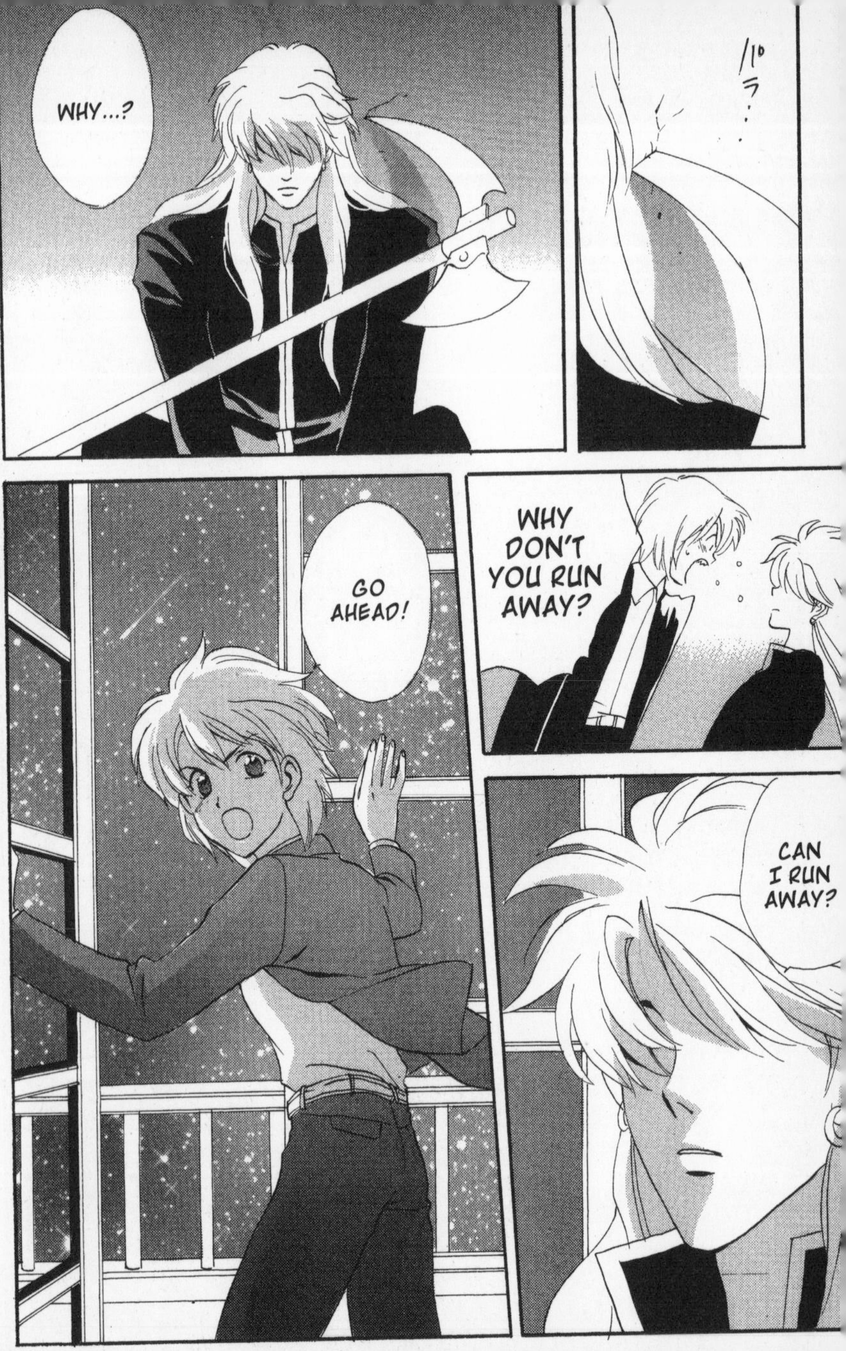
パラ・・・
WHY...?
WHY DON'T YOU RUN AWAY?
CAN I RUN AWAY?
GO AHEAD!

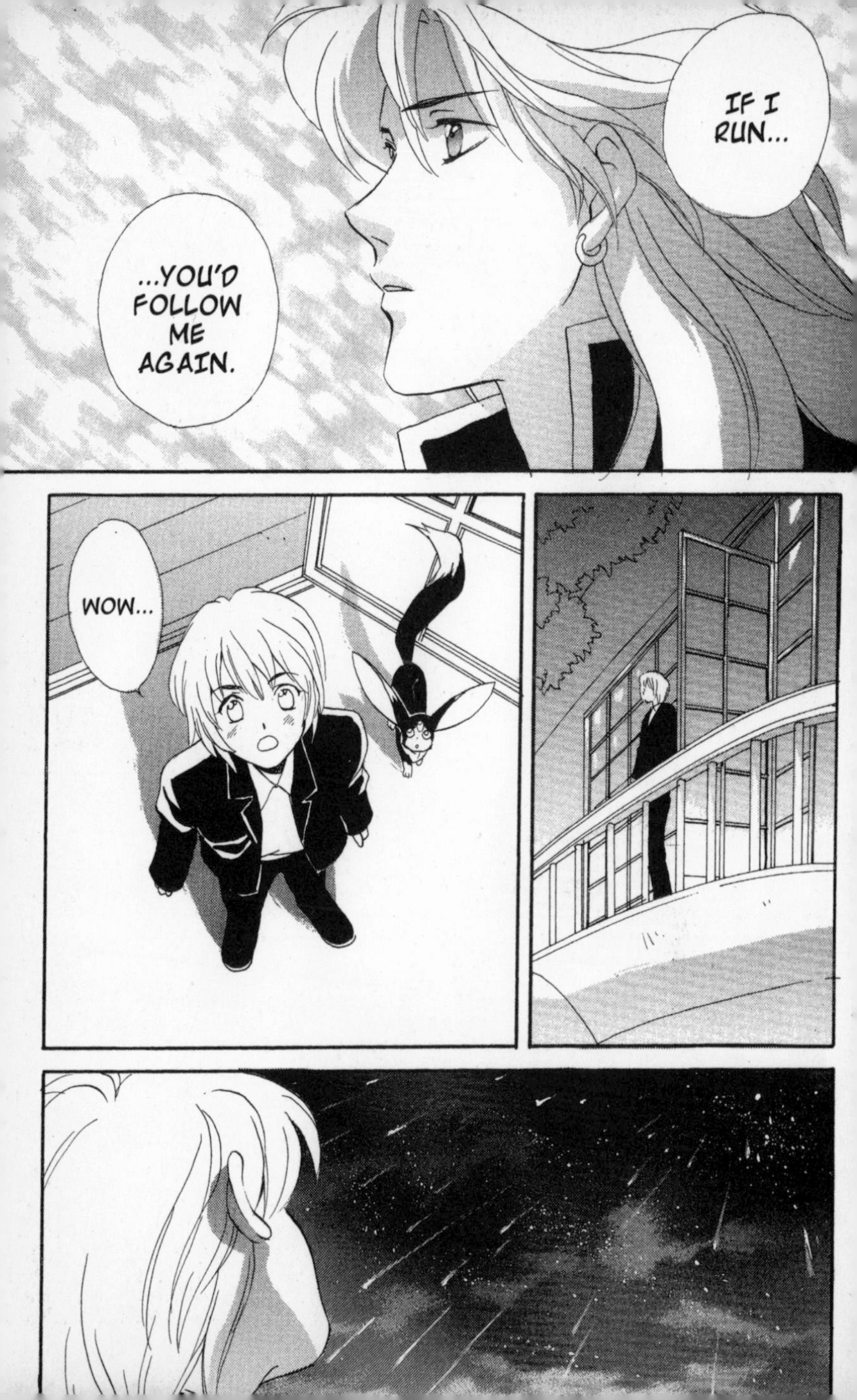
IF I RUN...
...YOU'D FOLLOW ME AGAIN.
WOW...

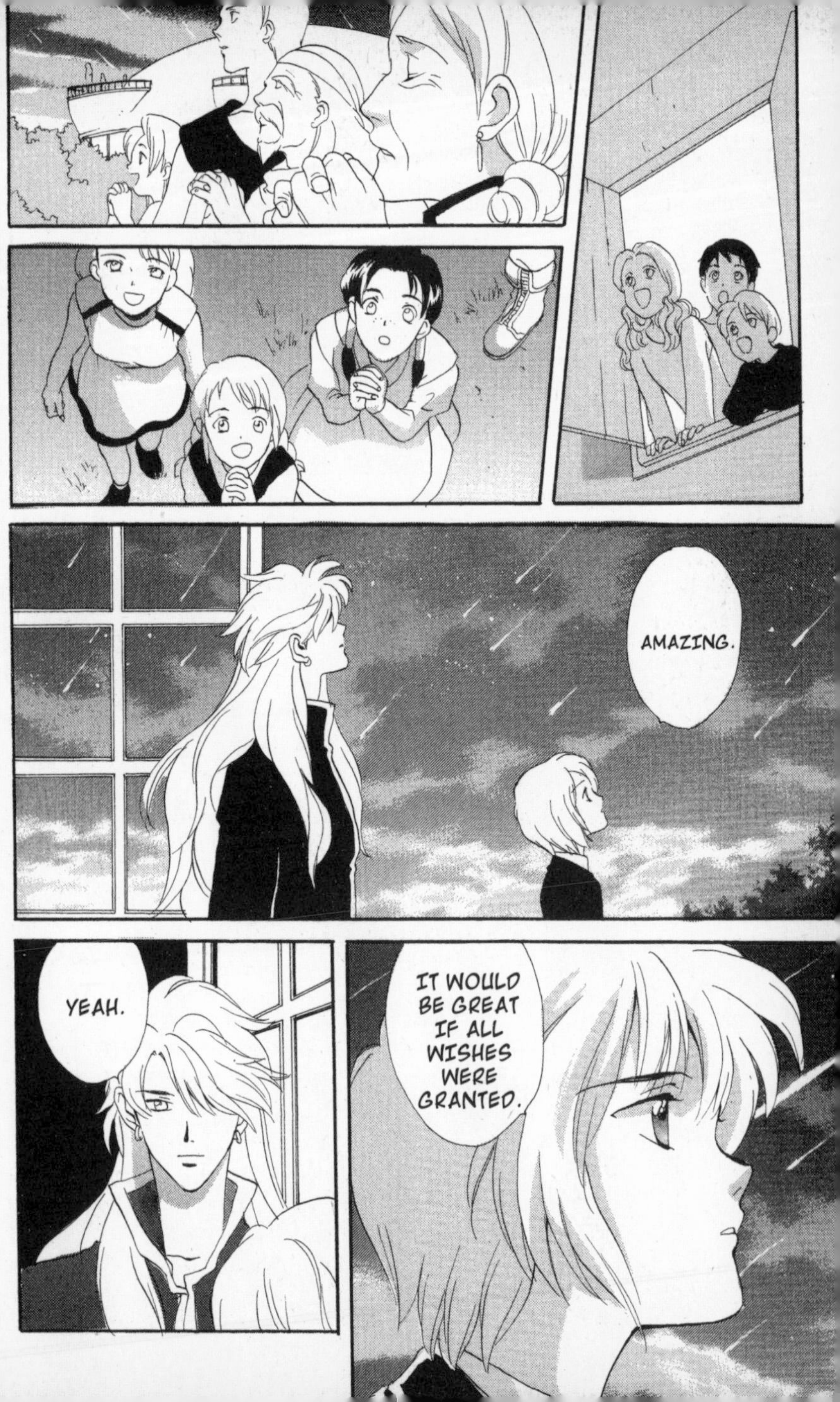
AMAZING.
IT WOULD BE GREAT IF ALL WISHES WERE GRANTED.
YEAH.

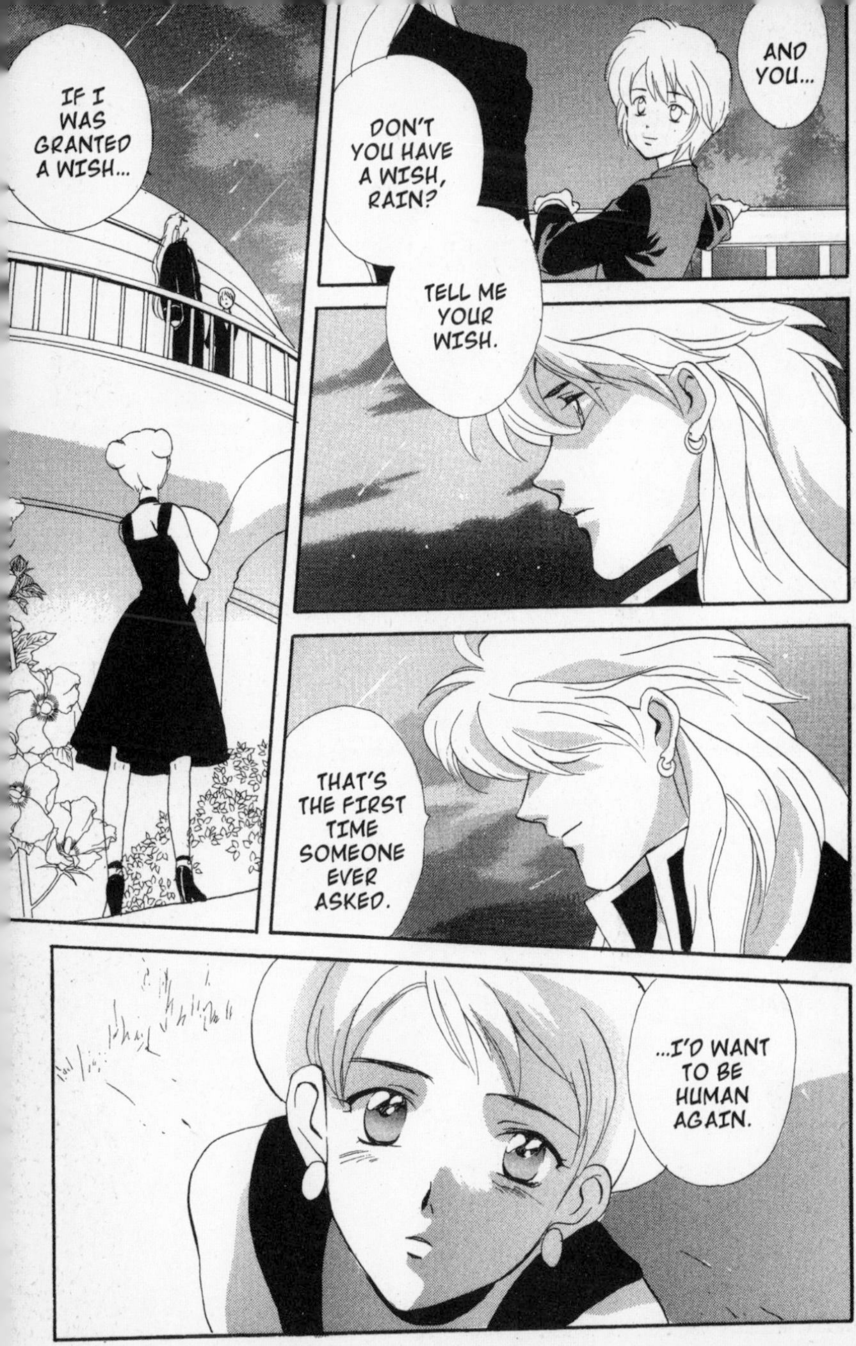
AND YOU...
DON'T YOU HAVE A WISH, RAIN?
TELL ME YOUR WISH.
THAT'S THE FIRST TIME SOMEONE EVER ASKED.
IF I WAS GRANTED A WISH...
...I'D WANT TO BE HUMAN AGAIN.

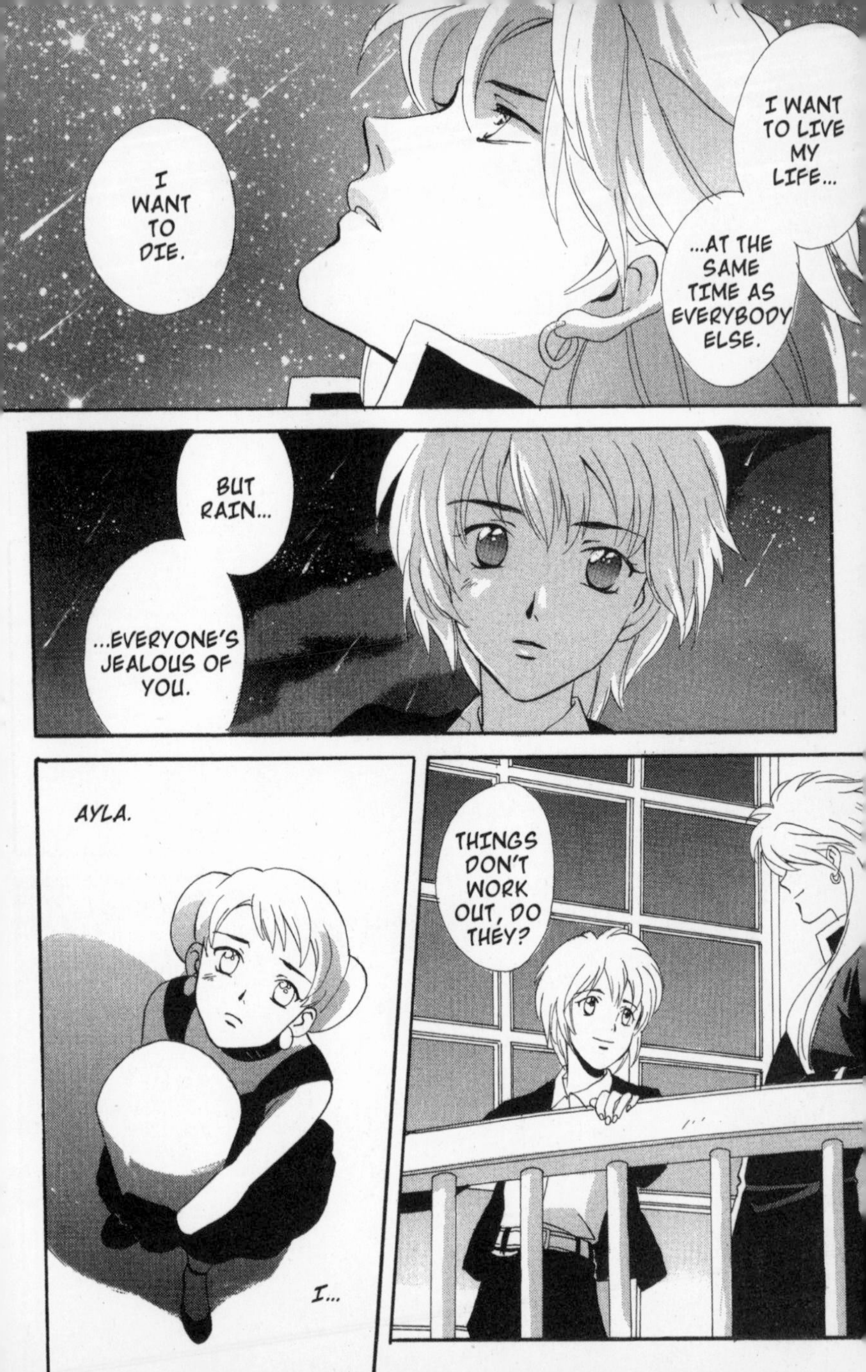
I WANT TO LIVE MY LIFE...
...AT THE SAME TIME AS EVERYBODY ELSE.
I WANT TO DIE.
BUT RAIN...
...EVERYONE'S JEALOUS OF YOU.
THINGS DON'T WORK OUT, DO THEY?
AYLA.
I...

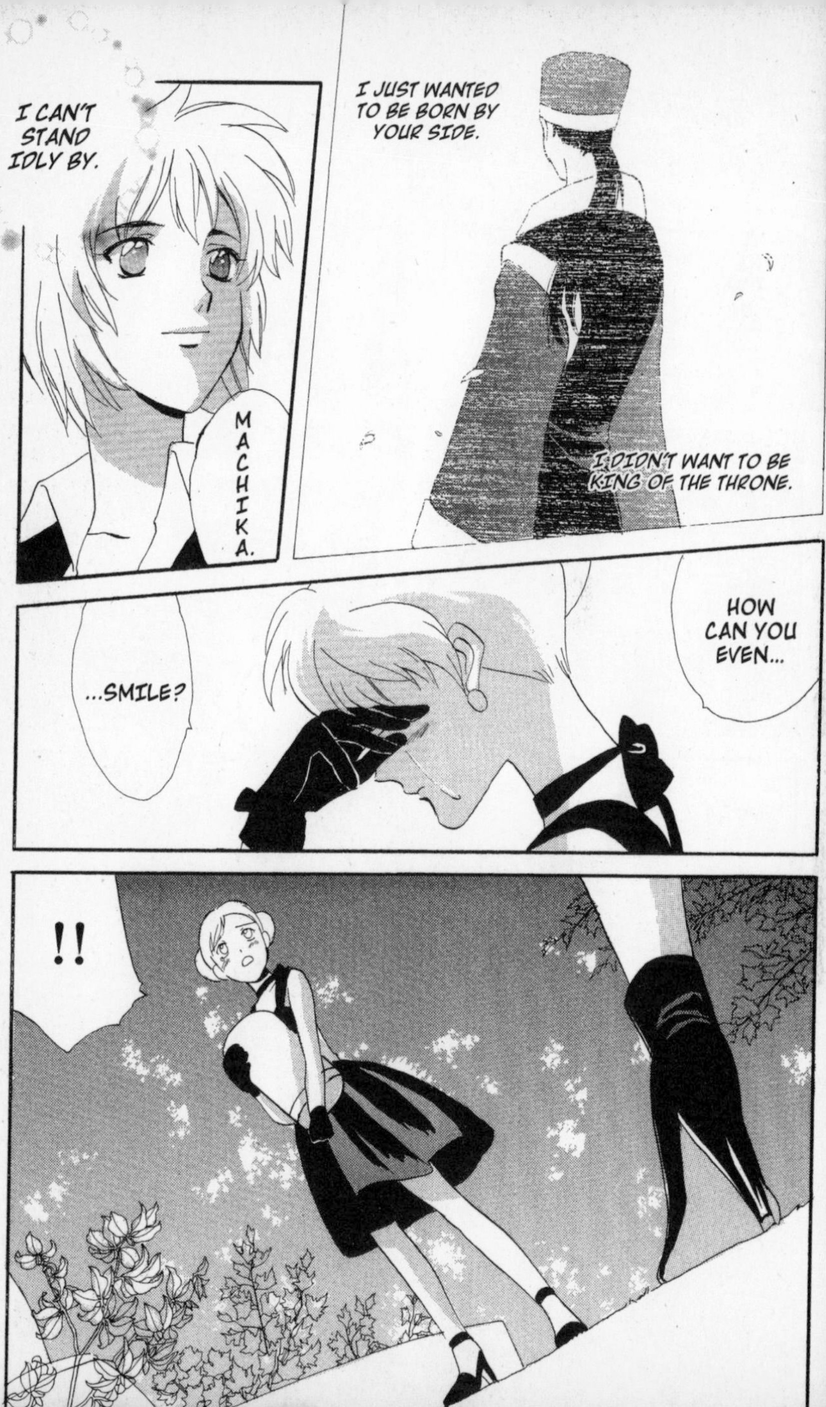

I JUST WANTED TO BE BORN BY YOUR SIDE.
I DIDN'T WANT TO BE KING OF THE THRONE.
I CAN'T STAND IDLY BY.
MACHIKA.
HOW CAN YOU EVEN...
...SMILE?
!!

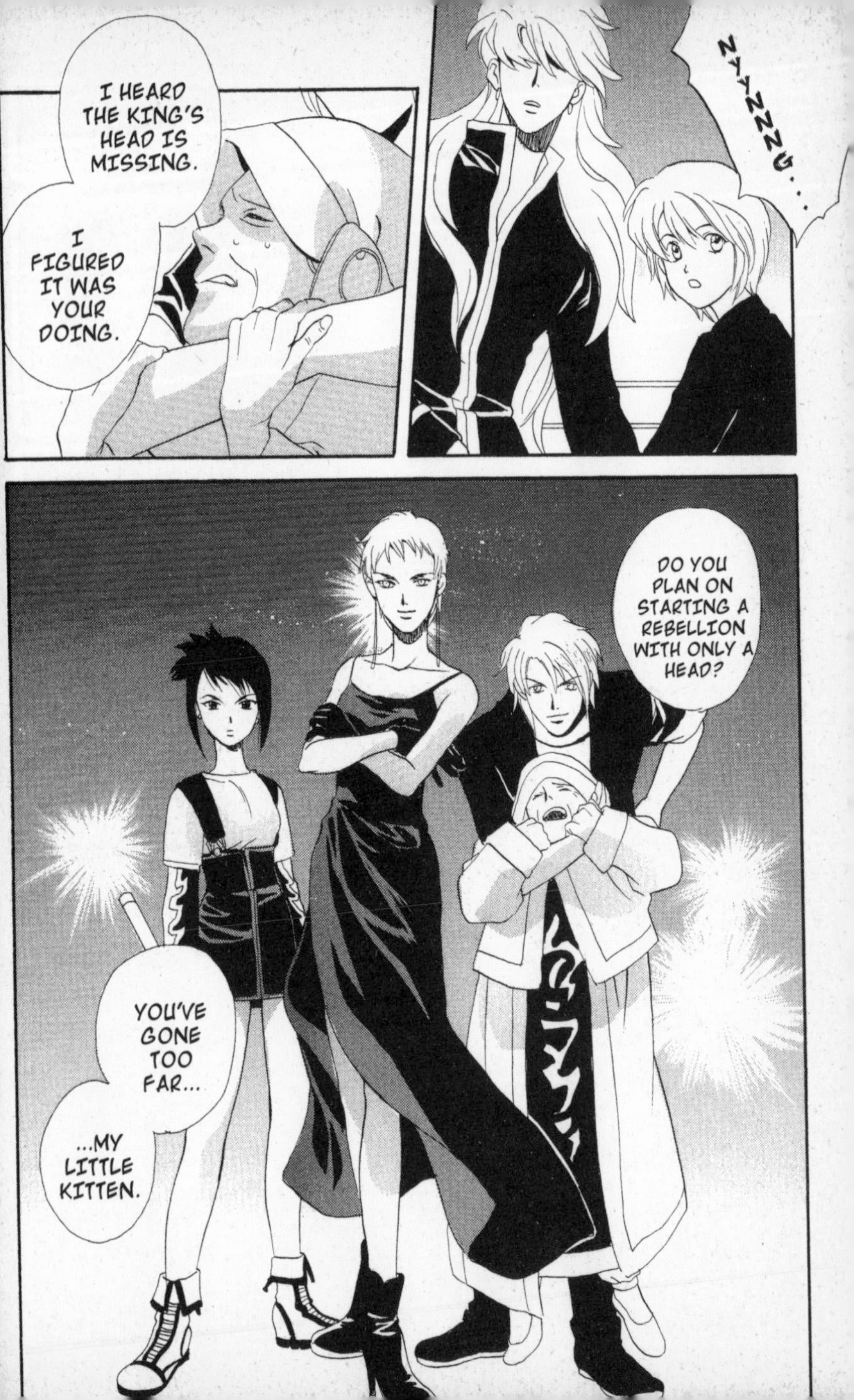
NYYNNNG...
I HEARD THE KING'S HEAD IS MISSING.
I FIGURED IT WAS YOUR DOING.
DO YOU PLAN ON STARTING A REBELLION WITH ONLY A HEAD?
YOU'VE GONE TOO FAR...
...MY LITTLE KITTEN.

SHAREM CORDELAN

AGE : 28
HEIGHT : 172CM
BLOOD TYPE : AB

COMMAND
FIGHT
BRIBERY
DROPPING HINTS

LV: 57
HP: 589/589
OFFENSE
STRENGTH: 71
DEFENSE
STRENGTH: 42
SPEED: 64
WIT: 89
LUCK: 42

EQUIPMENT
WEAPON: SADISTIC PIN HEEL /
        OFFENSIVE STRENGTH + 18
ARMOR: SEXY DRESS /
        DEFENSE STRENGTH - 2 (confuses opponent)
ACCESSORY: LEATHER GLOVES /
        QUEEN-NESS + 8

DEATHBLOW TECHNIQUE COMMAND

STOMP (when opponent is down)   ⬇Ⓚ

BAD-ASS MOTHER   Ⓟ+Ⓚ+Ⓖ

REGAL   ⓅⓅⓅⓀⓀ

USING THE REACH OF HER BEAUTIFUL LEGS, SHE WILL ATTACK
FROM MIDDLE OR LONG RANGE. I BETTER BE CAREFUL, IF I GIVE
TOO MANY HINTS TO THE READER, SHE'S GOING TO KILL ME.

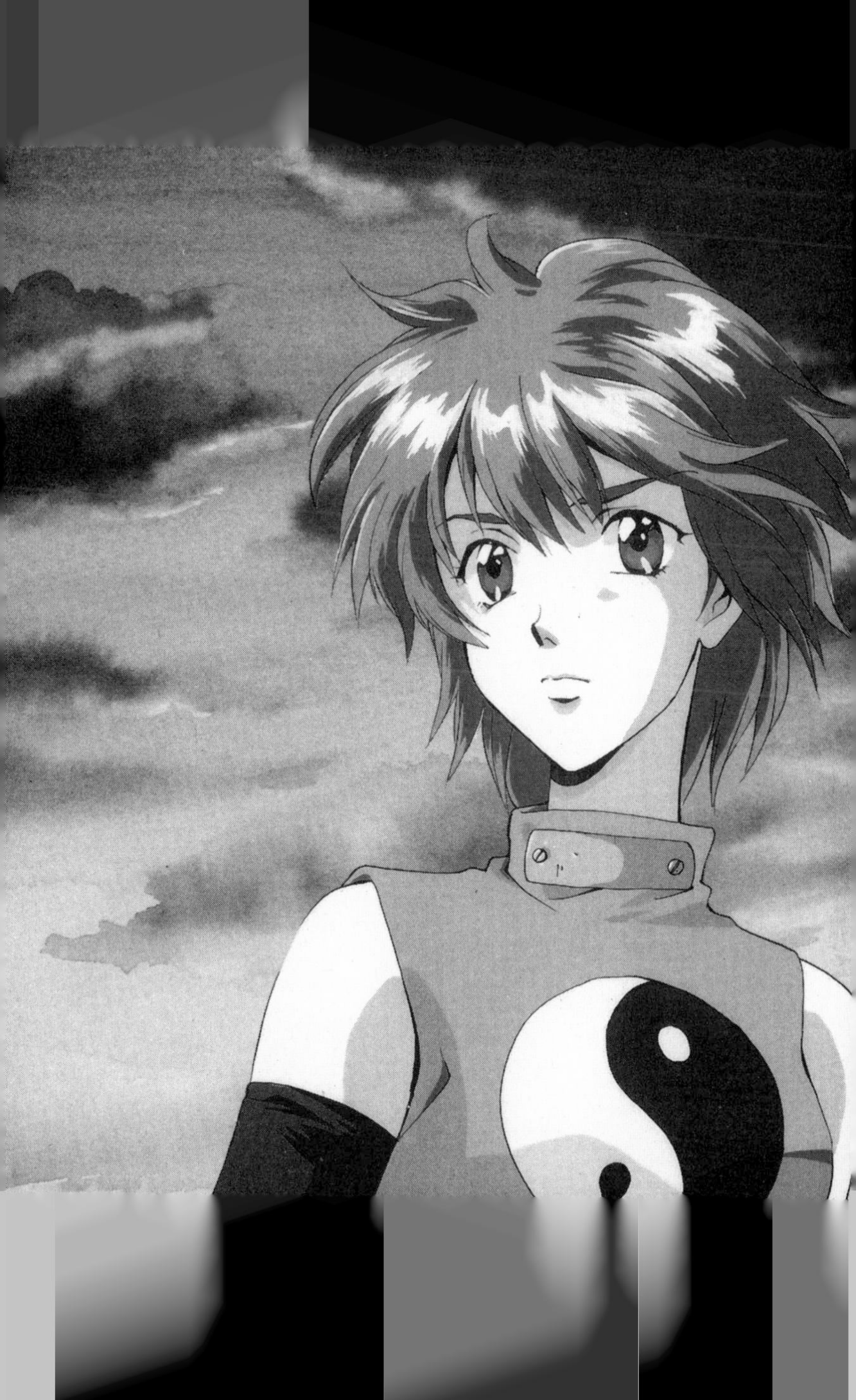

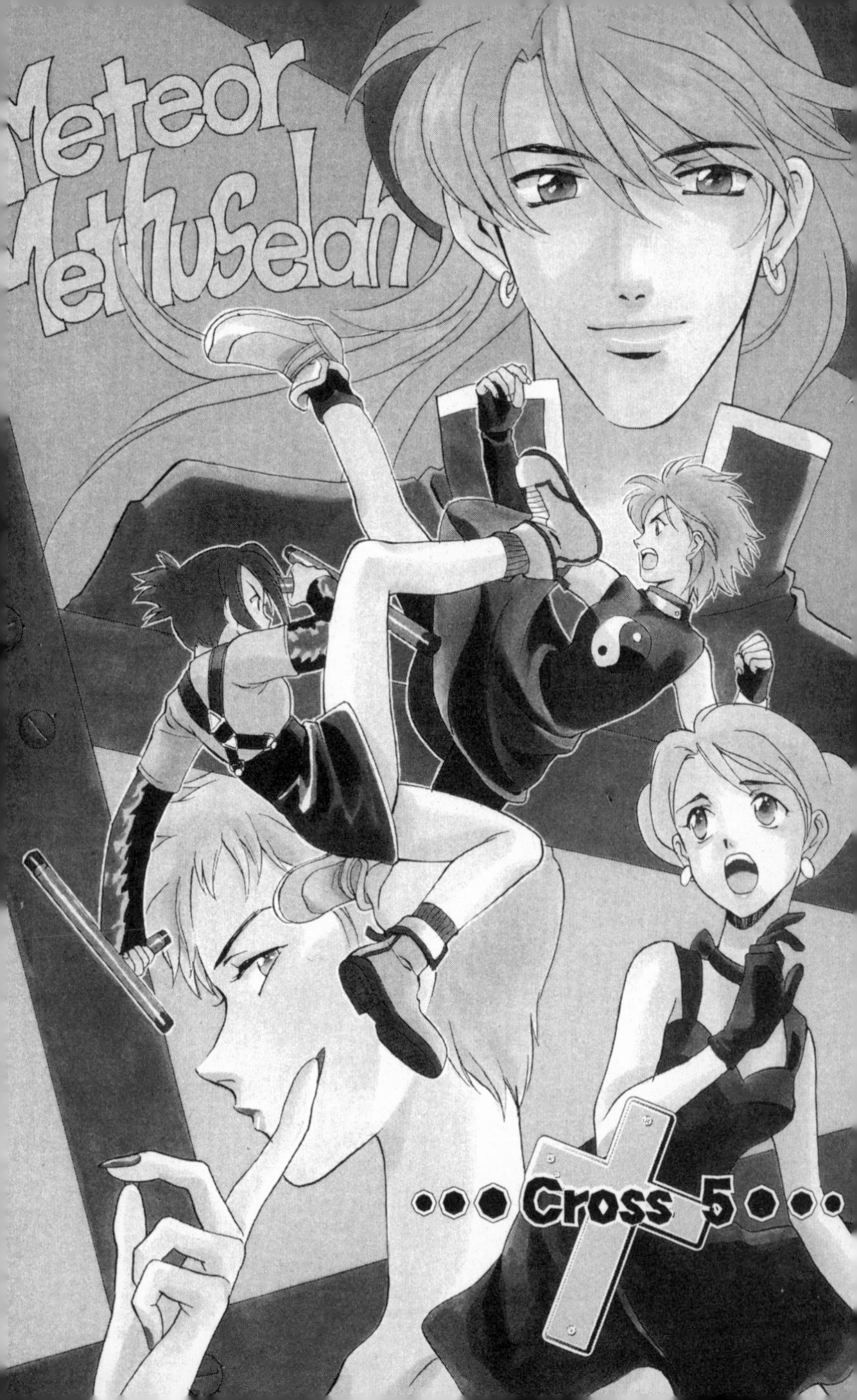
Meteor Methuselah
Cross 5

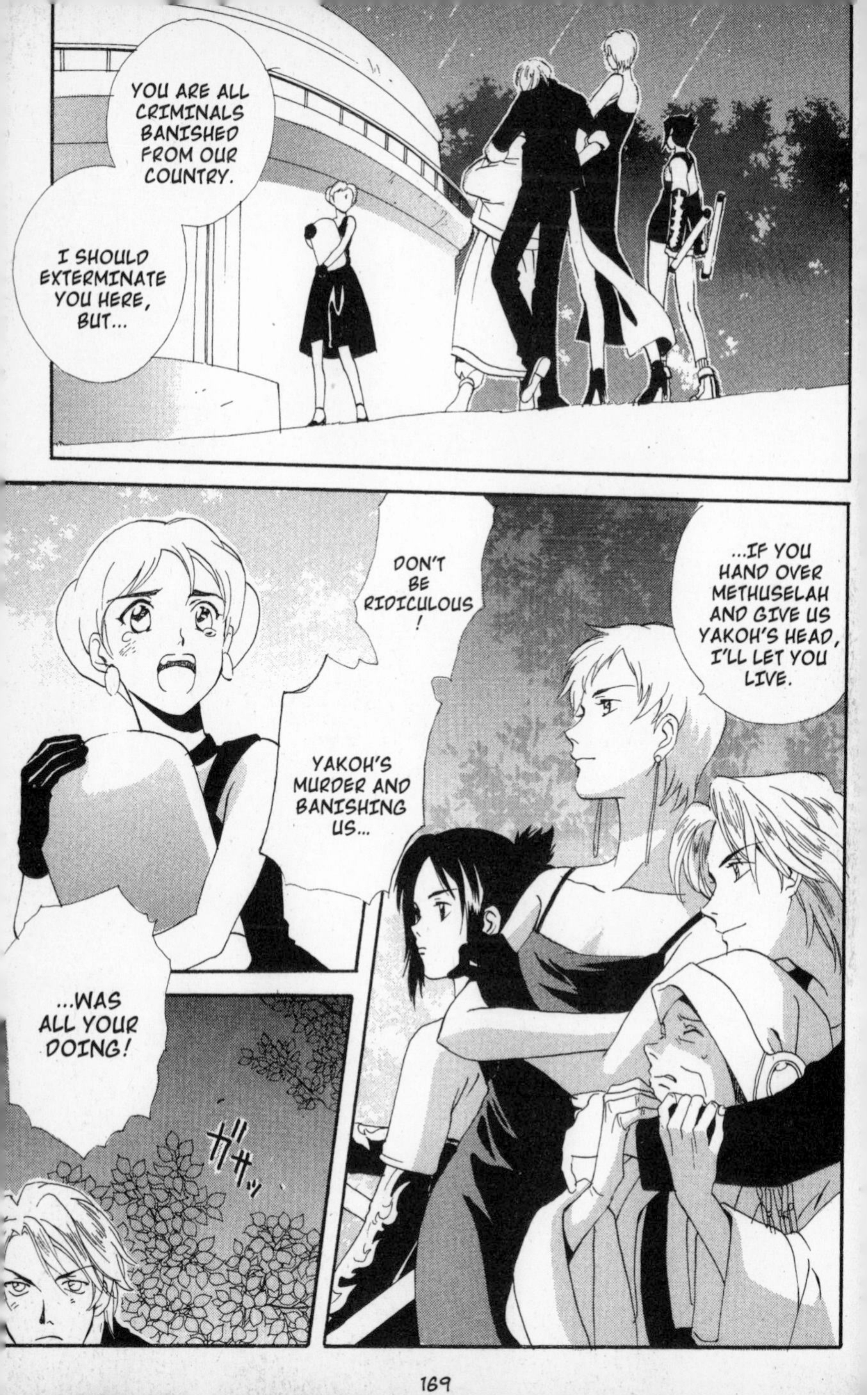
YOU ARE ALL CRIMINALS BANISHED FROM OUR COUNTRY.
I SHOULD EXTERMINATE YOU HERE, BUT...
...IF YOU HAND OVER METHUSELAH AND GIVE US YAKOH'S HEAD, I'LL LET YOU LIVE.
DON'T BE RIDICULOUS!
YAKOH'S MURDER AND BANISHING US...
...WAS ALL YOUR DOING!
ガサッ

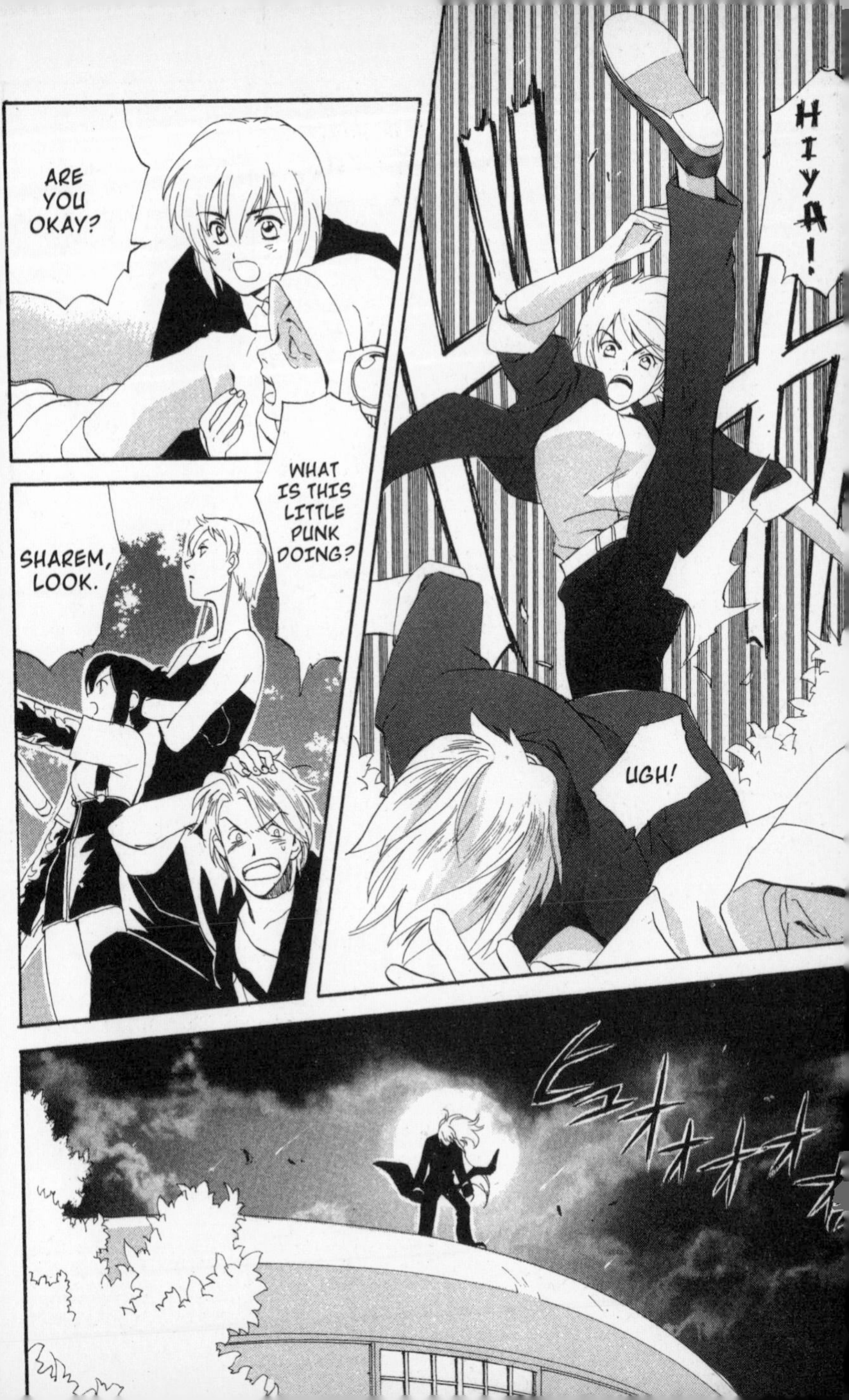
HIYA!
UGH!
ARE YOU OKAY?
WHAT IS THIS LITTLE PUNK DOING?
SHAREM, LOOK.

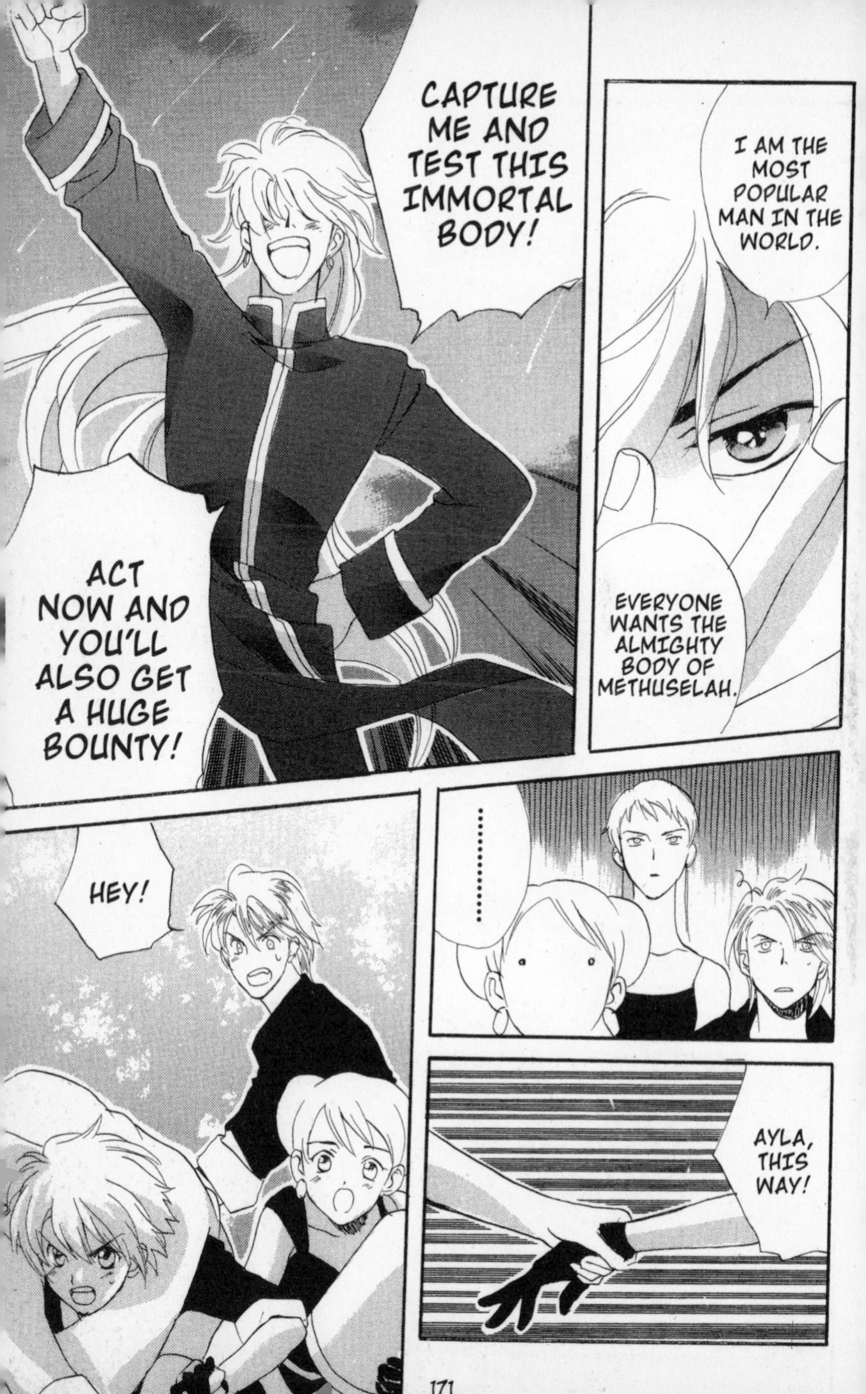
I AM THE MOST POPULAR MAN IN THE WORLD.
EVERYONE WANTS THE ALMIGHTY BODY OF METHUSELAH.
CAPTURE ME AND TEST THIS IMMORTAL BODY!
ACT NOW AND YOU'LL ALSO GET A HUGE BOUNTY!
......
AYLA, THIS WAY!
HEY!

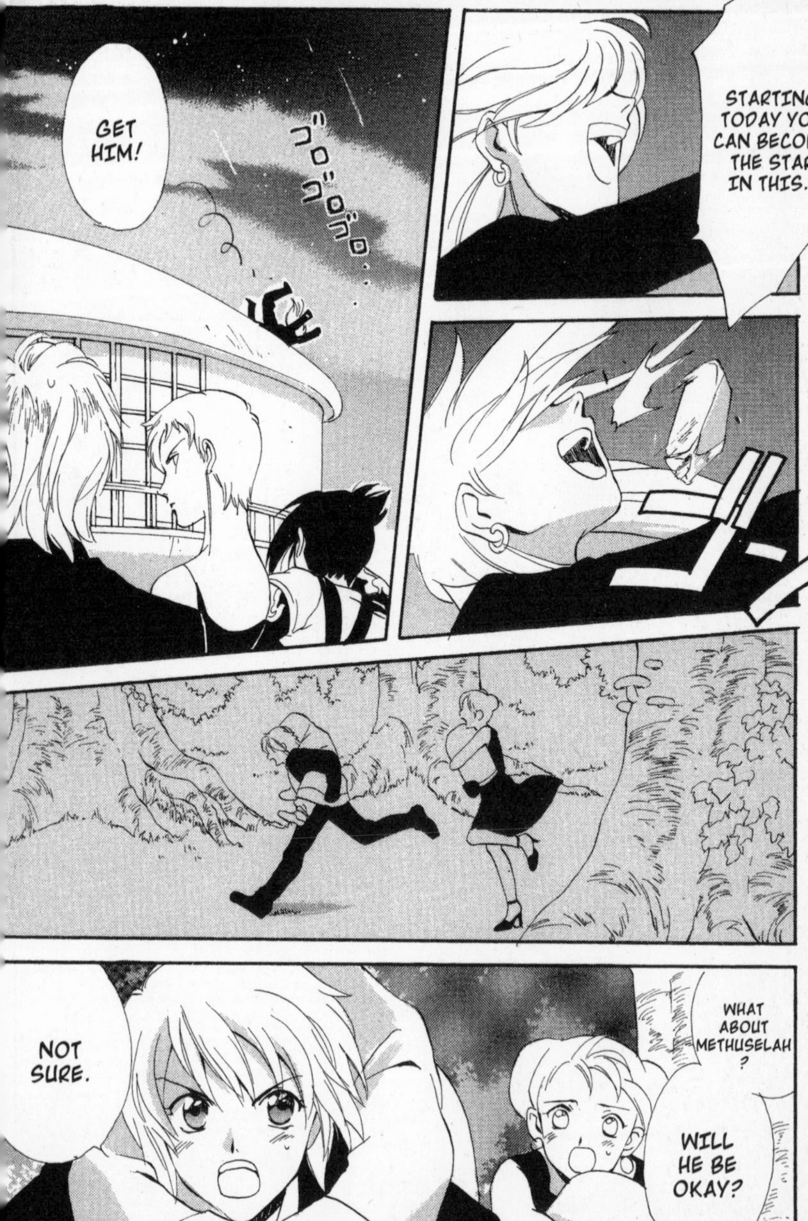
STARTING TODAY YOU CAN BECOME THE STAR IN THIS...
GET HIM!
ゴロゴロゴロ・・
WHAT ABOUT METHUSELAH?
WILL HE BE OKAY?
NOT SURE.

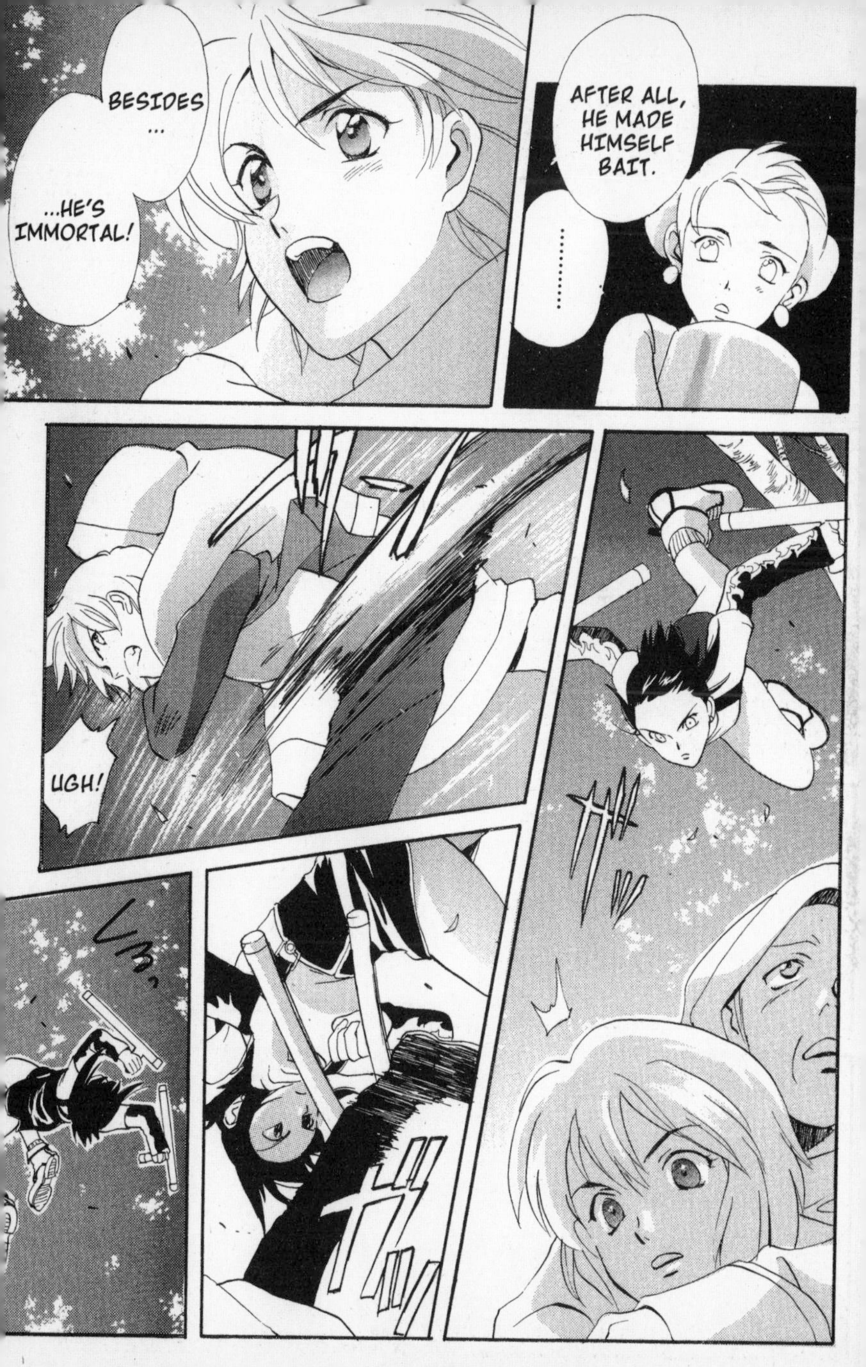
AFTER ALL, HE MADE HIMSELF BAIT.
......
BESIDES ...
...HE'S IMMORTAL!
UGH!
...

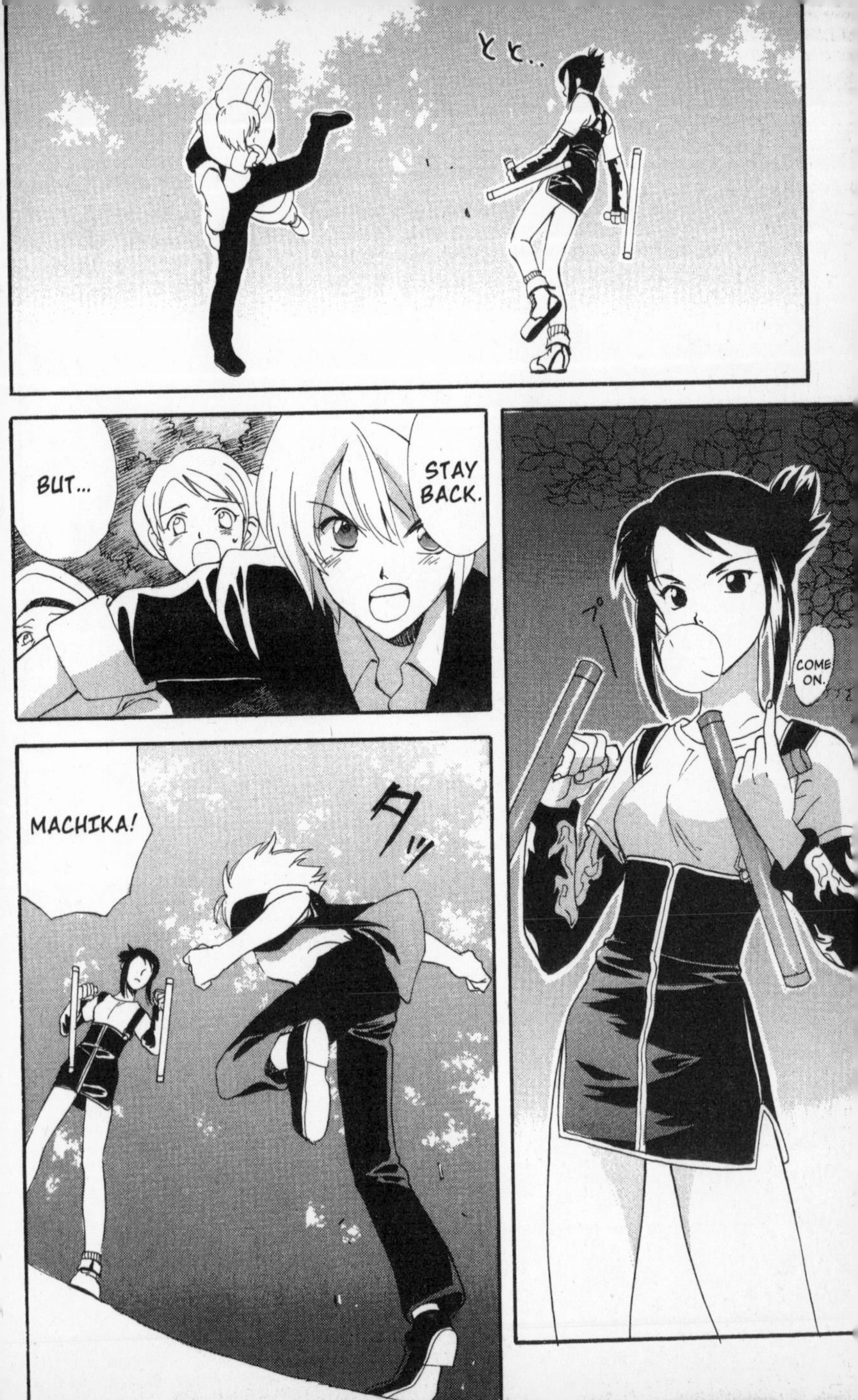
とと..
プ
COME ON.
STAY BACK.
BUT...
タッ
MACHIKA!

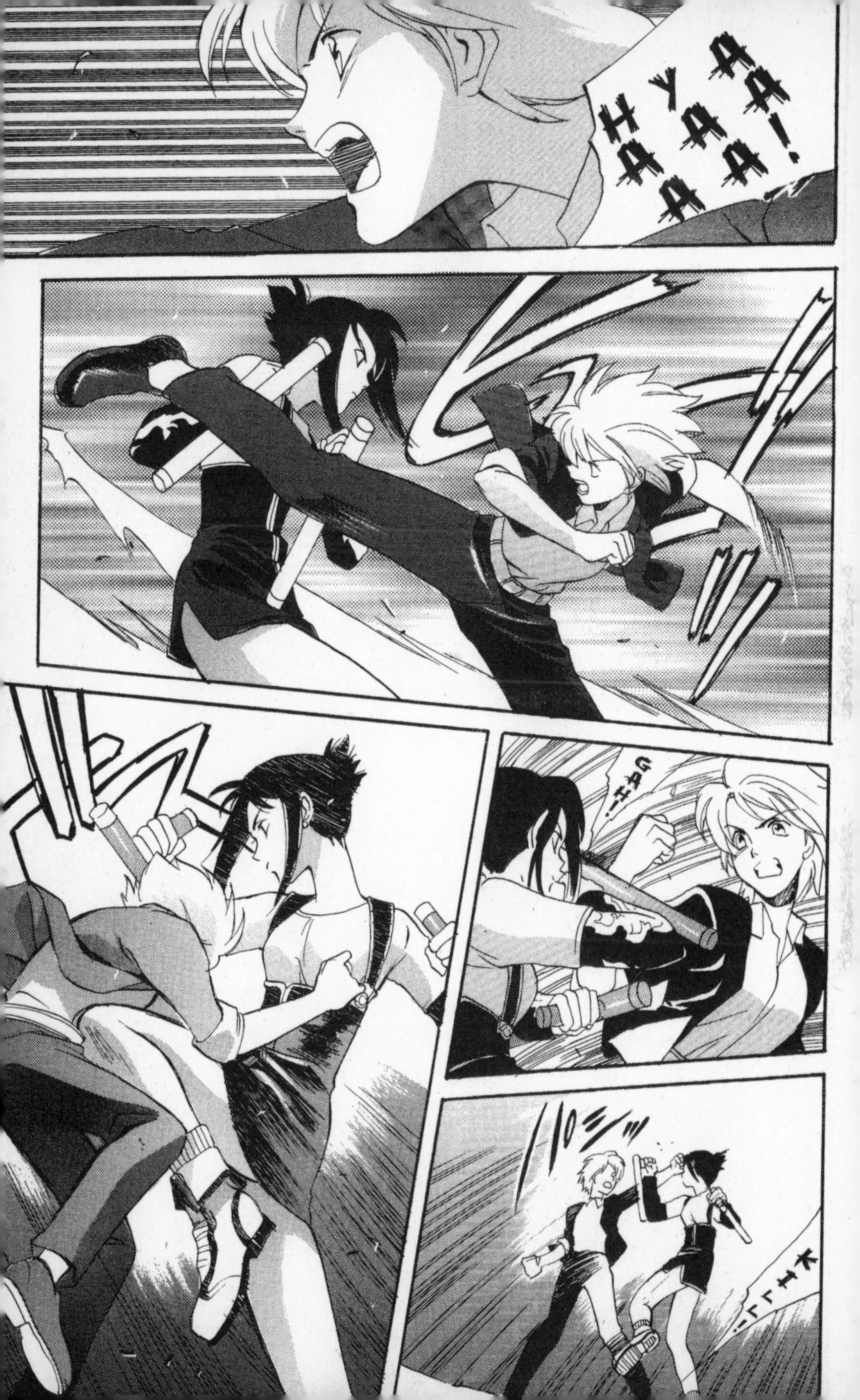
HYAAAAAAA!
GAH!

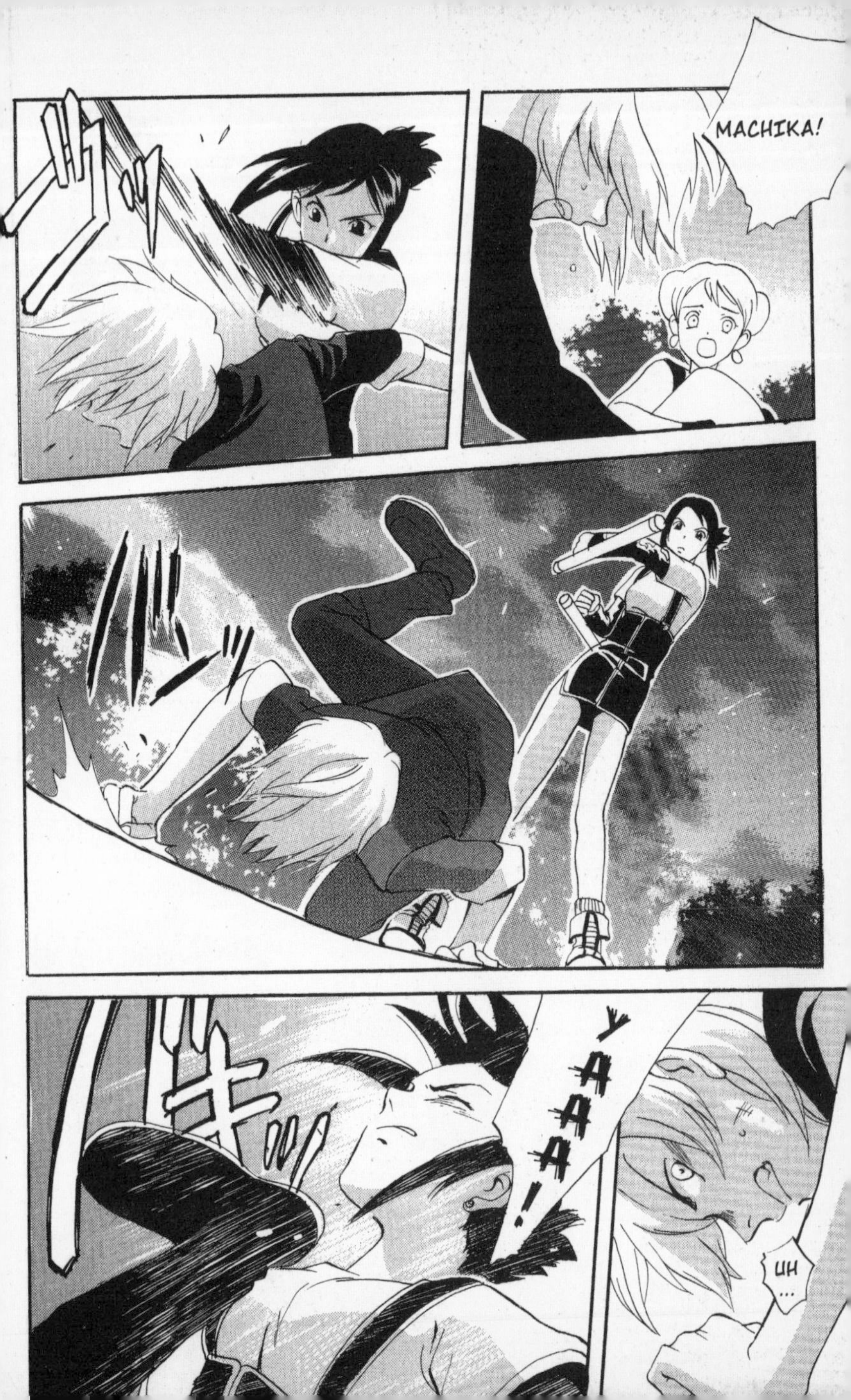
MACHIKA!
YAAAAA!
UH...

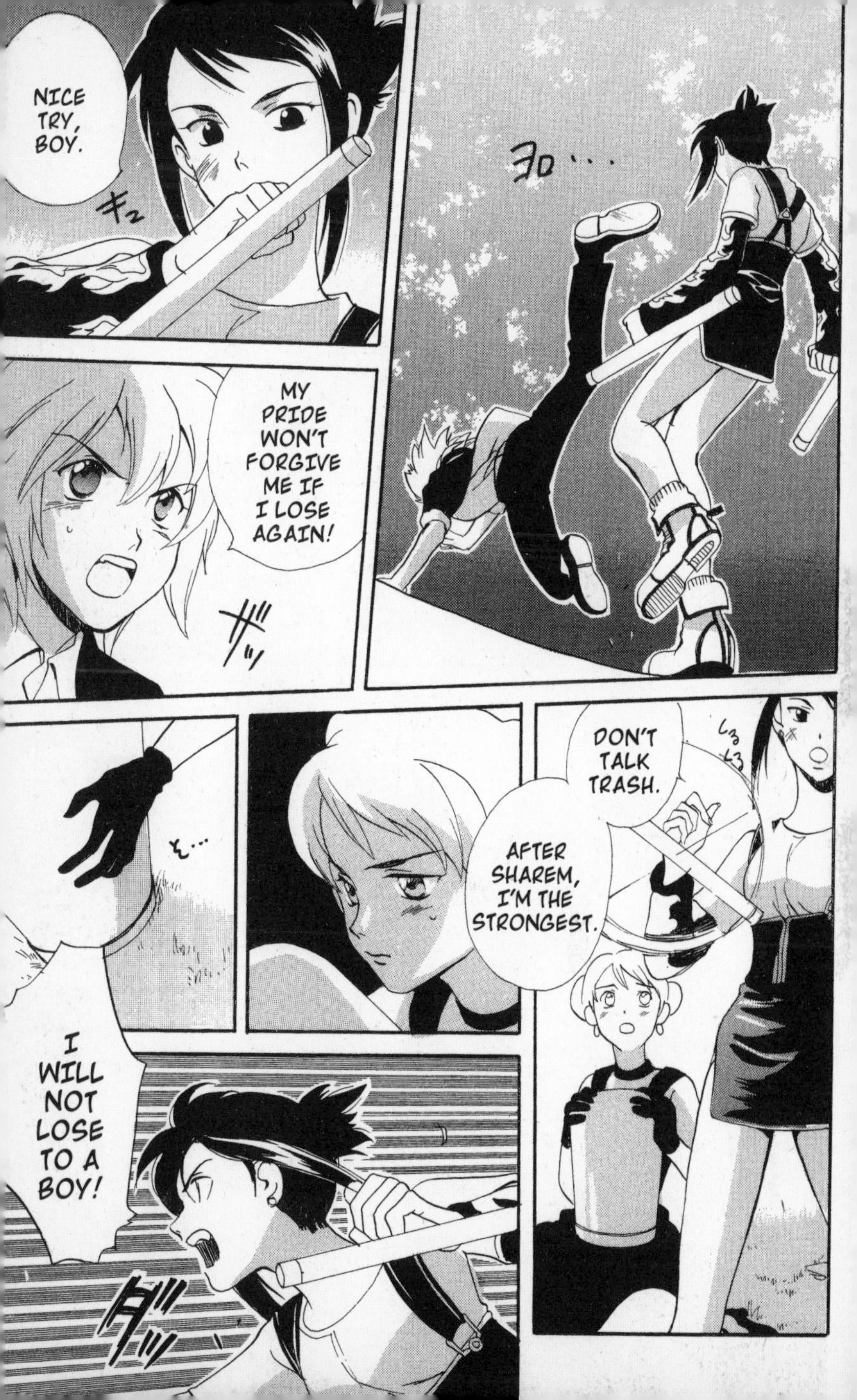
ヨロ…
NICE TRY, BOY.
MY PRIDE WON'T FORGIVE ME IF I LOSE AGAIN!
DON'T TALK TRASH.
AFTER SHAREM, I'M THE STRONGEST.
I WILL NOT LOSE TO A BOY!

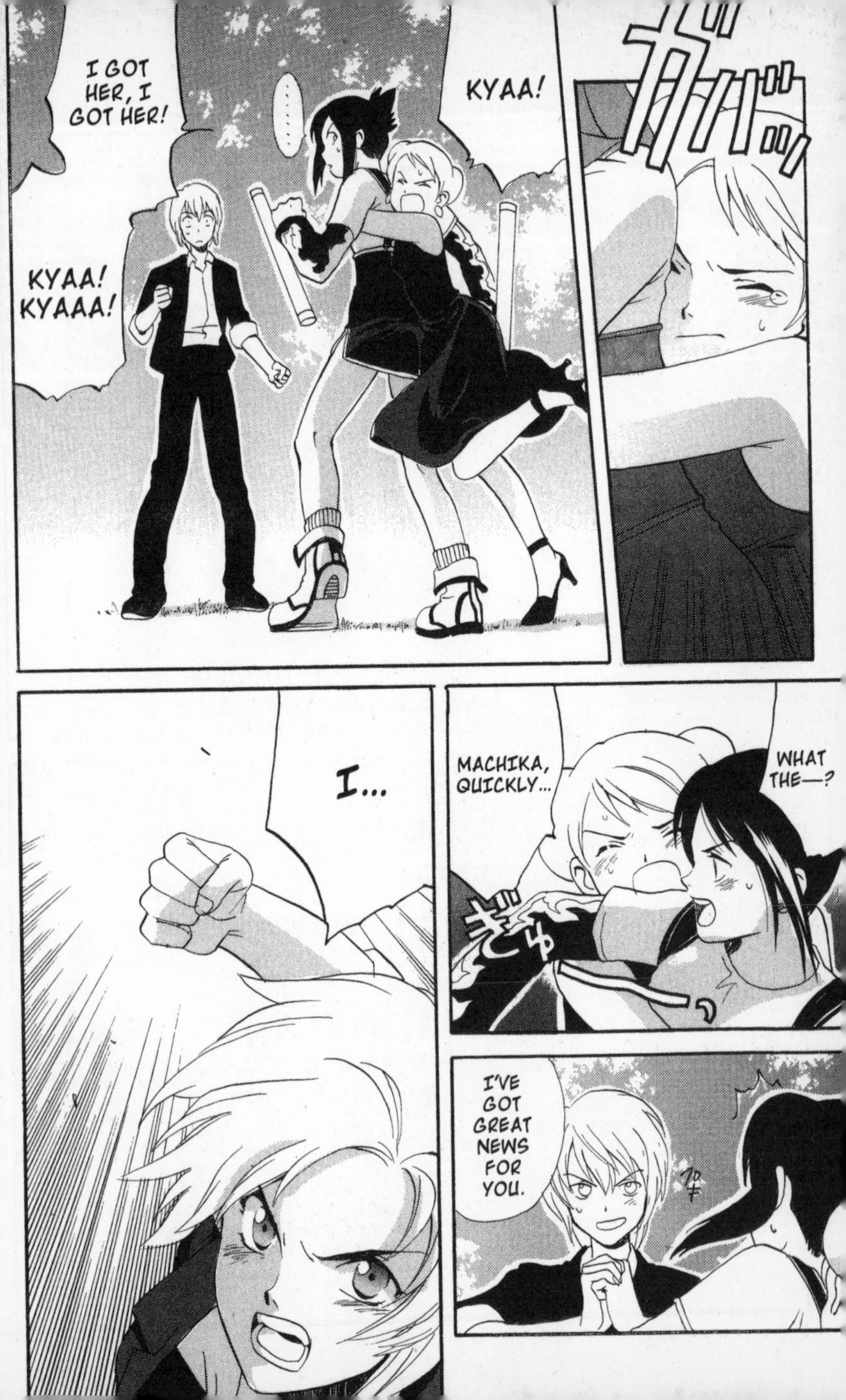
ガバッ
KYAA!
...
I GOT HER, I GOT HER!
KYAA! KYAAA!
WHAT THE—?
MACHIKA, QUICKLY...
ぎゅ
I'VE GOT GREAT NEWS FOR YOU.
I...

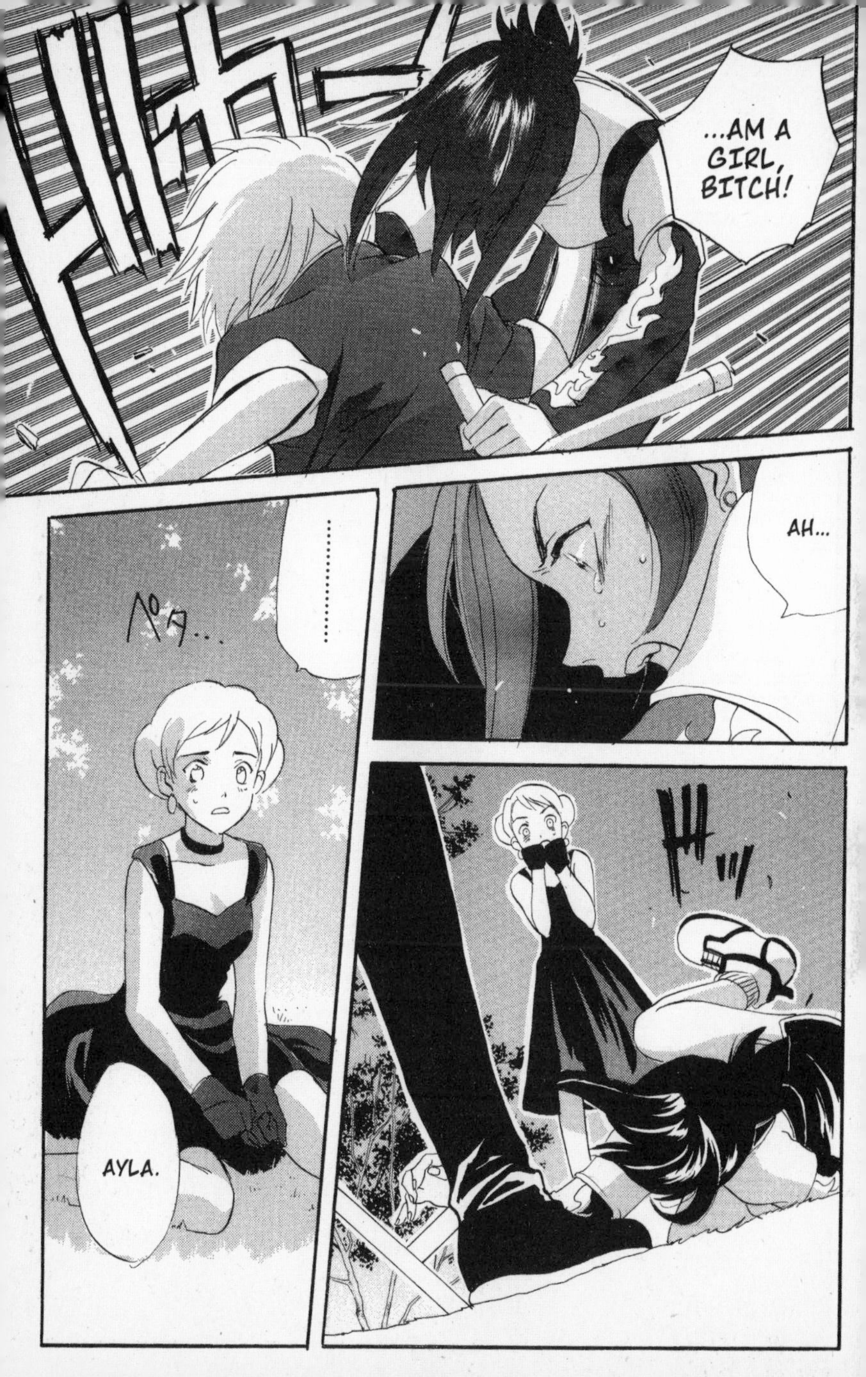

...AM A GIRL, BITCH!
AH...
......
AYLA.

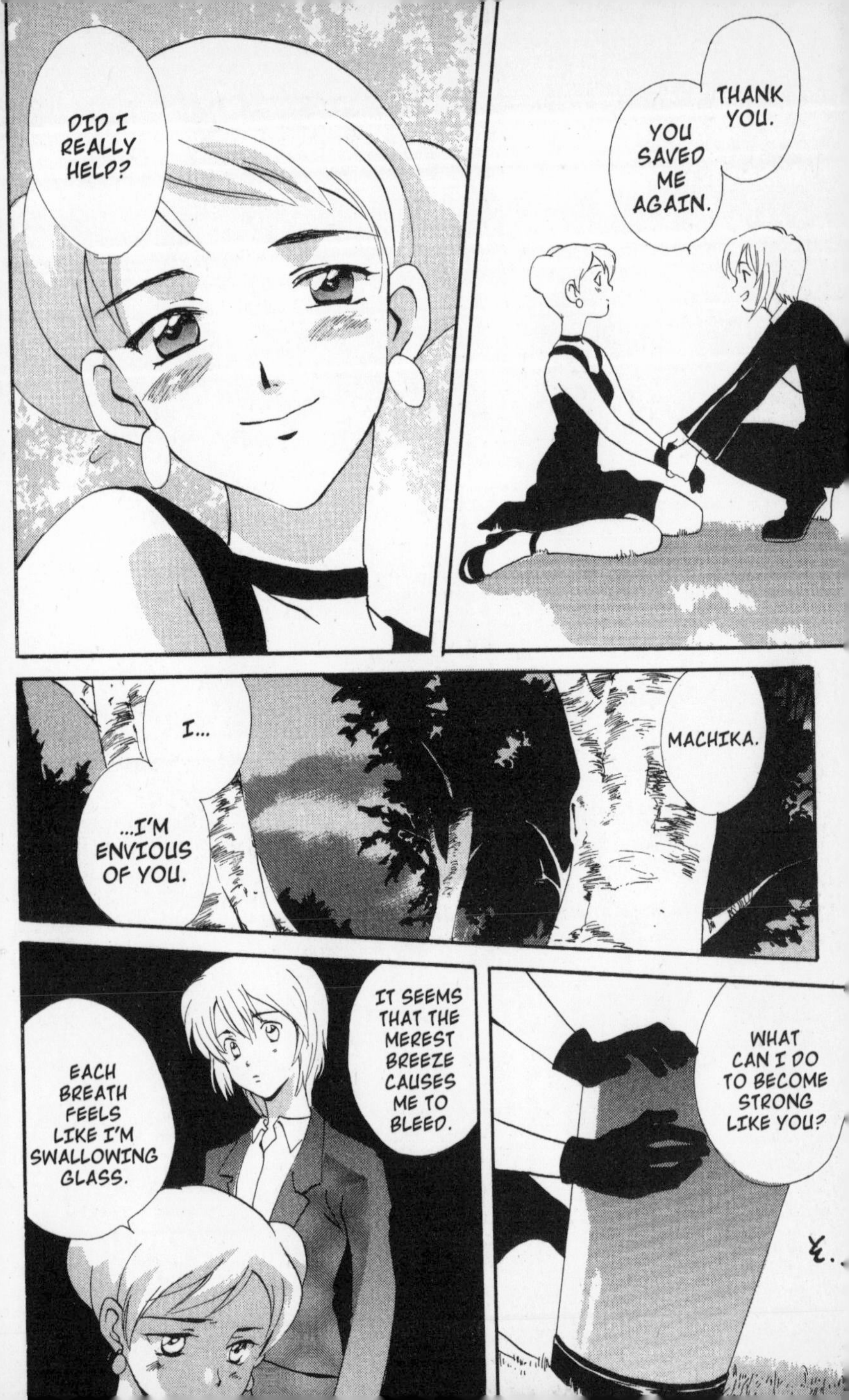
THANK YOU.
YOU SAVED ME AGAIN.
DID I REALLY HELP?
MACHIKA.
I...
...I'M ENVIOUS OF YOU.
WHAT CAN I DO TO BECOME STRONG LIKE YOU?
IT SEEMS THAT THE MEREST BREEZE CAUSES ME TO BLEED.
EACH BREATH FEELS LIKE I'M SWALLOWING GLASS.

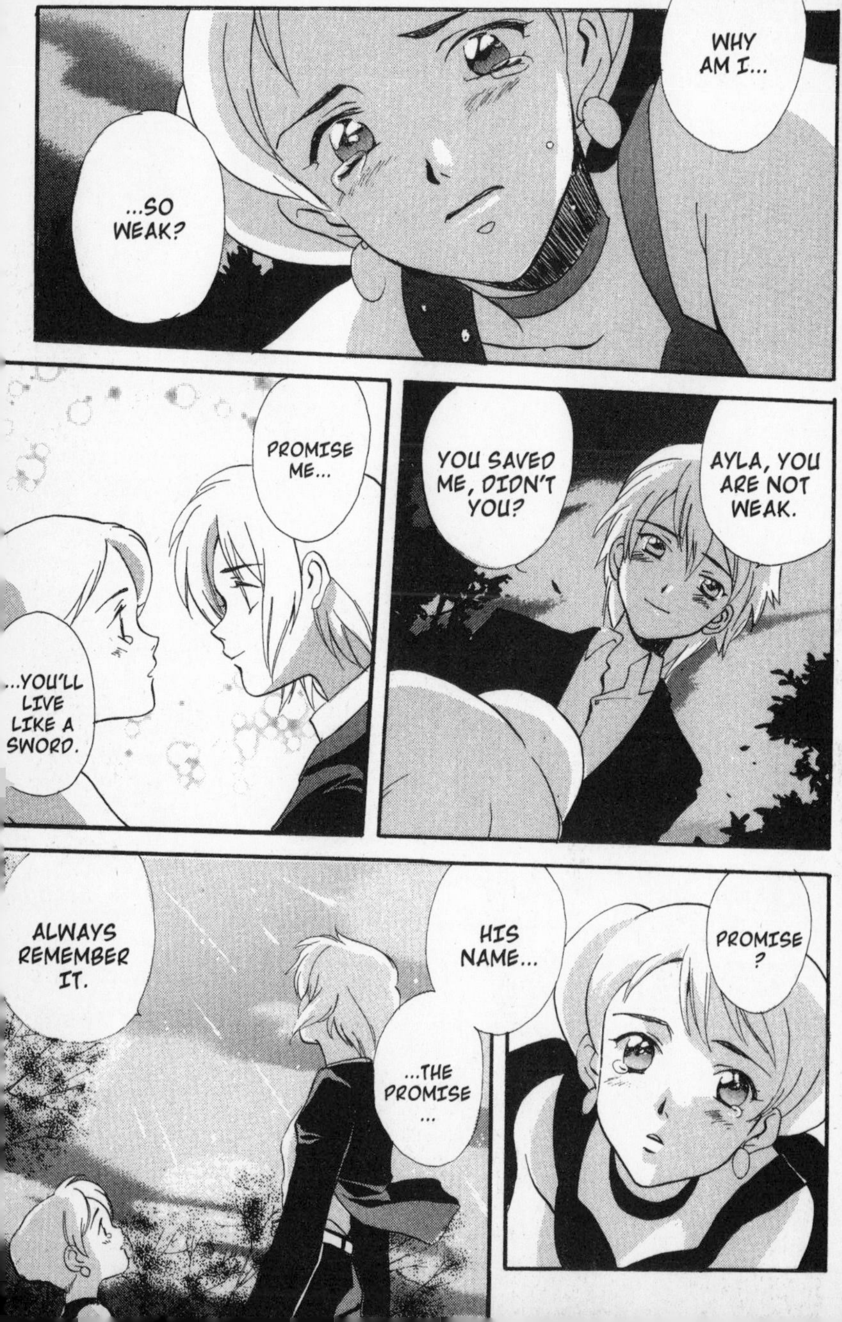
WHY AM I...
...SO WEAK?
AYLA, YOU ARE NOT WEAK.
YOU SAVED ME, DIDN'T YOU?
PROMISE ME...
...YOU'LL LIVE LIKE A SWORD.
PROMISE?
HIS NAME...
...THE PROMISE ...
ALWAYS REMEMBER IT.

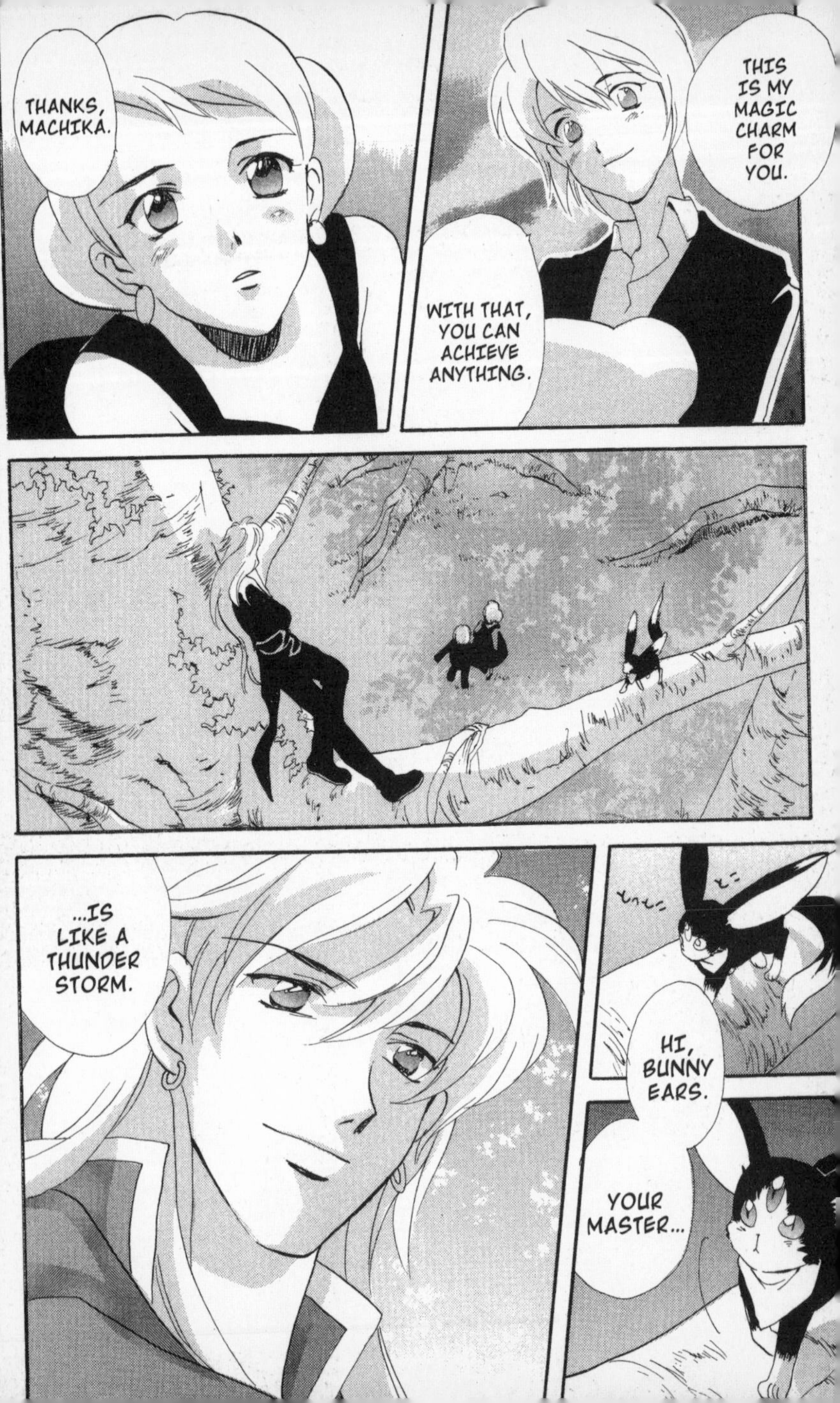
THIS IS MY MAGIC CHARM FOR YOU.
WITH THAT, YOU CAN ACHIEVE ANYTHING.
THANKS, MACHIKA.
HI, BUNNY EARS.
YOUR MASTER...
...IS LIKE A THUNDER STORM.

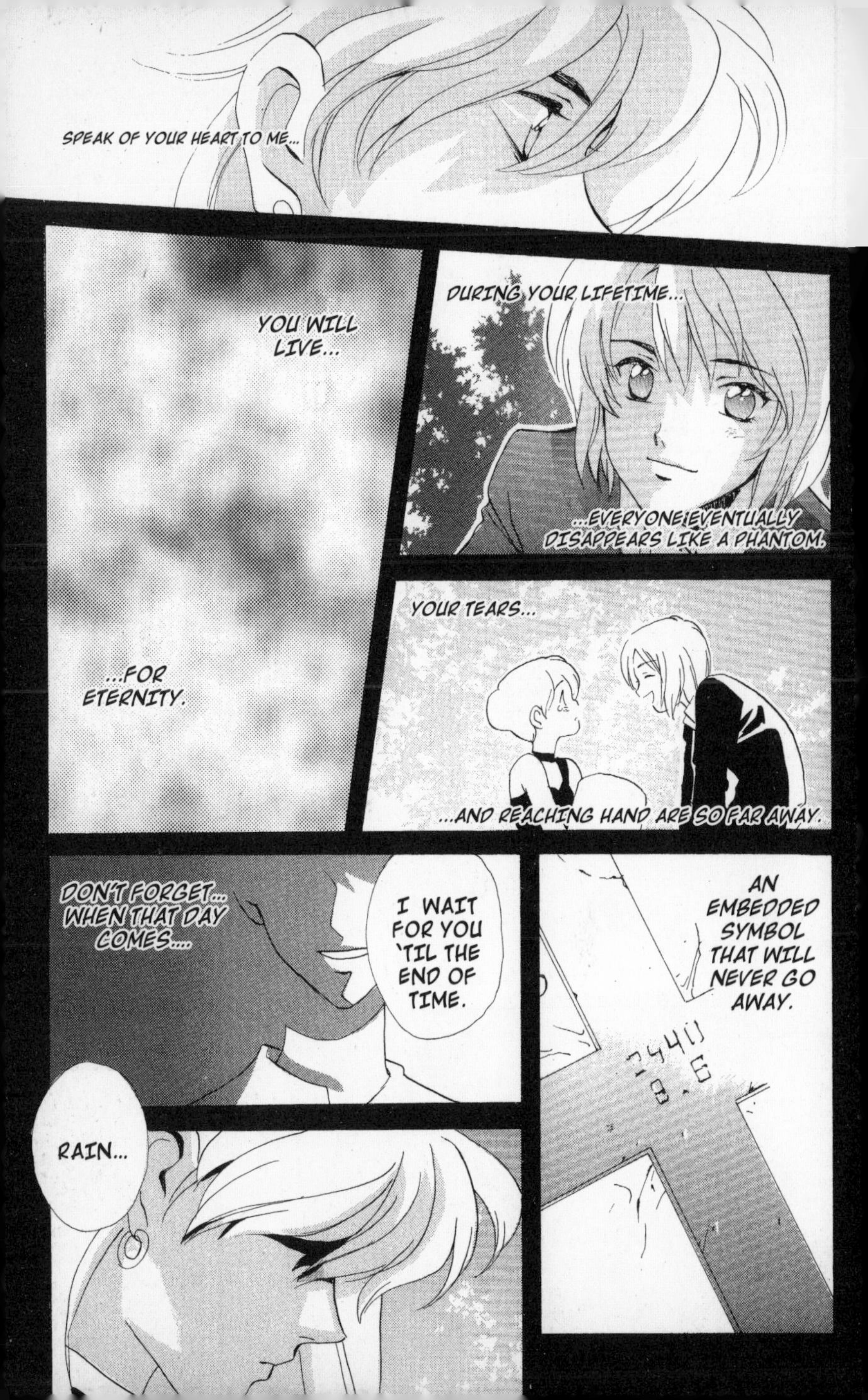
SPEAK OF YOUR HEART TO ME...
DURING YOUR LIFETIME...
...EVERYONE EVENTUALLY DISAPPEARS LIKE A PHANTOM.
YOUR TEARS...
...AND REACHING HAND ARE SO FAR AWAY.
YOU WILL LIVE...
...FOR ETERNITY.
AN EMBEDDED SYMBOL THAT WILL NEVER GO AWAY.
I WAIT FOR YOU 'TIL THE END OF TIME.
DON'T FORGET... WHEN THAT DAY COMES....
RAIN...

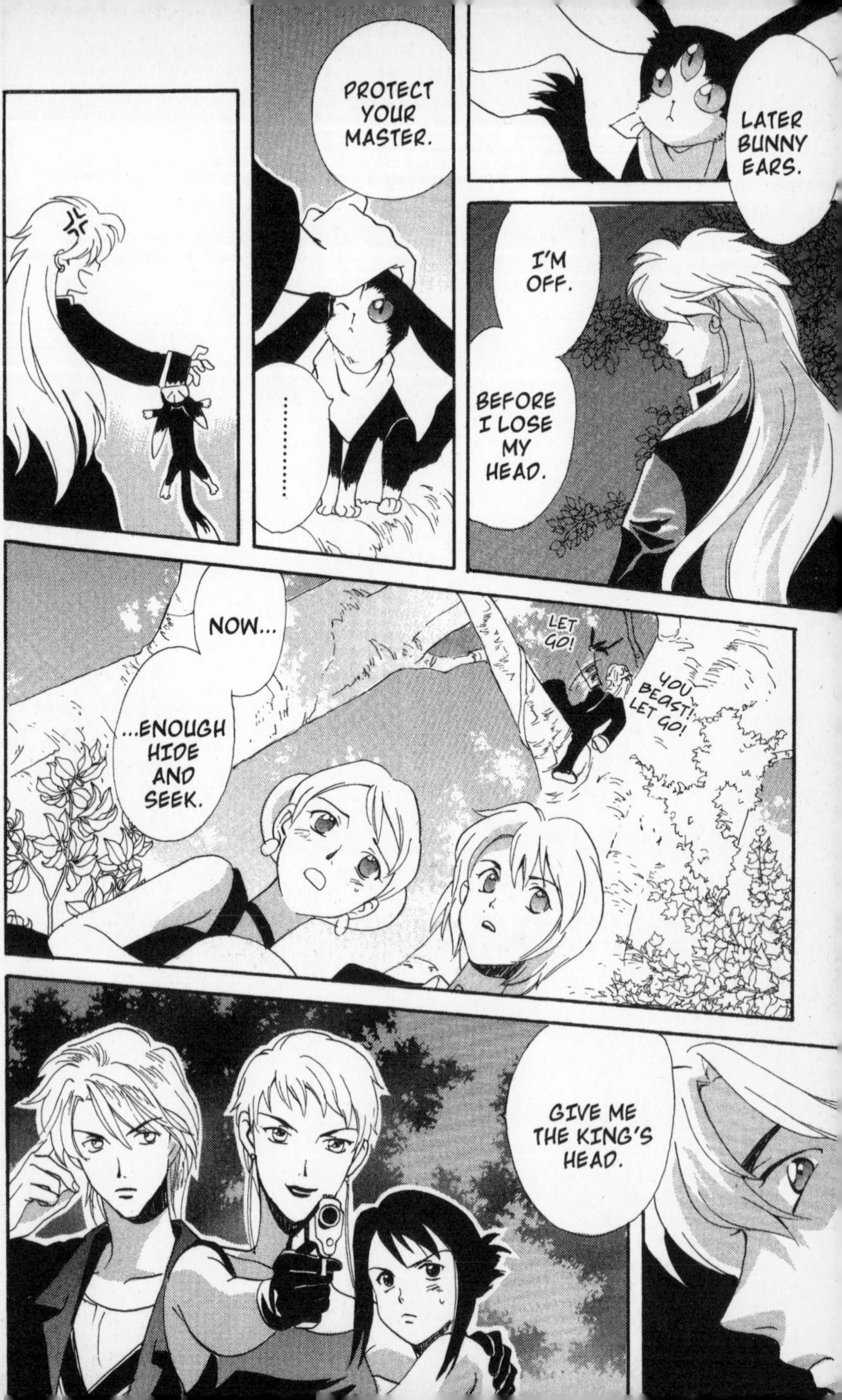
LATER BUNNY EARS.
I'M OFF.
BEFORE I LOSE MY HEAD.
PROTECT YOUR MASTER.
......
LET GO!
YOU BEAST! LET GO!
NOW...
...ENOUGH HIDE AND SEEK.
GIVE ME THE KING'S HEAD.

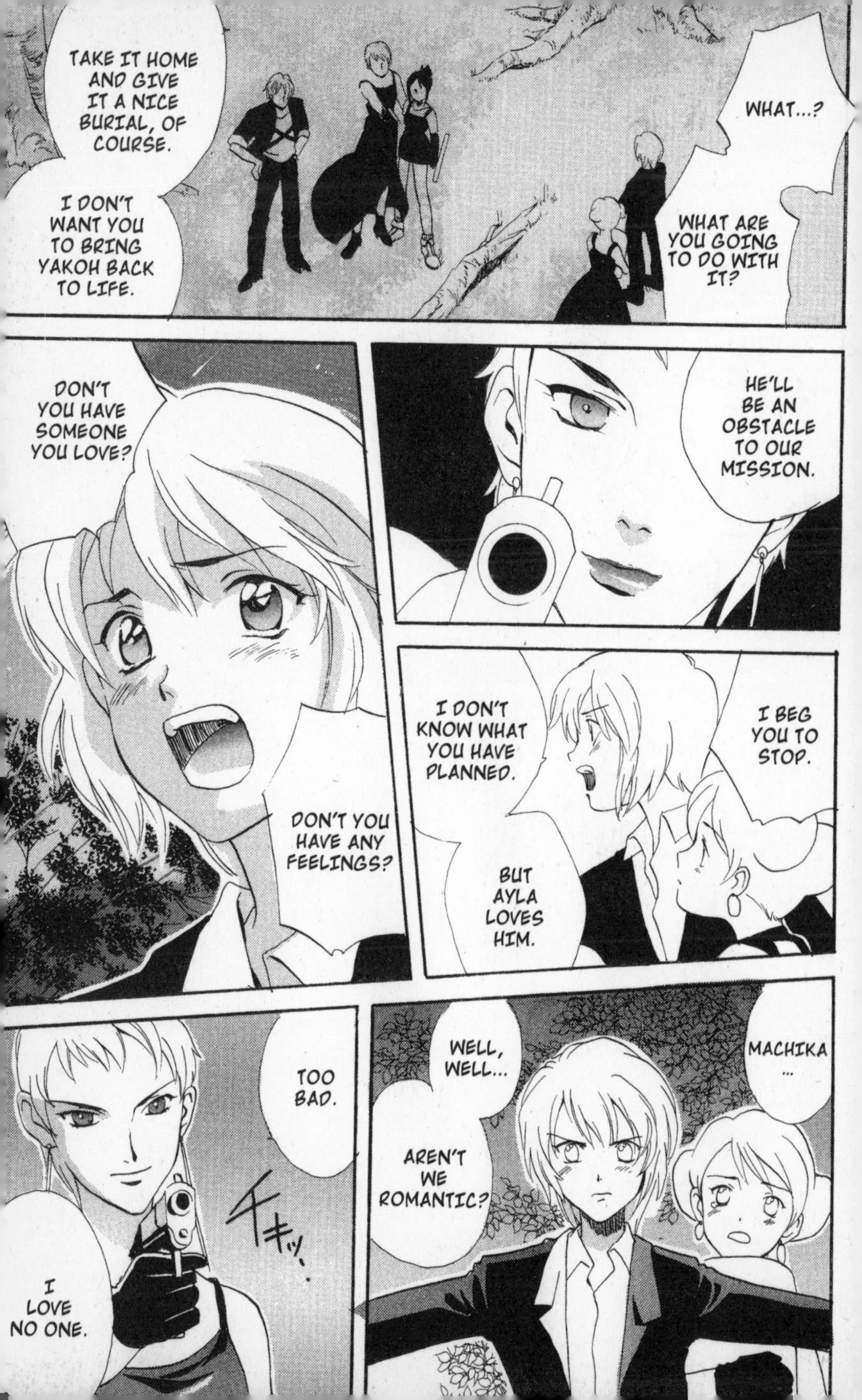
WHAT...?
WHAT ARE YOU GOING TO DO WITH IT?
TAKE IT HOME AND GIVE IT A NICE BURIAL, OF COURSE.
I DON'T WANT YOU TO BRING YAKOH BACK TO LIFE.
HE'LL BE AN OBSTACLE TO OUR MISSION.
I BEG YOU TO STOP.
I DON'T KNOW WHAT YOU HAVE PLANNED.
BUT AYLA LOVES HIM.
DON'T YOU HAVE SOMEONE YOU LOVE?
DON'T YOU HAVE ANY FEELINGS?
MACHIKA ...
WELL, WELL...
AREN'T WE ROMANTIC?
TOO BAD.
チキッ
I LOVE NO ONE.

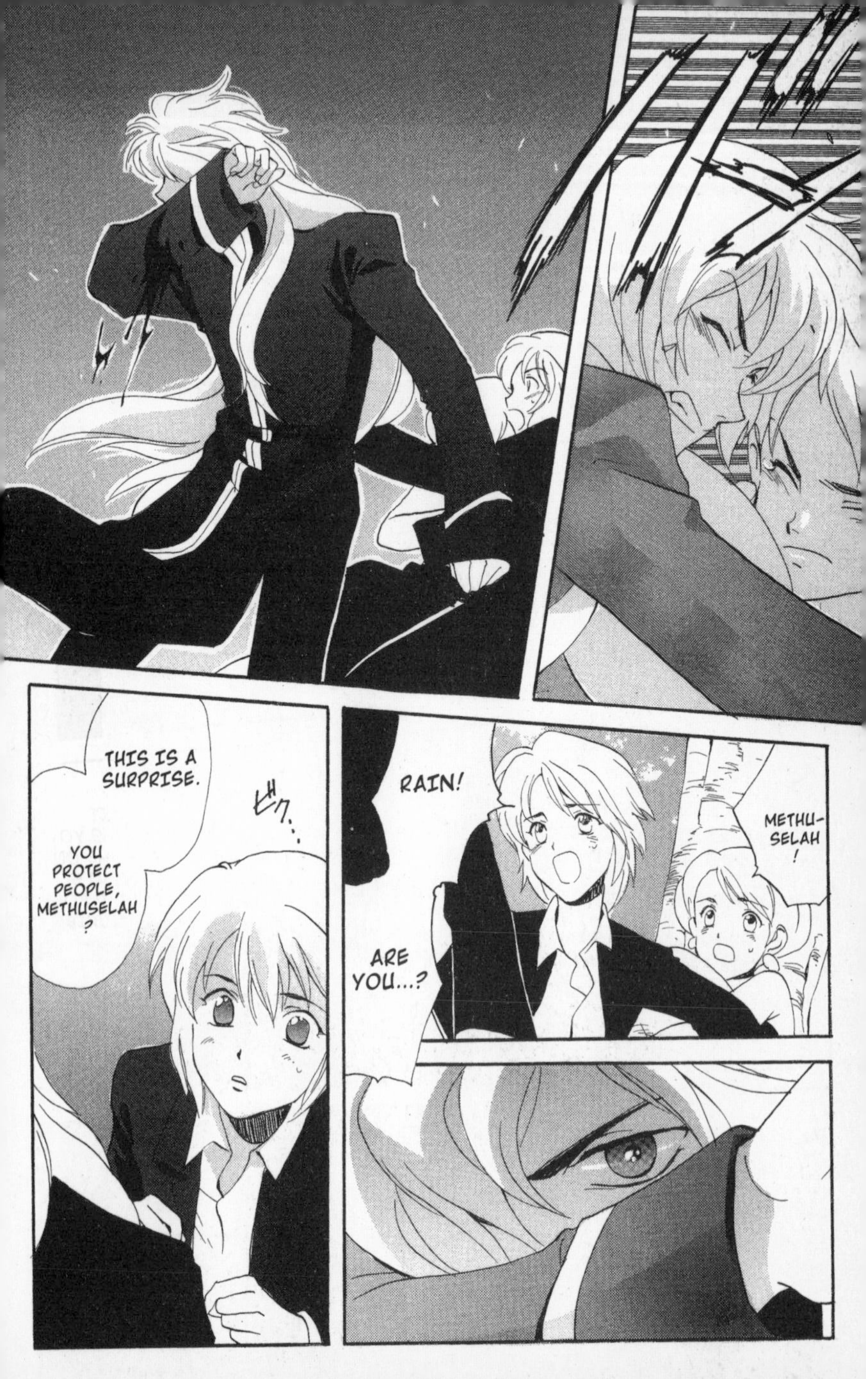
RAIN!
METHU-
SELAH
!
ARE YOU...?
THIS IS A SURPRISE.
YOU PROTECT PEOPLE, METHUSELAH?

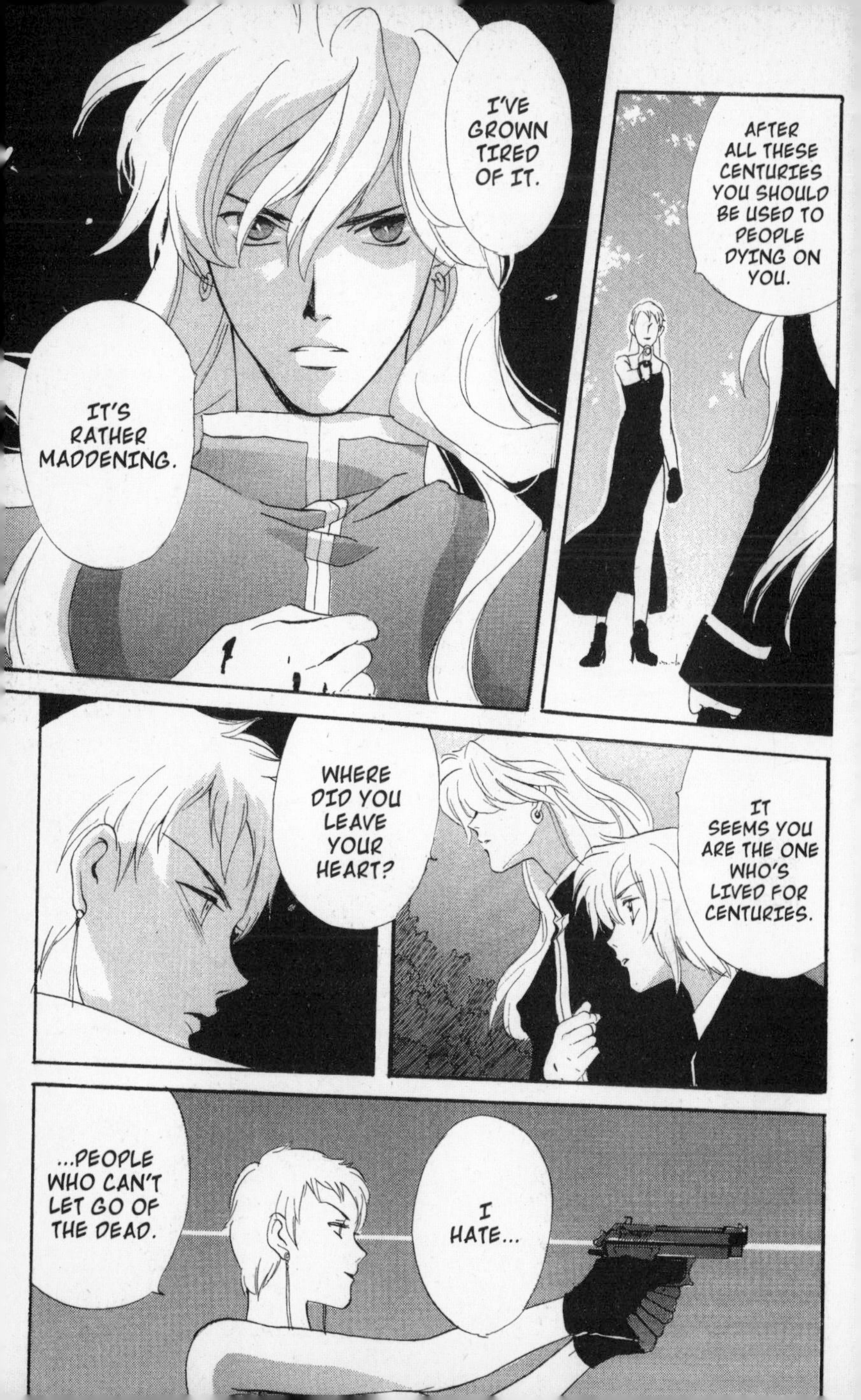
AFTER ALL THESE CENTURIES YOU SHOULD BE USED TO PEOPLE DYING ON YOU.
I'VE GROWN TIRED OF IT.
IT'S RATHER MADDENING.
IT SEEMS YOU ARE THE ONE WHO'S LIVED FOR CENTURIES.
WHERE DID YOU LEAVE YOUR HEART?
I HATE...
...PEOPLE WHO CAN'T LET GO OF THE DEAD.

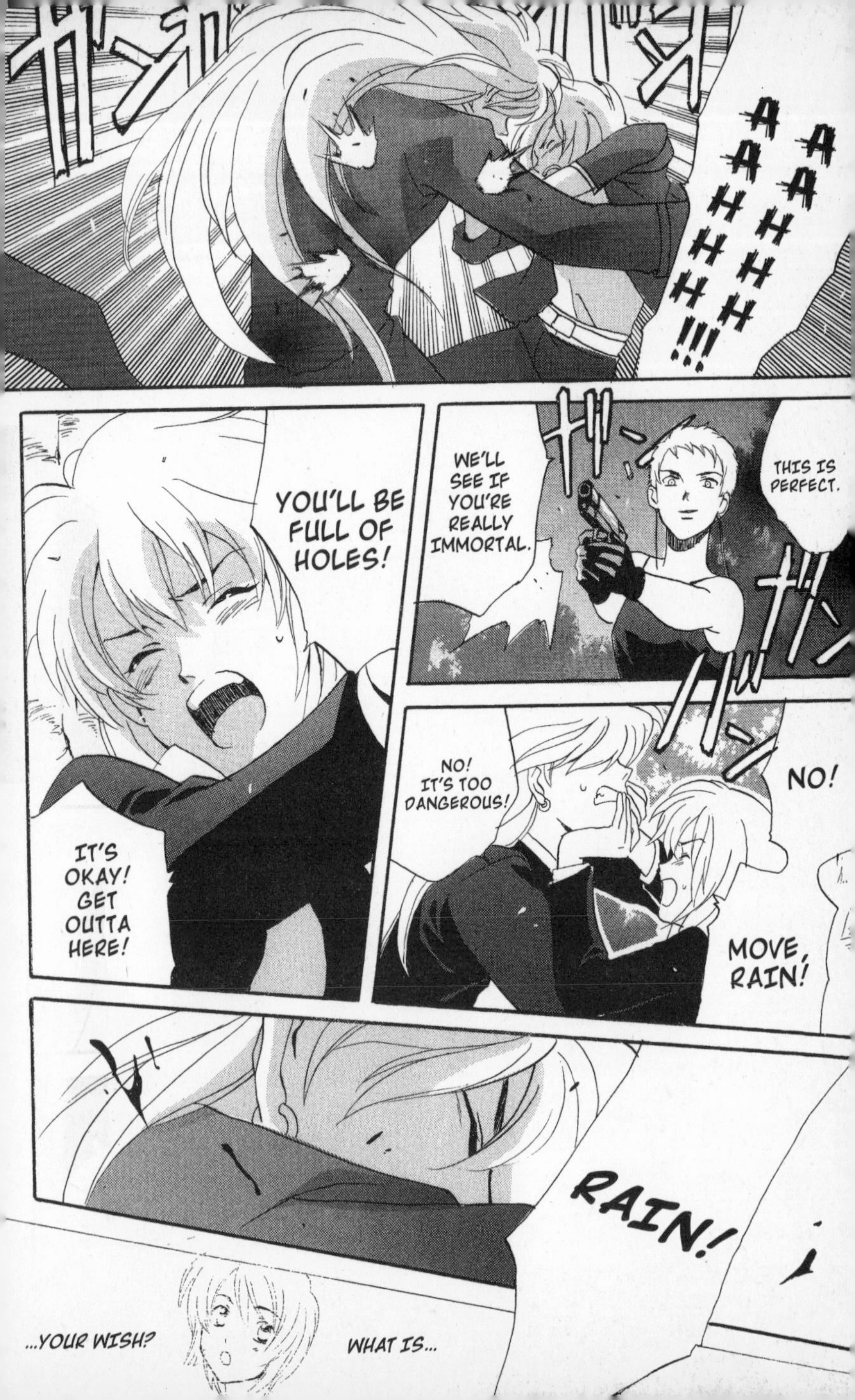
AAAAHHHHHHH!!!
THIS IS PERFECT.
WE'LL SEE IF YOU'RE REALLY IMMORTAL.
NO!
MOVE, RAIN!
NO! IT'S TOO DANGEROUS!
YOU'LL BE FULL OF HOLES!
IT'S OKAY! GET OUTTA HERE!
RAIN!
WHAT IS...
...YOUR WISH?

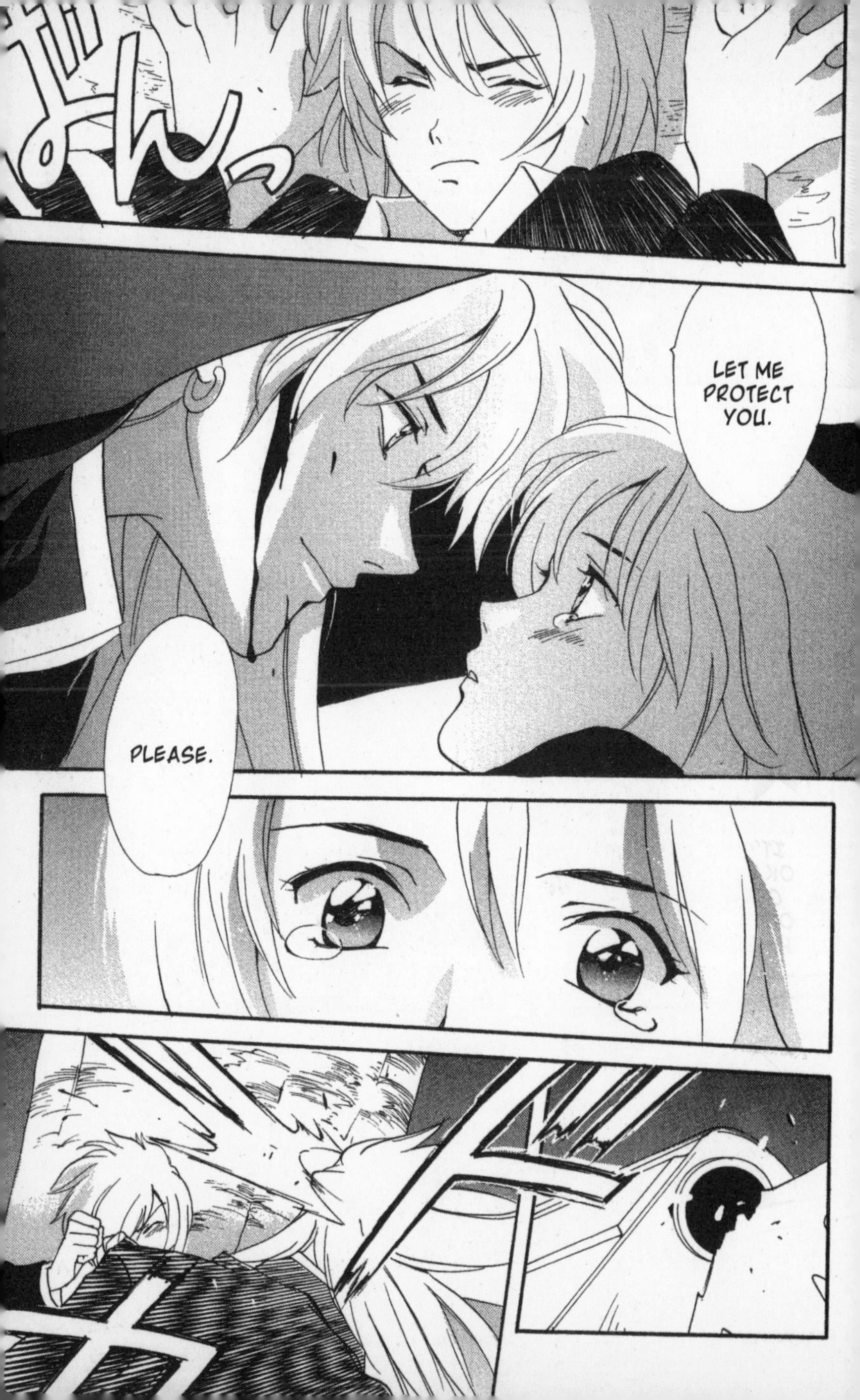
LET ME PROTECT YOU.
PLEASE.

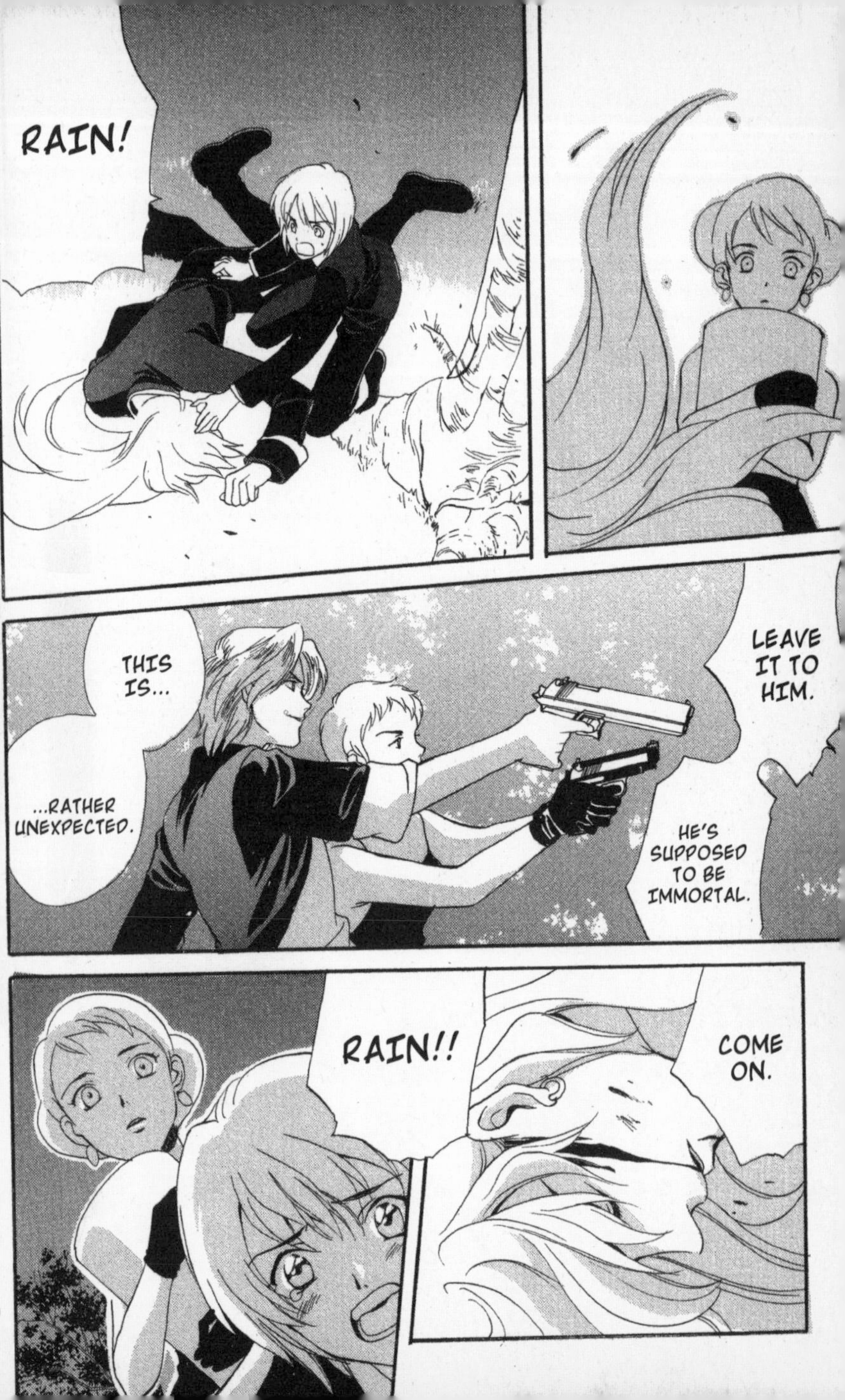
RAIN!
LEAVE IT TO HIM.
HE'S SUPPOSED TO BE IMMORTAL.
THIS IS...
...RATHER UNEXPECTED.
COME ON.
RAIN!!

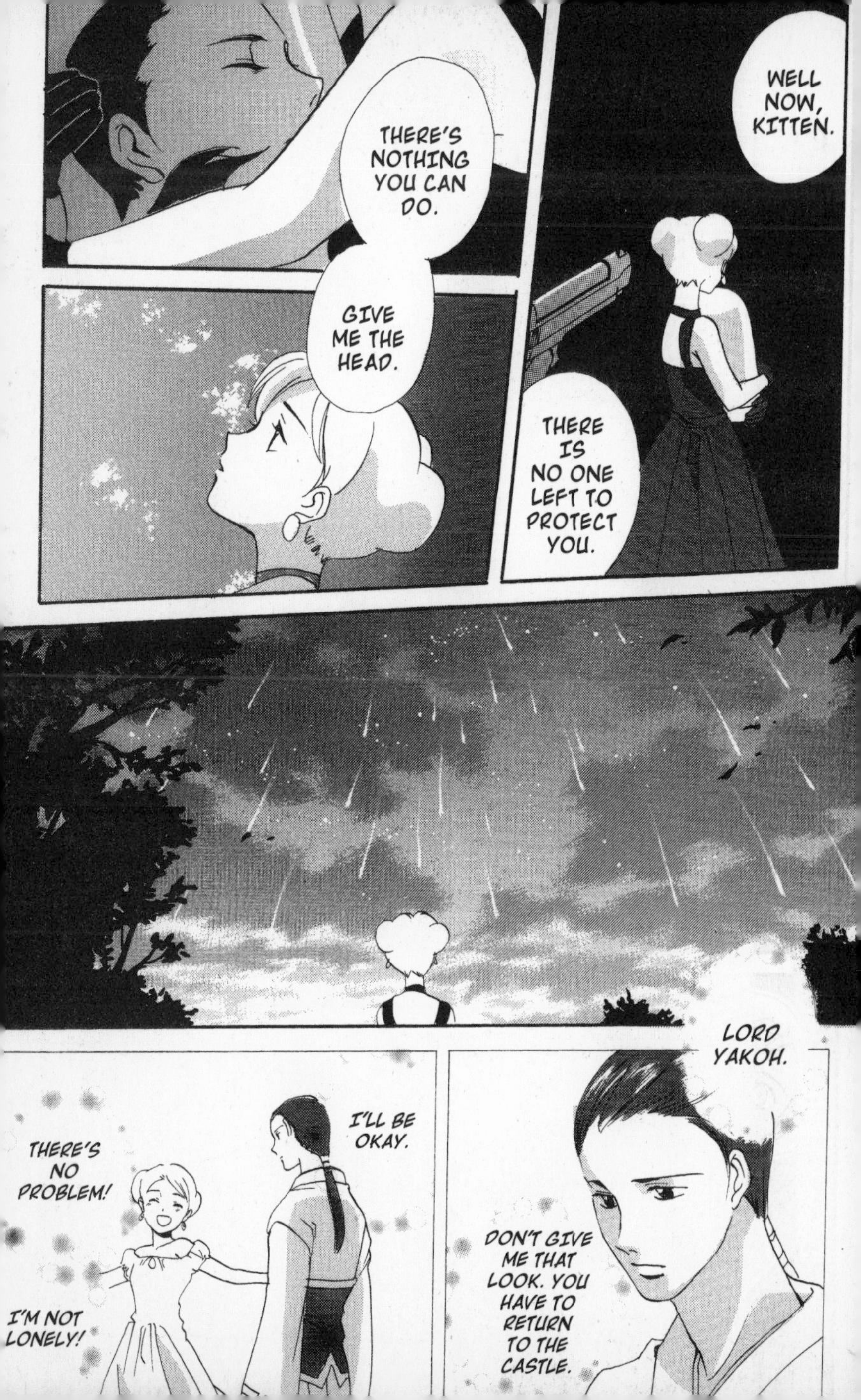
WELL NOW, KITTEN.
THERE IS NO ONE LEFT TO PROTECT YOU.
THERE'S NOTHING YOU CAN DO.
GIVE ME THE HEAD.
LORD YAKOH.
DON'T GIVE ME THAT LOOK. YOU HAVE TO RETURN TO THE CASTLE.
I'LL BE OKAY.
THERE'S NO PROBLEM!
I'M NOT LONELY!

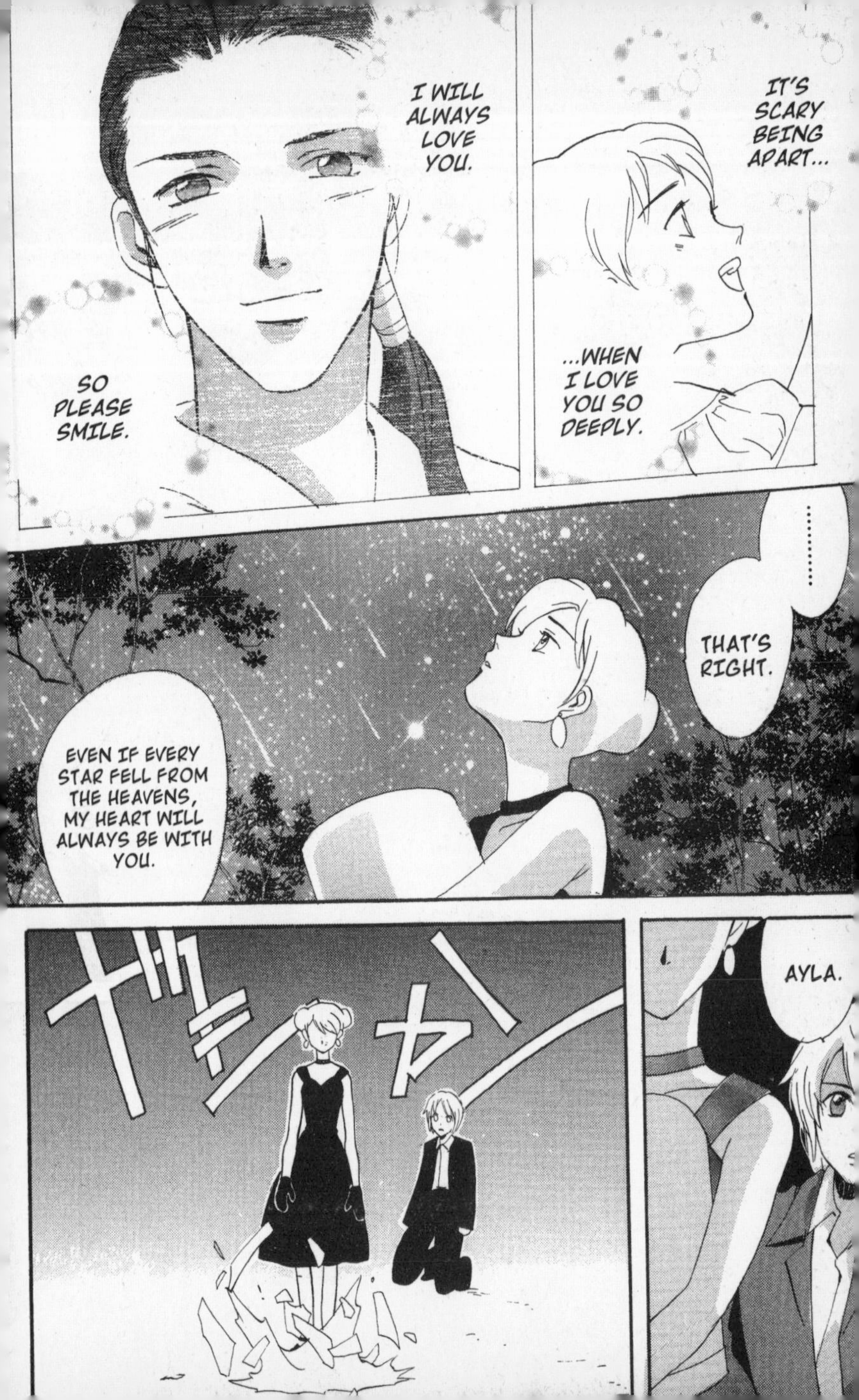
IT'S SCARY BEING APART...
...WHEN I LOVE YOU SO DEEPLY.
I WILL ALWAYS LOVE YOU.
SO PLEASE SMILE.
......
THAT'S RIGHT.
EVEN IF EVERY STAR FELL FROM THE HEAVENS, MY HEART WILL ALWAYS BE WITH YOU.
AYLA.

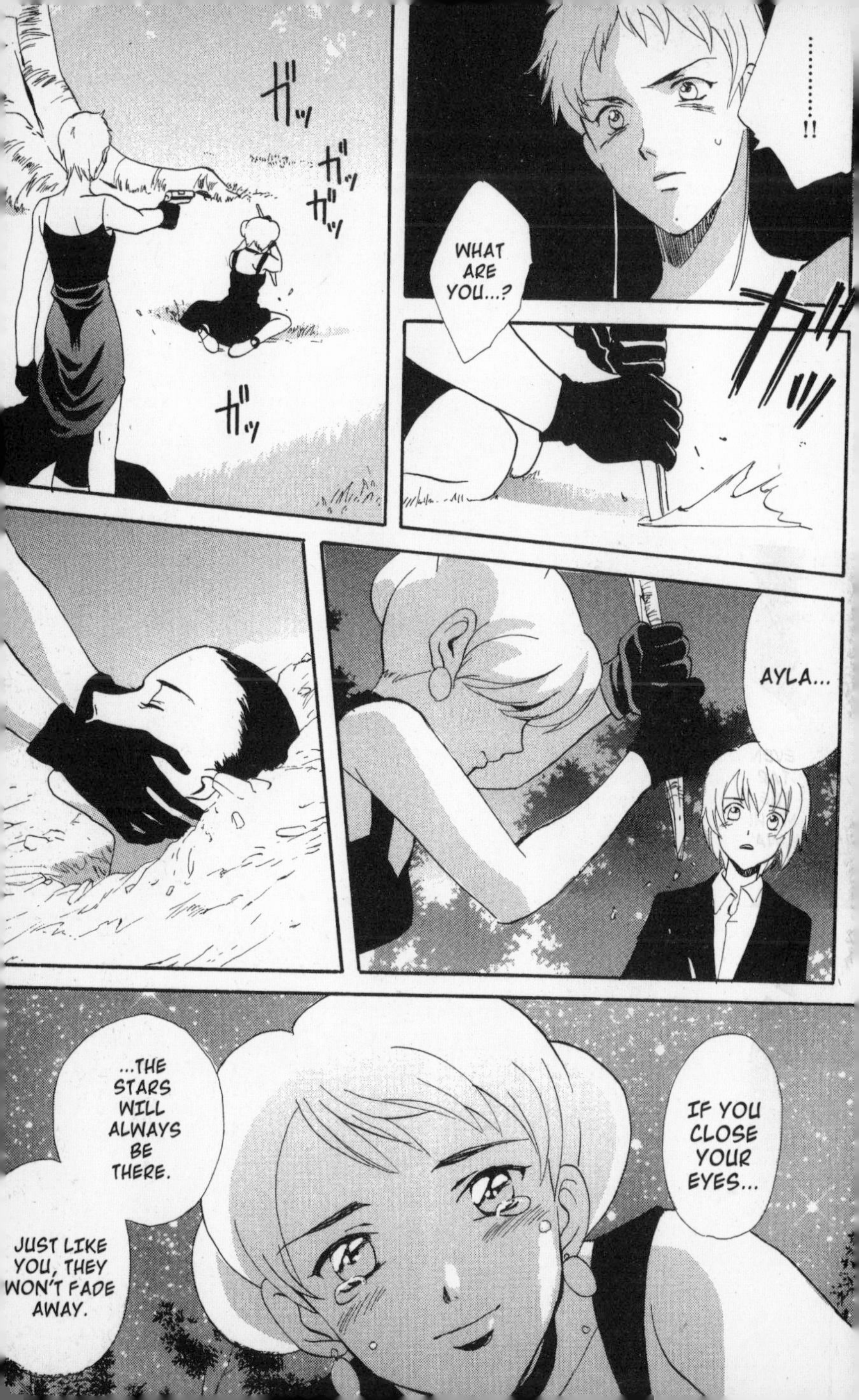

……!!
WHAT ARE YOU...?
ガッ
ガッ
ガッ
ガッ
ガッ
AYLA...
IF YOU CLOSE YOUR EYES...
...THE STARS WILL ALWAYS BE THERE.
JUST LIKE YOU, THEY WON'T FADE AWAY.

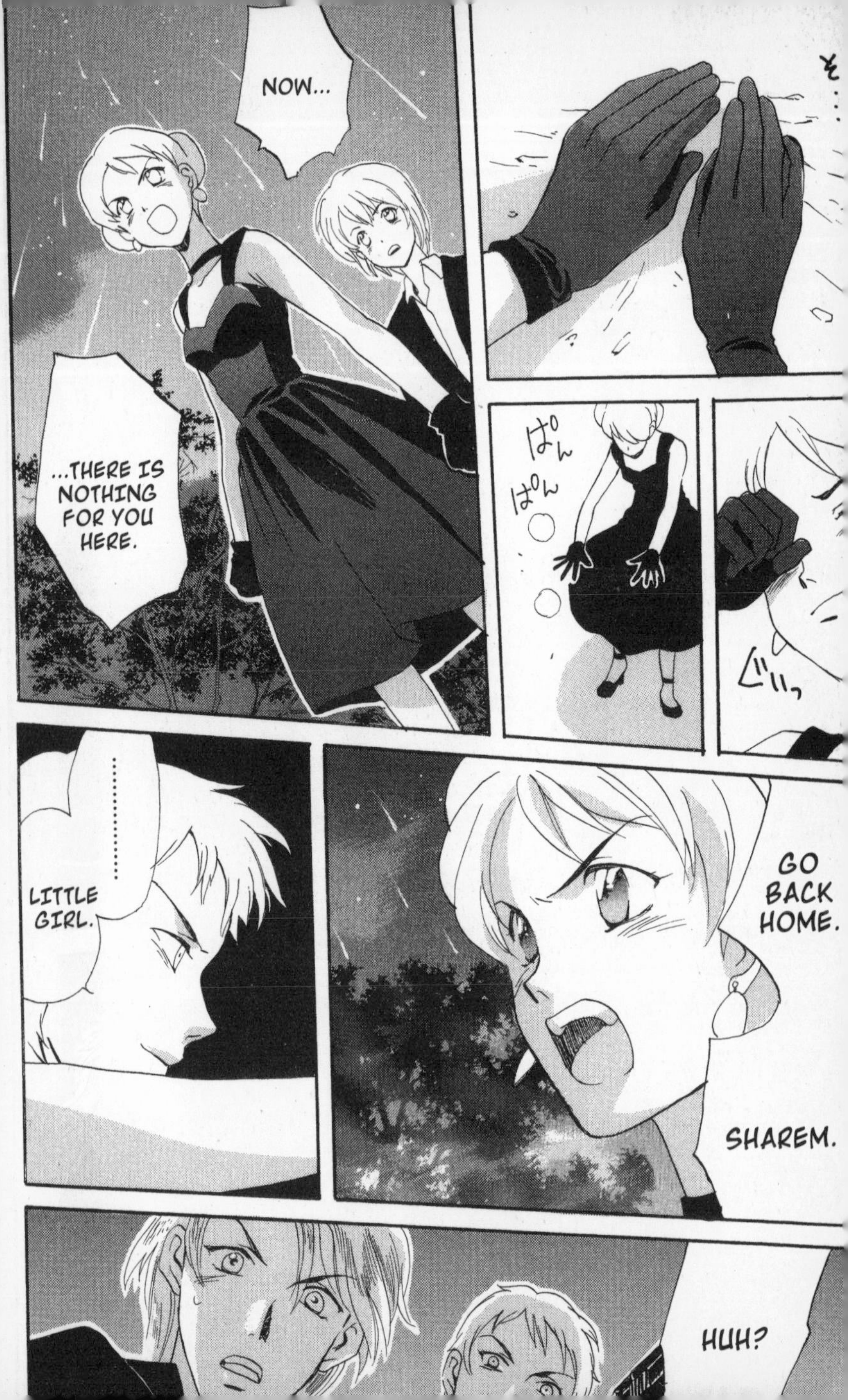
そ…
ぐいっ
ぱん
ぱん
NOW...
...THERE IS NOTHING FOR YOU HERE.
GO BACK HOME.
SHAREM.
......
LITTLE GIRL.
HUH?

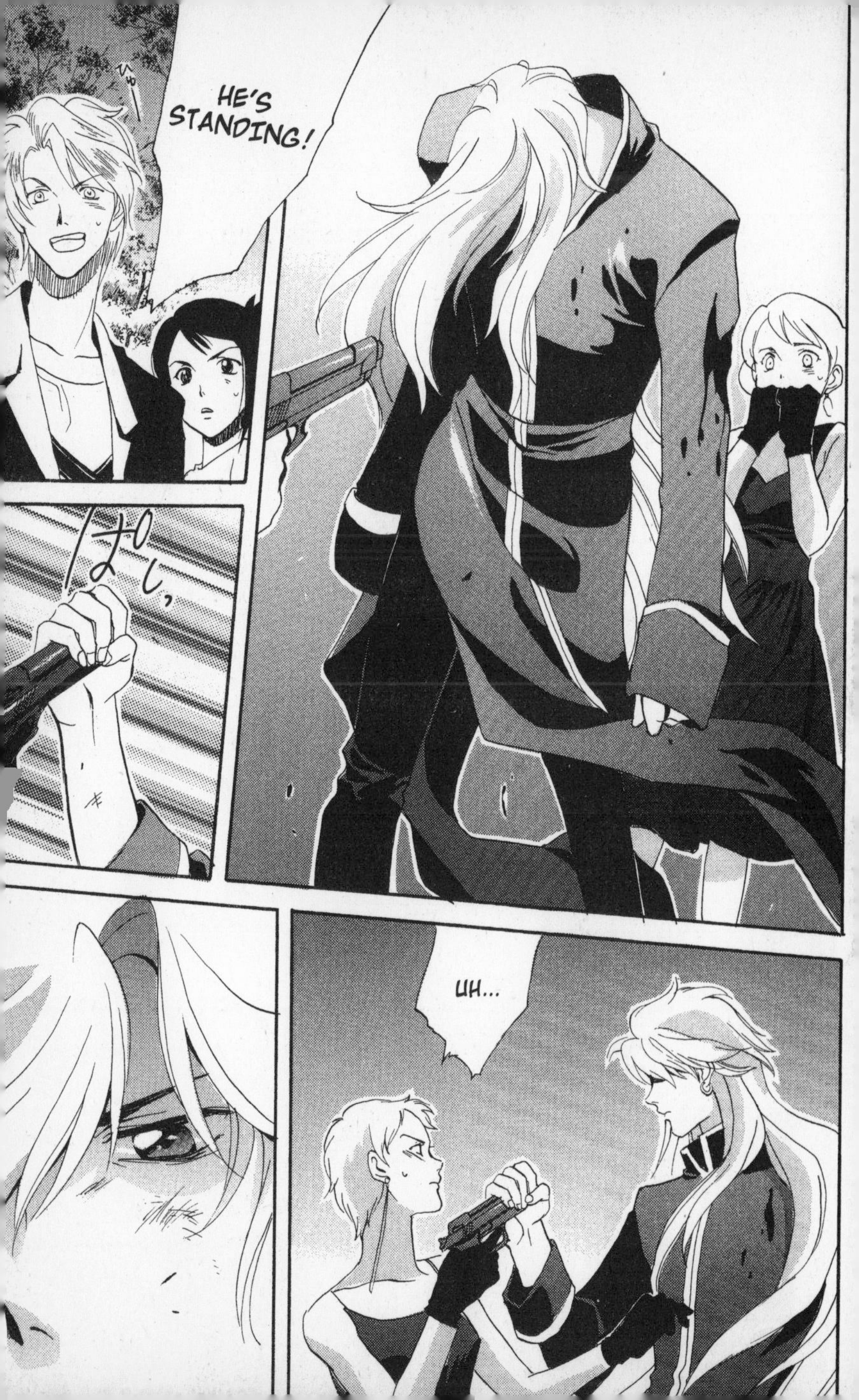
HE'S STANDING!
はし,
UH...

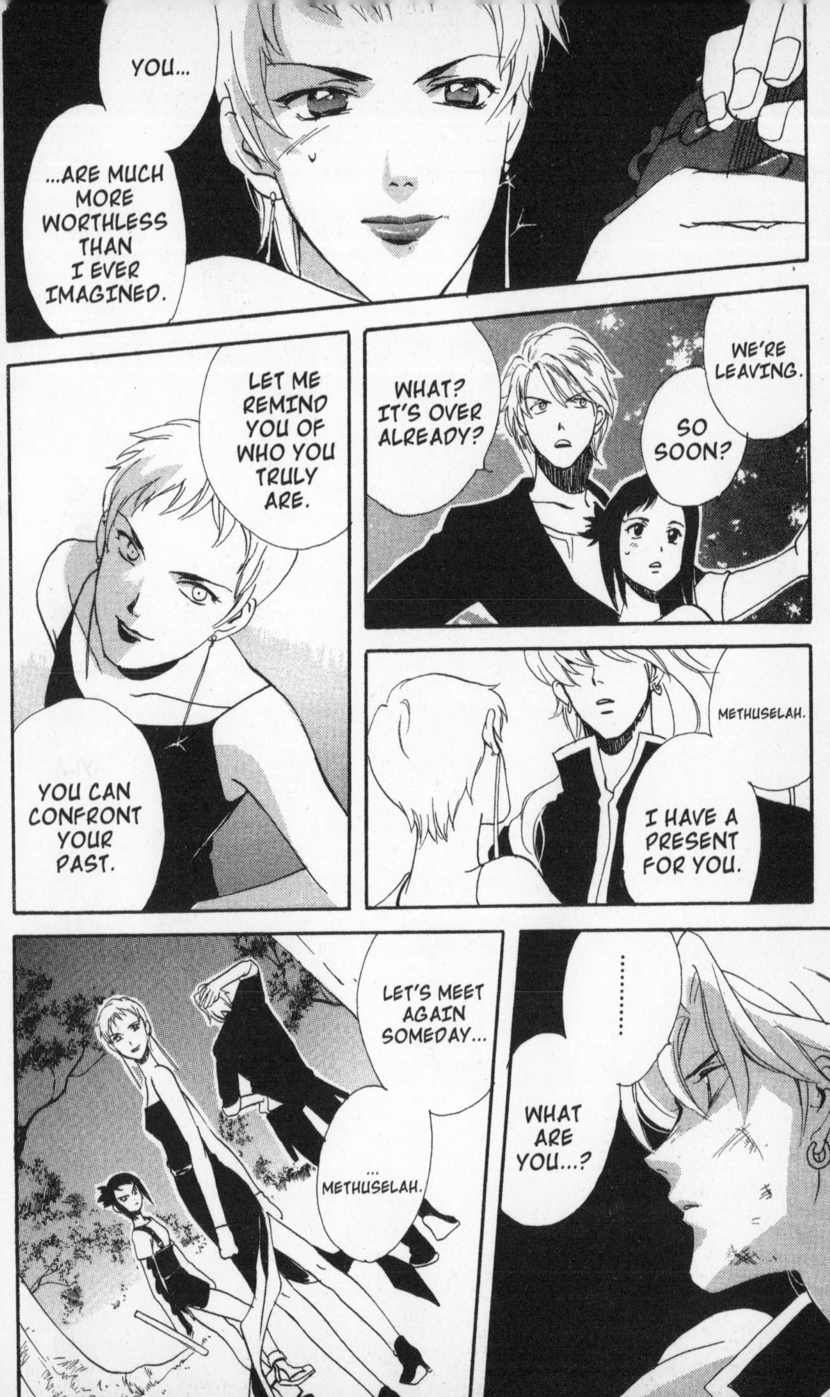
YOU...
...ARE MUCH MORE WORTHLESS THAN I EVER IMAGINED.
WE'RE LEAVING.
SO SOON?
WHAT? IT'S OVER ALREADY?
METHUSELAH.
I HAVE A PRESENT FOR YOU.
LET ME REMIND YOU OF WHO YOU TRULY ARE.
YOU CAN CONFRONT YOUR PAST.
......
WHAT ARE YOU...?
LET'S MEET AGAIN SOMEDAY...
...METHUSELAH.

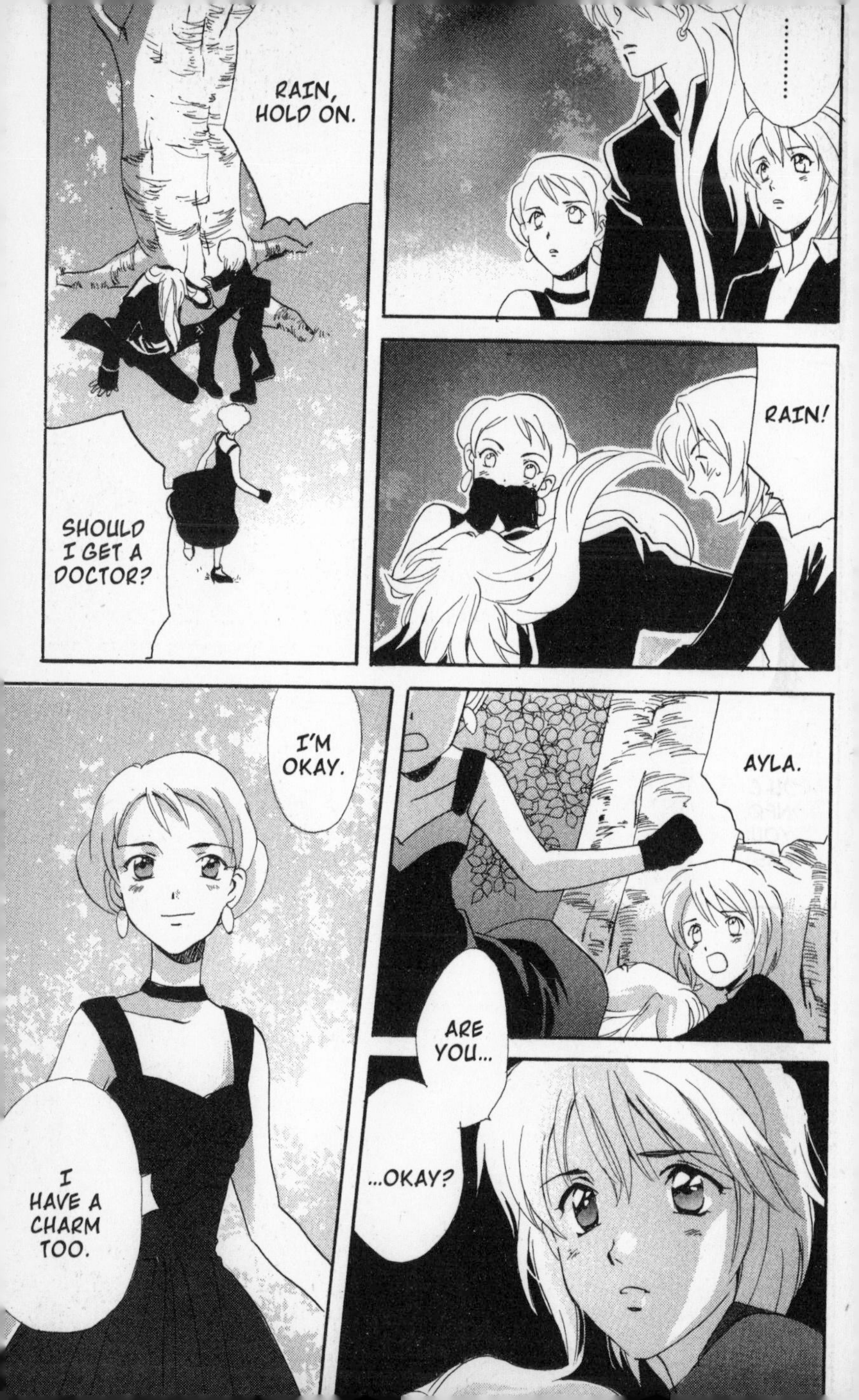
……
RAIN!
RAIN, HOLD ON.
SHOULD I GET A DOCTOR?
AYLA.
ARE YOU...
...OKAY?
I'M OKAY.
I HAVE A CHARM TOO.

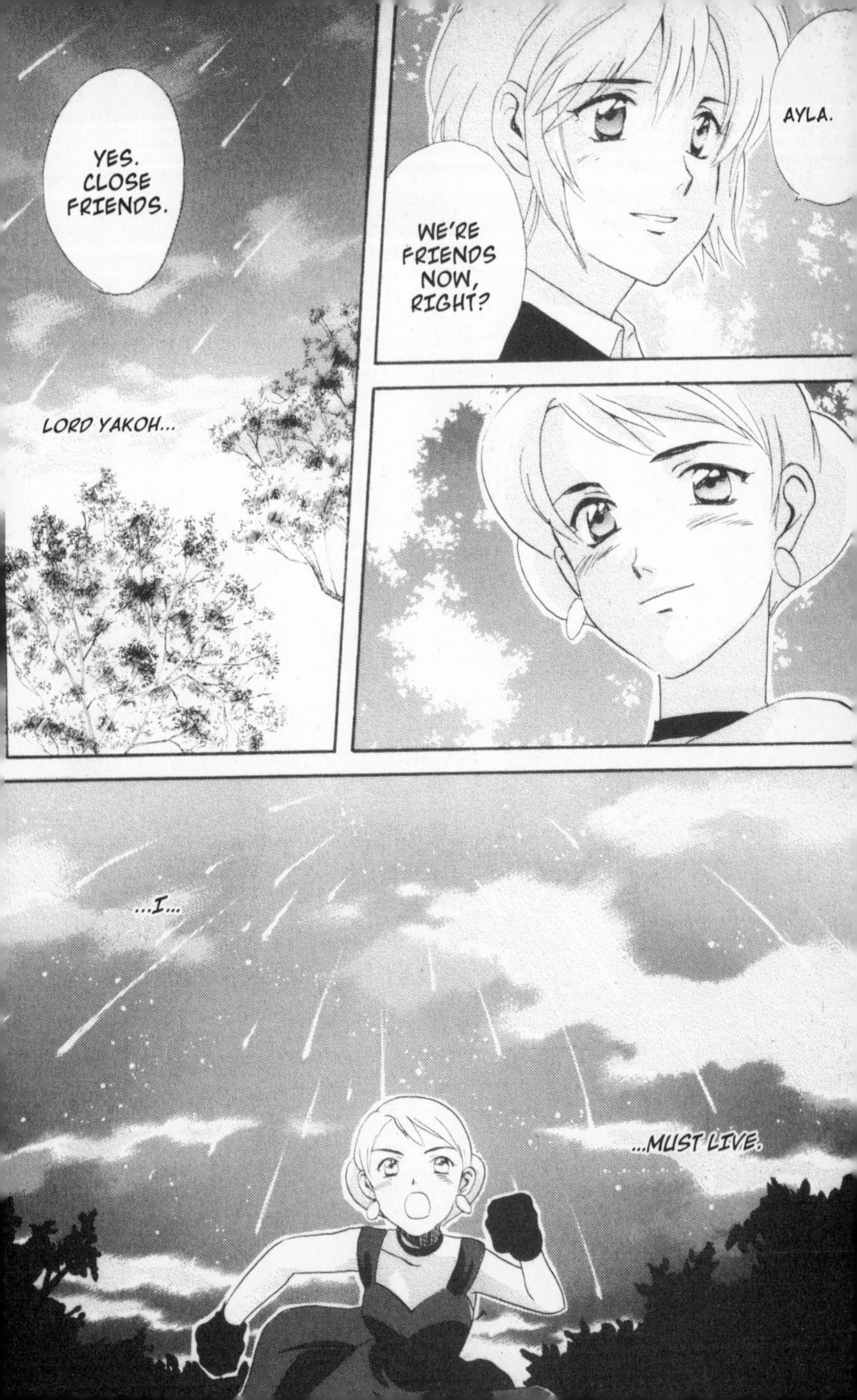
AYLA.
WE'RE FRIENDS NOW, RIGHT?
YES. CLOSE FRIENDS.
LORD YAKOH...
...I...
...MUST LIVE.

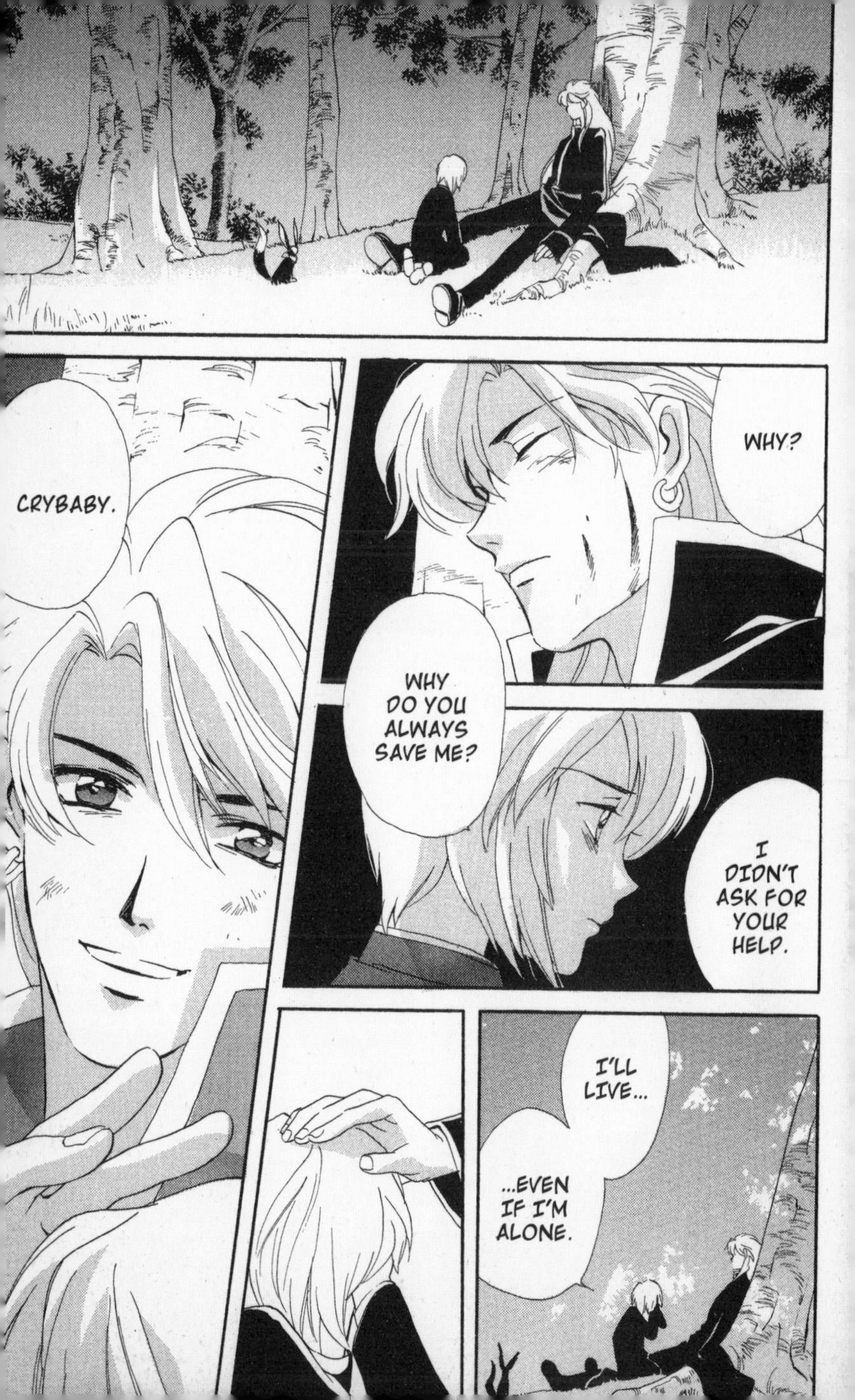
WHY?
WHY DO YOU ALWAYS SAVE ME?
I DIDN'T ASK FOR YOUR HELP.
CRYBABY.
I'LL LIVE...
...EVEN IF I'M ALONE.

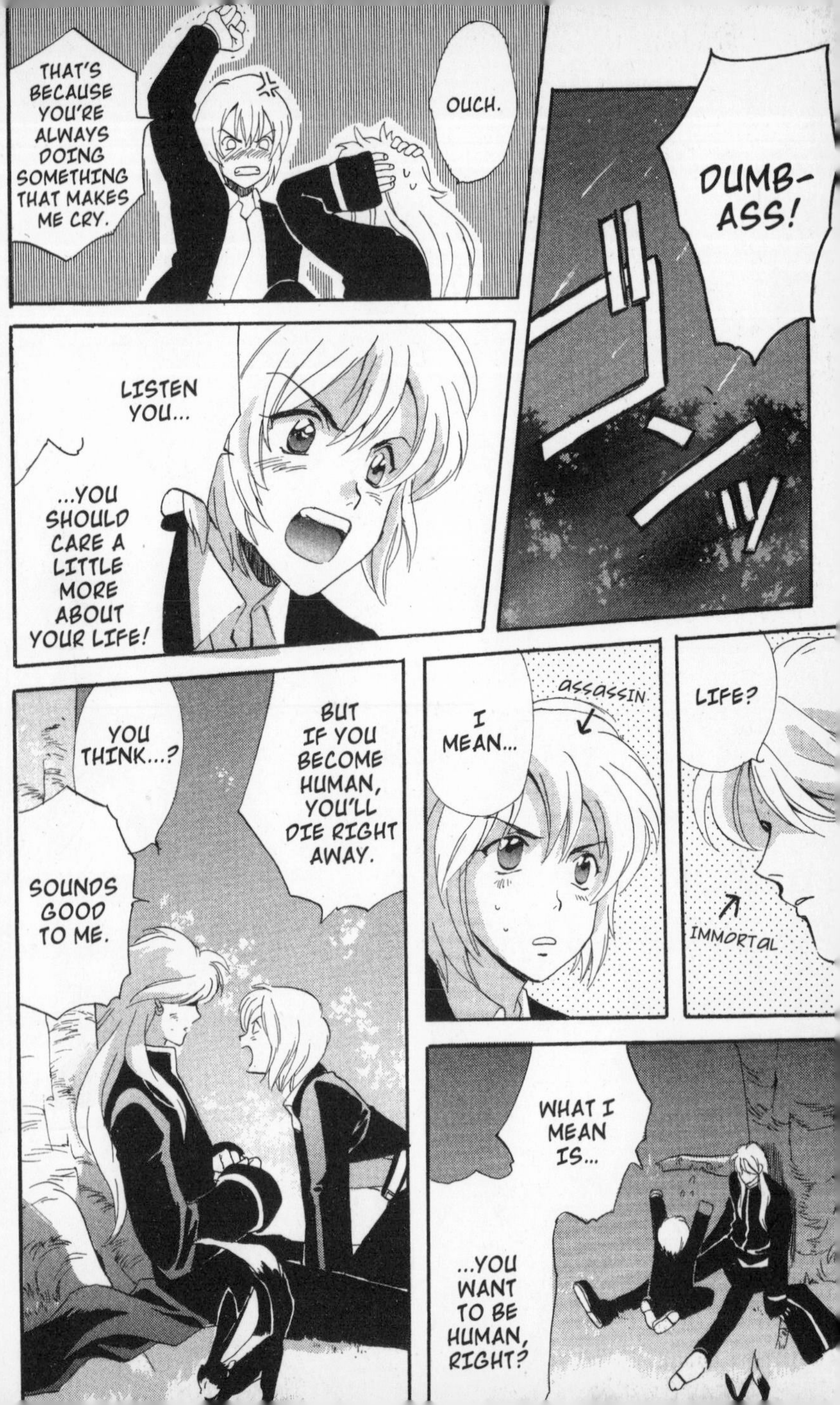
DUMB-ASS!
OUCH.
THAT'S BECAUSE YOU'RE ALWAYS DOING SOMETHING THAT MAKES ME CRY.
LISTEN YOU...
...YOU SHOULD CARE A LITTLE MORE ABOUT YOUR LIFE!
LIFE?
IMMORTAL
I MEAN...
assassin
WHAT I MEAN IS...
...YOU WANT TO BE HUMAN, RIGHT?
BUT IF YOU BECOME HUMAN, YOU'LL DIE RIGHT AWAY.
YOU THINK...?
SOUNDS GOOD TO ME.

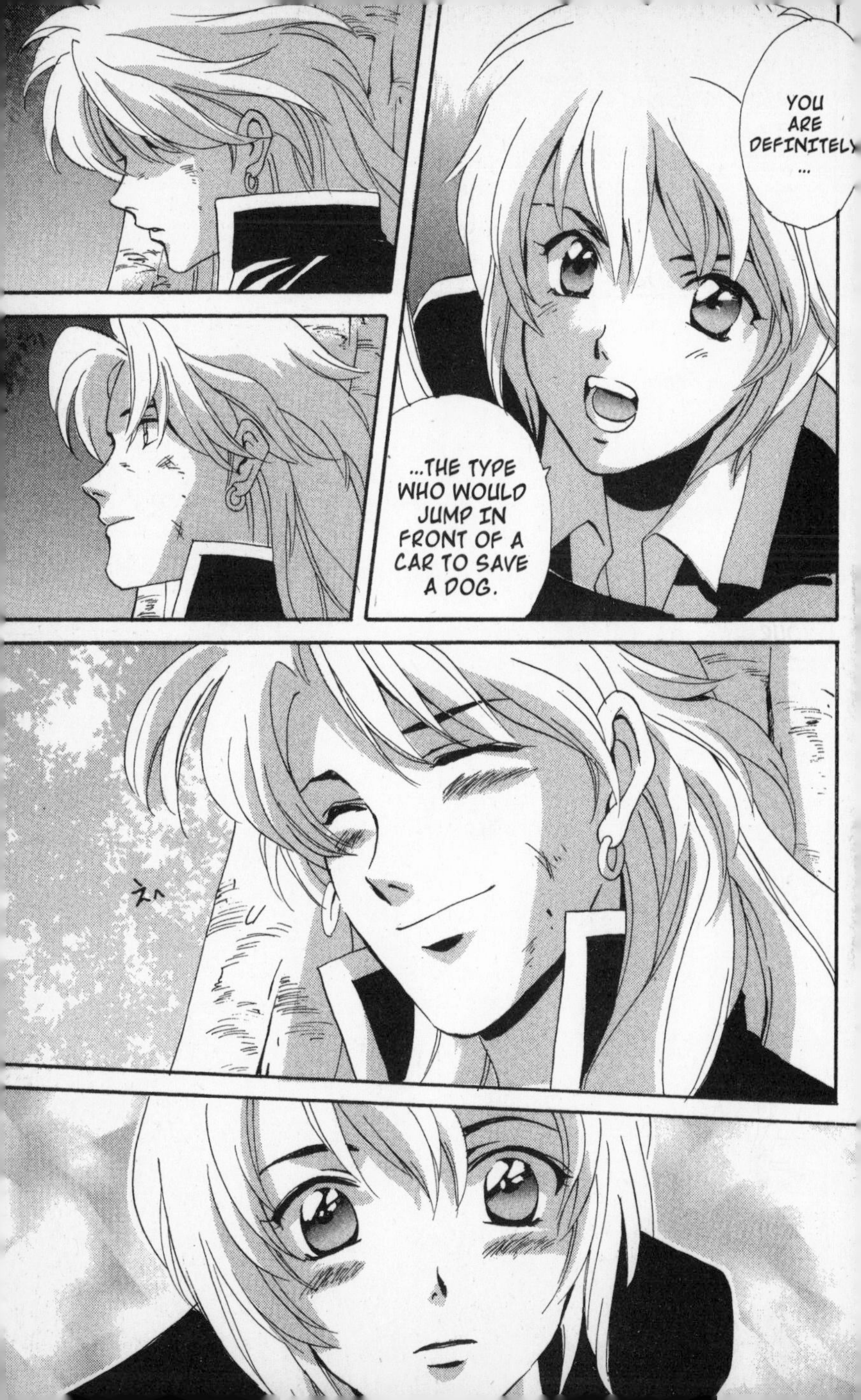
YOU ARE DEFINITELY ...
...THE TYPE WHO WOULD JUMP IN FRONT OF A CAR TO SAVE A DOG.
えへ

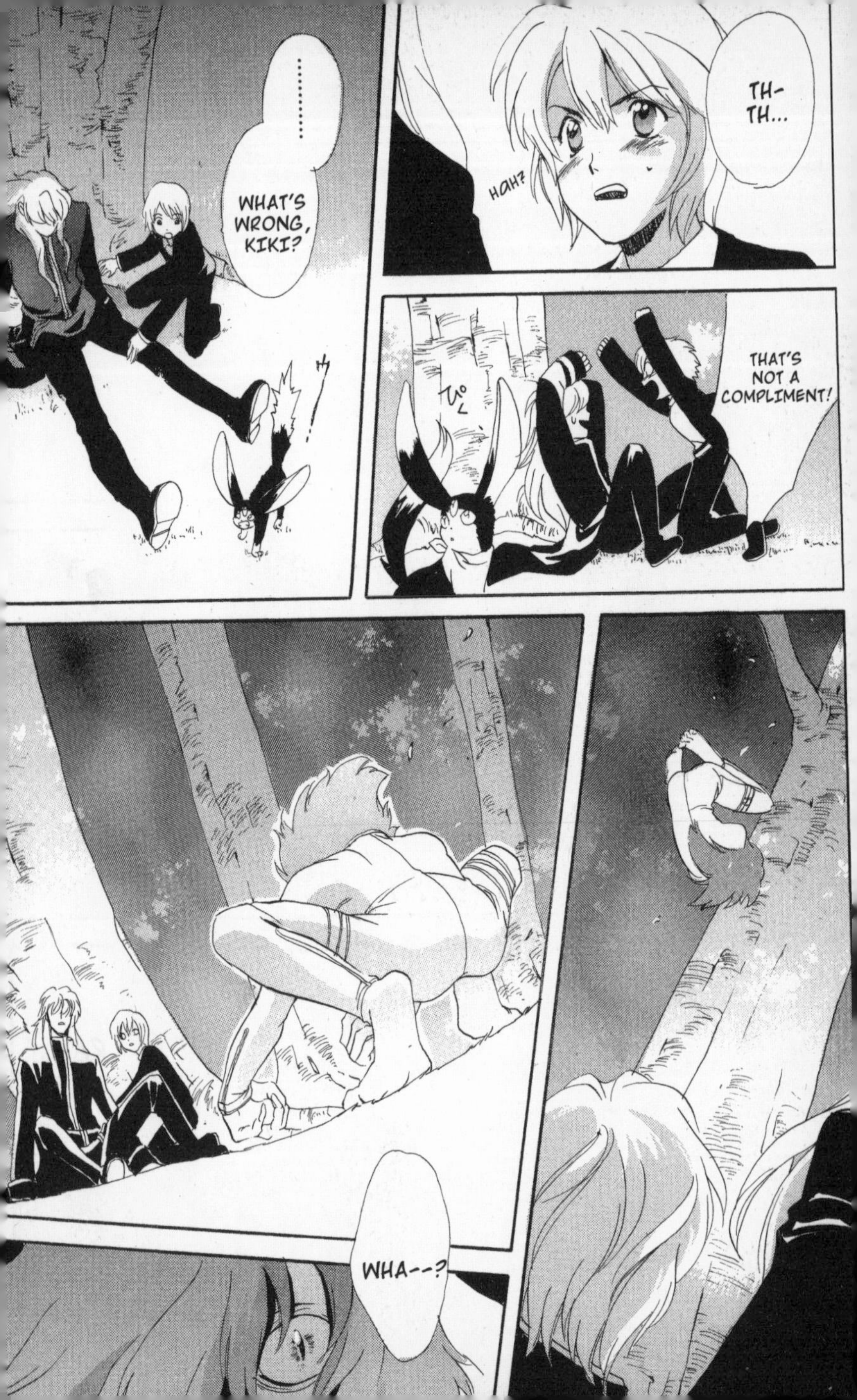
TH- TH...
HAH?
THAT'S NOT A COMPLIMENT!
ぴく
......
WHAT'S WRONG, KIKI?
WHA--?

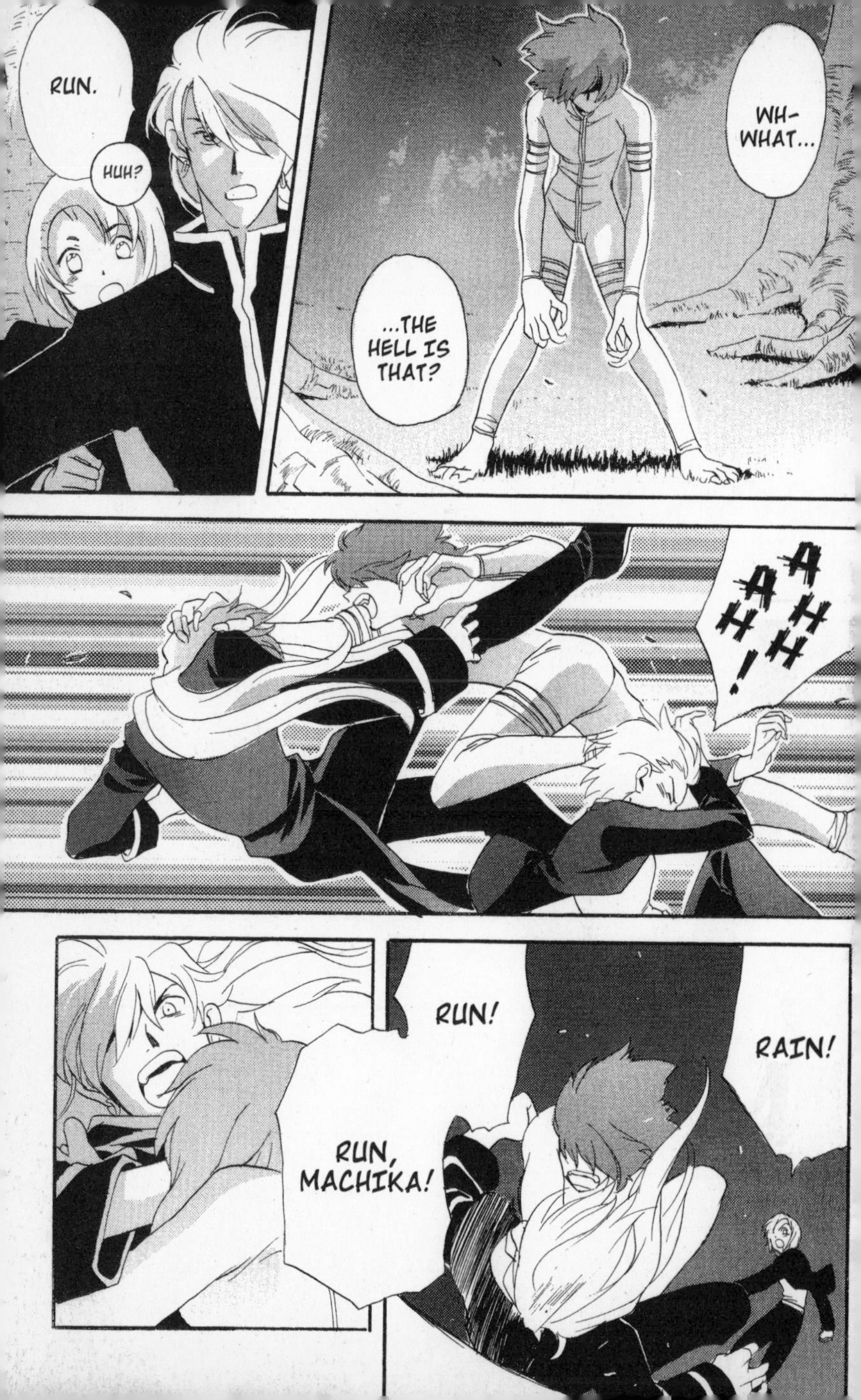
WH- WHAT...
...THE HELL IS THAT?
RUN.
HUH?
AHHH AHH!
RAIN!
RUN!
RUN, MACHIKA!

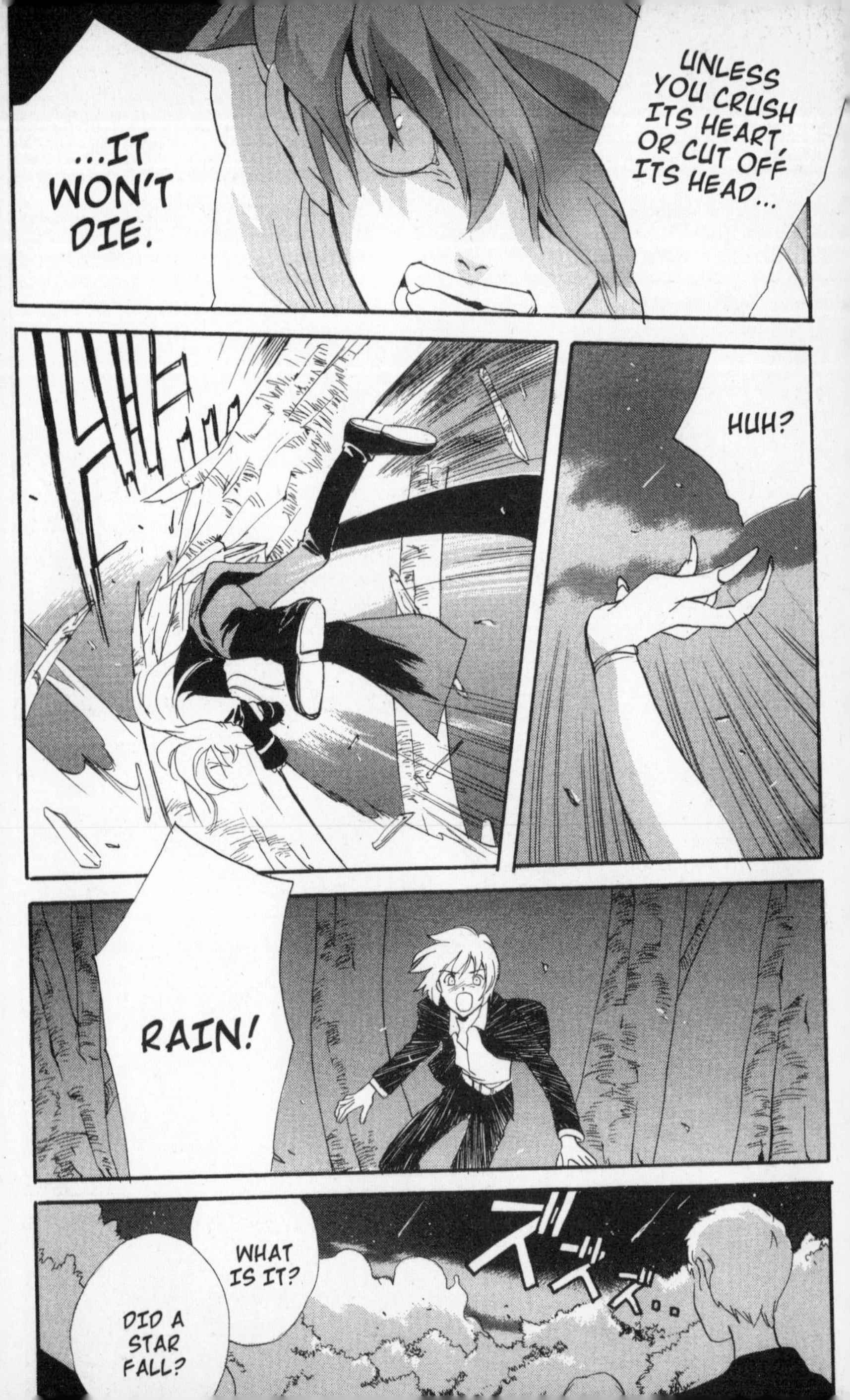
UNLESS YOU CRUSH ITS HEART, OR CUT OFF ITS HEAD...
...IT WON'T DIE.
HUH?
RAIN!
WHAT IS IT?
DID A STAR FALL?

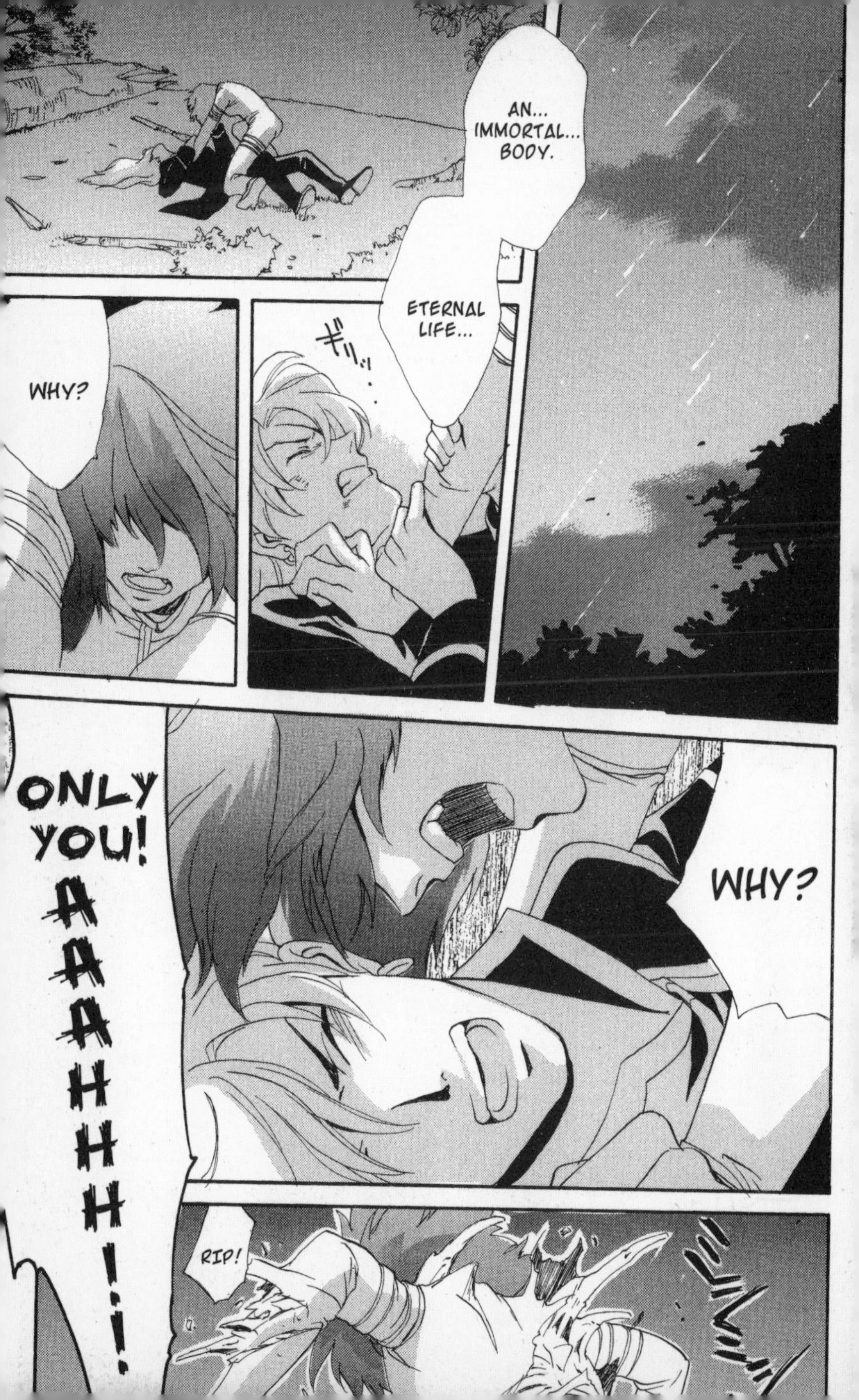
AN... IMMORTAL... BODY.
ETERNAL LIFE...
ギリッ
WHY?
WHY?
ONLY YOU! AAAHHHH!!!
RIP!

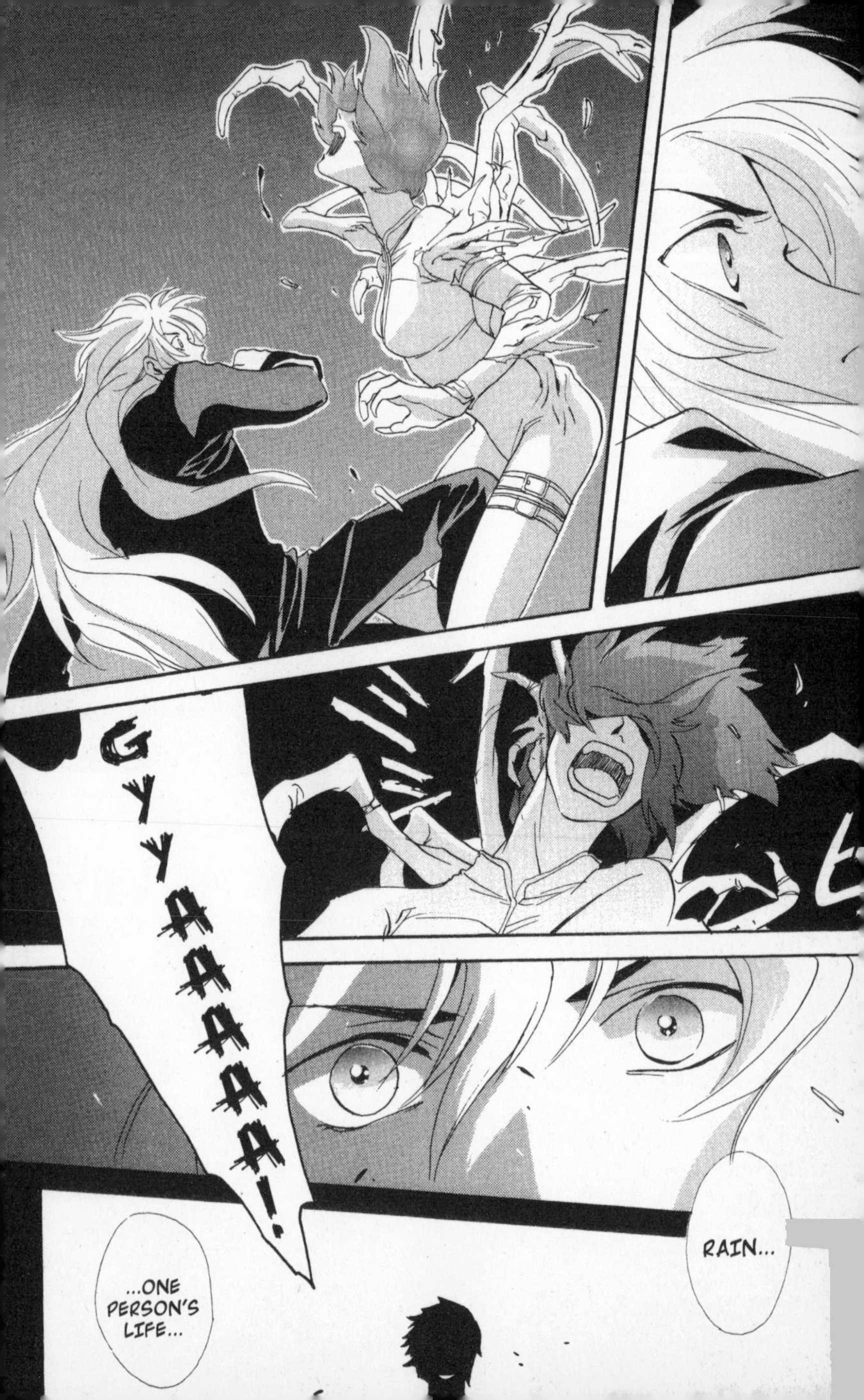
GYAAAAA!
RAIN...
...ONE PERSON'S LIFE...

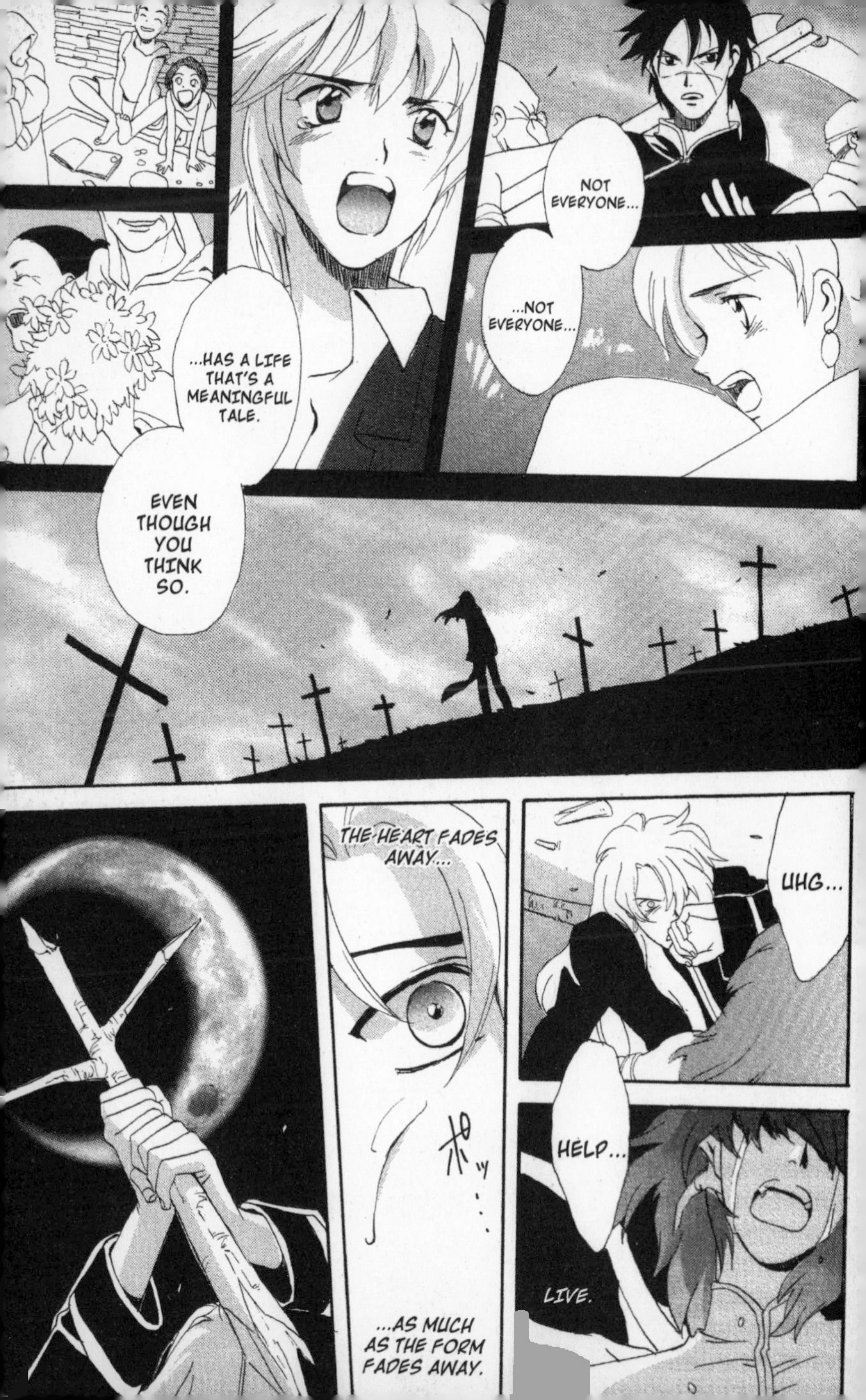
NOT EVERYONE...
...NOT EVERYONE...
...HAS A LIFE THAT'S A MEANINGFUL TALE.
EVEN THOUGH YOU THINK SO.
UHG...
HELP...
LIVE.
THE HEART FADES AWAY...
ポッ
...AS MUCH AS THE FORM FADES AWAY.

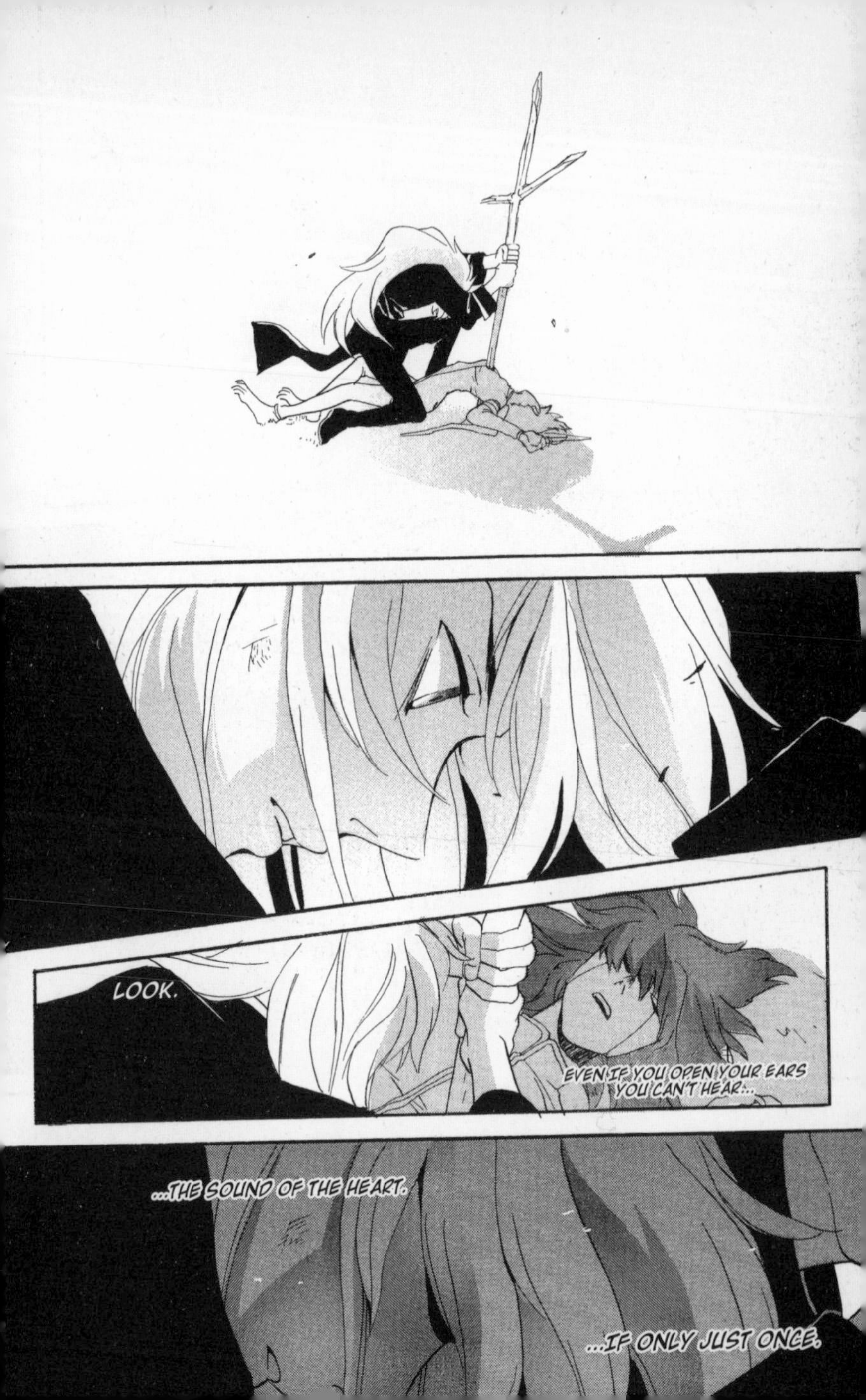
EVEN IF YOU OPEN YOUR EARS YOU CAN'T HEAR...
LOOK.
...THE SOUND OF THE HEART.
...IF ONLY JUST ONCE.

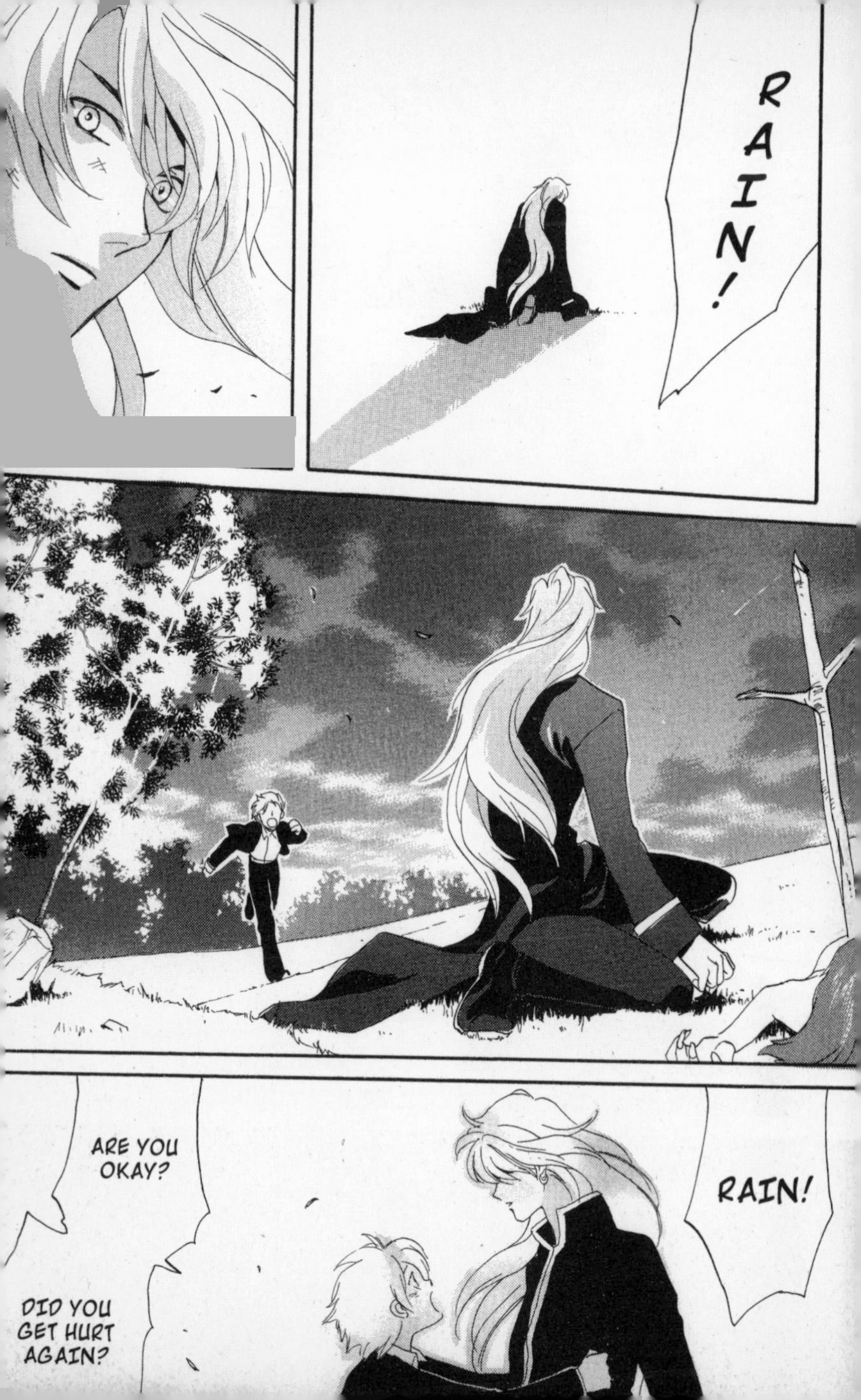
RAIN!
RAIN!
ARE YOU OKAY?
DID YOU GET HURT AGAIN?

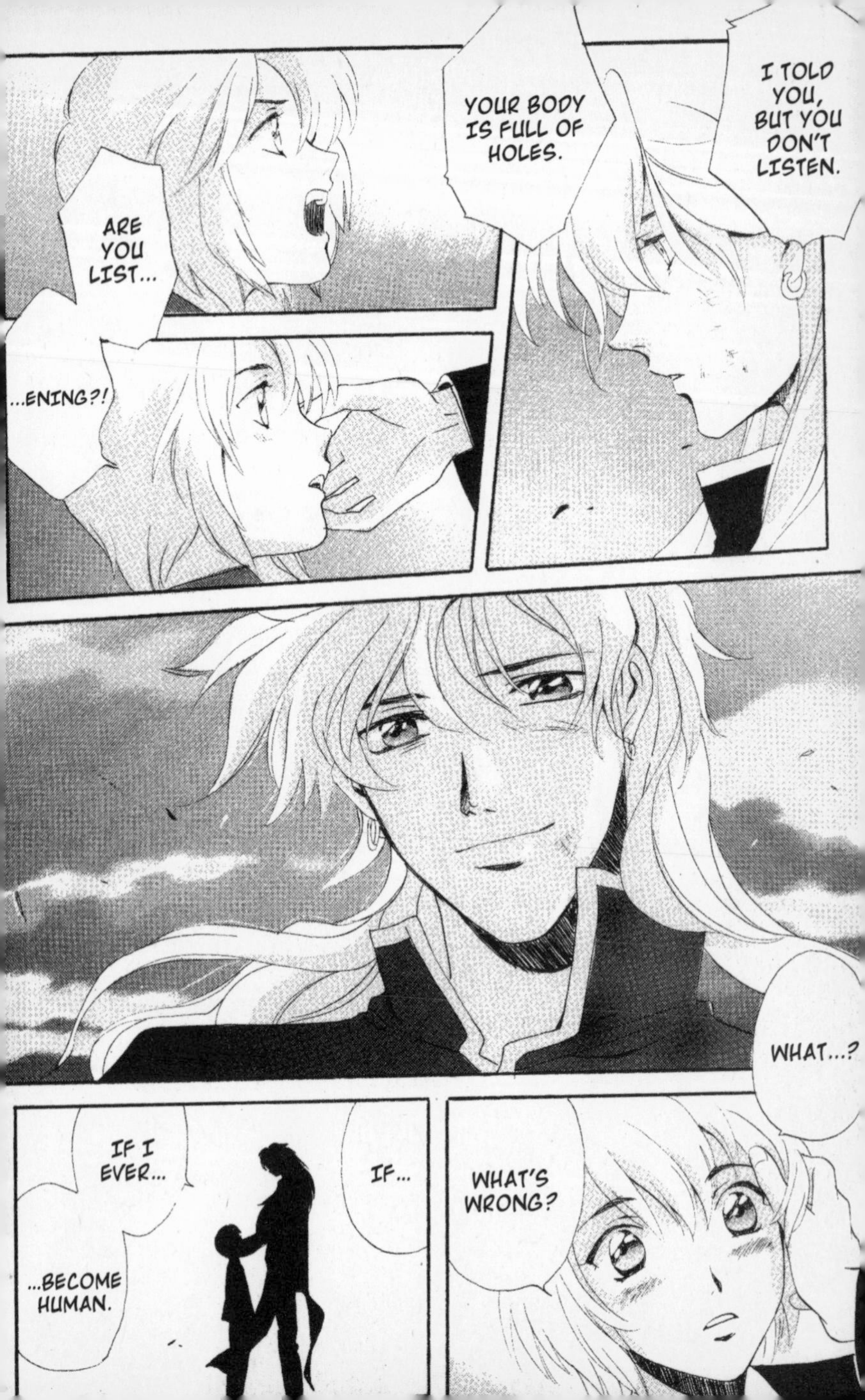
I TOLD YOU, BUT YOU DON'T LISTEN.
YOUR BODY IS FULL OF HOLES.
ARE YOU LIST...
...ENING?!
WHAT...?
WHAT'S WRONG?
IF...
IF I EVER...
...BECOME HUMAN.

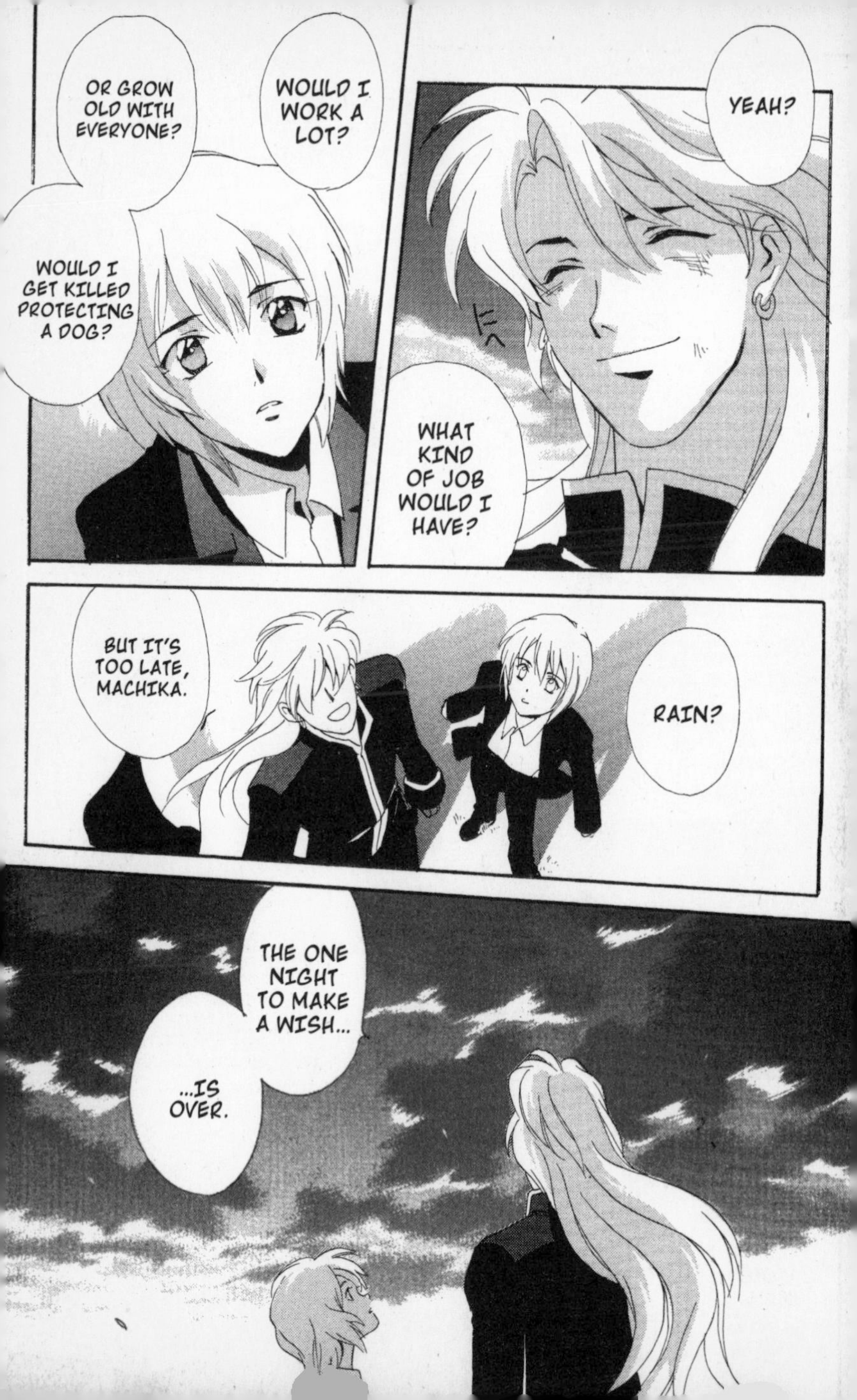
YEAH?
WHAT KIND OF JOB WOULD I HAVE?
WOULD I WORK A LOT?
OR GROW OLD WITH EVERYONE?
WOULD I GET KILLED PROTECTING A DOG?
RAIN?
BUT IT'S TOO LATE, MACHIKA.
THE ONE NIGHT TO MAKE A WISH...
...IS OVER.

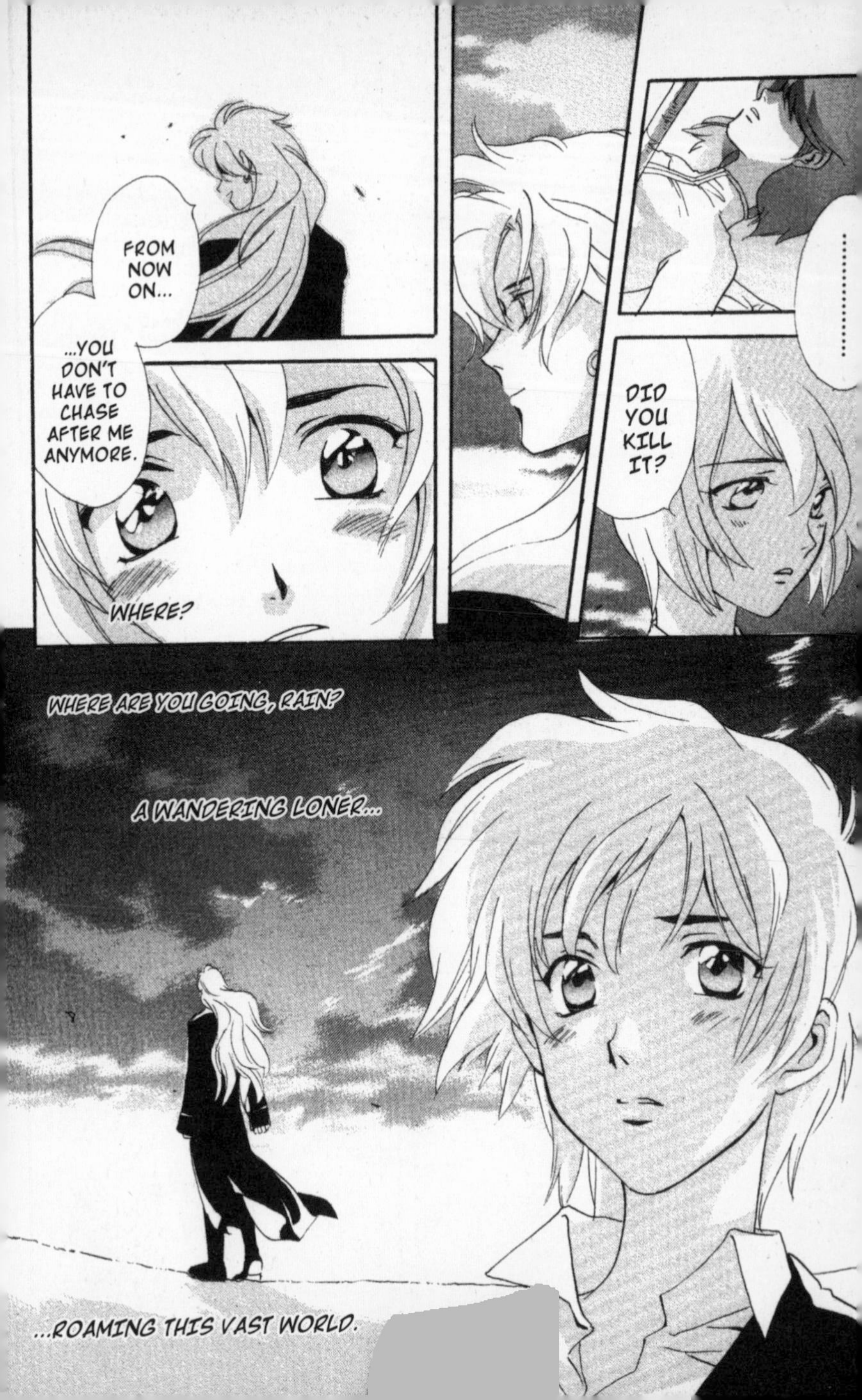
......
DID YOU KILL IT?
FROM NOW ON...
...YOU DON'T HAVE TO CHASE AFTER ME ANYMORE.
WHERE?
WHERE ARE YOU GOING, RAIN?
A WANDERING LONER...
...ROAMING THIS VAST WORLD.

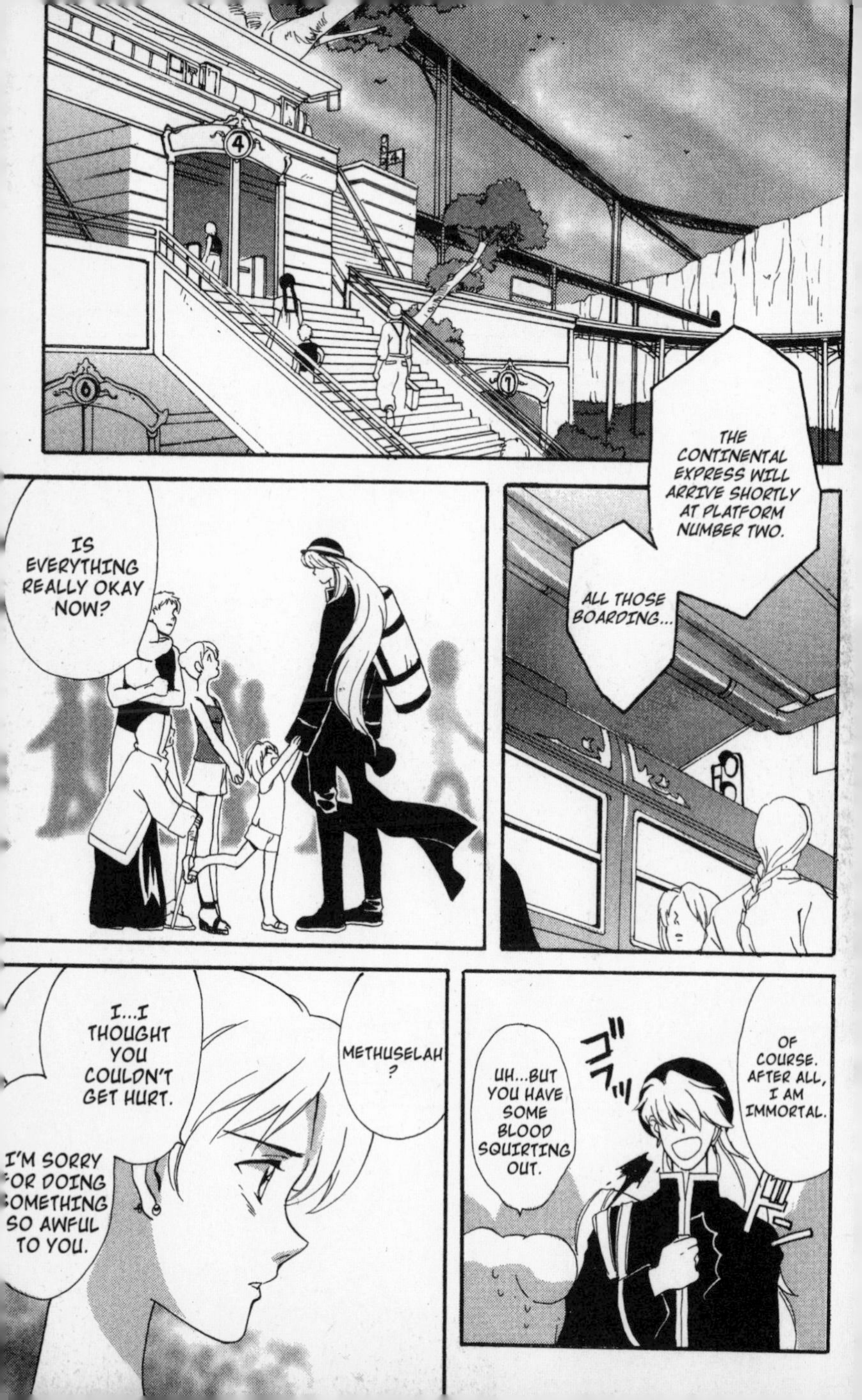
THE CONTINENTAL EXPRESS WILL ARRIVE SHORTLY AT PLATFORM NUMBER TWO.
ALL THOSE BOARDING...
IS EVERYTHING REALLY OKAY NOW?
OF COURSE. AFTER ALL, I AM IMMORTAL.
ゴフッ
UH...BUT YOU HAVE SOME BLOOD SQUIRTING OUT.
METHUSELAH?
I...I THOUGHT YOU COULDN'T GET HURT.
I'M SORRY FOR DOING SOMETHING SO AWFUL TO YOU.

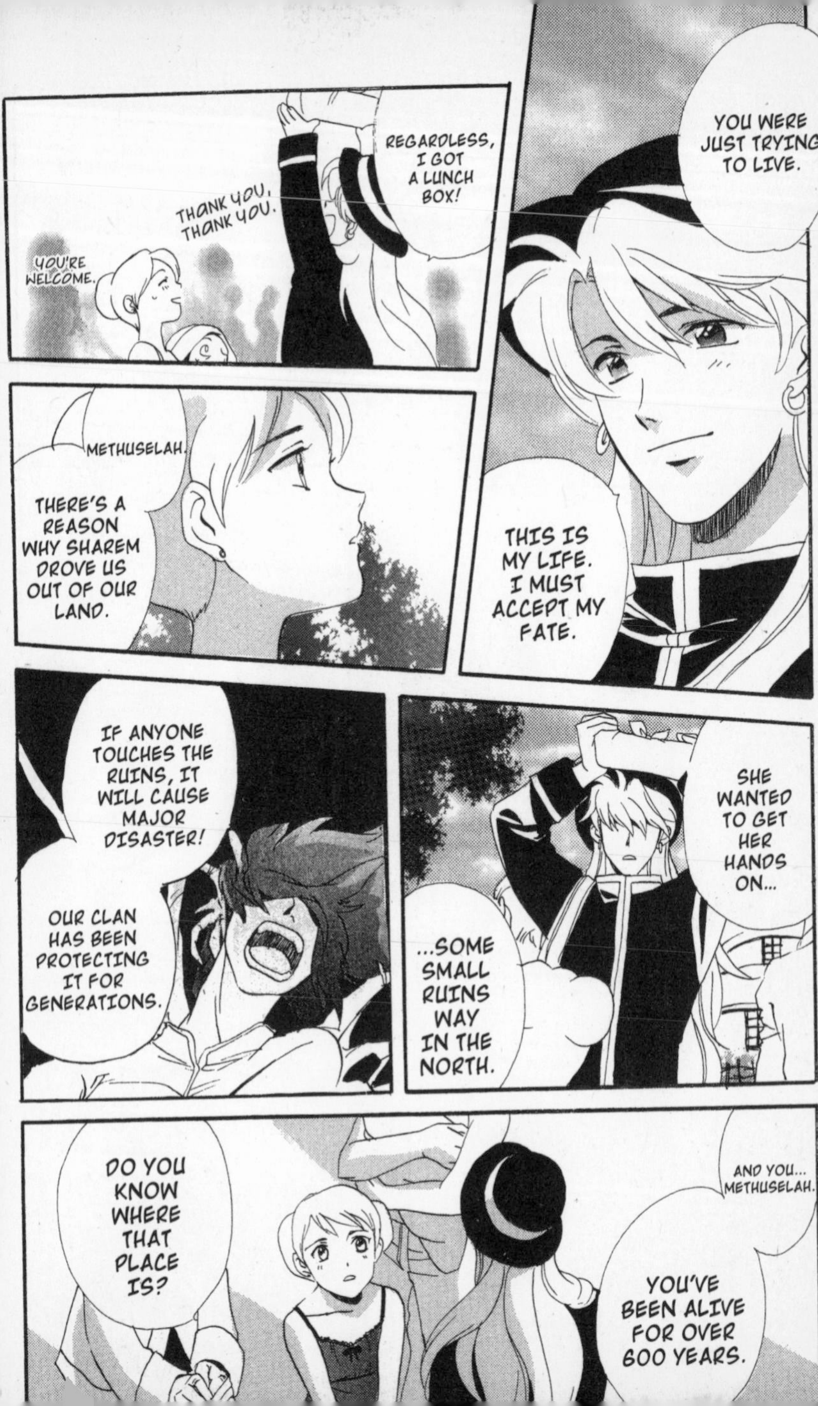
YOU WERE JUST TRYING TO LIVE.
THIS IS MY LIFE. I MUST ACCEPT MY FATE.
REGARDLESS, I GOT A LUNCH BOX!
THANK YOU, THANK YOU.
YOU'RE WELCOME.
METHUSELAH.
THERE'S A REASON WHY SHAREM DROVE US OUT OF OUR LAND.
SHE WANTED TO GET HER HANDS ON...
...SOME SMALL RUINS WAY IN THE NORTH.
IF ANYONE TOUCHES THE RUINS, IT WILL CAUSE MAJOR DISASTER!
OUR CLAN HAS BEEN PROTECTING IT FOR GENERATIONS.
AND YOU... METHUSELAH.
YOU'VE BEEN ALIVE FOR OVER 600 YEARS.
DO YOU KNOW WHERE THAT PLACE IS?

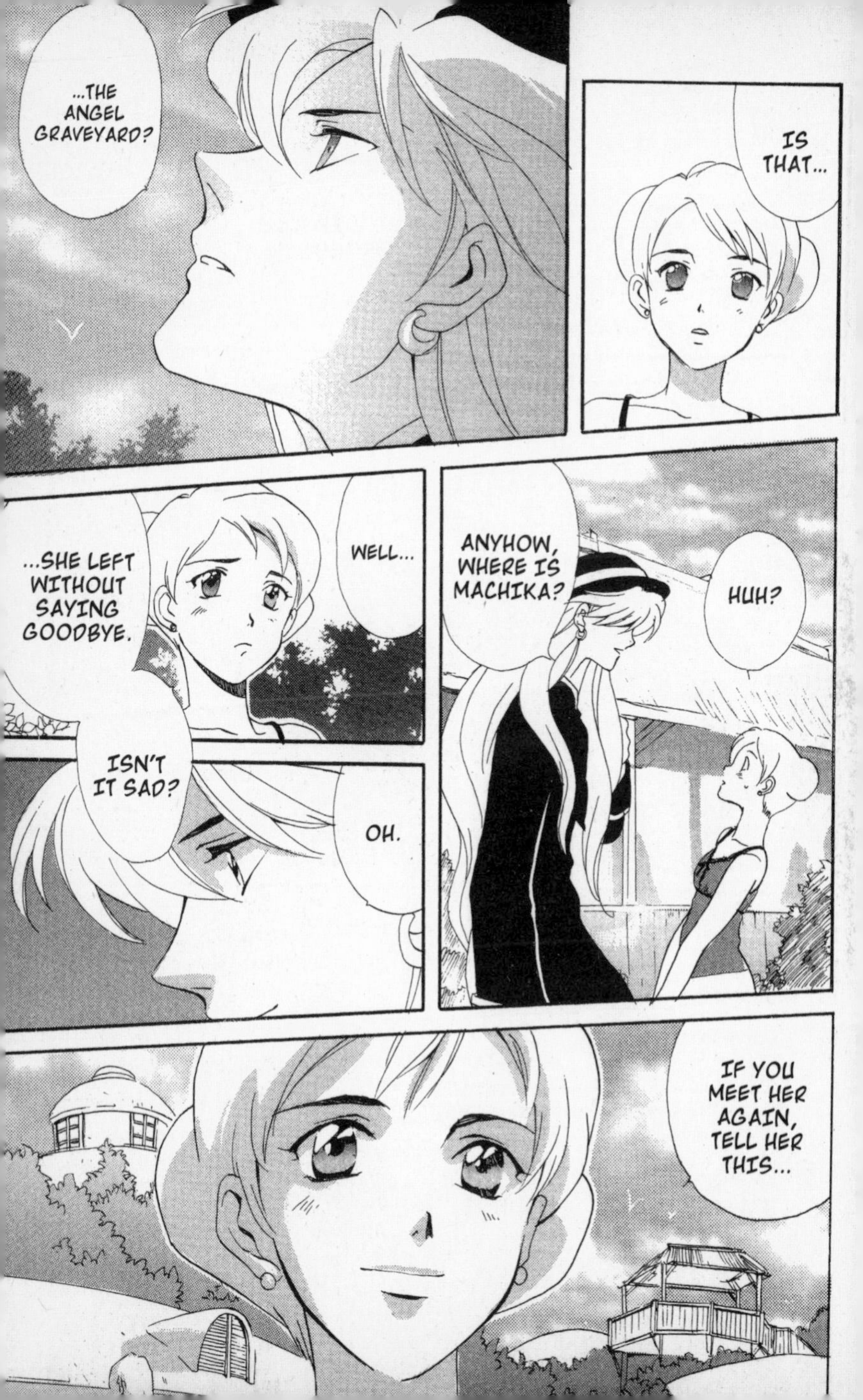
IS THAT...
...THE ANGEL GRAVEYARD?
ANYHOW, WHERE IS MACHIKA?
HUH?
WELL...
...SHE LEFT WITHOUT SAYING GOODBYE.
OH.
ISN'T IT SAD?
IF YOU MEET HER AGAIN, TELL HER THIS...

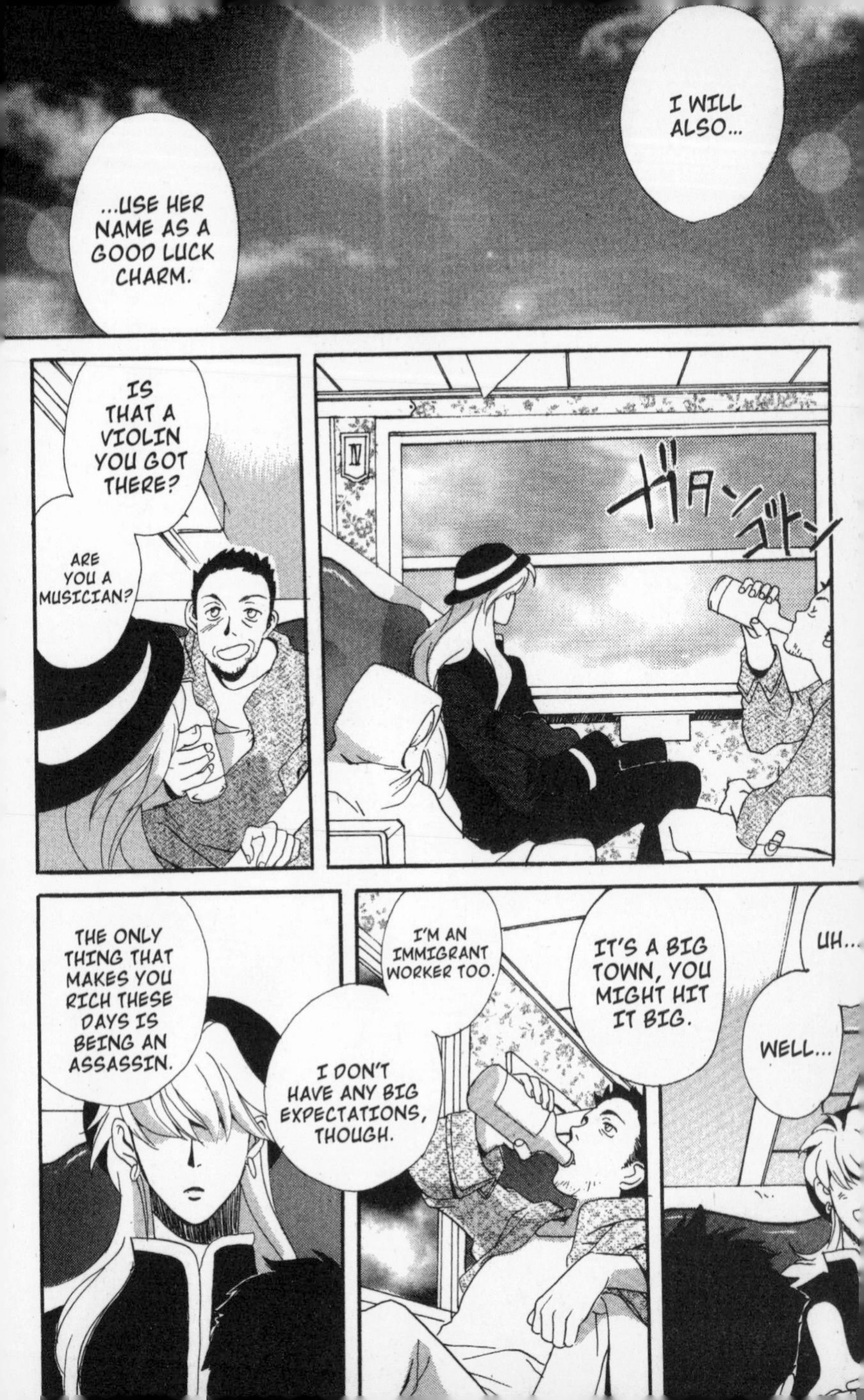
I WILL ALSO...
...USE HER NAME AS A GOOD LUCK CHARM.
ガタン ゴトン
IS THAT A VIOLIN YOU GOT THERE?
ARE YOU A MUSICIAN?
UH...
WELL...
IT'S A BIG TOWN, YOU MIGHT HIT IT BIG.
I'M AN IMMIGRANT WORKER TOO.
I DON'T HAVE ANY BIG EXPECTATIONS, THOUGH.
THE ONLY THING THAT MAKES YOU RICH THESE DAYS IS BEING AN ASSASSIN.

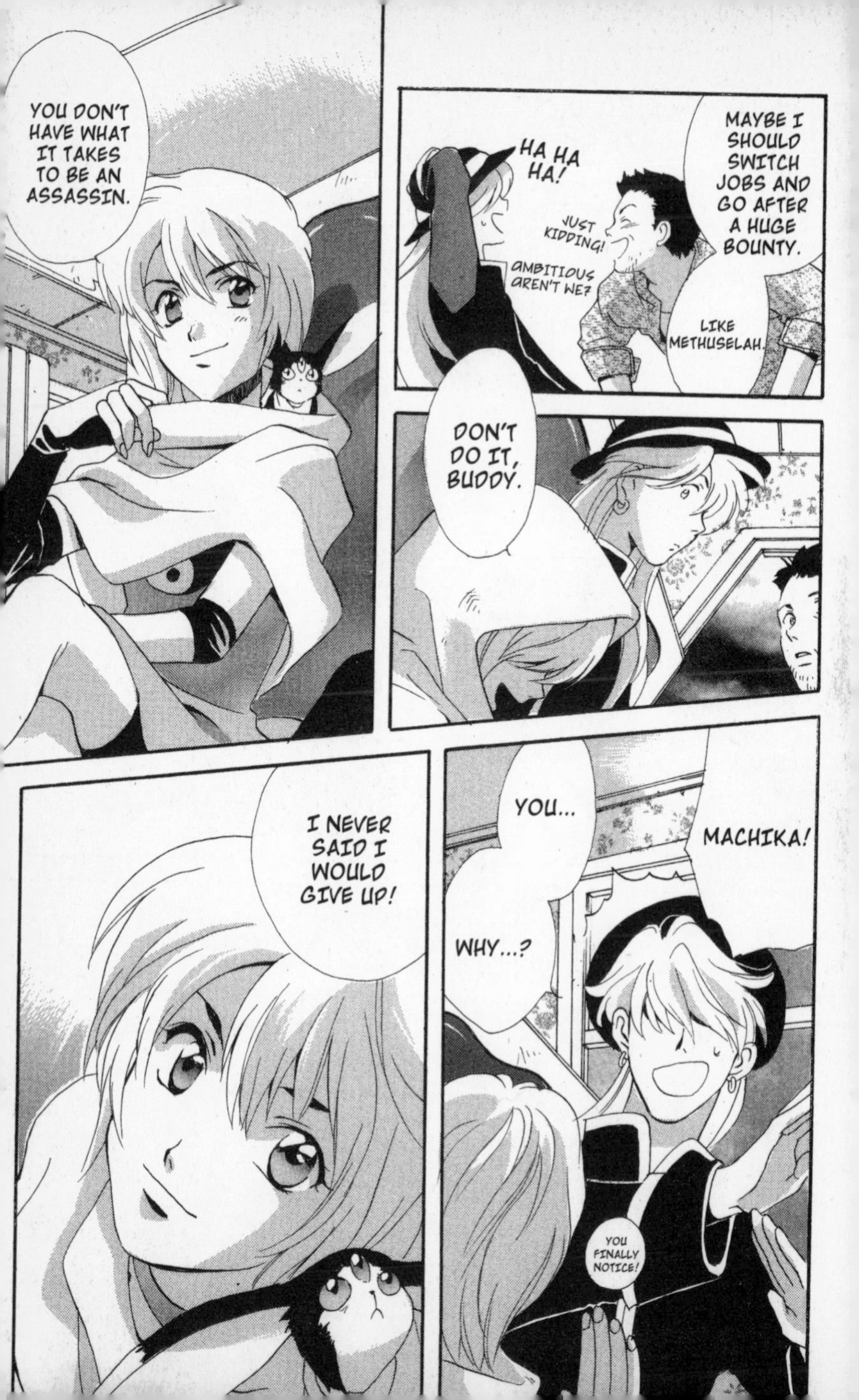
MAYBE I SHOULD SWITCH JOBS AND GO AFTER A HUGE BOUNTY.
LIKE METHUSELAH.
HA HA HA!
JUST KIDDING!
AMBITIOUS AREN'T WE?
DON'T DO IT, BUDDY.
YOU DON'T HAVE WHAT IT TAKES TO BE AN ASSASSIN.
MACHIKA!
YOU...
WHY...?
YOU FINALLY NOTICE!
I NEVER SAID I WOULD GIVE UP!

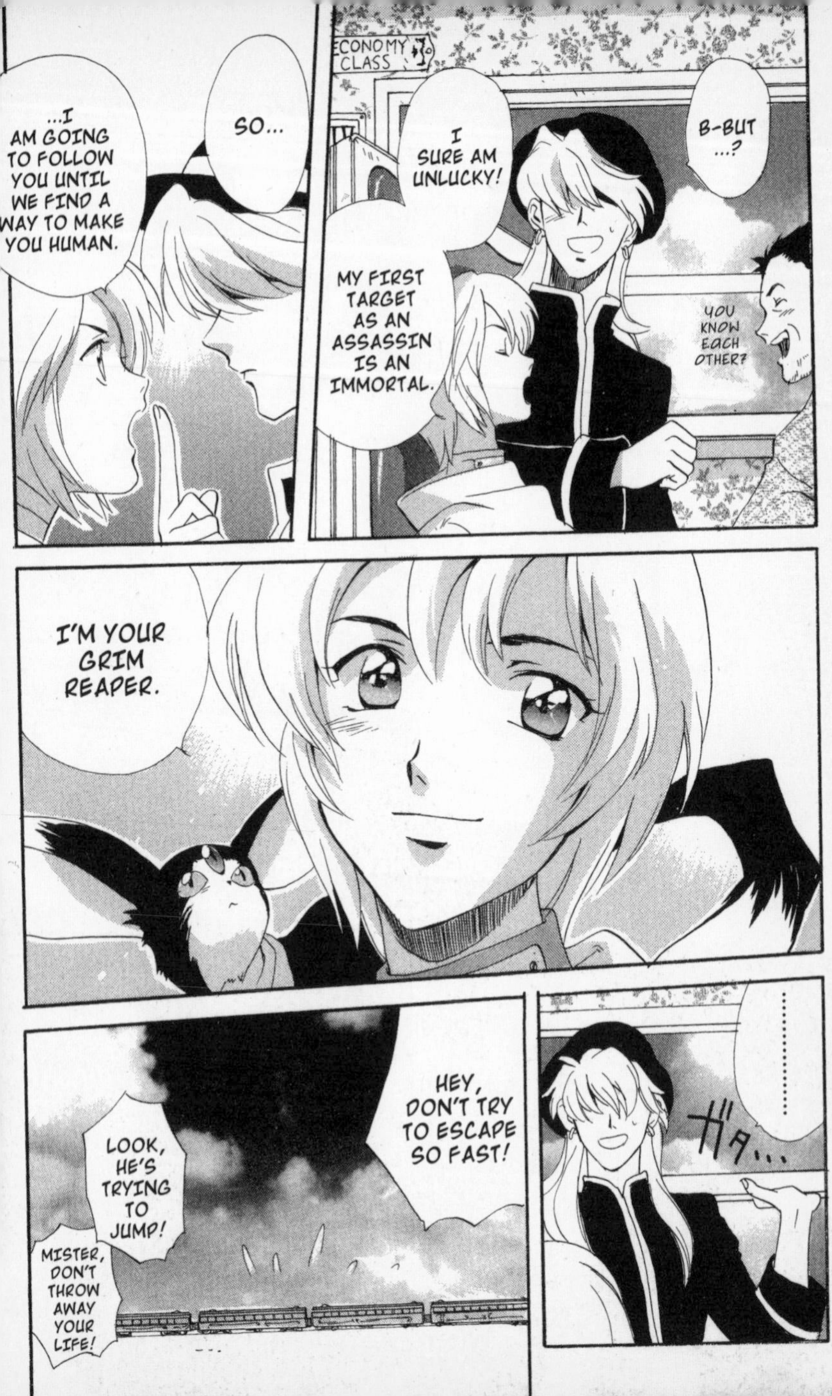
ECONOMY CLASS
B-BUT ...?
YOU KNOW EACH OTHER?
I SURE AM UNLUCKY!
MY FIRST TARGET AS AN ASSASSIN IS AN IMMORTAL.
SO...
...I AM GOING TO FOLLOW YOU UNTIL WE FIND A WAY TO MAKE YOU HUMAN.
I'M YOUR GRIM REAPER.
......
ガタ...
HEY, DON'T TRY TO ESCAPE SO FAST!
LOOK, HE'S TRYING TO JUMP!
MISTER, DON'T THROW AWAY YOUR LIFE!

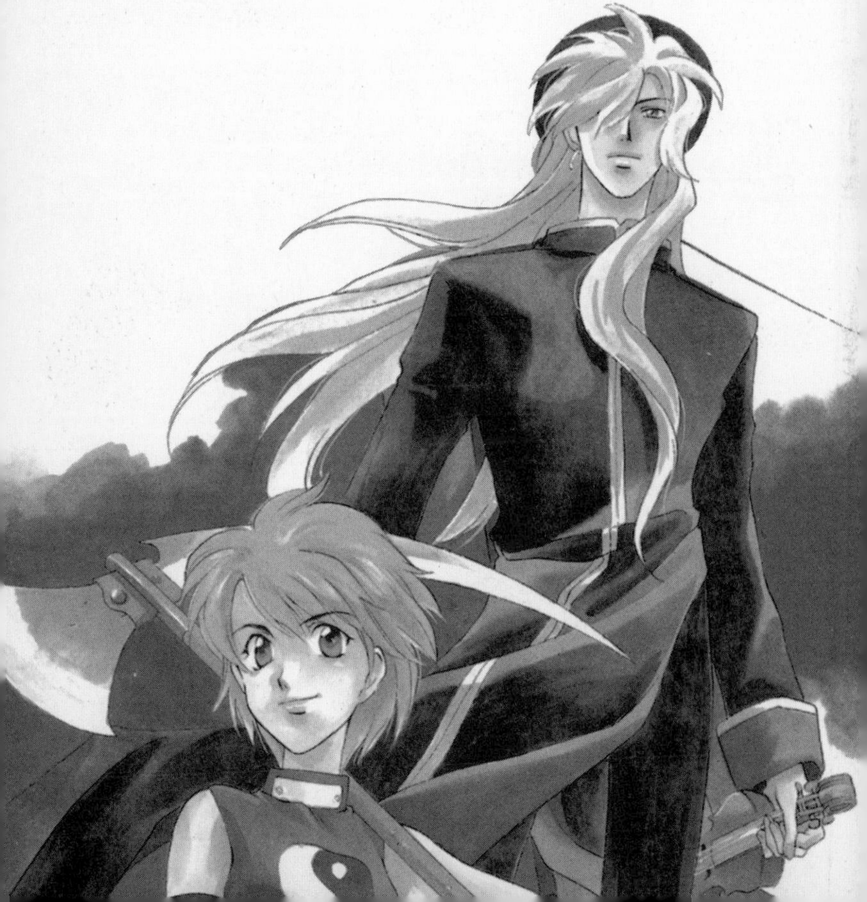

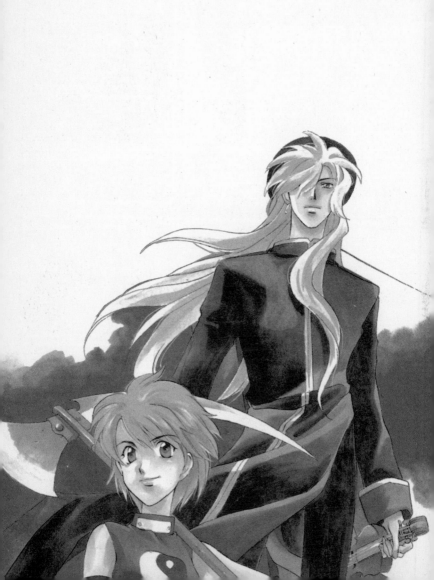

ZOL BALFALTIN

AGE : -
HEIGHT : 170CM
BLOOD TYPE : A

COMMAND
FIGHT

LV: 75
HP: 978/978
OFFENSE
STRENGTH: 114
DEFENSE
STRENGTH: 97
SPEED: 74
WIT: 29
LUCK: 31

EQUIPMENT

WEAPON: GRIM REAPER'S SICKLE /
    OFFENSE STRENGTH + 38
ARMOR: GRIM REAPER'S CLOTHES /
    DEFENSE STRENGTH + 32
ACCESSORY: BABY FACE /
    LOWERS OPPONENT'S
    DEFENSE STRENGTH

DEATHBLOW TECHNIQUE COMMAND

PREACH HIT   Ⓟ repeatedly

PUNISH   ⇨Ⓚ

HEAD CUTTING   ⇨ⓅⓅⓅ↙ⓀⓀ
DANCE

THE MAN WHO APPEARS IN THE FLASHBACK SCENES BETWEEN
MACHIKA AND RAIN. HE ATTACKS PEOPLE WHO DON'T LISTEN
TO HIS SERMON BY LIFTING THEM UP AND PERFORMING THE
HEAD-CUTTING DANCE.

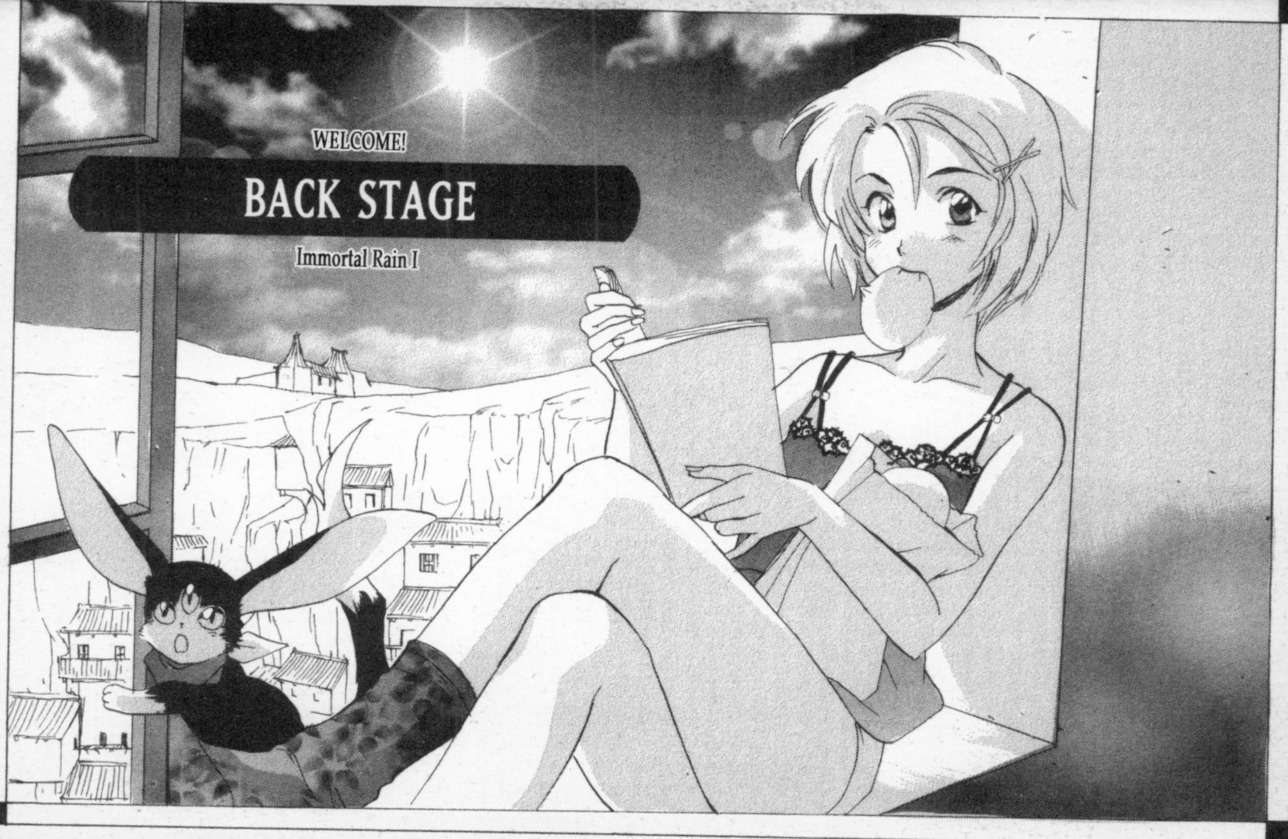
WELCOME!
BACK STAGE
Immortal Rain I

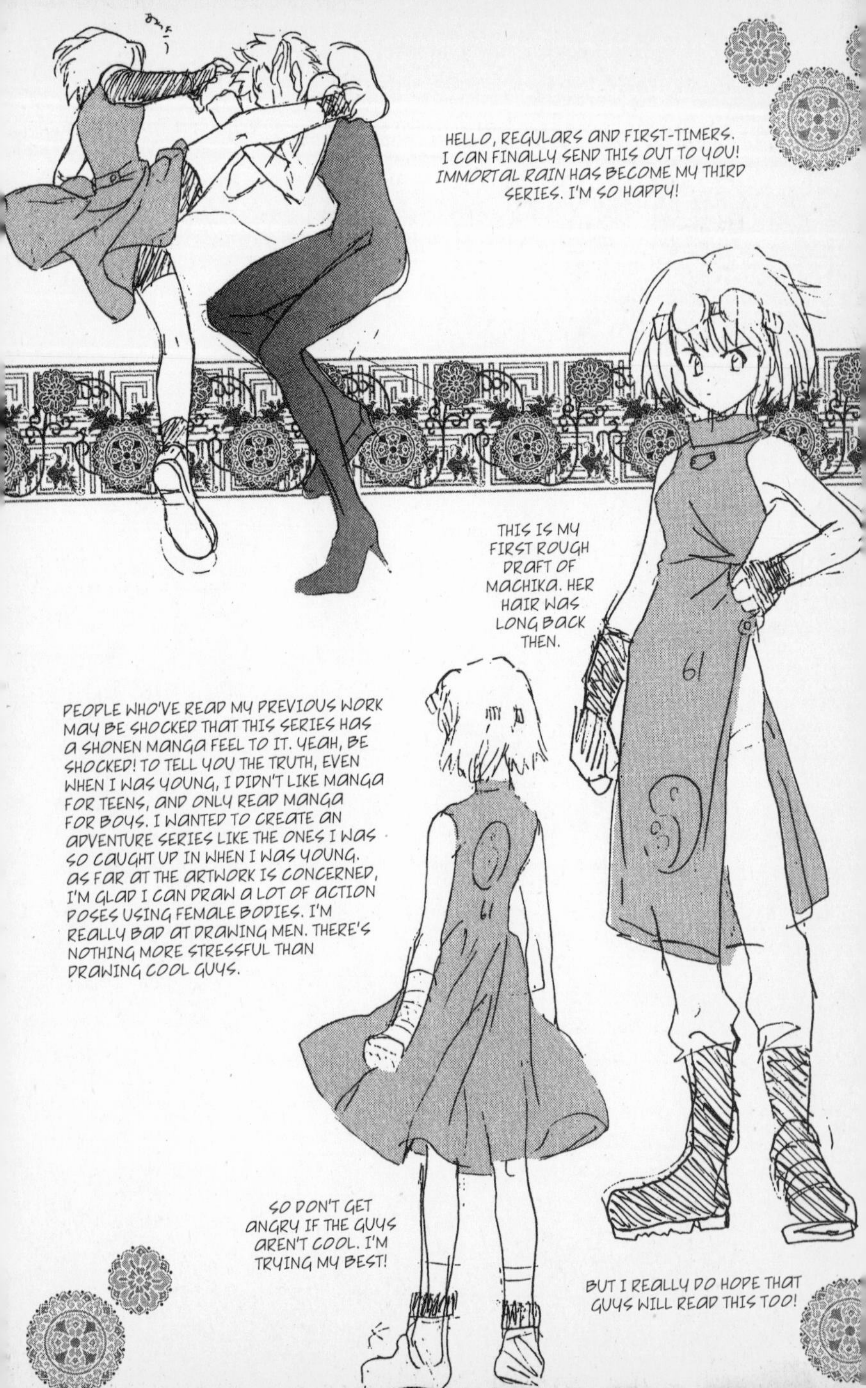
HELLO, REGULARS AND FIRST-TIMERS. I CAN FINALLY SEND THIS OUT TO YOU! IMMORTAL RAIN HAS BECOME MY THIRD SERIES. I'M SO HAPPY!
THIS IS MY FIRST ROUGH DRAFT OF MACHIKA. HER HAIR WAS LONG BACK THEN.
PEOPLE WHO'VE READ MY PREVIOUS WORK MAY BE SHOCKED THAT THIS SERIES HAS A SHONEN MANGA FEEL TO IT. YEAH, BE SHOCKED! TO TELL YOU THE TRUTH, EVEN WHEN I WAS YOUNG, I DIDN'T LIKE MANGA FOR TEENS, AND ONLY READ MANGA FOR BOYS. I WANTED TO CREATE AN ADVENTURE SERIES LIKE THE ONES I WAS SO CAUGHT UP IN WHEN I WAS YOUNG. AS FAR AT THE ARTWORK IS CONCERNED, I'M GLAD I CAN DRAW A LOT OF ACTION POSES USING FEMALE BODIES. I'M REALLY BAD AT DRAWING MEN. THERE'S NOTHING MORE STRESSFUL THAN DRAWING COOL GUYS.
SO DON'T GET ANGRY IF THE GUYS AREN'T COOL. I'M TRYING MY BEST!
BUT I REALLY DO HOPE THAT GUYS WILL READ THIS TOO!

HE HAS AN UMBRELLA BECAUSE INITIALLY, HE'S SUPPOSED TO BE THE RAIN MAN. HIS NAME MAY BE A REMNANT OF THAT. I FORGET.

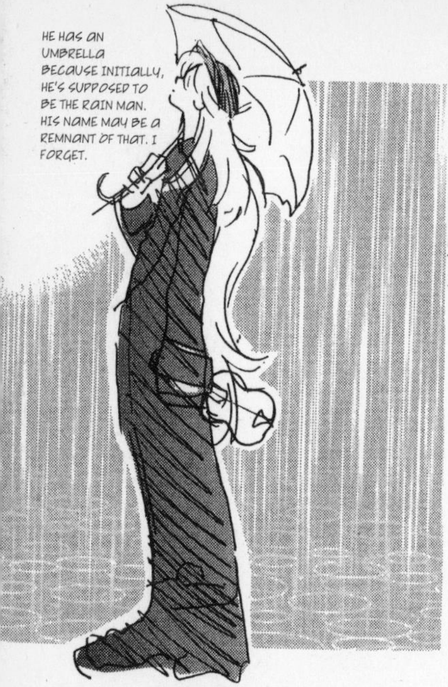

I'VE ALWAYS WANTED TO WRITE A STORY OF SOMEONE WHO WAS WAITING FOR SOME FATEFUL DATE THEY HAD IN MIND. WHY THIS SUDDEN RANDOMNESS? ENTHUSIASM BROUGHT ME THIS FAR. BUT, WE KEEP MOVING FORWARD. LIFE IS LIKE WALKING A TIGHTROPE. IT'S SCARY. THANK YOU FOR YOUR LETTERS. I ALSO RECEIVE TAPES TOO. ACTUALLY, I LIKE MUSIC MORE THAN MANGA. IF THERE ISN'T COOL MUSIC PLAYING, I CAN'T WORK!

IMMORTAL RAIN WAS WRITTEN TO MUSIC LIKE YELLOW MACHINE GUN AND COCCO.

A ROUGH SKETCH BEFORE GETTING SERIALIZED. HE WASN'T SO DIPPY YET.

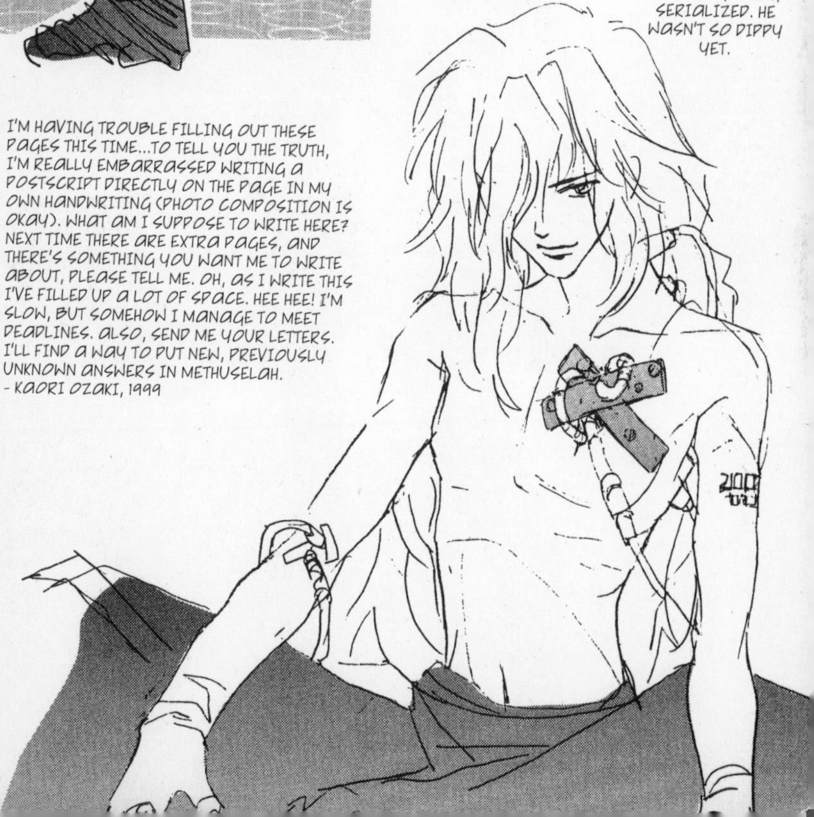

I'M HAVING TROUBLE FILLING OUT THESE PAGES THIS TIME...TO TELL YOU THE TRUTH, I'M REALLY EMBARRASSED WRITING A POSTSCRIPT DIRECTLY ON THE PAGE IN MY OWN HANDWRITING (PHOTO COMPOSITION IS OKAY). WHAT AM I SUPPOSE TO WRITE HERE? NEXT TIME THERE ARE EXTRA PAGES, AND THERE'S SOMETHING YOU WANT ME TO WRITE ABOUT, PLEASE TELL ME. OH, AS I WRITE THIS I'VE FILLED UP A LOT OF SPACE. HEE HEE! I'M SLOW, BUT SOMEHOW I MANAGE TO MEET DEADLINES. ALSO, SEND ME YOUR LETTERS. I'LL FIND A WAY TO PUT NEW, PREVIOUSLY UNKNOWN ANSWERS IN METHUSELAH.

- KAORI OZAKI, 1999

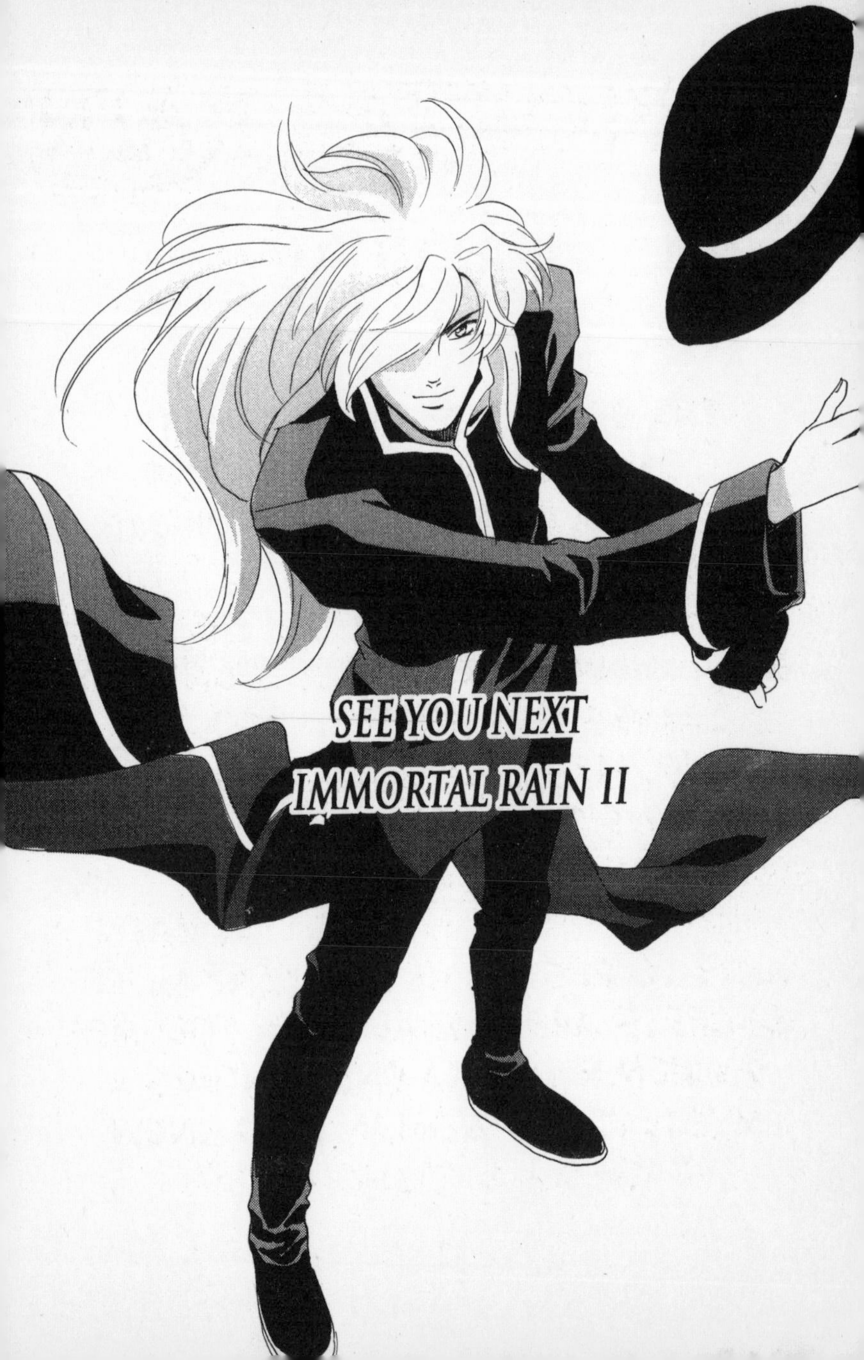
SEE YOU NEXT
IMMORTAL RAIN II

IMMORTAL RAIN

PREVIEW

THE SECRET OF IMMORTALITY
CONTINUES WHEN RAIN AND
MACHIKA BOARD A TRAIN WHERE
THEY MUST BATTLE A BANDIT OF
DESERT PIRATES SENT BY THE EVIL
SHAREM. WHEN RAIN ACCIDENTALLY
LEAVES HIS BELOVED VIOLIN
BEHIND, MACHIKA GOES BACK FOR IT
TO PROVE TO RAIN THAT SHE IS THE
ULTIMATE WARRIOR AFTER ALL! CAN
SHE DO IT ALONE? OR WILL RAIN
HAVE TO RESCUE HER AGAIN? MORE
SECRETS ARE REVEALED IN VOLUME
2 WHEN MACHIKA ENCOUNTERS A
MYSTERIOUS WOMAN WHO KNEW
RAIN AS A YOUNG CHILD!

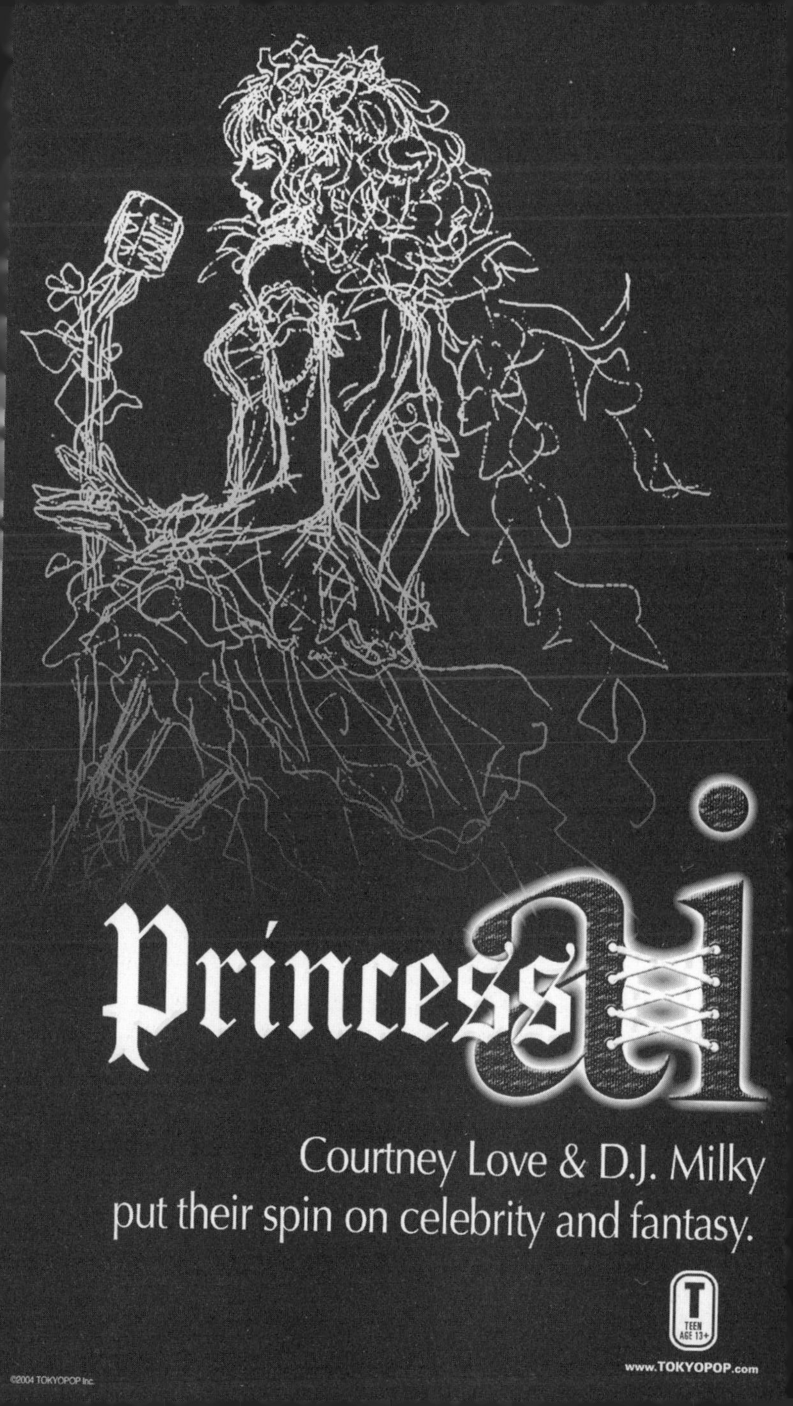
Princess Ai
Courtney Love & D.J. Milky
put their spin on celebrity and fantasy.
T TEEN AGE 13+
www.TOKYOPOP.com
©2004 TOKYOPOP Inc.

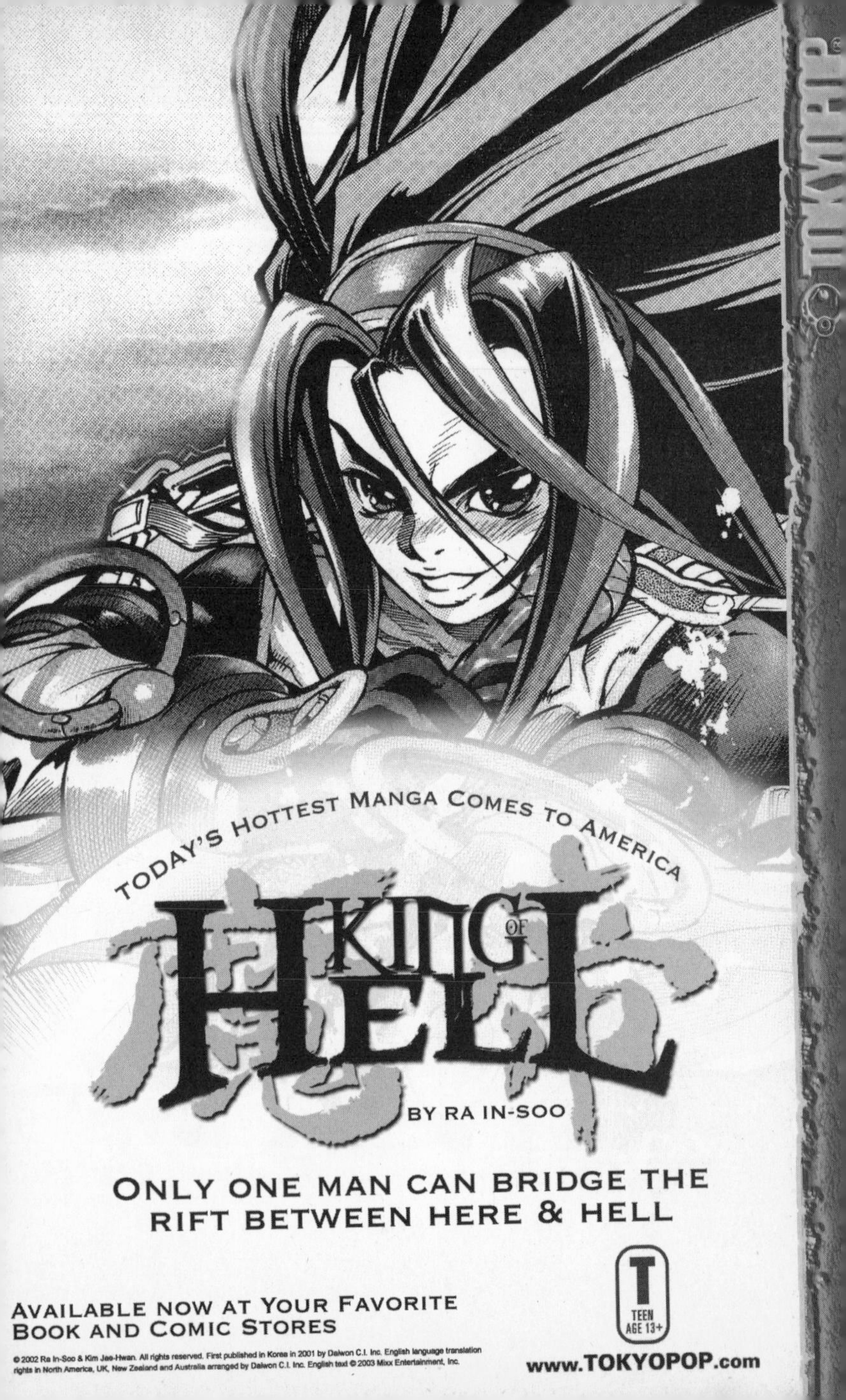
TOKYOPOP
TODAY'S HOTTEST MANGA COMES TO AMERICA
KING OF HELL
BY RA IN-SOO
ONLY ONE MAN CAN BRIDGE THE RIFT BETWEEN HERE & HELL
AVAILABLE NOW AT YOUR FAVORITE BOOK AND COMIC STORES
T TEEN AGE 13+
© 2002 Ra In-Soo & Kim Jae-Hwan. All rights reserved. First published in Korea in 2001 by Daiwon C.I. Inc. English language translation rights in North America, UK, New Zealand and Australia arranged by Daiwon C.I. Inc. English text © 2003 Mixx Entertainment, Inc.
www.TOKYOPOP.com

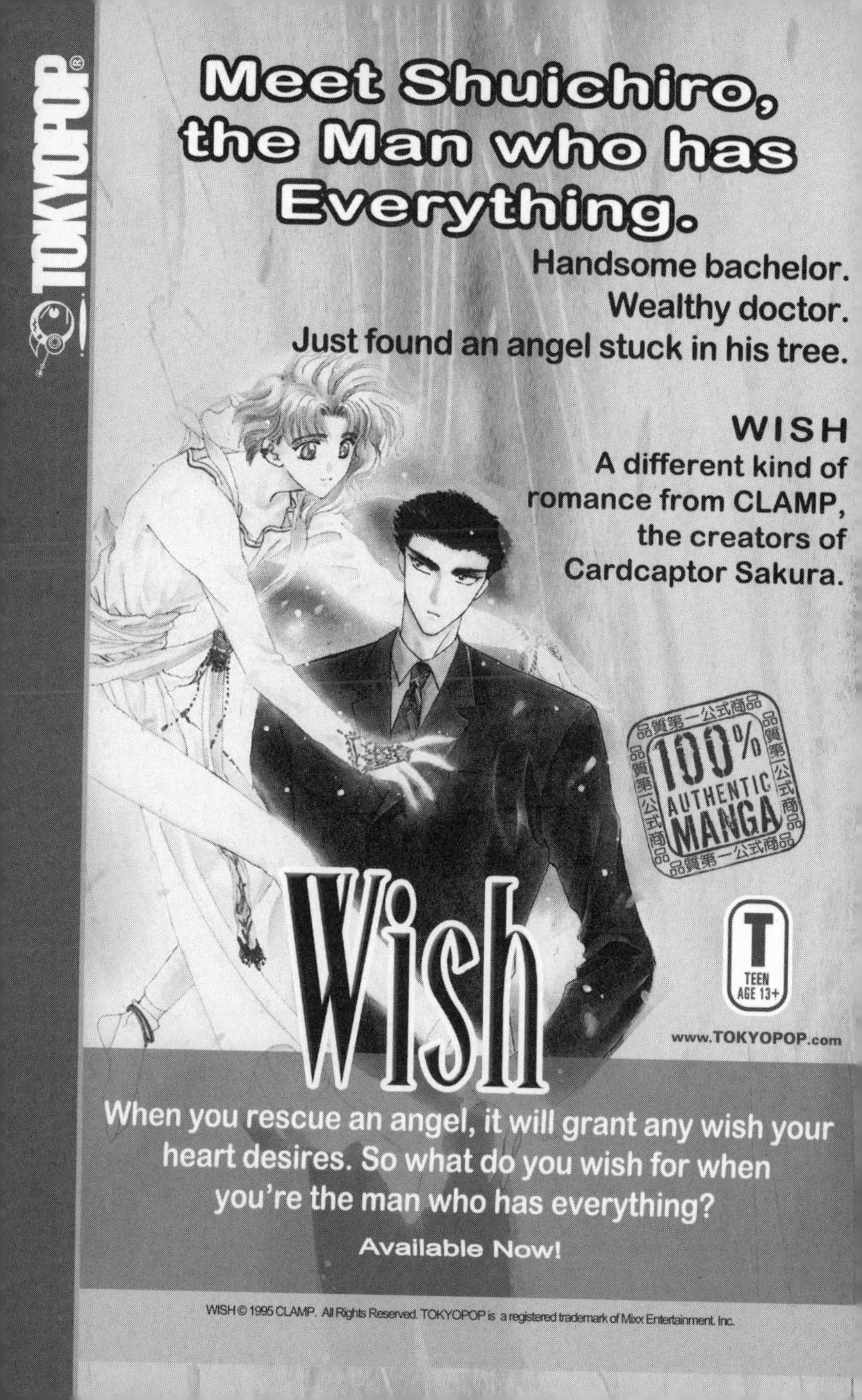
TOKYOPOP®
Meet Shuichiro, the Man who has Everything.
Handsome bachelor.
Wealthy doctor.
Just found an angel stuck in his tree.
WISH
A different kind of romance from CLAMP, the creators of Cardcaptor Sakura.
品質第一公式商品 100% AUTHENTIC MANGA
Wish
T TEEN AGE 13+
www.TOKYOPOP.com
When you rescue an angel, it will grant any wish your heart desires. So what do you wish for when you're the man who has everything?
Available Now!
WISH © 1995 CLAMP. All Rights Reserved. TOKYOPOP is a registered trademark of Mixx Entertainment, Inc.

ALSO AVAILABLE FROM ☺TOKYOPOP

**For more
information visit
www.TOKYOPOP.com**

02.03.04T

ALSO AVAILABLE FROM TOKYOPOP

MANGA

.HACK//LEGEND OF THE TWILIGHT
@LARGE
ABENOBASHI: MAGICAL SHOPPING ARCADE
A.I. LOVE YOU
AI YORI AOSHI
ANGELIC LAYER
ARM OF KANNON
BABY BIRTH
BATTLE ROYALE
BATTLE VIXENS
BRAIN POWERED
BRIGADOON
B'TX
CANDIDATE FOR GODDESS, THE
CARDCAPTOR SAKURA
CARDCAPTOR SAKURA - MASTER OF THE CLOW

CHOBITS
CHRONICLES OF THE CURSED SWORD
CLAMP SCHOOL DETECTIVES
CLOVER
COMIC PARTY
CONFIDENTIAL CONFESSIONS
CORRECTOR YUI
COWBOY BEBOP
COWBOY BEBOP: SHOOTING STAR
CRAZY LOVE STORY
CRESCENT MOON
CULDCEPT
CYBORG 009
D•N•ANGEL
DEMON DIARY
DEMON ORORON, THE
DEUS VITAE
DIGIMON
DIGIMON TAMERS
DIGIMON ZERO TWO
DOLL
DRAGON HUNTER
DRAGON KNIGHTS
DRAGON VOICE
DREAM SAGA
DUKLYON: CLAMP SCHOOL DEFENDERS
EERIE QUEERIE!
ERICA SAKURAZAWA: COLLECTED WORKS
ET CETERA
ETERNITY
EVIL'S RETURN
FAERIES' LANDING
FAKE
FLCL
FORBIDDEN DANCE
FRUITS BASKET
G GUNDAM
GATEKEEPERS

GETBACKERS
GIRL GOT GAME
GRAVITATION
GTO
GUNDAM BLUE DESTINY
GUNDAM SEED ASTRAY
GUNDAM WING
GUNDAM WING: BATTLEFIELD OF PACIFISTS
GUNDAM WING: ENDLESS WALTZ
GUNDAM WING: THE LAST OUTPOST (G-UNIT)
HANDS OFF!
HAPPY MANIA
HARLEM BEAT
I.N.V.U.
IMMORTAL RAIN
INITIAL D
INSTANT TEEN: JUST ADD NUTS
ISLAND
JING: KING OF BANDITS
JING: KING OF BANDITS - TWILIGHT TALES
JULINE
KARE KANO
KILL ME, KISS ME
KINDAICHI CASE FILES, THE
KING OF HELL
KODOCHA: SANA'S STAGE
LAMENT OF THE LAMB
LEGAL DRUG
LEGEND OF CHUN HYANG, THE
LES BIJOUX
LOVE HINA
LUPIN III
LUPIN III: WORLD'S MOST WANTED
MAGIC KNIGHT RAYEARTH I
MAGIC KNIGHT RAYEARTH II
MAHOROMATIC: AUTOMATIC MAIDEN
MAN OF MANY FACES
MARMALADE BOY
MARS
MARS: HORSE WITH NO NAME
METROID
MINK
MIRACLE GIRLS
MIYUKI-CHAN IN WONDERLAND
MODEL
ONE
ONE I LOVE, THE
PARADISE KISS
PARASYTE
PASSION FRUIT
PEACH GIRL
PEACH GIRL: CHANGE OF HEART
PET SHOP OF HORRORS
PITA-TEN
PLANET LADDER
PLANETES

STOP!

This is the back of the book.
You wouldn't want to spoil a great ending!

This book is printed "manga-style," in the authentic Japanese right-to-left format. Since none of the artwork has been flipped or altered, readers get to experience the story just as the creator intended. You've been asking for it, so TOKYOPOP® delivered: authentic, hot-off-the-press, and far more fun!

DIRECTIONS

If this is your first time reading manga-style, here's a quick guide to help you understand how it works.

It's easy... just start in the top right panel and follow the numbers. Have fun, and look for more 100% authentic manga from TOKYOPOP®!